African OriginS
Of The Major
"Western Religions"

African Origins Of The Major Western Religions

Published 1991 by

Black Classic Press

Published with the permission of the author. Cover art by Tony Browder, rendered from the original cover design by Yosef ben–Jochannan. We are indebted to both Malik Azeez for preparing the Select Bibliography and Noni Ford for preparing the Index for the B.C.P. edition of this work.

Originally published by Alkebu–lan Books Associates

Library of Congress Catalog Card Number 90–82689

ISBN 0–933121–29–6

Printed on acid free paper to assure long life

Founded in 1978, Black Classic Press specializes in bringing to light obscure and significant works by and about people of African descent. If our books are not available in your area, ask your local bookseller to order them. Our current list of titles can be obtained by writing:

Black Classic Press
c/o List
P.O. Box 13414
Baltimore, MD 21203

A Young Press With Some Very Old Ideas

African Origins
Of The Major
"Western Religions"

By
Yosef A.A. ben-Jochannan

AFRICAN ORIGINS OF THE
MAJOR "WESTERN RELIGIONS"

by: Yosef ben-Jochannan

Chairman, African Studies Department:
The Harlem Preparatory School of New York
N.Y.C., N.Y.

Visiting Professor of History:
State University College at New Paltz, New Paltz, N.Y.

Adjunct Assoc. Professor of History: Pace College, New York
(New York City and Westchester Campus).

Instructor of History: Marymount College, Tarrytown, New York.

Formerly Cultural and Historical Consultant to the Permanent
African Missions of the United Nations Organization.

Dedicated To: the innocently recent born and those yet-to-be
born African and African-American infants who must one day take
their place in mankind's world as the inheritors of the religions
their forebearers created, hoping that they may become the forces of change to bring this world to its equilibrium once more...

CONTENTS:

COVER DESIGN: SYMBOLIC GLOSSARY

 * = God: Ra - Sun God of the Nile.
Sunburst

 ▲ = Symbol of the first principles of religion. Coffin Texts.
Pyramid with All Seeing Eye.
 ☥ = God: Damballah Ouedo, Voodoo. West African.
Rooster.
 ☥ = Key of Life of the Mysteries. Grand Lodge of Luxor.
Ankh, Nile Valley Cross.
 ✝ = God: Jesus Christ. Christianity.
Cross, Westernized Version.
 ☥ = God: Traditional African religions.
Cross, Nile Valley and Central Africa.
 ✡ = God: Yaweh. Hebrewism (Judaism).
Star of David.
     = God: Al'lah. Islam.
Crescent of Tigris and Euphrates.

iv

All Faith is <u>false</u>, all Faith is <u>True</u>
    Truth is the shattered mirrors strewn
In myriad bits; while each believes
    his little bit the whole to own

From:
THE KASIDAH of ḤAJI ABU el-YEZDI
(as transl. by Sir Richard F. Burton)

Everytime I had the good fortune to research into someone's religion I found "God" to be the image of the people to whom the religion belongs; that is providing its philosophical concepts are indigenous; not colonial. The colonialism referred to is not essentially one of conqueror nor is it one of the conquered in the sense of troops and land, but of <u>slaves</u> and <u>masters</u>; in this case, <u>slaves</u> who have seen the shackles which bound their bodies removed for over one-hundred years, but not those of their mind.

Because of their mental enslavement to Judaism, Christianity, and Islam, the Africans and African-Americans who have for one reason or another been forced to abandon their own indigenous religions, need to know their role in either of these three. As a person of African origin, I feel that it is my obligation to enter this field, where so many non-Africans have before me entered to speak and write about me. In so doing, I shall show that Judaism, Christianity, and Islam are as much African as they are Asian in origin, and in no sense what-so-ever European as the title, "WESTERN RELIGIONS" suggests; that the terms "<u>Semitic</u>" and "<u>Hamitic</u>" - as they are presently applied to the early founders of these religions - are <u>racist</u> in character and intent. The sole purpose is to deny the existence of that which most Europeans and European-Americans call "<u>Negro</u>," "<u>Africans South of the Sahara</u>" and "<u>Bantu</u>," among other such nomenclatures of contempt in the development of religion and thought in ancient North Africa - particularly Sais (Egypt). But the fact still remains with respect to the origin of religion, that there would have been no Egyptian civilization (High-Culture) had the Africans - the so-called "Negroes" - of the Upper Nile Valley and Central Africa not migrated north along the more than four-thousand and one-hundred (4,000) miles long Nile River into Sais; equally there could be no "Judaism, Christianity" or "Islam" (the daughter, grand-daughter and great-grand-daughter of the African God "RA" and the "Mysteries"), all three being outgrowths of the Egyptian Religion, as shown in the "Coffin" and "Pyramid" Texts in the

BOOK OF THE DEAD; and OSIRIS.[1]

The revelations in this work show that the Reverend Martin
Luther's[2] revolt against Papl Roman Christianity, as well as
Judaism and Islam, remained stagnantly rhetoric until the
Reverend Dr. Martin Luther King, Jr. (no relationship to the
above) introduced into it the element of "non-violence" he
copied from the Hindu teacher, philosopher, lawyer and
statesman - Mahatma ("the Sacred One") Mohandas Karamchand
Gandhi.[3] And even though Dr. King tried to invoke the "ancestral
worship" method of calling upon the "spirit world" (in
Christianity - "Saints"),[4] like his God - Jesus Christ, he was
not to be heard by an irreligious nation of people whose Gods
appear to be machines of mass production.

The traditional religions of the indigenous African peoples
and their descendants which are notoriously called "paganism"
and "fetishism"[5] by antagonists of the so-called "Western
Religions," are in fact the forerunners of Nile Valley religions;
therefore, they are the creators of the "Mysteries of Sais"
(Egypt), Kush (Ethiopia) and Nubia (Sudan). This is shown in
the text of this volume, along with the fact that the "Mysteries"
were developed from the ancient religious rites of the indegenous
Africans who once occupied the lands around the major "great
lakes" of Central Africa and along the head-waters of the Nile
River.[5a] That civilization in Alkebu-lan (Africa) travelled
from south to north with the flow of the Nile River and all its
component parts. With them they brought religion[6] and
philosophy, all of which existed thousands of years before the
first nation in Europe, Greece, came into being.

The similarity between existing religious practices in
parts of West, Central, East and South Africa with that of the
ancient indigenous Africans of Sais (Egypt), is not coincidental,
but instead, is common to the heritage which began along the
"great lakes" of Central Africa and the head-waters of the Nile
River, as shown in this work.

There are people today around the world who have suffered
similarly from European and European-American imperialism - aided
and abetted by the leaders of Judaism and Christianity - who also

actively engaged in slavery by sanctioning its institution through twisted quotations from their own versions of that which is called "The Holy and Sacred Scriptures."[7] Therefore, information of the nature found in this work may be considered of current importance; but there was never a period in the history of mankind when they were of 'no importance.' It is shown that most Europeans and European-Americans have consistently used the same information revealed in this work disguised as what they choose to call "Greek Philosophy"[8] and "Western Religions;"[9] titles of direct Caucasian (White) oriented ethnic superiority. The mere titles by themselves suggest the exclusiveness of European and European-American (White) peoples only.[10] It is recognized, however, that this may not be sufficient reason to speak out against this type of academic dishonesty, according to those who wish not to "rock the boat" of the established order of things, although knowing that "truth" is not being served. But the main purpose of this work is to show that there is another phase to the greatness that is still "MOTHER AFRICA," the MOTHER OF MANKIND, a sort of "GARDEN OF EDEN,"[11] also to provide another perspective in Africa's major contribution to world civilization which may well assist in rearranging the present and future tenets of religious thought.

CREDIT:

A work of this dimension could not be possible without the assistance from others. My sincerest appreciation in this regard is extended to Mr. George Simmonds, my associate instructor, at the Harlem Preparatory School of New York, for re-checking the documents and factual information; and to Miss

viii

Doris Mosely for her general contributions and checking the entire manuscript for its scholarly excellence. My youngest daughter Collette Makeda, who read the manuscript with regards to its easy flow of information, has been extremely helpful in many other ways.

My many friends at the various centers of contact and learning in Harlem, especially those whom I meet constantly at the Arthur Olonzo Schomburg Collection of the Countee Cullen Branch of the New York City Public Library, and the Lecture Series of the Library, have been more than an inspiration for the little more than two years needed to prepare this work. There are countless others, who in many different ways, I am indebted to; to them, I also extend my joy in the completion of this task. Hopefully, this work means to them the beginning of a better understanding of the contributions of the peoples of African origin to the entire world civilization.

Yosef ben-Jochannan

> "No positive religion that has moved man has
> been able to start with a tabula rasa, and express
> itself as if religion were beginning for the first
> time, in form, if not in substance. The new system
> must be in contact all along the line with the
> older ideas and practices which it finds in
> possession. A new scheme of faith can find a
> hearing only by appealing to religious instincts
> and susceptibilities that already exist; and it
> cannot reach these without taking account of the
> traditional forms in which all religious feeling
> is embodied, and without speaking a language which
> men accustomed to these old forms can understand...."

The above is the manner in which Robertson Smith began his

classic study entitled "RELIGION OF THE SEMITES." But Mr. Smith's

words could be extended to include, that....'no major religion

of today is exclusive of moral and philosophic concepts of any

of the peoples with whom it had contact in its earliest develop-

ment.' This would, of course, give credit to those African and

Asian predecessors who were the ones that really began the

religions which are today called "Judaism" (Hebrewism), "Chris-

tianity and Islam" (Mohammedism) - formerly "Mohametism."

If what has been said so far could become common knowledge,

the general public would have no difficulty in recognizing that

much of what they read in their Torah (Jewish Holy Book or Five

Books of Moses), Christian Holy Bible (any version - Roman

Catholic or Protestant and Christian Scientist) and Moslem

(Muslim) Koran or Quran, would be conceded to be of African

origin, as well as Asian, and adopted later by Europeans and

European-Americans before they arrived in the Americas - the

"New World." But as long as racism remains the basis upon which

these religions are taught, rejection of the indigenous African

and Asian peoples' contribution to them shall continue to be

x

camouflaged into the authorship of those who did least to start them, but most to continue them as their own exclusive domain.

To say at this time that "Moses," of the Hebrew (Jewish) religion and peoples, was an indigenous African (Black or Negro"), would create a catastrophic consternation among theological racists and bring down all sorts of "anti-Semitic" charges by the same people who equally as strenuously would admit that "Moses was born in Egypt," at the same instance, forgetting that Egypt is in Africa. Why? Because Egypt, in most European-American minds, is some sort of a mythical place remote from any place near Africa. This would not stop them from saying that "Moses was found floating down the Nile River in a bulrush basket,"[2a] conveniently forgetting that the Nile River's source begins in Uganda; also that there are two Niles, the White and the Blue; and that the White Nile is more than four-thousand miles long, flowing northwards through Sudan (Nubia) and Egypt (Sais) and finally emptying into the Mediterranean (Egyptian) Sea. They seem to forget that the Blue Nile's main source of water comes from the Ethiopian Highlands - at Lake Tana; and that the other source of the Nile - the Atbara River, also starts in the Ethiopian Highlands and flows into Sudan - where it joins both the Blue and White Niles.

The "TEN COMMANDMENTS" spoken of in each of the so-called "WESTERN RELIGIONS'" moral code of ethics are based upon extensions of philosophical developments by the indigenous Africans - the so-called "Negroes" and "Bantus" - of the Nile Valley civilizations from pre-recorded history. The laws that say ..."THOU SHALT NOT KILL..., etc." and "THOU SHALT NOT

STEAL ..., etc."[2] were used in Egypt (Sais) and Ethiopia (Kush or Cush) thousands of years before the birth of Moses of the Hebrew (Jewish) Torah. Yet these two laws, including all of the other ten that make up so-called "Western Religions'" basic moral codes, are still being taught as if the first time they ever came to the knowledge of mankind was when they were allegedly "... given to Moses on Mount Sinai." At least, this is the manner in which they are presently taught in Europe, the Americas and wherever European and European-American religious and economic controls are in evidence.

It will be shown that the statements so far may hold true with regard to the almost successful attempts to make all philosophical concepts in the major religions cited as beginning with the usually mentioned "Greek Philosophy" and "Greek Philosophers." In this sense the Greeks are treated as if they were in no way whatsoever influenced or taught by the Egyptians, Ethiopians, and other indigenous Africans along the Nile Valley - whence the philosophical concepts, now called "Greek Philosophy", were originated - thousands of years before the creation of the Greek nation. In this regard, Professor G. G. M. James, in his book entitled "STOLEN LEGACY," states on the title page:

> "The Greeks were not the authors of Greek Philosophy, but the people of North Africa, commonly called the Egyptians."

Strange as it may seem, the ancient Egyptians are being called "Caucasian" by most European and European-American educators; purposefully ignoring Herodotus' description of them in his book, THE HISTORIES - Book II.

xii

Count Constantine Francis Chassebeuf DeVolney, who personally visited Egypt in 1789 C.E. from his native France (Europe), wrote in his book, RUINS OF EMPIRES - published in 1802, the following:

> The earth, under these holy lands, produces only thorns and briers. Man soweth in anguish, and reapeth tears and cares. War, famine, pestilence, assail him by turns. And yet, are not these the children of the prophets? The Mussulman, Christian, Jew, are they not the elect children of God, loaded with favors and miracles? Why, then, do these privileged races no longer enjoy the same advantages? Why are these fields, sanctified by the blood of martyrs, deprived of the ancient fertility? Why have those blessings been banished hence, and transferred for so many ages to other nations and different climes?

Count Volney's questions could be asked of the Africans who are today being called "Negroes, Bantus, Hottentots, Bushmen, Pygmies," and a host of other degrading terms, whose ancestors were responsible for the development of the religions mentioned herein; starting with the worship of the Sun God - RA, then passing on to the Gods - "Jehovah, Jesus Christ" and "Allah." The first question must be:

> How much longer are we to remain outside of the religions we originated in our "Mysteries" in Egypt and other High-Cultures along the Nile?

The answer in this case would be simple. At least, the peoples of Africa can still point to such religious works as recorded in the BOOK OF THE DEAD (translated from its original Hieroglyph by Sir E. A. Wallis-Budge); FACING MOUNT KENYA by

---

* Latest edition, Volney's Ruins of Empires, p. 7, Truth Seeker Company, New York, 1950.

Jomo Kenyatta, the edited works in Janheinz Jahn's MUNTU. Of
course there are countless others that show the variety of
depth in the philosophical concepts of African traditional
religions - Judaism, Christianity and Islam, presently being
analyzed.

In the BOOK OF THE DEAD, the origin of "Heaven" and "Hell"
are clearly seen to be nothing more than places, poor ones at
that, of the indigenous Africans of Egypt's "NETHER WORLD"
and "MYSTERIES" developed along the Nile Valley, all of which
stemmed from civilizations that preceded the birth of the first
Haribu (Hebrew of Jew) - Abraham (Avram or Abram) centuries before
the creation of the first Hebrew nation - Palestine. Therefore,
in this work, the God RA is shown to be the "...jealous God..."
who wants "... no other Gods before me...," etc. This, the
Hebrews copied in Egypt and changed in the following manner:

Thou shalt have no Gods before me, sayeth Yvah.[7]

In the case of the Reverend Placide Temples' book, BANTU
PHILOSOPHY, this Roman Catholic priest failed miserably to dispel
the confusion in his own mind to prove that there are basic
philosophical concepts in traditional African religions on an
equal level of spiritual consciousness to Judaism, Christianity
or Islam, yet he continued to show how much better Christianity[8]
(his own religion) is than any of the so-called "Bantu" religions
and "Bantu" thoughts he examined.

Janheinz Jahn, who claims no special religious affiliation
or preference in his work, attempted to show many basic
philosophical elements in a few traditional African religions
which are comparable to the three religions called "Western

xiv

<u>Religions.</u>" In his book, MUNTU: The New African Culture, pages
29-30, as translated by Marjorie Grene, Grove Press, Inc., New
York, 1961, from its original work in German entitled -
MUNTUS, published by Eugene Diederichs Verlag, Dusseldorf,
Germany, 1958; Mr. Jahn gives the following account on Voodoo:

I. OLD ACCOUNTS OF THE CULT

Voodoo! Word of dark vowels and heavily
rolling consonants! Voodoo! Mysterious nocturnal
sound of drums in the Haitian mountains of abominations they have read about! Voodoo, idolatry,
sorcery; Voodoo, epitome of all impiety, all
depravity and terror, witches' Sabbath of the
infernal powers and ineradicable heresy! What is
it all about?

Some people have tried to dervie the word
from the dance of the Golden Calf (veau d'or),
and it has also been related to the heretical
side of the Waldensians (Vaudois) who were
reputed to practice witchcraft. In fact, the
whole practice of witchcraft in the Middle Ages
was called 'vaudoisie.'

The word is written in many different ways:
Vaudou, Vaudoux, Vodoo, etc., but it comes from
Dahomey in West Africa, where it means 'genius,
protective spirit'; in the Fon language it is
'Voduh' and in Ewe 'Vudu.' The name of the cult,
like the cult itself, is of West African origin,
for the Haitians for the most part come from there.
The reason why it was the religious conceptions of
Dahomey in particular that came to prevail in
Haiti is apparent from a London report of 1789
which tells us that ten to twelve thousand slaves
were exported yearly from the Kingdom of Dahomey.
The English exported only seven to eight hundred
of these, the Portuguese about three thousand and
the French the remainder, in other words more than
six to eight thousand a year, who were shipped to
the French Antilles, above all the Saint Dominique,
as the principal French colony of Haiti was then
called.

The earliest indication of the survival of
African cults in Haiti we owe to an anonymous
French report, which says: 'The slaves are strictly
forbidden to practice the dahce which in Surinam is

called "Water-Mama" and in our colonies "Mae d'Agua"
(Water Mother). They, therefore, make a great secret
of it, and all we know is that it highly inflames
their imaginations. They make immense efforts to
do evil things. The leader of the plot falls into
such transports that he loses consciousness.'

Moreau de Saint-Mery, an enlightened scholar,
lawyer, and politician who was born in Martinique
and practised law for nine years in Haiti before
playing an important part in the French revolution,
employed the leisure hours of the North-American
exile forced on him through his quarrel with
Robespierre in describing in detail the geographical,
social, and political conditions in Haiti.

In his works of several volumes this relative
of the Empress Josephine describes, among other
things, a Voodoo ceremony. 'According to the
Arada Negroes, Voodoo means a great supernatural
being, a snake that knows the past and the present,
and through the medium of the high priestess and
of a Negress, foretells the future. These two are
called King and Queen, Master and Mistress, or
Papa and Mama.'

The meeting takes place, he says, only
secretly and at night, far from profane eyes.
The initiated put on sandals and wrap themselves
in red cloths. The King and Queen wear girdles.
A chest, through the boards of which one can see
the snake, serves as an altar. The faithful
present their wishes, then the Queen leaps upon
the chest, falls at once into a trance, begins to
prophesy and gives her commands. Sacrificial gifts
are brought; the King and Queen receive them. The
receipts are used to meet the expenses of the
community and to assist needy members. Then follows
an oath similar to that at the opening of the
meeting and 'as fearful as the first,' an oath of
secrecy and obedience.

Jahn's details of a "Voodoo ceremony" on pages 42 and 43

of his book show very clearly the common relationship between

traditional concepts in Judaism, Christianity, Islam and Voodooism

which most twentieth-century moderns do not know exist. He

continues on:

In the Voodoo ceremony the first loa to be
invoked is Legba. He is the lord of roads, and
streets, the Hermes of the Voodoo Olympus, the
protector of crossroads and doors, the protector
of the herd. His wife Ayizan, is the Goddess of
the markets and the highest goddess of the Arada
Olympus. Legba's symbol, his veve, is the cross
- a cross which has, however, only its form, not
its meaning, in common with the Christian cross.
The vertical board means the deep and the heights,
the street of the loas, the invisible ones. The
foot of this vertical world-axis is rooted in the
waters of the deep. Here on the 'island under the
sea' is Guinea, Africa, the legendary home; here
the loas have their permanent places, from which
they hasten straight upward to the living. Every
vertical, above all every stee, and especially the
poteau-mitan in the hounfort, symbolizes the 'tree
of the Gods' which unites the damp earth, from
which all things spring, with heaven. The horizontal
bar of the cross signifies the earthly and the human
world. Only at the crossroad, where the human and
divine axes meet, does contact with divinities take
place. And this crossroad is guarded by Legba. In
Dahomey and Nigeria he is the interpreter of the
gods who translates the requests and prayers of
men into their language. In Haiti he has the
function of opening the barriere that separates
men from the loas. He is invoked in the vanvalou
- rhythm and dance.

The music and song of the dance are very similar in purpose

to that of the so-called "storefront churches" of Harlem. Thus

the following from Jahn's description above.

        Aitibo LegbaLuvri laye pu mwe
        Papa Legba, luvri baye pu mwe
        Luvri baye pu m'kapab ratre
        A tu bon Legba ouvre la barriere pour moi
        Papa Legba, ouvre la barriere pour moi
        Ouvre la barriere pour me faire capable
        de rentre

There are many more stanzas to this song; however, the

reason for not showing the entire song, is due to the fact that

the main purpose of noting it was not to learn the entire song,

only to get an insight into the projection of man and his God

as seen in the Voodoo ceremonial dance and song.

On the island of Cuba, not too far from Haiti, Voodooism becomes "Maniquismo" - a name which carries in the mind of most European-Americans the synonymous meanings of "black magic," "satanism," "idolatry," "heathen superstition," etc.[9] Fernand Ortiz, one of the foremost writers on this subject known to European-Americans, disclaimed any religious origin whatsoever for "Maniquismo" in his book, LA AFRICANIA DE LA MUSICA FOLKLORICA DE CUBA, La Habana, 1950. Ortiz called it:

> A secret society, a kind of a free masonry, to which only the initiate, who has sworn his allegiance, may belong.

Ortiz, who is of Roman Catholic Christian origin, overlooked the fact that Christianity is still a "secret society" in many lands today; and that it too was once so labeled everywhere. It was, and still is, a religion to which only the "initiates," who have sworn their allegiance, may belong. But Ortiz's position is typically what happens when an exponent of one (or no) religion pretends to write an 'unbiased analysis' of another person's religion.

If one is to take Ortiz's premise as the criteria for what is a "religion" and what is a "secret society," then the baptism (Christening) and confirmation rites of the Christian initiations must be omitted, equally circumcision of the Jews and Moslems, also, the exclusion of women from direct worship with their men in Orthodox Judaism and Islam. Or, are these not "secret rites?" Are they not special requirements in which only "sworn" members alone may rightfully indulge?

The opinions and expressions already shown are but a mere sampling of how religious personalities see each others' religion,

xviii

not only how they see each other in religious roles; but how
they also deny the existence of each other's "God." Of course
the indigenous Africans, the so-called "Negroes, Niggers," etc.,
and their descendants are not even entitlted to have the respect
of being capable of creating a religion with common philosophical
idealism, much less having a God which does not secure the
endorsement of those European and European-American judges who are
in charge of the department of certification of fitness and
qualification of religions and Gods. Since there are no African
or African-Americans allowed on the 'Board of God certifiers,'
due to their inferior color and race, the traditional African
religions must then remain "secret societies," while the
certifiers' religions – Judaism, Christianity, sometimes Islam,
receive 'the good God and religious seal of approval';all others
are damned to the pagan depth of inferiority, and only can they
expect to see God if they abandon their pagan God and heathen
religion for one of the approved religions, preferably Christianity.

The Africans and their descendants (Black People) everywhere
need not defend their traditional religious philosophies and
philosophers upon the approval of European and European-American
standards; neither shall this work even try to so do. Why?
Because within the three most accepted religions in Europe and
the Americas – Judaism, Christianity and Islam, often called
"Western Religions," Africans have been the founders of said
religions and their teachings along with the Asians hundreds
of years, in some cases thousands of years before they were
known to the peoples of Europe. The fact that within the last

three to four hundred years the role of the indigenous Africans in thes major religions has been carefully and purposefully denied, suppressed, and in most cases, omitted, will not stop the "truth" about their indigenous African origins from coming to the surface. In light of all that has been so far stated, further revelation of the general and specific role certain Africans had in the founding of all three religions - Judaism, Christianity and Islam - is being retold; all in the objective of "setting the record straight," or revealing the truth.

Hopefully, from this work, knowledge about some of the major indigenous African contributors and their descendants in the founding and development of Judaism, Christianity (an extension of Judaism) and Islam (an extension of Judaeo-Christianity) would spread to those who do not now know that the religion they practise and the God they worship are as much African (Black) as they are Asian (Yellow and Brown) and/or European (White).

Since Christianity, the European-American version of it, is the major religion in the Americas - the Caribbeans included - it is the center of focus to which this work must mainly address itself; moreover, because the vast majority of African peoples and their descendants - both in the Western Hemisphere and Africa - are critically conditioned and/or affected by it.

Islam, the major contender with European and European-American oriented Christianity for the minds of the African and African-American people, will of necessity receive particular consideration with regards to its foundation - which is so intensely African (Ethiopian in particular) in structure.
xx

Judaism, which today has very little or no real influence on any large segment of the African peoples anywhere, due primarily to the inhuman pressures brought upon the indigenous Hebrews of Africa by Christian and Islamic missionaries in their conversion crusades, will nevertheless be carefully examined with regards to its previous control and influence on many indigenous African societies; equally for its indigenous African origins will be highlighted.

As the clamor for "violent" or "non-violent" action[10] challenges the moral fibre of this Anglo-Saxon Greek-centric-oriented United States of America, many noted religious "prophets" within the major Black communities asserted themselves as "spiritual leaders," all of whom believed they had received some sort of a calling from a Caucasianized "God." The most noted of these are listed in the order in which they appeared on the national or international scene, thus, Father (Peace) Divine, Rabbi Wentworth Mathews, Prophet "Sweet Daddy" Grace, Prophet Elijah Mohammed, and the Reverend Dr. Martin Luther King, Jr. To these must be added the name of the Honorable Marcus Moziah Garvey. He was not a minister of the gospel; yet it was he who brought a different dimension to African-American Christianity which no other Black man in this area of the world has ever attempted.

The men above, all of African origin, have produced an immeasurable impact on that which is labeled today "Judeo-Christian civilization" and "white-power-structure" (government) names which are used synonymously with the "United States of America."

In the case of Father Divine, he gave Jesus Christ much
more of a humanistic posture than any of his contemporaries.
On the other hand, the Prophet Elijah Mohammed, reportedly of
a former Baptist preacher background, debunked European-
American style Christianity and Judaism as currently practised.
Not only has the Prophet removed his followers from what he
called,

> The hypocrisy of the white devil's religion
> ..., etc.,

but he also modernized the Moslem Koran (Qu'ran)

> to suit the needs of the Asiatic Black
> peoples... etc.,

according to the message being given to the "dead Negroes" his
followers desire to save. This is a basic tenet in the "Nation
of Islam" - the correct name for the so-called "Black Muslims."

The Honourable Marcus Garvey, late President-General of
the Universal Negro Improvement Association, Inc. (U.N.I.A.),
started a new Christian philosophy, and made Jesus Christ appear
Black for the people who worshipped him throughout the Harlems
of the "Western world." Garvey took his image from the Jesus
Christ depicted in the Ethiopian Koptic (Coptic) Church - the
oldest Christian Church and nation in existence.

This work's ultimate goal is to show the definite links
between Ju Ju, Voodoo, and other exclusively indigenous
traditional African religions with Judaism, Christianity and
Islam, among other religions more commonly known to the European-
Americans, and of course, to those of other ethnic groupings.
It will also show that when Ju Ju and Voodoo, as well as other
traditionally African religions, meet the conversion efforts
xxii

of either three so-called "Western Religions" - Judaism, Christianity and Islam, the latter three must accommodate the first
two by adopting many aspects of the basic tenets in order to
keep the new converts. For this reason, and many others not
being mentioned here, it is virtually impossible to find an
African convert in Africa who has surrendered all of his or her
traditional culture and religious practices - especially customs
associated with ancestral worship and oracles - for European-
style Judaism and Christianity or Asian Mohametism (Islam).
Because of the same reason most African-American forms of
Judaism, Christianity and Islam take on concepts and emotional
outlets not common among their European-American religious
contemporaries of the three so-called "Western Religions."
However, no attempt whatsoever will be made to prove whether
Abraham, Moses, Jesus Christ, Mohamet, Bilal or Oledamre, and
any other Gods and prophets were Black, White, Yellow, Brown,
Red or technicolor; except in cases where they already have
been made to appear Caucasianized, and in fact, are known to
be African or of African origin. This work shall not attempt
to convey any special political, cultural, economic, moral or
religious message; nor shall it refrain from any area heretofore
considered to be controversial and anti-established order by
certain ethnic, religious or political groupings. If this
work were to receive the endorsement of everyone, then it is
certain that it has said nothing meaningful, by virture of the
subject matter alone.

AFRICAN ORIGINS OF THE MAJOR RELIGIONS ADOPTED BY THE
"WESTERN WORLD" shall seek out and report "truth" as it is

discovered in the pages of recorded history; also through personal knowledge and contact by the author; ...this is all it is intended to accomplish.

Scholarly excellence is the goal this work attempts to achieve. Thus, it is written on a level somewhere between the college sophomore and the generally articulate reading public, which is the primary academic prerequisite for this course of study.

For the reasons already stated there are very few footnotes on the pages of the text. The major notes are given at the rear of the book in sections entitled: "Notes for Chapter No. 1 Shango," etc. This method of documentation affords the reader a free flow of the information without having to be immediately distracted by footnotes, of which the average reader may or may not be interested. By the same token, the necessary notes and documentations are still available to the much more inquiring student or general reader who may desire to become involved in further research, or just to verify the author's sources of information and references. At specific points in the work, however, it became necessary to insert in brackets certain documentary or related notes and evidence as part of the integral whole of the free flowing information, all of which dealt with recorded events; otherwise the quality and uniqueness of this work would not have been maintained.

Lastly, another major objective of this work is to make the past relate to the living present by means of the materials presented. The old (past) should be relevant to the contemporary (present) in order that the new (future) can be best planned ,
xxiv

approached, and subsequently obtained; if this be not the reason for works such as this, but instead only its historic chronological findings, then this would have been a waste of good time and academic research.

The role of the Africans (sometimes called "Negroes, Bantus, Pygmies, Hottentots, Bushmen, Niggers" and a host of other such degrading terminologies) and their descendants in the field of religion, as in all other areas of human endeavour, is too often ignored, and in too many cases, completely denied. Because of this existing condition it is necessary, if for no other reason, to bring to the forefront, once more, a few of the African (Black) personalities that preceded the Reverend Dr. Martin Luther King, Jr. in trying to put religion into religious congregations and institutions.[11] It is also necessary to show many of them as the people who were most responsible for the origination of the philosophical concepts by which European-Americans and African-Americans are guided as "moral codes," all of which today is called ..."Western Religion" and "Western Philosophy."[12]

The events of the death of Minister El Hajj Malik Shabazz (Malcolm - X - Little) and the Reverend Dr. Martin Luther King, Jr. caused certain delay in the completion of this work which was more than three years in preparation. Those who knew of this work in its earliest stages will notice that Chapter V has been revised to meet the above events; and by doing so, the entire manuscript has had to be rewritten in many places. This new dimension has enhanced the current value of the material content.

However, it will be noted that none of the personalities mentioned in this work is rated over any of the others. If this were done, the purpose for which this work is created would have suffered beyond repair. In closing, and with respect to the major contributions of all of the Africans and people of African origin mentioned herein, the following African saying is given:

> ...An offspring without a spirit past is a being without an ancestral tie ....

author unknown

SHANGO: A SOURCE OF AFRICAN RELIGIONS

CHAPTER NUMBER ONE

"Pagaism, Voodooism, Witchcraft, Fetishism, Black Magic,
Obyah and Oledamare" are all but a mere sample of the many names
relegated to a few of the righteously sacred religions of solely
traditional indigenous African origin - according to most
European and European-American educators, theologians and
general missionaries who believe within themselves that they
have been ordained by some God or the other to save mankind
from "themselves." Although this messianic obsession is in
itself disgusting enough, these labels have become more and
more extremely offensive to the peoples of African origin who
cherish their ancient traditional religious heritage that has
survived Asian, European and European-American slavery and
colonialization. As such, this chapter, hopefully, endeavors
to point out some of the fundamentally indigenous African
moral, spiritual, and philosophical concepts in these religions
which are unknown to most foreigners, as well as to the vast
majority of the sons and daughters of the true "Garden of Eden"
- Alkebu-lan, which the Greeks and Romans renamed "Africa,"
along with other such nomenclatures.

Subsequent to the dawn of Zinjanthropus boisie, approximately
750,000 B.C.E., and possibly before this date, the indigenous
African peoples - the so-called "Negroes, Bantus, Bushmen,
Hottentots" and others bearing such labels of inferiority status
placed upon them by their slave masters and colonizers from Asia

1

and Europe - have been honoring a "superior force" or "being."
Sometimes this "force" or "being" is expressed in its material
sense, or in its un-seeable union in the "Spirit (Nether) World"
- equal to the Christian "Hell" and "Heaven", Muslim "Paradise,"
and Jewish "Hereafter."

Because of the concept of a "Spirit World" in most of the
traditionally indigenous African religions there are also "good"
and "bad" or "evil" ancestors and/or "omens." These could be
translated into "good" and "bad" angels and devils. Thus: The
Christian Devil - 'His Satanic Majesty' - would be as much a God
as would be Jesus Christ, Allah or Yvah; however, he would be a
"bad" or fallen God; "bad," not in the sense that the ancestor
himself would have been obnoxious, but in the order of his past
as "good" or "bad" things - equivalent to the role of a "bad"
Satan (the Devil, or Fallen Angel) with respect to a "good"
Jesus Christ, Jehovah or Allah. For the African's contention is:
if God alone can make all things, and control all things -
including man, then there must be at least one "good" God and
one "bad" God; or the one God is both "good" and "bad" in the
same instance.

Contrary to most European and European-American-style
Christian dogmatism, which expounds the racist belief that
"Black Afrcian" (Negro, Bantu, etc.) traditional religions are
solely "visualistic and idolistic," the fact is that most
indigenous African traditional religions of pre-slavery and
pre-colonial European and European-American periods that
survived are as fundamentally philosophical and spiritual as
the so-called "idealistic religions." The natural objects
2

used in said-African traditional religious practices to which
Christian and Moslem missionaries object, serve only to remind
the faithful of "divine presence"; and they are no different
in meaning than the exhibition of a Mogen David around a Jew's
neck, a Crucifix hanging on a Christian's chest, or a Ka'aba
(black stone from Ethiopia) concealed on a Moslem's person:[1]
all of which are "natural" (materialistic) "objects" to remind
them of their Gods.

Citations of an example of the above remarks are to be
found in the "libations" (sacrificial drinking) still being
practised by the indigenous Africans of traditionally African
religions. The extent of this custom is seen in the fact that
"the greatest of the Fathers of the Christian Church" - St.
Augustine (an indigenous African), the most noted of Christendom's
"moralists," commented on its usage in religious devotion quite
favorably. It is no less sacred, Augustine felt, than the
drinking of wine during the Christians' "Holy Communion" in
memory of the Last Supper (Passover Seder); or a Rabbi taking
his sips of wine on the Sabbath Eve (Omeg Shabat - Friday Evening).
Yet these fundamental mainstays in most traditional indigenous
African religious teachings have been employed in the "Mystery
Systems" of North, East, West, South,and Central Africa more than
three-thousand years before the birth of the Hebrew religion,
which is thousands of years before the African of Egypt - Moses -
supposedly left his native homeland on the Nile River banks to
resettle the African-Jews of Egypt in Canaan. Strange as it may
seem, the liberation of Canaan by the Hebrews would be an act of
imperialism and of genocide had it taken place in the 19th or

3

20th century C.E. Nevertheless, the mere fact that people have
said that God (Jehovah) ordered this colonialization of one
group of people, he made, by another, seems to justify said
barbarism in the minds of most, even today. If the Egyptians
should claim that God ordered them into the same area taken from
the Moabites, Hittites, Jebusites, etc., the same as he ordered
the Hebrews sometime ago, over three-thousand years ago, who
will believe them?

To say that the indigenous West Africans' involvement in
the use of alcoholic beverages (palm wine) for libations
(religious invocations or secular toastings) is the custom of
"pagans" and the "uncivilized," which is too often said, is to
label equally all "Westerners" who drink wine ceremoniously
in Hebrew or Christian rituals of being guilty of the same.
Then is it Godly when a White man drinks wine in a church or
synagogue, but unGodly in the case of a Black man?

In Voodoo ceremonies, Libation[2] marks the period when
certain rituals begin and others end. For example, the Libation
ritual during the ceremony that precedes the placing of
sacrificial foods on the main altar - Bagi (Holy of Holies) -
before the prayer of sacrifice,[3] also marks the entrance of the
Papa loa (High Priest). This custom is as common among the
African-Haitians as it is among the Whydahs of West Africa. In
Christian ceremonies, especially during Holy Communion, it is
customary for the attendants (mass boys, priests, etc.) to set
the altar with bread (host) in preparation of the recital of a
"pagan" ritual that demands:

4

"Take ye and eat this, Christ's body...," etc.

For wine (alcohol) it is:

"Drink ye this, Christ's blood...", etc.

The priest-or minister's first drink (libation) before he dips the host (Christ's body) into the wine (Christ's blood)[3a] and calls upon God (Christ's father) which is similar to invoking the spirit of the Yorubas of West Africa's God, Oledamare, and his Orishas (minor Gods). This is clearly stated in the..."Take ye this My blood, and drink in My memory," etc., a typically "paganistic" and "cannibalistic" ceremony if performed by Africans or African-Americans in Voodoo.[4] Is this ceremony not similar to the ancient custom when the Druids[5] of Northern Europe allegedly "...drank their enemies' blood and ate their brains to capture their spiritual and physical strength?"

Is there any major difference between the practice: When the Papa loa (High Priest - who is similar in rank to a Roman Catholic Bishop, Protestant Archbishop, Jewish Chief Rabbi, or Moslem Grand Iman) is aided by his subordinate Houngan (priest) and Mambo (priestess) at the beginning of the eating of the manges (sacrificial food) as the badgian (acolyte, or assistant to the High Priest) shakes the asson (rattle made from a hollowed gourde with dried corn kernel inside) three times while the members of his congregation respond by bowing their heads; and when a Roman Catholic Bishop in his ceremony during the Holy Communion; or when a priest acts as the Bishop's acolyte and shakes the chimer (incense holder) and the chimes signal the congregation to bow their heads to prayer,

5

while in the pursuing moments that follow the choir softly and
solemly sings as his wine (libation) is carefully poured for
him by his acolyte (badgian)?

Is the burning of sweet incense in Voodoo rituals "un-Godly,"
but "Godly" in Jewish, Christian,and Islamic ceremonies? If
this is true, then "Western Religions" incense is the right way;
and maybe the choir in their religious ceremonies - with its
organ and/or piano background music - is also the only one to be
rated "Godly." If "Western Religions'" choirs are the only ones
approved by the authorized Gods, it is only natural that the
Voodoo choirs with their background ogun (triangular instruments
beaten by sticks) and tambours (series of drums)[6] - must be
rendered "un-Godly." Why? Because a group of powerful men
(European and European-Americans) who dominate and control
religious propaganda ordained it so.

God - or Vodum, Jehovah, Oledamare, Jesus Christ, Allah,
and Baba Loas, neither one is less the divinity that enters and
seizes the righteous in a Pentecostal, Baptist, or Voodoo
ceremony because He or She is called by either one of these
names mentioned. In any of the fundamentally so-called "Save
Soul Churches" of African-American and European-American
sponsorship, one can easily note that Voodoo and Ju Ju have been
co-opted in many of their forms into the Judaeo-Christian setting
that is common to Christians and Jews in the United States of
America. Within this phenomenal development, the so-called
"Negro Spiritual" is the most common and acceptable "paganistic
incantation" to European-American Jews and Christians. Why?
Because they see such African-American incantations ("Negro
6

Spirituals") as religious entertainment by truly black-faced
minstrels ("Niggers," etc.).

Are the "Negro Spirituals" in any way a developmental
outgrowth of European-American-style Christianity? Or, are
they not an extension of indigenous African traditional
religious chants that underwent European and European-American-
style Jewish and Christian influences? The latter is definitely
the case. Of course this conclusion will be very heatedly
denied by those who wish not to be labeled - among other
things - "pagans, savages, uncivilized, cannibals," etc. But
the fact still remains that Ju Ju, Voodoo, Witchcraft,and Magic,
all basic elements within the so-called "Western Religions," have
been emphasized in the African-American (Black) owned and
controlled synagogues, churches,and mosques.

The history of the African-Americans' belated entrance into
European-American-style Christian Protestantism and Roman
Catholicism is in itself evidence that the Africans, who were at
the time chattel slaves of European and European-American Jewish
and Christian slavemasters, were not wanted by the in-groups
(the slavemasters). Could it have been possible that those
Africans (who were not aware of the fact that their fellow
indigenous Africans - such as Moses, St. Augustine, Bilal and
others - primarily made Judaism, Christianity,and Islam the mass
organizations they are) would have adopted the existing forms
of religious worship their slavemasters were using to enslave
them in toto? Not at all so. The mere fact that they were
forcibly excluded from all forms of Jewish, Christian,and Islamic

7

("Western Religions") religious worship; and that they were even persecuted and prosecuted for any attempt at practising either on their own, is further prime facie evidence that there is a distinctly different Judaism, Christianity, and Islam developed by the African-Americans that is not attributable and/or applicable to, and by, European-Americans.   The uniqueness of their common eating habits represents no major differences between the two groups. For example, the African-American was forced to develop an appetite for "chitterling, ham hocks, pig's ears, tails and feet." Why? Because all other parts of the pig, like all other edible animals, were reserved for the European and European-American slavemasters - Christian and Jewish - in and out of religion. In the case of the so-called "Western Religions," the Africans were even denied the right to read any book whatsoever, that is, including the Jewish or Christian "Holy Scripture," much less the Moslem's - which was not tolerated among the colonists, even after they became independent as the United States of America.

One must remember that the Africans, although crushed in their every attempt to participate within the culture of the bestial environment of slavery, did communicate with each other in the cotton fields and other places where they labored, through Voodoo, Ju Ju, and other richly spiritual and religious devotions they developed in their indigenous homeland - the continent of Alkebu-lan (Africa). The bestiality of their slavemasters further made them learn each other's religious songs and chants. This conglomerate of religious exultation, therefore, became the background for the later development which is today

8

erroneously called "Negro Spirituals," instead of African incantations, or Voodoo Chants. It is to be remembered that the slaves were Africans; not "Negroes." "Negroes" were originated by the European slavemasters, so was "Negroland" (See BLACK MAN OF THE NILE, by Yosef ben-Jochannan, Alkebu-lan Books, New York, 1970, Chapter I, pp. 1-48, and pp. 266-268.

There was nothing "Negro" about the development of the "Spirituals." They were developed by millions of Africans; not one of whom was a "free man"; not one a "citizen"; not one a "human being" under the laws of Great Britain up until 1776 C.E.; neither were they so considered after the American war of independence from Great Britain, nor after their Federal Constitution was written, and from thence through the 14th Amendment of said document in 1885 C.E.;[7a] and to a very great extent not even today in 1970 - more than 350 years after the first group of Africans were brought to the United States of America as indentured and chattel slaves.

Further proof lies in the fact that Africans on the European and European-American slave farms, plantations, or in the businesses and big houses sang their 'African Spirituals' and chanted their other Voodoo and Ju Ju praises to Africa's Gods long before they could even understand what the Gods of their European and European-American captors and slavemasters were all about. This European-style Christian God (Jesus Christ) was different to the Jesus Christ presented to them in Ethiopia before He was introduced to the Romans in Rome.

"Fare de well, fare de well...," etc., may be to most Black and White peoples in the United States of America today

9

some sort of poetically broken English. Yes! Certainly poetic,
and definitely broken in its English. Yet, it came from a
"Negro Spiritual" that had its origin in the savagery of the
Jewishless and Christianless slavemasters' sadistic cruelty and
genocide upon their helpless and defenseless African slaves.
"Fare de well, fare de well" that the blows from the master's
bull-whip, with its metal pellets, would not maim another
African slave if he (or she) was not lucky enough to die from
the blows instead. This is what these words that were composed
during the world's worst era of genocide by one group of mankind's
inhumanity towards the other (European and European-American
physical and mental enslavement of the African peoples in
Africa, the Caribbean Islands, and continental Americas) were
saying.

"Go down Moses, way down in Egypt's land, tell ole Pharoah[8]
let my people go...," etc., may in itself suggest Jewish (Hebrew)
origin. Yet, in fact, it was the poetic expression which was so
common in the Africans' rebellion of their disgust and contempt
for their Christian and Jewish slavemasters that were being
exulted. But, why did the slaves use the name of a fellow
indigenous African - Moses (a Haribu) - in their appeal for
freedom, and could not see the justice in their other fellow
African - Pharoah (King) Rameses II's reason for exiling his
fellow indigenous Africans of the Hebrew religion (Jews)?
Because of many reasons, most common of which are:

        (A) They did not know that Moses was an indigenous
             African, as they were.

10

(B)   Biblical Egypt had always been taught in
      churches and synagogues as a mythical place
      where Africans (whom the slavemasters
      renamed "Negroes") did not exist.

(C)   They were brainwashed into believing that
      the enslavement of the African Jews by their
      fellow African worshippers of the God Ra was
      an act against their God (Jehovah of the Jews,
      and Jesus Christ of the Christians); but
      their own slavery, on the other hand, was "the
      will of God."

(D)   And that their own enslavement was for their
      own benefit, since "slavery saved them from
      being eaten by their much more cannibalistic
      uncivilized pagan fellow Africans, who were
      not as fortunate as they were to... hear the
      message of God "(Jesus Christ).[8a]

The hatred implanted into the preceding words with regard
to Moses and his troubles with his fellow African, Pharoah
Rameses II, is still sung with greater passion in African-
American Churches than songs of their own enslavement – such as
"Ole Man River" and "Lift Every Voice and Sing."[9] In most of the
sophisticated so-called "middle class" minded "Negro Churches"
– such as the "Negro" Presbyterians, Anglicans, Roman Catholics,
Lutherans, Moravians, etc., these songs seem to be banned by a
kind of gentlemen's agreement to, hopefully, bury their historic
past memories of chattel slavery. In this manner, the
beneficiaries of slavery, their slavemasters' descendants, can
easily forget the fact that the slaves' labor, which created
said wealth, goes still unpaid.

"Lift Every Voice and Sing...," etc., begins the once
famous "Negro National Anthem" that was composed by the late
African-American – James Weldon Johnson. However, it is still
being sung among the less sophisticated African-Americans (Blacks)
who find no solace in its continued exclusion in European-America.

11

But, today it, too, has become a part of the Voodoo and Ju Ju
'African-American Spiritual' of the cultural revolution. It
too has been relegated to be sung only upon occasions when the
African-American is overshadowed by some white could of misery -
such as the cold-blooded murders of the Minister Malcom X
(El hajj Malik Shabazz) and the Reverend Dr. Martin Luther King,
Jr. But it must also give way to the much more popular
"...When I Die I'm Gonna Walk Al Over God's Heavun, Heavun,
Heavun...," etc., when the fallen brother or sister African-
American is a close and personal friend or blood relative. Why?
Because the latter song preaches resignation and satisfaction
with slavery; whereas the former slightly suggests a bit of
protest on the part of a people who are still in their state of
mental slavery, yet conscious enough to muster a bit of protest
in their struggle for self esteem.

Voodoo and Ju Ju chants, and testimonials, can be heard in
the preaching of the Last Sermon on the Mount that echoed:

> Free at last! Free at last! Great God
> Almighty, I'm Free at last..." "I've been up to
> the mountain top, and I've seen the Promised Land...,"
> etc.

But with a crashing booming BANG from an assassin's weapon of
violence the life of the man on the mountain - a by-product of
Voodoo and Ju Ju, along with European and European-Americanized
Judaeo-Christianity, the Reverend Dr. Martin Luther King, Jr.,
was "Free at last...." This man, who had melodiously mastered
his African chants, found only in the African-American (so-called
"Negro") Baptist Church and other "testimonial" sharing and
"Soul releasing" African forms of Christian experience around
12

the entire world, had also revived Voodooism and Ju Ju-ism -
even to the point of provoking the love of the God Oledamare
and His Orishas (minor Gods). This analysis may not find many
believers in its proclamations; but the fact remains that
Dr. King was typical in his approach as any Voodoo preacher
of today.

When Voodoo priests take a rooster in their divine
encantation and begin their dance to the God Damballah Ouedo
one can hear the same in the spiritual crescendo of the
tambourine and piano-playing that accompany the religious
dancing within the African-American testimonial that Dr. King
preached; particularly when Obyah and Voodoo spirits take hold
of their worshippers - to the extent that they floatingly move
into the ecstacy of religious trance. This form of Voodooistic
involvement has been adopted by thousands of European-Americans
of varied brahces of Christianity which are today called "sects"
by their much more "sophisticated" brethren, who prefer to
maintain their emotionless dried-up middle-class analytical
teachings of self-proclaimed "theologians" and "philosophers,"
who teach beyond and above the understanding of their parishioners,
mainly to show their academic skills, rather than deal with their
followers' earthly needs.

"SOUL!" ...This overplayed and maligned "exotic word" has
been removed from its Voodoo origin into an "Old Black Magic"[10]
and "Witchcraft" night-clubbing atmosphere, and from there to
the more popular and contemporary, but most contemptible,
meaning of "Black Comedy." Yet; "SOUL" was originally the

13

expression used in the religious ceremonial dance that once
entered, in a debased form, the European-American entertainment
world from the Caribbean as the "LIMBO DANCE."

The "Limbo," a religious ceremonial dance performed by
the priest of the Obyah rites in preparation for the adoration
ceremonies adulating masculinity before the initiation
proceedings of a young boy to be circumcized and start his road
into "manhood," is as sacred as a <u>Jewish Barmitzvah</u> or a
<u>Christian First Communion</u>. In this ceremonial exhibition, it
is said that:

> Man displays his greatest sense of power in
> his ability to coordinate in perfect unison his
> mind and body in graciously rhythmic movements,
> and as such reach perfect meditation with his
> God through the intervention of ancestral spirits
> from the spirit world.

But, why did the overlords and slavemasters from Europe and
Britain ban the "Limbo" in Africa and the Caribbean Islands?
Because they feared its "paganistic immorality" and the "Black
Magic" it was supposed to emit. They saw it as a form of
"heathenism"; of course, with a bit of cannibalism thrown in
for good measure, this reaction being typical of the so-called
"Christian Missionaries" that afflicted Africa and the indigenous
African peoples and their descendants for over the past 476 years
(1503-1970 C.E.)[*]

---

[*] 1503 or 1506 C.E. was the year the Right Reverend Bishop
Bartolome de Las Casas of the Roman Catholic Church had the King
and Queen of Spain and the Pope in Rome institute the infamous
"slave trade." Their first victims being Moors who had refused
to become Christians after they were toppled by the Christians.
The first number to be sent to Las Casas was 4,000. The original
slave port was located on the Island of Hayte (Haiti), which
the Spaniards had already renamed "Hispaniola."

14

In general, that which is presently called "Limbo Dance" came down to contemporary African-Americans by way of African Christianity which was adopted after Christinaity was infused with Ju Ju-ism and Voodooism in West Africa and the Caribbean Islands, before its arrival in the United States of America.

Is it not strange that in "Save Soul" or "Sanctified" dancing the dancers' knees are never crossed? Yes!. But only to those who do not know that "crossing the Knees" in a Voodoo dance is as much sacriligious as one trying to do a goose-step during a Jewish or Christian religious procession before the Ark of the Covenant or the Altar of Communion. The history of this most sacred religious tradition came down to the African-American and the African-Caribbean from generations succeeding generations (through action) even though not a single word was permitted to be written down; all of which was "inspired by God," the African God - "Voodum." One sees the same corollary in the Jewish, Christian, and Moslem traditional religious dances or movements of the priests, rabbis, ministers, and imams. This tradition, the "Limbo Dance," is as much the order of a God of Africa - through his "inspired Holy Prophets" that were called upon by His "angels," as the Gods of Europe and Asia who called upon Abraham, Moses, Jesus Christ, and Mohamet. Or is it that God, too, is guilty of "racism?" And that He, She or It, could never call upon an African to be one of the "Prophets?" Maybe it is that Oledamare, the God of the Yorubas and millions more of West Africa, is not the equal of Jehovah, Jesus Christ or Allah.

15

If the European and European-American can see beyond his

(or her) own narrow belief that he alone is perfect; and that

mankind did not have to call upon him to save humanity for any

God whatsoever, then, and only then, is it possible for him

to see the influence Ju Ju, Voodoo, Magic, Obyah, Witchcraft,

and most other forms of other peoples' religion and God that

preceded the creation of Judaism, Christianity, and Islam,

had on them in their own beginning, and now.

    In his book, BANTU PHILOSOPHY, the late Roman Catholic

priest - Placide Temples - wrote:[11]

IN SEARCH OF A BANTU PHILOSOPHY

1. Life and death determine human behavior.

    It has been often remarked that a European
who has given up, during his life, all practices
of the Christian religion, quickly returns to a
Christian viewpoint when suffering or pain raise
the problem of the preservation and survival or
the loss and destruction of his being. Many
sceptics turn, in their last moments, to seek
in the ancient Christian teaching of the West,
the practical answer to the problem of redemption
or destruction. Suffering and death are ever the
two great apostles who lead many wanderers in
Europe at their last moments to our traditional
Christian wisdom.

    In the same way among our Bantu we see the
evolues, the "civilized," even the Christians,
return to their former ways of behavior whenever
they are overtaken by moral lassitude, danger or
suffering. They do so because their ancestors
left them their practical solution of the great
problem of humanity, the problem of life and death,
of salvation or destruction. The Bantu, only
converted or civilized superficially, return at the
instance of a determining force to the behavior
activistically dictated to them.

    Among the Bantu and, indeed, among all primitive
peoples, life and death are the great apostles of
fidelity to a magical view of life and of recourse
to traditional magical practices.

1. Evolues: I preserve this term untranslated
for lack of a suitable English equivalent. It
signifies those who have passed out of the traditional
ways of life and thought of their own ethnic group
and have taken over those of the West. (C.K.)

Herein lies the basic problem in which so many European and

European-American-style Christian and Asian Moslem missionaries

and their African converts, also Jewish educators (Rabbinate),

find themselves hopelessly enthralled. Reverend Temples also

tried to be "impartial," he said. His claim being the same as

all others who professed Judaism, Christianity or Islam, and at

the same instance, pretend that their own prejudices can be

scholarly subdued sufficiently to make "impartial" analysis of

Africa's traditional religions. This premise is without a doubt

ridiculously preposterous. And it is seen in its ugliest pretext

by most Africans and African-Americans who are most affected by

it. How can a person believe in one God and be impartial in his

praises of another God of a different philosophy than his own?

The possessiveness of Reverend Father Placide Temples is

best seen in his claim that:

"In the same way among our Bantu, we see the
evolues, the "civilized," even the....," etc.

"Our Bantu" was not even given the usually dishonest

treatment of the quotation marks, which would have to some

extent, concealed the Reverend's personal bias and obvious and

apparent racism concerning the word "civilized."

Reverend Temples opened up his work on the very first

page, second paragraph, exhibiting what appears to be the same

type of gross racism and religious bigotry his work was

supposedly correcting.

17

The title of Chapter I, "IN SEARCH OF A BANTU PHILOSOPHY,"
is itself at least provocative, if not openly insulting to the
overwhelming majority of the peoples of Africa - the indigenous
population. Here is a professed "man of God" who allegedly came
to Africa to "civilize and Christianize the heathen Africans";[11a]
yet, he had to look for a "Bantu Philosophy." One can understand
the semantic problem, because the name "Bantu" in itself is a
creation of the racist colonial slavemasters who, like himself,
came originally from Europe, and later on, The United States of
America. This type of arrogance caused mass genocide to be
committed against the indigenous Africans, the slavers, and
colonizers renamed "Bantus" - along with other names such as
"Hottentots, Hamites, Pygmies, Negroes," etc. But Reverend
Placide Temples was very well aware of this part of history with
respect to his fellow colonialist administrators and European-
style Christian missionaires with whom he served, and those that
preceded him; all of them knowing too well the correct names the
indigenous Africans called themselves when they first arrived
in Africa. Nevertheless they forced the Africans to adopt what
they chose to call "Christian names" - such as "James, George,
Phillip," and other such names used by British and European
kings, who were some of the worst characters in world history.

Any group of people with a concept that created a God which
they have not seen, spoken to, or met, must have begun from a
philosophical premise. This is seen in the "Mysteries" the
Jews (Hebrews) copied from their fellow Africans of Egypt
(Sais) to produce their first Torah, which the Christians
subsequently copied from the Jews to create their "Holy Bible"
18

(all versions); and the Torah and Bible the Moslems later
adopted from the Christians and Jews to produce their Koran.
At least, the philosophy Father Temples could not find in
his "Bantu-God" (or Gods) is uniquely original to any of the
so-called "Western Religions." It was developed along with
other traditions and experiences the indigenous Africans had,
rather than upon European and European-American-style
Christian doctrines which had nothing in common with West,
South or Central African civilizations before the European
(White Man) arrived at these areas of Africa (Alkebu-lan).

On the other hand Jack Mendelsohn, a Unitarian Minister,
in the second "Preface" of his book entitled - "GOD, ALLAH
AND JU JU," used an entirely different approach in 1962 than
Temples did in 1954. He opened on pages 9 and 10 with the
following remarks:[12]

>"I accept African independence without
>reservations. This is my "bias" and it is well
>to state it at the beginning. I acknowledge
>also without reservations, the equal dignity
>of Africans. I believe that Africans are under
>no more obligation to justify their freedom and
>dignity than Westerners are. Nor are they under
>any less obligations. We - Africans and Westerners
>- are of the same species.
>
>In practical terms the outcome of African
>freedom will depend on many forces, some of
>which are purely African. Others, however, are
>much influenced by Western sentiments, conduct
>and relations with Africa.
>
>A good many of these forces are political and
>economic. They are written about profusely. But
>politics and economics are not the only forces
>shaping Africa's future. Religion is also a factor
>to be reckoned with, a vitally important one.
>Little enough has been written of it, especially
>in the broad fashion of this book.

19

Questions of profound significance for Africans
and for the sentiments of Westerners about Africa are:

What is the future of Christianity as the
religious commitment of Africa's rising leadership?

What is the future of Islam in the same context?

What normal base do African Elitists see being
built under the newly independent societies? What
do African intellectuals mean when they appeal to
traditional African spiritual values as such a base?
If magic is an inherent part of such traditional
values, how does it affect moral and intellectual
development?

What kind of religious and moral training does
the African intelligentsia advocate as part of the
educational process?

What does the concept of the separation of church
and state mean in modern African society?

How does religious commitment relate to the
overall style of life of African leaders?

What vital relevance is there, if any, in the
traditional African structure of "time," the unseen,
spirit world?

How does all of this relate to the allure of
Communism as an alternative spiritual force?

Before commenting on Mendelsohn's "Preface," it is necessary

to cite what he had to say in his dedication:

TO:

That small circle of men and women in each
African society, who hunger for what is essentially
African, even as they thirst for the best of the
world's learning and modernity. They are still few
in number, and are having no easy time of it.

"The small circle of men and women in each African society,"

etc., which Reverend Mendelsohn knows in his mind "...are still

few in number..." is conceivable, but not necessarily true, and

needs corroboration. The balance of his statement is just

another missionary's conclusion that appears prejudged to suit

20

the pattern of something-else dissimilar to that which he wrote in
the first paragraph of his "Preface" shown underscored for emphasis.

The extract from the "Preface," pages 9 and 10, as highlighted
by the last question. Thus:

> How does all of this relate to the allure of
> Communism as an alternative spiritual force?

Would it not be logical that the indigenous Africans should, now,
relate more so to their own traditional "Ju Ju" religion with its
built-in Communalism, which is much more highly advanced in terms
of human relations than that which is today called "democracy"
for their own religious solutions? Why is the question with
relation to the Africans' freedom always Communism more than
Capitalism, Islam, Judaism or Christianity - including
Unitariansim, neither of which is conducive to any of the
indigenous African civilizations in existence? Each of these
foreign "-isms" has had at least four hundred years in Africa,
except Communism, to prove itself in the eyes of the Africans
and has utterly failed.

On pages 21 and 22 Reverend Mendelsohn stated the following:

> What of the Christian missionary movement?
> Its slow but steady progress has now run headlong
> into the "new" Africa. The charges leveled
> against it are both humorous and biting.
>
> In their freewheeling moods, young Africans
> never seem to tire of retelling the old chestnut:
>
> "The missionaries came to us and said, 'We want
> to teach you to pray.' 'Good,' we said. 'We would
> like to learn to pray.' So the Missionaries told
> us to close our eyes. We closed our eyes, there
> was a Bible in our hands, but our land was gone!"

If the good Reverend believes that this is not true, he should read accounts by his own forerunners in the missionary field; especially "THE PLANTING OF CHRISTIANITY IN AFRICA," by C.P. Grove, New York, 1948-58, 4 Vols.

The Reverend continues:

> But there are also bitter words - words repeated endlessly across the breadth of Africa.
>
> "The Christian missionary movement was an attempt to quench the African spirit. It tried to turn Africans into European Christians. It kicked down our culture to show us which side God is on."
>
> "Missionaries are unrealistic about polygamy."
>
> "Wherever the white man still has the upper hand, the missionaries remain strangely tolerant of racial discrimination."
>
> "The missionaries drag their feet when it comes to training Africans for church leadership and authority."
>
> "The missions have been indifferent, even hostile toward African nationalism. There's been no real sympathy for the political aspirations gripping young Africans."

If Mendelsohn, at this late date in Christian missionary invovlement in Africa as an adjunct to colonialism, cannot understand why Africans would turn to any _ism_ other than "capitalism" and European or European-American-style "Christian-ism" from the above alleged comments, his slumber is very deep indeed. There is not an African old enough to reason who is not aware of the truth in the above charges; even Africans who have unfortunately joined what is being peddled as "Christianity" in Africa to this very day by "men of the cloth" from Europe and the United States of America - the so-called "African" or "Native Clergy" - know these facts. They know that imperialism,

22

colonialism, chattel slavery, and now neo-colonialism, were, and are, partners of European and European-American-style Christianity.

"Africa's Tarnished Cross" is the name selected by Mendelsohn for the chapter in which the preceding quotations are shown. But should it not be Europe and European-America's "Tarnished Cross?" Why insinuate that the Christian Cross, European and European-American-style, is at all African? The indigenous African peoples did not import this style of Christianity into Africa. It came there with the slavemasters and its co-colonialist mate - imperialism, which it nows desires to disavow. Why? Because it too is now under attack and being rejected for what it has proven to be, in fact, in the eyes of the Africans and their new nations. Yet Ethiopian (African) Christianity - formerly the "Koptic (Coptic) Church, the oldest Christian Church in the world, is still respected, and has no "Tarnished Cross."

"Religion In Africa Today," the subtitle of Mendelsohn's book, follows the usual order in which the traditional religions of Africa have been lowly rated by the missionaries, as shown in the pattern followed in his book's title - "GOD, ALLAH AND JU JU." Since Africa is the main theme or subject of the entire book, why not JU JU, GOD, AND ALLAH? And is Jesus Christ any more a GOD than JU JU and ALLAH? Furthermore, why should the Africans always follow everyone-else? The answer is already shown in the comments the alleged Africans repeated to Reverend Mendelsohn, which he seems not to comprehend. It is seen in its contemptuous accounts by his fellow missionaries who still contend that the Africans, who are not taken in by sky pilots who preach death

23

and not life, are "cannibals, heathens, pagans, one step near man," and the likes of such comments and labels.

Commenting on the expulsion of the French Roman Catholic Bishop - the Right Reverend Gerard de Milleville (who got booted from the Republic of Guineas 25 August 1962 by President Sekou Toure after he had served sixteen years of indulgence and support of French colonialism without once ever opposing it, and four years after the people of Guinea under the leadership of their president won their independence from France, which he could not adjust to) - Mendelsohn stated on pages 165 and 166 the following:

> This but one more in a continuing line of
> of flaring signals indicating that the Christian
> missionary enterprise in Africa is in serious
> trouble. Regardless of how valuable the missionary
> contribution to Africa has been, and might continue
> to be, the sentiment spreads among African leaders
> that the effort is no longer appropriate to their
> continent.

One must need say that Mendelsohm believes that the African leadership at one time or another considered European and European-American-style Christian missionaries "appropriate." He may be surprised to know that they are there, not because they were or are "appropriate," instead because they were, and still are, supported by the military might of the nations of Europe that imposed them upon the indigenous African peoples. And that this imposition was used to stomp out many indigenous traditional African religions of thousands of years duration. He continues nevertheless:

> "...Missionaries should not feel despondent
> about this," say Africans. "The intellectual and
> religious loaves they have cast upon the waters
> have returned in the form of nationalism and our

24

determination to run our own affairs. In that sense, missionaries have done their job well, and we thank them. Their devotion, including often enough even the sacrifice of their lives, has built schools and hospitals, and widened the horizons of our religious beliefs. Still they must go. Not that the needs of Africa in education, medicine, and spiritual growth are now met. Far from it."

Unfortunately Reverend Mendelsohn did not identify any of "the Africans" who supposedly made these profound statements of praises for the missionaries. Africans who were not aware of the systems of education in Africa before the coming of the White man from Europe (and later the Americas) in search of food, medicine, education, and other means of human comforts. But, again, the quotation marks act to remove the Reverend's own reactions, apparently only. However, his remarks seem to be in response to President Toure's statement of 27 August 1961, in which he said:

> "...no Catholic prelate will be accredited to Guinea, unless he is an African..."

President Toure's prohibition was rather mild in comparison to the general feeling of other Africans in high positions, who have witnessed the courtship and marriage between Christian missionaries and their church to the colonial administrators, and of course to the heads of the various Christian orders in their national headquarters of the national governments to which they pledge unfailing loyalty - while claiming God's (Jesus Christ's) endorsement. This is best seen in the case of all missionary groups, by virtue of the colonial and neo-colonial powers' authority - through force or economic stronghold on the African nations, which are further perpetuated in each case where there is a sanctioned state religion, generally that which the former

25

colonizer set up before leaving physically - **of Christianity,**
European or European-American-style. As a result, this type
of religious structure and the Europeanized Africans who
operate them are obligated for continued leadership and control
by the former slavemasters and colonizers. If for no other
reasons, this is one of the major ones which the present
leadership prefers not to have continued. Unfortunately the
Reverend Mendelsohn is not the only "Christian" who wants to
see Christianity in Africa at all costs, irrespective of the
Africans opinion about it. Like most of his colleagues, the
missonary sees new hospitals, schools, medicine, and other such
material values being of greater importance to the Africans than
the price the Africans had to pay for these things. This is
providing one is to accept the position that the Africans had
none of these facilities before colonialism. It would be
foolish to take time in refuting this ancient colonialist Tarzan
and Jane type of Stanley and Livingstone mythology.

One has to learn that the re-Africanization of African
things that were Europeanized for over four hundred years also
includes the so-called "Western Religions," and in particular
those which are still being passed off as "Christianity," which
in reality are nothing more than the religious accomodation of
what is also called today "Western democracy" or the "Free World
system of economic individualsim." Again, it is quite unfortunate that the Africans are so much underated by Communists and
Capitalists alike, each believing that his way is the only way
to the answer to mankind's problem, each forgetting that each
man, including Africans, can think for himself; and that it was
26

gun powder, not Jesus Christ, Allah, Jehovah, Marx, Mao or any other God that made the Africans slaves for over four-hundred years. Therefore the African God OLEDAMARE, once more in the history of Africa, becomes as much a recognized "SUPREME BEING" in Nigeria and other parts of Africa as the Gods "JEHOVAH, ALLAH" and "JESUS CHRIST" are elsewhere, and as they were in Africa from the beginning of the infamous slave trade until political independence in Africa, a fact which too many Christian missionaries cannot yet accept. This recognition is actually saying that OLORUM is the "Master of the Nether World" (owner of Heaven) as much as Jesus Christ, Jehovah and/or Allah. And, of course, that He also rules over every man in the universe from his "joyous heaven"; just as He maintains a wretched "spirit world" for those that fail Oledamare. Also, that "OLEDAMARE IS THE GOD OVER ALL OTHER GODS." Yes, this, the Africans of this religion hold true, according to their "God-inspired men." A noted African scholar and author dealt with this same problem in the following dialogue:

> "You say that there is one supreme God who made heaven and earth," said Akunna on one of Mr. Brown's visits. "We also believe in Him and call Him Chukwu. He made all the world and the other gods."
>
> "There are no other gods," said Mr. Brown. "Chukwu is the only God and all the others are false. You carve a piece of wood - like that one," (he pointed at the rafters from which Akunna's carved Ikenga hung), "and you call it a god. But it is still a piece of wood."
>
> "Yes," said Akunna. "It is indeed a piece of wood. The tree from which it came was made by Chukwu, as indeed all minor gods were. But

27

He made them for His messengers so that we
could approach Him through them. It is like
yourself. You are the head of the church."

"No," protested Mr. Brown. "The head of
my church is God Himself."

"I know," said Akunna, "but there must be
a head in this world among men. Somebody like
yourself must be the head here."

"The head of my church in that sense is in
England."

"That is exactly what I am saying. The head
of your church is in your country. He has sent
you here as his messenger. And you have also
appointed your own messenger, and servants. Or
let me take another example, the District
Commissioner. He is sent by your king."

The above drama took place in the classic work, THINGS
FALL APART,[13] by Mr. Chinua Achebe of Nigeria, West Africa.
This story relates how a European missionary first entered
a particular village in Eastern Nigeria during the early 1900's
and tried to change the peoples from their own traditional
African God that served them faithfully for thousands of years
for his own God from Europe, of whom these Africans knew
nothing. It also deals with the value of the living "Oracle"
(prophet) in African life, as against the belief in appealing to
"saints" (dead people) in European and European-American-style
Christianity. But the crux of the above dialogue is seen in the
fact that the missionary had the audacity to come into Eastern
Nigeria and condemn the peoples' God, calling it "...a piece of
wood." He forgot that they could see their God, at least,
which was more than he could say for his. Moreover, they knew
where to find their's when they wanted his service; but could he
find his when he wanted service?

28

The dialogue continued along the line that is still commonly used by Christian, Moslem, and other foreign missionaries in their attempt to belittle the traditional Gods of Africa while, at the same instance, honoring their own Gods of Europe, Asia, and the United States of America — Jesus Christ and Allah in particular. In this regard Mr. Achebe continues:[14]

> "You say that there is one supreme God who made heaven and earth," said Akunna on one of Mr. Brown's visits. "We also believe in Him and call Him Chukwu. He made all the world and the other Gods."
>
> "There are no other gods," said Mr. Brown. "Chukwu is the only God and all others are false. You carve a piece of wood...", etc., etc.

Mr. Brown repeated everything he had stated above in this visit. Here, as one looks back at the last five paragraphs on page 25, it is seen that the indigenous Africans defended their religions with as much vigor as did the foreign European-style "Christian missionaries," like Mr. Brown, try to sell their's. Mr. Achebe continues further in the next paragraphs:[15]

> "They have a queen," said the interpreter on on his own account.
>
> "Your queen sends her messenger, the District Commissioner. He finds that he cannot do the work alone and so he appoints kotma to help him. It is the same with God, or Chukwu. He appoints the smaller gods to help Him because His work is too great for one person."

Not being able to convince Mr. Akkunna (the African) that his God — "JESUS CHRIST" — was a superior diviner to "CHUKWU," Mr. Brown (the European from England) resorted to economic (White) power, which was always available to the colonialist Christian missionaries to whip Africans who would not convert into line. This method of forced conversion was always used whenever the

29

missionaries' logic about their European-styled blonde Jesus
Christ failed to convince and convert the Africans through
non-violent persuasion. Mr. Achebe continues:[16]

> "In this way, Mr. Brown learned a good deal
> about the religion of the clan and he came to the
> conclusion that a frontal attack on it would not
> succeed. And so he built a school and a little
> hospital in Umufia. He went from family to
> family begging people to send their children to
> his school. But at first they only sent their
> slaves or sometimes their lazy children. Mr. Brown
> begged and argued and prophesied. He said that the
> leaders of the land in the future would be men and
> women who had learned to read and write. If
> Umufia failed to send her children to the school,
> strangers would come from other places to rule
> them. They could already see that happening in
> the Native Court, where the D. C. was surrounded
> by strangers who spoke his tongue. Most of these
> strangers came from the distant town of Umuru on
> the bank of the Great River where the white man
> first went.
>
> In the end, Mr. Brown's arguments began to have
> an effect. More people came and learned in his
> school, and he encouraged them with gifts of singlets
> and towels. They were not all young, these people who
> came to learn. Some of them were thirty years old
> or more. They worked on their farms in the morning
> and went to school in the afternoons. And it was
> not long before the people began to say that the
> white man's medicine was quick in working. Mr. Brown's
> school produced quick results. A few months in it
> were enough to make one a court messenger or a court
> clerk. Those who stayed longer became teachers; and
> from Umufia laborers went forth into the Lord's
> vineyard. New churches were established in the
> surrounding villages and a few schools with them.
> From the beginning religion and education went hand
> in hand.
>
> Mr. Brown's mission grew from strength to strength
> because of its link with the new administration; it
> earned a new social prestige. But Mr. Brown himself
> was breaking down in health. At first he ignored the
> warning signs. But in the end Mr. Brown had to
> leave his flock, sad and broken.

"...religion and education went hand in hand." These are
the words Mr. Achebe used to describe the manner in which Mr.
Brown was able to capture the affection of the Africans to his
God - Jesus Christ. In other words, if the Africans wanted to
eat they had to have the required education and skills of their
imposed colonialist masters in the "...new government..." To
secure such needed food and educational skills they were forced
to fall into the waiting outstretched arms of the missionaries
whose religion, European-style Christianity, they had rejected.
They were caught by the age-old African proverb that says:

> Jumping from the log to the fire is a
> fatal solution to the problem.

One is to assume that the European God - Jesus Christ in
this specific case - inspired His missionaries to use whatever
violation of His "TEN COMMANDMENTS" (which Moses was supposed to
have received on Mount Sinai, but in fact co-opted from the
"Negative Confessions")*they felt fitting in any conversion
situation, providing it led to the acquisition of new converts.
This was the preferred manner in which God (Jesus Christ) and
Allah won converts from the Gods - Ju Ju, Oledamare, Chukwu,
and others in every part of Africa from the beginning of the
slave trade to the present late 20th century. However, this
method is certainly overshadowed by chattel slavery, when
Africans by the millions were beaten into accepting European-
style Christianity by their slavemasters - many of whom were
ordained ministers of the church, many also being captains of

---

* The relationship between Moses and the "Negative Confessions"
is detailed in Chapter III of this work.

slave ships and owners of same. The most notorious of the slave ship owners and captains was the Reverend John Hawkins of the Church of England (Anglican Church), whose flagship was named JESUS CHRIST de LOBIC.[17] But one must remember that there was also another European-style Christian missionary, the Most Reverend Bishop Bartolome de Las Casas of the Roman Catholic Church, who in circa 1503 or 1506 C.E. was responsible for the institution of slave trading from Africa to the "New World." The first of such African slaves were the dethroned Moors from Spain, more than 4000 of whom were shipped to the Island of Hayte, which the Spaniards had already renamed "Hispaniola."[17]

Looking back to the Reverend Placide Temples book, BANTU PHILOSOPHY, one sees certain fundamentals which are said to be the basis for Ju Ju, Voodoo, Shango, Damballah Quedo, and all other African, European, Asian and American religions; yet they cannot be accepted as such by European and European-American religionists. Why? Because one man sees the other man's God or religion as being inferior to his own. His God is no better than his own image of himself. If he feels that an African is less than a European or European-American, he must also assume that his God must have also made the same conclusion. Therefore the Jews are "...the chosen people..."[17a] for Jews and Christian alike. But, are they "the chosen people" for the Moslems, Hindus, Budhists, Yorubas, or even Christians who claim no Jewish ethnological tie with the so-called "Jewish race"[17b] one hears so much about of late? Emphatically not. In conjunction with this point the Reverend Placide Temples noted:

32

The <u>white man</u>,* a new phenomenon in the Bantu world, could be conceived only according to pre-existing categories of Bantu thought. He was, therefore incorporated into the universe of forces, in the position therein which was congruent with the logic of the Bantu ontology. The technological skill of the white man impressed the Bantu. The white man seemed to be the master of great natural forces. It had, therefore, to be admitted that the white man was an elder, a superior human force, surpassing the vital force of all Africans. The vital force of the white man is such that against the "manga" or the application of active natural forces as the disposition of Africans was without effect.

Herein lies a basic error on Temples' part. He obviously underestimated the ethics of the Africans, which he like all of the other colonialist called "Bantus," - hospitality to all strangers, in which reverence for another's religion is too often mistaken by foreign missionaries as being the Africans' expression of "fear." The same holds true for any foreigner in their midst who may be able to perform material feats which they have not yet done.

Outlining what he chooses to call "The General Laws of Vital Causability," Temples listed the following:[19]

    I. Man (living or deceased) can directly reinforce or diminish the being of another man.

    Such vital influence is possible from man to man; it is indeed necessarily effective as between the progenitor, superior vital force - and his progeny - an inferior force. This interaction does not occur only when the recipient object is endowed, in respect of the endowing subject, with a superior force, which he may achieve of himself, or some vital external influence, or (especially) by the action of God.

---

* Temples was himself a "white man." He was only expressing his own "chosen people's" myth. Did not the so-called "Bantu" have a color like the "White Man?" Should the Africans he called "Bantus" not be called "Black men?" Is it not true that "white" is as much a color as "black?" Why this type of racism in religion?

II. The vital human force can directly influence inferior force-beings (animals, vegetables or minerals) in their being itself.

III. A rational being (spirit, names, or living) can indirectly upon another rational being by communicating his vital influence to an inferior force (animal, vegetable, or mineral) through the intermediary of which it influences the rational being. This influence will also have the character of a necessarily effective action, save only when the object is inherently the stronger force, or is reinforced by the influence of some third party, or preserves himself by recourse to inferior forces exceeding those which his enemy is employing.

Temples had to journey all the way to Africa and involve himself in a major study in order that he might understand if there is a philosophical basis for any African traditional religion. Upon what basis could the Africans rest their traditional religions other than a spiritual philosophy? However, Temples' type of missionaries are still active in the Harlems of the United States of America; as they are still frequented by so-called "Christian" and "Islamic" missionaries, all of whom express freely their utter contempt for the African-Americans' right to practice Voodoo, Magic, and Ju Ju as they are being presently practised in the thousands of "Store Front Churches" where Oracles[19a] called "prophets" chant Christian songs, dispense Voodoo herbs and conduct burnt offerings while they make anointing oils; all of which one can find in the Hebrew (Jewish) Torah, Christian Holy Bible, and Moslem Koran.

While sweet burnt-incense fills the air of the "Store Front Churches" and "Oracles" move into their incantations to communicate with the "Spirit World" the words are Christian but the ceremony Voodoo. The blessing of charms and anointment with oils and myrrh are as much Voodooistic as they are Judaic,

34

Christian, or Islamic.

The Third Book of Moses, Leviticus, speaks of the paganistic "burnt offerings," which are in every sense the same as in most Voodoo, JU Ju, and Shango or Obyah feasts. Thus Leviticus states:[20]

> 1. The Lord called Moses, and spoke to him from the tent of meeting, saying, 2. Speak to the people of Israel, and say to them, when any man of you brings an offering to the Lord, you shall bring your offering of cattle from the herd or from the flock.
>
> 3. If his offering is a burnt offering from the herd, he shall offer a male without blemish;* he shall offer it at the door of the tent of meeting, that he may be accepted before the Lord; he shall lay his hand upon the head of the burnt offering, and it shall be accepted for him to make atonement for him. 5. Then he shall kill the bull before the Lord; and Aaron's sons the priests shall present the blood, and throw the blood around about against the altar that is at the door of the tent of meeting. 6. And he shall flay the burnt offering and cut it into pieces; 7. and the sons of Aaron the priest shall put fire on the altar, and lay wood in order upon the fire; 8. and Aaron's sons the priests shall lay the pieces, the head, and the fat, in order upon the wood that is on the altar; 9. but its entrails and its legs he shall wash with water. And the priests shall burn the whole on the altar, as a burnt offering, an offering by fire, a pleasing odor to the Lord.
>
> 10. If his gift for a burnt offering is from the flock, from the sheep* or goats, he shall offer a a male without blemish; 11. and he shall kill it on the northside of the altar before the Lord, and Aaron's sons the priests shall throw its blood against the altar around about. 12. And he shall cut it into pieces, with its head and its fat, and the priest shall lay them in order upon the wood that is on the fire upon the altar; 13. but the entrails and the legs

---

* This custom is still being maintained by the Beta Israel (Black Jews, or Falasa) of Ethiopia, East Africa. They perform this sacrifice on Yum Kippur, Rosh Hashanah, and Pesach (Day of Atonement, New Year, and Passover).

he shall wash in water. And the priest shall offer
the whole, and burn it on the altar; if it is a
burnt offering, an offering by fire, a pleasing
odor to the Lord.

In Leviticus, under the "LAW OF PEACE OFFERINGS," it is
also written:[21]

> 32. If he brings a lamb as his offering for a
> sin offering, he shall bring a female without
> blemish, 33. and lay his hand upon the head of the
> sin offering, and kill it for a sin offering in the
> place where they kill the burnt offering. 34. Then
> the priest shall take some of the blood of the sin
> offering with his finger and put it on the horns
> of the **altar of the** burnt offering, and pour out
> the rest of its blood at the base of the altar.
> 35. **And all** its fat he shall remove as the fat of
> the lamb is removed from the sacrifice of peace
> offerings, and the priest shall burn it on the
> altar, upon the offerings by fire to the Lord;
> and the priest shall make atonement for him for the
> sin which he has committed, and he shall be forgiven.

In the United States of America palms are still being burned
as "burnt offerings" on Ash Wednesday of each year, and the sign
of the Crucifix painted with the ashes from the palm on the
forehead of each of the faithful in a "pagan cermony" that is
older than the Christian religion. The ceremony of the "burnt
offering" and "burnt palms" are as old as the origin of its
Voodoo origin, just as the sacrifice of the "first male lamb"
of its unblemished mother was an ancient Egyptian ceremonial
tradition for cleansing the soul thousands of years before an
Egyptian named Moses even knew he was going to be born, much
less receive a set of laws at Mt. Sinai. This ceremony is equal
to the rooster that is sacrificed to the God - Damballah Ouedo -
in Voodooism, or the God - Oledamare - of the Yoruba religion
to please His Orishas (minor Gods).

36

In the book, AFRICAN MYTHOLOGY, the author - Reverend Godfrey Parrinder, states that the Dogons of Western Africa, around
the bend of the Niger River, south of Tombut (Timbuktu or Timbuctoo), have a religion that is comparable in mythology and spirituality to Judaism, Christianity, and Islam (the so-called "Western
Religions").

Explaining the Dogon's religion, which Reverend Parrinder
said was revealed to him by one of their sages named "Ogotemme-
li on permission from the Elders (headmen), he wrote:[22]

> In the beginning of the one God, Amma, creat-
> ed the sun and moon like pots, his first inven-
> tion. The sun is white hot and surrounded by eight
> rings of red copper, and the moon is the same
> shape with rings of white copper. The stars came
> from pellets of clay that Amma flung into space.
> To create the earth, he squeezed a lump of clay,
> as he had done for the stars, and threw it into
> space. There it spread out flat, with the north
> at the top, and its members branched out in dif-
> ferent directions like the body, lying flat with
> its face upwards.
>
> Amma was lonely and drew near to the female
> earth to unite himself with it. But his passage
> was barred by a red termite hill. He cut
> this down and union took place, but the interfer-
> ence made it defective and instead of twins being
> born, which would have been natural, a jackal was
> born instead. This jackal was a trouble to him
> afterwards. The myth justifies female circumcis-
> ion, which is practised by the Dogon and many
> other African peoples.
>
> There was further union between God and Earth
> and twins were born. They were like water and
> green in color. Their top half was human and the
> bottom half snake-like. They had red eyes and
> forked tongues, sinuous arms without joints, and
> their bodies covered with short green hair, shin-
> ing like water. They had eight members and were
> born perfect. These two spirits were called Nummo,
> and they went up to heaven to get instructions
> from God, since he was their father and they were
> made from his essence which is the life-force of
> the world, from which comes all motion and energy.
> This force is water and the Nummo are in all water,

or seas and rivers and storms, in fact they
are water. They are also light and emit it
constantly.

When the Nummo spirits looked down from
the sky they saw Mother Earth, naked and in
disorder. So they came down bringing the
bunches of fibres from heavenly plants which
they made into tow bunches to clothe the
Earth in front and behind like a woman. The
fibres were moist of the essence of the Nam-
mo spirits. By means of this clothing the
Earth obtained a language, elementary but
sufficient for the beginning.

The jackal, deceitful first born of God, was
jealous of his mother's possession of language.
He seized the fiber skirt in which the language was embodied. The Earth resisted this sinful attack and hid in her own womb, symbolized
as an ant hill in which she changed into an ant.
The jackal pursued her, and although the Earth
dug down deep, she was not able to escape. The
jackal seized his mother's skirt, gained the
power of speech, and so he is able to reveal
the plans of the Supreme Being to diviners.

The result of this unfilial attack was the
defilement of the Earth, and Amma decided to
create live beings without her.But when he had
formed their organs the Nummo spirits saw that
there was a danger of twin births disappearing.
So they drew a male and a female outline on the
ground, on top of one another. And so it was,
and has been ever since, that every human being
has two souls at first, man is bi-sexual. But a
man's female soul is removed at circumcision,
when he becomes a true man; and the correspond-
ing event happens to a woman at excision. The
myths continue with the coming of the first man,
and though they still refer back to God, they
will be considered later under a separate heading. Meanwhile the gifts of God to man occur in
a number of myths.

If the above story, with all of its universality in the explanation of man's origin, is a myth, what is the story about
"Adam and Eve" and "creation" in the First Book of Moses (Genesis) following?[23]

1 In the beginning God created the heavens
and the earth, 2 The earth was without form

and void, and darkness was upon the face of the
deep; and the Spirit of God was moving over the
face of the waters.

3 And God said, "Let there be light;" and
there was light. 4 And God saw the light was
good; and God separated the light from the
darkness. 5 God called the light Day, and the
darkness he called Night. And there was evening as there was morning one day.

6 And God said, "Let there be a firmament
in the midst of the waters, and let it seper-
ate the waters from the waters." 7 And God
made the firmament and seperated the waters
which were under the firmament from the waters
which were above the firmament. And it was so.
8 God called the firmament Heaven. And there
was evening and there was morning, a second day.

9 And God said, "Let the waters under the
heavens be gathered together into one place, and
let the dry land appear." And it was so. 10 God
called the dry land Earth, and the waters that
were gathered together he called Seas. And God
saw that it was good. 11 And God said, "Let the
Earth put forth vegetation, plants yielding
seed, and fruit trees bearing fruit in
which is their seed, each according to its kind,
upon the Earth." And it was so. 12 The Earth
brought forth vegetation, plants yielding seed
according to their own kinds, and trees bearing
fruit in which there is seed, each according to
its kind. And God saw that it was good. 13 And
there was evening and there was morning, a third
day.

The story continues with the making of "light, seasons,
stars, birds, sea monsters, other living creatures," etc. But in
verse 24 it begins to take on animals and other forms which man
deals with daily. Thus the making of cattle, man, etc.:

24 And God said, "Let the Earth bring forth
living creatures according to their kinds;
cattle and creeping things and beasts of the
Earth according to their kinds." And it was so.
25 And God made the beasts of the Earth according to their kinds and the cattle to their kinds,
and everything that creeps upon the ground according to its kind. And God saw that was good.

Following the "creation" of everything-else the Jewish Je-

hovah, Christian Jesus Christ, and Moslem Allah, with the help of

one or more persons, created man - called "Adam," according to
the following:

> 26 Then God said, "Let us* make man in our
> own image after our own likeness; and let him
> have dominion over the fish of the sea, and over
> the birds of the air, and over the cattle, and
> over all the Earth, and over every creeping
> thing that creeps upon the Earth." 27 So
> God created man in his own image, in the image
> of God He created him; male and female He creat-
> ed them. 28 And God blessed them, and God said
> to them, "Be fruitful and multiply, and fill the
> Earth and subdue it; and have dominion over the
> fish of the sea and over the birds of the air
> and over every living thing that moves upon the
> Earth." 29 And God said, "Behold, I have given
> you every plant yielding seed which is upon the
> face of all the Earth, and every tree with seed
> in its fruit; you shall have them for food. 30
> And to every beast of the Earth, and to every
> bird of the air, and to everything that creeps
> on the Earth, everything that has the breath of
> life, I have given every green plant for food."
> And it was so. 31 And God saw everything that
> He had made, and behold it was very good. And
> there was evening and there was morning, a
> sixth day.

Still not satisfied with what he had already created, God
decided to create a woman called "Eve" for His "Adam."[25] The act
continues in the following manner, according to the story:

> 15 The Lord God took the man and put him in
> the Garden of Eden to till it and keep it. 16
> And the Lord God Commanded the man, saying,
> "You may freely eat of every tree of the garden;
> 17 but of the tree of knowledge of good and evil
> you shall not eat, for in the day that you eat
> of it you shall die."

> 18 Then the Lord God said, "It is not good
> that the man should be alone; I will make him
> a helper fit for him. 19 So out of the ground
> the Lord God formed every beast of the field
> and every bird of the air, and brought them to
> man to see what he would call them; and what-

* "US" is plural (more than one). Who was God speaking to when He
said "LET US MAKE MAN IN OUR OWN IMAGE......," etc.?It could not
have been Jesus Christ as some tried to indicate; he was not born.

40

ever the man called every living creature,
that was its name. 20 The man gave names
to all cattle, and to the birds of the air,
and to every beast of the field; but for the
the man there was not found a helper fit for
him. 21 So the Lord God caused a deep sleep
to fall upon the man, and while he slept
took one of his ribs and closed up its place
with flesh; 22 and the rib which the Lord
God had taken from the man He made into a woman and brought her to the man. 23 Then the
man said,

"This at least is bone of my bones and
flesh of my flesh; she shall be called woman,
because she was taken out of Man."

24 Therefore a man leaves his father and
his mother and cleaves to his wife, and they
become one flesh. 25 And the man and his wife
were both naked, and were not ashamed.

From this point on many things happened; but the
most important - so far as this citation is concerned, a ..."serpent tempted Eve...," etc., in the Garden of Eden; Adam and Eve
then "...ate the forbidden fruit...," etc.; they found out they
were "...naked,and covered their nakedness...," etc.; God followed by chasing them"from the Garden of Eden;" Eve repeatedly became
pregnant and delivered her three oldest children, all sons. Thus:
Cane and Abel, the former killed the latter and **was** driven from
the Garden of Eden into "...the land of Nod, east of Eden...,"
etc., where he "...knew his wife and she conceived and bore Enoch."
This entire drama did not in anyway include Eve's third son, Seth.
Strangely enough, God must have made more people beside Adam and
Eve elsewhere in order for Cain to have found himself a wife when
he arrived in Nod. It could not have been his mother, the only woman in the world at the time according to the story, because she
was not bannished with him; and she did not **have** any daughter up
to the time of Cain's bannishment.[26]

41

Before analyzing these myths - the creation of man by another God should be examined. For this Jomo Kenyatta, long **before** becoming President of the Republic of Kenya, East Africa, wrote the following in the most authoritative book on the subject entitled - FACING MOUNT KENYA.[27] It is a deep searching anthropological work with which he tried to acquaint Europeans and European-Americans of the traditions, beliefs, and customs of his own ethnic grouping - the Gikuyu people. He wrote:

THE CONCEPTION OF A DEITY

The Gikuyu believes in one God, Ngai, the creator and giver of all things. Ngai moobi wa indo ciothe na mohei kerende indo ciothe. He has no father, mother, or companion of any kind. His work is done in solitude. Ngai ndere ithe kana nyina, ndere gethia kana gethethwa. He loves or hates people according to their behaviour. The creator lives in the sky. Ngai eikaraga matuine, but has temporary homes on earth, situated on the mountains, where he may rest during his visits. The visits are made with a view to carrying out a kind of "general inspection," koroora thi, and to bring blessings and punishments to the people. Korehere ando kiguni kana gitei.

The common name used in speaking of the Supreme Being is Ngai; this name is used by three neighboring tribes, the Masai, the Gikuyu, and Wakamba. In prayers and sacrifices Ngai is addressed by the Gikuyu as Mwene-Nyaga (possessor of brightness). This name is associated with Kere-Nyaga (the Gikuyu name for Mount Kenya), which means: That which possesses brightness, or mountain of brightness.

The mountain of brightness is believed by the Gikuyu to be Ngai's official resting-place, and in their prayers they turn towards Kere-Ngai and, with their hands raised towards it, they offer their sacrifices, taking the mountain to be the holy earthly dwelling-place of Ngai. Kenyororokero na kehuroko kia Mwene-Nyaga - literally, "descending and resting - or dwelling-place of God."

The Being thus described cannot be seen by ordinary mortal eyes. He is a distant Being

and takes but little interest in individuals
in their daily walks of life. Yet at the cris-
es of their lives he is invariably called upon.
At the birth, initiation, marriage, and death
of every Gikuyu, communication is established
on his behalf with Ngai. The ceremonies for
these four events leave no doubt as to the importance of the spiritual assistance which is
essential to them.

Of the Gikuyu's Holy Place (which is the equivalent, in deed,
of any Hebrew synagouge, Christian church or Islamic mosque) Mr.
Kenyatta wrote:[28]

> Apart from the official abode of Mwene-Nyaga
> at Kere-Nyaga on the north, there are minor
> homes such as Kea-Njahe (the mountain of the
> Big Rain) on the east; Kea-Mbiroioro (the mount-
> ain of Clear Sky) on the south; Kea-Nyandarwa
> (the mountain of Sleeping Place or Hides) on the
> west. All these are regarded with reverence as
> great places and mysteries symbolic of God, Mana-
> ge na orior wa Ngai. The Gikuyu who has no "tem-
> ples made with hands," selects huge trees, gener-
> ally mogumo or motamayo and mokoyo trees, which
> symbolise the mountains. Under these trees he wor-
> ships and makes his sacrifices to Mwene-Nyaga.
> These sacred trees are regarded in the same manner
> as most Christians regarded churches - as the
> "House of God."

On the origin of the Gikuyu people, Mr. Kenyatta stated:[29]

> According to the tribal legend, we are told
> that in the beginning of things, when mankind
> started to populate the earth, the man Gikuyu,
> the founder of the tribe, was called by the Mo-
> gai (the Divider of the Universe), and was giv-
> en as his share the land with ravines, the riv-
> ers, the forests, the game and all the gifts
> that the Lord of Nature (Mogai) bestowed on man-
> kind. At the same time, Mogai made a big moun-
> tain which he called Kere-Nyaga (Mount Kenya), as
> the resting place when on inspection tour, and
> as a sign of his wonders. He then took the man
> Gikuyu to the top of the mountain of mystery,
> and showed him the beauty of the country that
> Mogai had given him. While still on the top of
> the mountain, the Mogai pointed out to the Gikuyu
> a spot full of fig trees (mikoyo), right in the
> centre of the country. After the Mogai had
> shown the Gikuyu the panorama of the wonderful
> land he had been given, he commanded him to

descend and establish his homestead on the selected place, which he named Mokorwe wa Gathanga. Before they parted, Mogai told Gikuyu that, whenever he was in need, he should make a sacrifice and raise his hands toward Kere-Nyaga (the mountain of mystery), and the Lord of Nature will come to his assistance.

Gikuyu did as was commanded by the Mogai, and when he reached the spot, he found that the Mogai had provided him with a beautiful wife whom Gikuyu named Moombi (creator or moulder). Both lived happily, and had nine daughters and no sons.

Gikuyu was very disturbed at not having a male heir. In his despair he called upon the Mogai to advise him on the situation. He responded quickly and told Gikuyu not to be perturbed, but to have patience and everything would be done according to his wish. He then commanded him, saying: "Go and take one lamb and one kid from your flock. Kill them under the big fig tree (mokoyo) near your homestead. Pour the blood and the fat of the two animals on the trunk of the tree. Then you and your family make a big fire under the tree and burn the meat as a sacrifice to me, your benefactor. When you have done this, take home your wife and daughters. After that go back to the sacred tree, and there you will find nine handsome young men who are willing to marry your daughters, under any condition that will please you and your family."

Gikuyu did as he was directed by the Mogai or Ngai, and so it happened that when Gikuyu returned to the sacred tree, there he found the promised nine young men who greeted him warmly. For a few moments he could not utter a word, for he was overwhelmed with joy. When he had recovered from his emotional excitement, he took the nine youths to his homestead and introduced them to his family.

The strangers were entertained and hospitably treated according to the social custom. A ram was killed and a millet gruel prepared for their food. While this was being made ready, the youths were taken to a stream nearby to wash their tired limbs. After this, they had their meal, and conversed merrily with the family and then went to bed.

Early the next morning Gikuyu rose and woke the young men to have their morning meal with him. when they finished eating, the question of marriage was discussed. Gikuyu told the young men that if they wished to marry his daughters he could give his consent only if they agreed to live in his homestead under a matriarchal system.

44

The young men agreed to this condition, for
they could not resist the beauty of the Gikuyu
daughters, nor the kindness which the family
had showed them. This pleased the parents, for
they knew that their lack of sons was not going
to be recompensed. The daughters, too, were
pleased to have male companions, and after a
short time all of them were married, and soon
established their own family sets. These were
joined together under the name of Mbari ya Moombi, i.e. Moombi's family group, in honour of
their mother Moombi.

The nine small families continued to live
together, with their parents (Gikuyu and Moombi) acting as the heads of the Mbari ya Moombi. As time went on, each family increased
rapidly, and Gikuyu and Moombi had many grand
and great-grandchildren. When Gikuyu and Moobi
died, their daughters inherited their movable
and immovable property which they shared equally among them.

Further examination of other indigenous traditional African

religions should not be necessary at this time. One should be able,

at this point to observe that the extent of mythology regarding "cre-

ation" within African religions is no more or no less than within

Judaism, Christianity, and Islam. Yet, no one in either religion

would concede that the other is as much God-created as his or

hers. Why? Because of Man's drive to be the "master of all he sur-

veys." As such, all that he is associated with must be superior

to that of others who do not belong to his in-group.

The biological explanation of how a son came to the family

of Moombi - according to the Gikuyu - is not only logical, but

modern in its application for twentieth-century thinking man. It

certainly bears more to reality than God taking "earth" or "clay"

and moulding man into existence. But the Gikuyu's story is sup-

posedly "mythological paganism;" whereas, the "earth" and "clay"

story of the Jews and Christians, also the Moslems, is "...God—

inspired words" passed down through "...His holy prophets and writers." At least, these are the teachings one hears from the earthly representatives of Judaism, Christianity,and Islam. Why? Because of the same egotism mentioned before; along with its nat- ural outgrowth - modern racism - that infiltrated and corrupted them to the extent that "God" is seem in terms of "black" and "white."

Since each theologian is within his own authoritative rights to interpret the alleged "Holy words of God," that is depending upon which God is being used at the time - the"holy words" - can say anything the exhorter desires "God" to have said.

Inevitably, the following question always arises:"If Jesus Christ is not the only one and true God, then why are so many people Christians?" Of course this question worked the other way when there was no Jesus Christ, then there must have been no Christian God. But amongst Christians this type of logic is con- fusing and, therefore, "sacrilegious." If "sacrilegious," it is more than likely "pagan."

The premise of a Good or Bad, True or False, religion is the cardinal problem which makes it almost impossible for many re- searchers to report freely, and without bias, on their findings about the traditional African Gods within Voodoo, JuJu, Obyah, Magic, Witchcraft,and all other traditional African religions re- legated to "Animism" by European and European-American-style Christian religionists, Jewish "chosen people," and Moslem Jihad- ists and other paternal and maternal "protectors" of their African and African-American ("Negro") children. This must be done, of course, because people of African origin supposedly lack the ne -

46

cessary capacity of the "large brain" which is only to be found in "Caucasians" of Europe and European-America. At least this seems to be the basic premise upon which traditional African religions have been degraded by most who now label themselves "Westerners" in place of their formerly prestigious..."Caucasians."[29a]

Upon further examination of the Dogon's God, one noted that in the creation of heaven and earth "clay" was also used. But according to the same Dogons, man was not made from "clay,"but:

"...the stars came from pellets of clay that Amma" (God) "flung into space."[32]

It is further revealed that:

"...Amma was lonely and drew near to the female Earth to unite himself with it."[31]

The same sexual relationship between God and a female existed in Judaism, Christianity and Islam; as seen in the following:

"...Then God said, let us make man in our image, after our likeness...," etc.

Obviously, God would not likely make man in his "own image" with another male. But this traditional myth seems to be common among "Western peoples." Whether or not the traditional African religions' "US" as animal or thing, it is always "female." This so-called "primitive" or "pagan" rationalization was, and still is, said to be naturally "instinctive." And no high degree of academic sophistication was necessary for ancient man to have deduced such a rationale. Yet, everywhere in Africa "original man" is shown to have had a "mother."

The concept of "Sacred Trees" within the religions of the Yorubas of Nigeria, Gikuyu of Kenya, Nbundus of Angola (Ngola),

47

Twa (the so-called "Pygmies") of the Congo, and Burundi are embodied with "soul." Because "trees" do eat, move, and do other
things like most animals - man included; as such most indigenous
Africans recognized them as having "spirit." This is the reason
some Africans can be seen praying for forgiveness whenever they
must cut down a tree. This custom gives rise to the reason why
most Christian missionaries from Europe and European-America
mistakenly assume that "...Africans worship trees."

A "spirit" is not "paganistic" when "Westerners" apply it
to man. Yet, it is when Africans suggest that "...there is a
spirit world" in which their ancestors enter after death, and
which guard them. If "...God is a spirit," at times; and man is
the spitting"image of God," then one should easily see why ancestors become "spirits" in African traditional religions. Obviously,
the Africans seem to be employing the same mythological concepts
built into the so-called "Western religions" (as written); whereas most Europeans, European-Americans (Jews and Christians), and
Asians (Moslems) would prefer that said "paganistic customs"
could be extracted from their own religion's "Holy Book." But, to
do this would leave Christianity, Judaism, and Islam without
"Saints, Spirits, Prophets, Ghosts, Angels," and a host of other
fantastics which are so commonly found within Voodoo, JuJu, Magic,
and the entire gamut of what is being called African "pagaism"
and "animism;" and of course one cannot forget the much more
usual terms - "heathenism" and "cannibalism."

> In the beginning the one God, Amma, created
> the Sun and Moon like pots, his first invention
> ...," etc.;[32]

48

according to the Dogons of West Africa.

In the beginning God created the heavens and the earth...," etc.[35]

according to the Jews, Christians, and Moslems of the United States of America.

Ngai, the creator and giver of all things...," etc.[35]

according to the Gikuyu of Kenya, East Africa. But, what makes the creation of either of these Gods of West Africa and East Africa (Anima and Ngai) any less than the creation by the Gods of North Africa and West Asia (Yvah or Jehovah and Jesus Christ). In each of the three examples shown, the Gods of Africa and Asia created the "Sun, Moon, Heavens, Earth," and " all things." The Gods born in Asia, Jesus Christ and Allah, adopted what the God of North Africa - RA (the Sun God)- passed on to the African Jews before their Pesach (Passover) to establish their own God - Yvah (Jehovah).

The course of the latter chain of events spanned a period of approximately 1,854 years; i.e. c1232 B.C.E., when Moses tried to flee his native country Sais (Egypt) and copied the laws he adopted from his fellow indigenous Africans of Sais, which he allegedly re-established at Mt. Sinai.[36] In 1 C.E. fellow Jews became disenchanted with the way things were progressing from the year c1232 B.C.E. in the worship of Yvah and created a new God in the person of one "Jesus Christ." But Jesus Christ "...did not come to bring a new religion...," etc.(Christianity), "...only to correct it ..." (Judaism).[37] It was only Jesus Christ's martyrdom which, thereby, created the "Christians" (the Greek "Kristos, or followers of the anointed one). But in 622 C.E. (or A.H. 1) -

"the Year after the Hegira" - Mohamet of Arabia, a former camel driver, condemned both Jews and Christians for failing the "One God" he called "Allah" (from the ancient Arabian Goddess Al'lat that was worshipped in Arabia for thousands of years before Mohamet's birth)[37a] and established Islam at the Oasis of Yathrib - Medina, and thereby, re-established the continuation of the "Mysteries," Judaism, and Christianity in Mecca during 632 C.E. (A.H. 10).[38]

In examining that which has been misnomered "Western Religions," one finds no European or European-American playing any role whatsoever in the creation of any of the "God-heads." And there is no indication that any of the dramas of creation took place in any part of Europe. All of the dramas, so far mentioned, having took place in Asia-Minor (today's Middle East), the Arabian Peninsula of Western Asia, North Africa, West Africa, and East Africa. This, of course, is not to imply that there was no creation by a God of (or in) Europe. What it does say, however, is that none of the Gods, prophets, or founders of any of the three religions - Judaism, Christianity, and Islam - the so-called "Western Religions," was indigenous to Europe (a Caucasian, or White man). It is further saying, that Judaism and Islam, both, had indigenous Africans in the leadership roles from the first day of their recorded origin. In Judaism, after Abraham, Isaac, and Jacob, it was Moses and his fellow indigenous African-Jews of Egypt, and those in Kush (Cush or Ethiopia) where Moses married one of his many wives - which made his sister (Miriam) and brother (Aaron) protest.[39] Islam had Mohamet - whose grandfather was of African origin, and his closest advisor and co-founder of Islam - an Afri -

50

can from Ethiopia (Kush or Abyssina) named Hadzart Bilal ibn
Rahbab.[40]

How do all of these avenues to the Gods relate to African-
Americans throughout the Americas and their African influenced
so-called "Western Religions?" They have created a sense of re-
ligiosity which is not to be found within any European-American
religious settings. This same sense of religion is reflected in
the "Blues" - the sorrowful testimonial that found its way into
"Jazz." [4a] Because of this influence Mahalia Jackson and Aretha
Franklin, both African-Americans, can sing the "Star Spangled
Banner" (the National Anthem of the United States of America)
like no European-American can, with "Soul." But behind this Voodooistic background is a Baptist, Aretha's father, a very well
known Christian Minister who saw to it that she was brought up in
his church's choir. Mahalia Jackson, also,Dinah Washington, Sarah
Vaughn,and many other well known Black singers of equal billing
were brought up in very similar backgrounds of church and choir.
For in the Black, or African-American, Baptist background (like
its African Methodist Episcopate) the basic elements in Voodoism
have always dominated all forms of music by African-Americans,
just as it has controlled the "spiritual" and "Blues," and of
course "Jazz ."

In Haiti, Cuba, Trinidad, Puerto Rico, Jamaica,and other islands of the Caribbean (West Indies) - along with the South American mainland - Voodoo, JuJu, Shango, Ngai, Damballah Ouedo, Obyah,
and Magic compete in the open for the minds of European-Americans,
Europeans, Africans, African-Americans,and the indigenous peoples
(misnomered "Indians"). Because of this the Roman Catholic Church

51

and other Christian "sects," including Protestantism, were forced
to embrace much of these traditionally "African spiritualistic
mysticism." Not only have they adopted said traditional African
religious customs, they were also forced to adopt many traditional religious customs of the indigenous peoples.

In the Black communities of the United States of America
local "store front churches" have become the true centers of un-
inhibited Voodoistic expressions. There, one can purchase all
sorts of roots; from "Love John the Conqueror" to "Blood Root."
Oils are equally available, from "Snake Oil" to plain old Palm
Oil." "Grave yard dirt" and "African Red Clay" can be had at a
little extra cost. "Metallic charms" are blessed by "prophets" and
other diviners; just as medallions and crucifixes are blessed by
Roman Catholic priests, Black Stones (Ka'aba) by Moslem imans, and
Mogen Davids by Jewish rabbis. Burnt incense also fills the air
as African and African-American spirituals and other imported religious songs from Brazil, the Caribbean Islands,and West Africa
play to the softly dim-lit room full of worshipers waiting to communicate with the "Nether World" (Next World, Ancestral World).
Needless to say, charlatans have invaded the world of the "Mysteries," which some find to be extremely financially lucrative.
Here also "Black Magic"* is abused by too many who do not know
with what they are fooling. These highly sophisticated indigenous
African traditional religious rites have been deemed "Witchcraft"*
by ill wishers and the ignorant; mostly because such charlatans

---

* The terms "Witchcraft" and "Witch Doctor," neither of which is
common to people of African origin, are the creations of those
who can find no time to respectfully investigate for the sake of
truth and enlightenment.

have professed to be able to:

> "...perform evil deeds through Black Magic in religion...," etc.

"Witchcraft" is as much scientific as the religious rites of Mrs. Mary Baker Eddy's "Christian Science."[40a] Its "Witch Doctors" are as much "scientists" as the Christian scientist "practitioners." Yet, the "Reading Rooms" of the Christian Science organization meet with revered acceptance and tolerance by Jews, Christians, and Moslems alike. On the other hand, Voodoo and other indigenous African traditional religions must suffer the disgusting designation of "Occult," to say the least; and must settle for an occasional Steinway Hall Auditorium or some off limit place where landlords seldom could rent other than for manufacturing lofts.

Even with all of the clamour for Islam, and the flight from Judaism and Christianity, a small but ever increasing band of African-Americans turn to one of the religions of their forefathers - the Yorubas of West Africa - and give praise to God - Oledamare (and others). Thousands more turn to Damballah Ouedo and Voodoo through their contact with priests from Haiti, Cuba, Brazil, and other parts of the Caribbeans, South America and Africa. A good number of local African-Americans have also become priestesses and priests of high rank and recognition among international brotherhood of their faith. These priestesses march along in the fineries of their office with their priests along Seventh Avenue, Harlem, New York City, once more on Sundays; just as priests, rabbis, imans, ministers, nuns, and others dress up in their habits of the so-called "Western Religions." With the rank of their offices embroidered in their clothing or other ob-

jects of said authority held in their hands, they lead the
faithful in the playing of skin and wind instruments at varied
places in the "Harlems" of the United States of America.

What made these African-Americans return to the traditional
religions of their Motherland - Alkebu-lan (Africa by the Greeks
and Romans) - and turn their backs on Judaism, Christianity,and
Islam, in spite of all the adverse propaganda against them? The
answers are many; some of which follows:

> "A search for indentity; A sense of pride; A de-
> termination to have their own thing; A sense of
> belonging; To be able to say," at last, "this is
> mine, which I have created and have always kept
> sacred."

These things are very well true; for what is "pride" without
ownership (community or private)?

Another aspect of the renaissance in indigenous African traditional religions presently spreading over the African-American
communities, especially in the northern and eastern urban centers,
of the United States of America is to be found in the following
words:

> "...And God created man in His own image, and
> His own likeness...," etc.

But for the first time in over four-hundred years African-
Americans have "a Black God" or "Gods" to whom they could relate
like the European-Americans related to the "White God" image provided by Michaelangelo and all of the theologians of the various
seminaries and yeshivas - whom they found in JuJu, Voodoo, Damballah Ouedo, "Black" Magic,and others. This revival, however, is not
consistent with the Doctor of Divinity's statement, that:

> "...In modern times new religions have come into
> every part of Africa. Islam and Christianity bring

54

new doctrines, morality, history, scripture, and universalism."[41]

Such seeming arrogance only tends to convey that "morality" and the other values he mentioned were not in Africa before the appearance of his people - the Europeans and/or Asians from Arabia. Therefore, that which is being revitalized among the African-Americans is foreign, rather than African. Yet, it existed hundreds of years before the African - Bilal - made Islam what it is today; and before that when Tertullian, St. Cyprian, St. Augustine, and other Africans modernized Christianity; and of course when Moses made Judaism a religion from the document - the "Neggative Confessions" - he co-opted from his fellow Africans of the religion of the God Ra.

The biased presumption that the indigenous Africans had to await the arrival of the European colonialist missionaries to acquire "morality, culture, scriptures, and universalism" is a value judgment that is inconsistent with ancient traditional laws and customs governing every aspect of indigenous African communal and religious living. For example; the "monogamy" versus "polygamy" issue within African-Christianity and Judaism highlights the point in question. Whereas European, American, and even Israelis, Judaism and Christianity have now classified polygamy as being "immoral", even though there are no written comments to this effect in the "Holy Books;" but the vast majority of African peoples of the same religions have retained it. The African peoples have asked, including those who are Jews (Israelites), Christians, and Moslems:

> " Why is polygamy "immoral" now, and it was not when Abraham and all of the other "prophets" es-

tablished its "morality?" Did God order the change?

On the other hand the Africans, including officials within the laity and clergy of Christianity, now demand that:

> Polygamy must again become acceptable to those who set the rules and mores within Roman Catholicism and Protestantism.

Those indigenous Africans involved with Judaism, the "Black Jews[42] of Ethiopia - the Beta Israel or Falashas, have refused to make any change to suit Jews from Europe and the United States of America who have succumbed to this "Western" social and moral custom - "monogamy" - that had its origin in Germany. They have supported the Yemenite Jews,[43] now in Israel, against the European-American and European "power structure" within the orthodox rabbinate of Israel on this issue.

Polygamy is a fundamental part of most indigenous African religions' "myths" and "morality." It also supports the entire civil and social structure of the vast majority of family living and the philosophy for life in most African societies. Its interruption by European And European-American-style Christian missionaries, who attempted to stomp it out beginning from their involvement with the slave trade and the founding of colonialism in the continent of Africa, caused untold suffering as millions of families were destroyed - thereby the destruction of the entire fibre of many clans, tribes, and in many cases, nations. Why? For the sole purpose of imposing values and standards, which included monogamy; all of which the Europeans and European-Americans, because of some uknown reason, believed that some God or Gods endowed them with the rights to set the entire world in their

own image. However, they were not willing to show **why polygamy**
is moral in their own "Holy scriptures" and not "moral" in the
Africans "Holy scriptures." And in so crushing the Africans polygamous societies they also showed a perverted picture of their
own God - Jesus Christ, who was presented to the African peoples
in the worst example of a prostituted Christian teaching and
scripture any where. Jesus is shown as a "celibate," who shows
no sense what-so-ever of the masculinity a male is supposed to
have. He was always shown with an **aura** of homosexuality, to the
point of always being afraid to be around women, and of course
always overwhelmed by men; all of this effort being carried out
in order to show how much better it is to be a celibate than a
polygamist. Never-the-less, they did not tell the legal monogam-
ist with his illegal polygamous harem (the common behavioral
pattern in most "Western societies"). Neither have they shown that
the two other God-heads , Jehovah and Allah, have endorsed the
morality of polygamy over monogamy. This cannot be denied, as
each and everyone of the "prophets" and other"holy men" in the
Jewish (Hebrew) Torah and the Moslem Koran practiced polygamy,
King Solomon of Israel being the master harem keeper of them all.
There are provisions in the Hebrew, Christian,and Moslem "scrip-
ure" dealing with a man's duty to his wives within **polygamous**
union; also rules governing the manner in which each **wife is to** be
selected and treated - which also included the treatment of women who were slaves and their masters cohabited with them and
made them pregnant.

To say "...there was no scripture...." in any African religion is to deny the existence of religious scripture in Koptic and

57

Gheese in the oldest Christian religious group in history - the
Egyptian and Ethiopian Christian churches; not to mention man's
earliest religious script - hieroglyphs- from North Africa, a
script that became the basis for all religions following; or the
writing the Twe people of Liberia, West Africa, once used for all
purposes - stopping only when they were converted to Islam and
adopted Arabic in place of their own language, by force. In the
strictest usage of the word "scriptures," with relationship to
the root "script," there are very few European languages with
their own "Script." Yet "scripture,"[44] as it is commonly used in
its religious significance among the masses, does not necessarily
have to be in written form, as all "scripture" stems from oral
tradition of half-truths, myths, beliefs,and partial history.
Among the Yorubas of Nigeria, West Africa; Fulanis of Sierra Le-
one and Akan, also of West Africa; Agikuyu of Kenya, East Afica;
and the Djukas of Surinam (formerly called "Dutch Guiana") of
South America; also hundreds of other nations, the masses recite
their common scripture in Voodoo, Black Magic, Obyah, Witchcraft,
Damballah Ouedo and other traditional African religious rites .
"Scripture," in the loose sense of the word usage, was no less
handed down from one to the other in the indigenous African religions than they were among any other group of people - Europeans and European-Americans included. Before their Jewish, Christ-
tian,and Moslem (the so-called "Western Religions") religious writings ("scriptures") they were rehearsed and memorized, then put
into writing by allegedly "God inspired men." Must one assume
that such teachings (history plus myths) were not "scriptures"
before, and until, they were written by people who lived hundreds
58

of years after the events they were reporting occured? Is it not
true that the so-called "scriptures" were being taught by the
forerunners that started these religions, most of whom were not
even conscious at the time that they were "God inspired men?" If
not; then the same recognition is due Voodoo and JuJu religious
"scriptures," and all other religious "scriptures" of other non-
European peoples throughout the Planet Earth. For it must be remembered that very few "European languages" developed their own
"script," and could have existed in their present form were it not
for Arabic "script" - from whence their characters (alphabet) are
derived.

As for "universality," which the good Doctor of Divinity -
Reverend Parrinder - also claimed African religions lacked before
the arrival of the Europeans as slavemasters and colonizers, both
groups represented also as European-style Christian missionaries
(all together as a combined institution of imperialism), he is
correct in his observation. However, this is providing that he
took into account - which he did not - that proselytizing through
military force (armed violence), as employed by the European colon-
ialists - the so-called Christian missionaries included - during
their six"Crusades" in Africa and Asia, has never been done by any
African religious group under the pretense of following their
"scriptures." And that none of the indigenous African religious
leaders ever led their adherents in the extermination of millions
of peoples and placed them into chattel slavery because they did
not accept JuJu, Shango, Voodoo, or any other African religion or
God-head. This is not to say, however, that the indigenous Africans did not fight wars among themselves, and that many had relig-

59

ious implications. Like all other groups, including the Europeans who are still fighting among themselves in Europe in ways unimaginable to the average African, the Africans - too - have fought each other. But the Africans never joined in forced conversion of others to any of their religions which are of solely traditionally indigenous character. Why? Because in each case such is forbidden by religious "scripture" passed down in oral tradition. Only in this sense they may have failed to show the type of "universality" the good Reverend was seeking to find, and obviously could not find anywhere in Africa. Yet, each and every African religion has been accessible to anyone who wishes to embrace one or the other. For example: As powerful as the Empire of Ethiopia once was, even to the point of expanding her colonial empire to the Ganges River in India, Asia, she did not force her religion upon the Indian people she conquered; the same not being true when the various European empires conquered the same are of Asia and others. This type of arrogance on the part of the European missionaries, that they were ordained to save the world, was never one of the human failings of the Americans, and they have many.

If "universality" involves what the leaders of European and European-American-style Christianity and Asian Islam did to the peoples of Africa from the 7th through 20th century C.E. in the name of "Jesus Christ" (God) and "Allah," the Africans, hopefully, must remain religious isolationists. But, if on the otherhand, it means carrying their message to those who are freely willing to heed, then and only then, JuJu, Voodoo, Oledamare, Baba Loa, Damballah Ouedo, and all other indigenous traditional Gods and relig-
60

ions of Africa shall continue to be "universalist" in their outlook on the needs of man for a common religion; that is if such
is needed. And who is to decide that all of mankind is to worship "One God?" Who has been given the answer to all?

The God - Oledamare, of the Yoruba religion, is emphatic in
his demand that:

> "...every man must heed My Orishas (minor Gods)."

Baba Loa on the otherhand claimed:

> "...I am the God of all Gods, and Master of all
> that moves, stand still, and ever was...," etc.

If the last two Gods were not **universal** in their declarations
with as much equivalent righteousness as the Jewish, Christian,
and Moslem Gods (Jehovah, Jesus Christ, Allah), all of whom allegedly stated:

> "...I am a jealous God, thou shalt have no other
> Gods before me...," etc.[45]

What is it that makes the last three Gods of the so-called
"Western Religions" command "true authority" and the others "falsehood?" Man. Yet each of these God-heads (African, Asian) has been
acclaimed to be the "...one and only true God, ruler of the universe...," etc. And that"all other Gods" are inferior to them.

Another of the basic religious foundations without which
there would be no Judaism or Islam is "circumcision,"[46] a sacred,
social and religious rite in each and every indigenous traditional African society - including the ancient Nile Valley Africans
that carried into Sais (Egypt) in order that the Hebrews could
copy it and pass it to others under their influence. The only
difference between all of these religions with regards to"circumcision"being _time_ (the age the initiate male , or in some cases

61

female,has to be for the ceremony to be performed). On the otherhand, this rite -"circumcision"- is carried to the female in many
African societies as part of the traditional religious ceremonies
under the name of "excision,"[47] a rite that is uncommon in either
of the so-called "Western Religions." Of course European-style
Talmudic Judaism, Christianity,and Islam frown upon "excision" as
a "heathen practice." But the Hebrews - Beta Israel (Children of
the House of Israel), misnomered "Falashas or Falasa, of Ethiopia,
East Africa - one of the oldest groups of Torahdic (tradition-
ists) Hebrews today - still practice "excision." Why? Because
there are no prohibitions mentioned or implied in the original
Five Books of Moses - commonly called "TORAH" which the Chris -
tians' version called "OLD TESTAMENT." Jehovah, Jesus Christ,and
Allah are all moot on the issue of "excision;" whereas JuJu, Voodoo, Oledamare, Ngai and other African Gods are quite definite
in its approval.

>"But man's female soul is removed at circumcision
>when he becomes a true man; and the corresponding
>events happen to a woman at excision...," etc.

The above quotation comes from Reverend Geoffrey Parrinder,
D.D., in his book - AFRICAN MYTHOLOGY,[48] as he attempted to described the Dogons belief in creation. Yet one can see the same
illusions in the "Adam and Eve in the Garden of Eden" drama in
this critique which the good doctor sees as "myth" in the case
of the African religions, but to which he is completely blinded
in his own - Christianity (Unitarianism). It is to be remembered
that "God" (the Hebrew or Jewish Jehovah) "took a rib from Adam
and made Eve...," etc. (mythical magic).[49] In this mythological sex
transplant it was from male to female; in the case of the Afri-
62

cans "mythological excision" or sex transplant it was both ways –
male to female and female to male, through circumcision and excision respectively. If the Judaeo-Christian Gods (Yahweh and
Jesus Christ)"made man from the clay of the earth," and then
took "a rib from the man" (Adam) and "made a woman" (Eve); why
is it impossible for any traditional African God to do a much
more reasonable feat through "circumcision" and/or "excision?" Because it was not so stated in the "Holy scriptures" written by
European Jews and Christians, and in that which was later written by Arab Moslems with modifications to suit Arabic culture.
Strangely enough even Abraham's (the first Hebrew or Jew) "circumcision"(the method of which the Hebrew learnt from the Africans of Egypt) made his conversion from alleged "heathenism" or
"paganism" to "purity" (Hebrewism); "circumcision"being one of
the most basic ceremonies in a man becoming a Hebrew (Jew). But
millions upon millions of indigenous Africans, for thousands upon thousands of years before the birth of the first Hebrew –
Abraham, had to pass through "circumcision"or "excision." Yet it
is to be remembered that in the City of Ur, Chaldea (Chaldees),
where Abraham was born, the people there were already using the
methods of both "circumcision" and "excision" which they had
adopted from the Africans of Egypt and Ethiopia; both of these
countries at the time being the leader of world culture. This
custom was carried on by way of Abraham's son – Isaac,and his
grandson Jacob,[49] neither of whom were Caucasian as one is made
to assume these days. The descendants of these first Hebrews had
to practice the same when they arrived in Egypt and lived along
the banks of the Nile River (Blue and White) and the Atbara River.

These "purification rites" (circumcision and excision) were integral parts of every African civilization (High-Culture) throughout the entire continent of Alkebu-lan (Africa), in particular
along the more than 4,100 mile - long Nile River, all of which
have been written on various papyri in existence in museums all
over Europe, the United States of America, Britain, North Africa
and East Africa (Ethiopia). Is it that the Gods of Egypt and
other parts of Alkebu-lan did not know what they were doing before Abraham was born, became a man, and then found his new God -
Yahweh (Jehovah, Yavh, Almighty God) - who had to confirm that
what the Africans were doing is correct, i.e. "circumcision", but
not "excision?" Or is it not true that the " my God is better than
your God " hypocrisy is what makes one story "mythology" and the
other " sacred writings (scripture) by inspired men of God?" And
is it not equally true that they all say, "I believe"[49] it is so;
not "I know" it is so? In general, what makes the European, European-American, and Asian "I believe" divine (Godly) and that of the
African and African-American devilish (unGodly)? The answer is
very simple. It is plain and simple RACISM and RELIGIOUS BIGOTRY,
otherwise called by its first nomenclature - "WHITE SUPREMACY."
But stranger than fiction, millions of those who could not register as "Caucasians" for many generations in the United States
of America,but can do so now, joined their new fellow "Caucasians"
in said "racism" and"religious bigotry,"yet they continue to yell loud
er whenever those whom they tend to degrade counteract.

"Oledamare - God of the Orishas - God over all other Gods -
brother of the God Ra, the representative God of ONE who gave
birth to the Gods of Judaism and Christianity and Islam (Yahweh,
64

Jesus Christ and Allah), rules Supreme over the universe " (according to the followers of his worship - the Yoruba-speaking Africans of West Africa, the African-Caribbeans and the African-Americans in the United States of America; especially at their temples in Harlem, New York City, New York. Here in Harlem Yoruba priests and priestesses can be seen in their habits of white and other colors - according to their rank. "ALAFIA" their greetings say; "ALAFIA" their parting (Welcome to all; and, farewell). As-salaam alechem or Shalom - in Arabic and Hebrew. What is the major difference? Languages. The first is strictly African; the second African-Asian mixture; the latter strictly Asian; not one of them European or European-American; yet they are of the major religions being discussed in this work.

Obyah, Voodoo, JuJu, Ngai, "Black" Magic, Judaism, Christianity, Islam, etc., are all names of religions in which mankind (all colors, including white) tries to find the answer to the unknown factor responsible for life itself. Herein among these names various groups of mankind daily murder (commit genocide) each other under the pretext of "...carrying the true message of God." Each preaching "...thou shalt not kill...," etc., whenever one person dares to think of killing a fellow human being. Each claiming that "...God is on our side..." whenever the killing is called "WAR" - at which time thousands, sometimes millions, are slaughtered in the name of "nationalism" and "patriotism to God and country." This tragic behavior pattern of humans is best highlighted when either of these groups carrying the same religious label begin to fight among themselves; each side claiming "God's" endorsement. Thus: One sees this dilemma in the biblical split between Judah and

65

Israel (Palestine), the civil war between Hebrews, with Yahweh
(Jehovah, Almighty God) on both sides; Germans against English
(both Christians), with Jesus Christ on both sides; Turks against
Arabs (both Moslems), with Allah on each side. Yet in Nigeria's
civil war, in West Africa, it was Oledamare, Allah vs. Jesus Christ,
on their sides, and helping each. In this latter case the Gods –
Oledamare and Allah defeated Jesus Christ (the central government
forces defeated the break-away Eastern Region forces), the final
outcome should have then indicated that "...the will of God had
prevailed." Or does the "...will of God" only "prevail" when
Jehovah or Jesus wins? From the reaction to the so-called
"Nigerian – Biafran War," in the United States of America, with
respect to the alleged "genocide of the Nigerian race over the
Ibo race," "God" did not "prevail." Why? Because the prevailing
God did not contemplate the type of ending said war took. The
"race war" they dreamed up fizzled; just as their theory of
Northern, Western, and Southern Nigerians being of one "race" and
fellow Nigerians of the Eastern Region being of another "race."
Yet, and still, these same people cannot see their own "race
war" in the United States of America.

In the book, MAN AND HIS GODS, by Homer W. Smith, he wrote:[50]

THE GREAT MOTHER

From remote antiquity, the Egyptian knew well
enough they could not indicate upon their maps the
actual location of mountains which upheld the sky.
They maintained the cosmological fiction because
it was elastic, the invisible pillars of heaven
being easily pushed farther afield as knowledge
of new lands was brought home by venturesome wanderers.
Yet it was with a certain justice that the men of this
Old Kingdom considered their country to be the center
of the world, themselves to be the only civilized
beings, for at the farthest limits of their travels they found only barbarians to whom the finer

arts of agriculture, masonry, sculpture, painting and the like were quite unknown. The Egyptians, moreover, were never great explorers,
their expeditions being confined to the upper
reaches of the Niles or the Red Sea coast, or
at farthest venturing across the Ithmus of Suez
into the Sinai Peninsula. Consequently even the
country of Syria which lay immediately beyond
the wedge of Sinai remained for them an almost
unknown land until the period of the New Empire
when Thotmes brought its western edge under the
double crown.

"...members of the Old Kingdom considered their country to be
the center of the world, themselves to be the only civilized beings...," etc., according to the above report by Mr. Smith. This
is quite a revelation, when one considers that the European and
Asian (Jewish, Christian or Moslem) peoples followed the Africans
from whom they modeled their own religions. Count C. C. Volney
supports Mr. Smith's position in his own book - RUINS OF EMPIRE,
as he wrote:

" All religions originated in Africa."[51]

To indulge in extensive detailing of the differences or similarities between that which is being called "Western Religions"
and those still remaining solely traditional and indigenous to
Africa could only result in a fruitless game of rhetoric. However,
it must be made very clear that the Africans, those who are very
much cognizant of their historical heritage, do not hold Judaism,
Christianity or Islam in any higher esteem than they hold their
own religions which have not been corrupted by slavery, colonialism or cultural genocide. It is therefore only befiting that Mr.
Homer W. Smith's book, MAN AND HIS GODS, be quoted in this regards
at least once more.[52] Thusly:

EPILOGUE

As the fallen angel, man would be ludicrous.

As an intelligent animal, he has reason to be
proud because he is the first who can ask himself, "Whither, Why, and Whence?" and confident
because he can know himself as a creature of
earth who has risen by his own efforts from a
low state. If he would rise higher he must be
true to earth, he must accept that he is its
creature, unplanned, unprotected and unfavored,
co-natural with all other living creatures and
with the air and water and sunlight and black
soil from which their dynamic pattern has been
fabricated by impersonal and indifferent forms.
In every wish, thought and action he is seeking
to escape the same protoplasmic disquietude that
impels the meanest flesh crawling beneath his
feet. He must find his values and his ends en-
entirely within this frame of reference.

Mr. Smith continued with his "Epilogue" as he cited the crux

of the answer to the argument between 'which religion is right or

wrong.' He wrote:[53]

As an intelligent creature he explores his
world and here is the first value that is uniquely his: he is more intelligent than any other
creature, and from intelligence fired by curiosity comes knowledge, and from knowledge come power and the manifold satisfactions by which he
surpasses all his fellow creatures. The sequence
has led him to abondon the forest and the cave
for the purposes and plans. But the need for
knowledge has burdened him with the ethnic of
truth, to lie willingly to himself or others, to
that which is suspect, however tentatively he
holds to truth, is to forfeit his opportunity
and jeopardize his dreams. This is the essence
of all philosophy: to cherish truth for its
uniquely human value to search for it, to test
and retest it by conscious effort, to communicate it, to be guided by it, to base upon it all
purposes and plans.

In the following paragraph Mr. Smith's conclusion was reached,

as he wrote:[54]

But he who has purposes and plans must take a
choice, no other can make it for him. A proper
view of man finds no place for a priori 'should'
or 'ought' or any categorical imperative, but
only for this: that if a man so acts, that is
his action and his alone. This is the essence
of all morality: a man is responsible for the
consequences of whatever choice he makes. The

68

degree to which he recognizes this and acts accordingly is a measure of his biological maturity.

This chapter is being closed with "... the last act of the Osirian drama, the weighing of the 'heart' in the scales of Thoth ...," etc., as taken from the BOOK OF THE DEAD, the 125ᵗʰ Chapter - also known as the "NEGATIVE CONFESSIONS." One will see the similarity between that which is today called the "TEN COMMANDMENTS OF MOSES" and source of its origin - the "HYM OF ADORATION TO THE GOD OSIRIS;" as follows:[55]

1) I have not done iniquity.
2) I have not committed robbery with violence.
3) I have done violence to no man.
4) I have not committed theft.
5) I have not slain man or woman.
6) I have not made light the bushel.
7) I have not acted deceitfully.
8) I have not purloined the things which belonged to the God.
9) I have not uttered falsehood.
10) I have not carried away food.
11) I have not uttered evil words.
12) I have not attacked man.
13) I have not killed the beasts which are the property of the Gods.
14) I have not eaten my heart (i.e., done anything to my regret).
15) I have not laid waste ploughed land.
16) I have never pried into matters.
17) I have not set my mouth in motion against any man.
18) I have not given way to anger concerning myself without cause.
19) I have not defiled the wife of a man.
20) I have not committed transgression against any party.
21) I have not violated sacred times and seasons.
22) I have not struck fear into any man.
23) I have not been a man of anger.
24) I have not made myself deaf to words of right and truth.
25) I have not stirred up strife.
26) I have not made no man weep.
27) I have not committed acts of impurity or sodomy.
28) I have not eaten my heart.
29) I have not abused no man.

69

30) I have not acted with violence.
31) I have not judged hastily.
32) I have not taken vengeance upon the God.
33) I have not multiplied my speech overmuch.
34) I have not acted with deceit, or worked wickedness.
35) I have not cursed the king.
36) I have not fouled water.
37) I have not made haughty my voice.
38) I have not cursed the God.
39) I have not behaved with insolence.
40) I have not sought for distinctions.
41) I have not increased my wealth except with such things as are my own possessions.
42) I have not thought scorn of the God who is in the city.

Note that this "Drama" took place approximately more than one-thousand three-hundred years to one-thousand three-hundred and fifty years (1,300 to 1,350) before Moses was supposedly driven out of Western Sais (Egypt) to the Eastern limits - Mt. Sinai - by Pharoah Rameses II between c1225 and 1232 B.C.E. An account of this document was discovered written on a black basalt-slab (stone) in the ruins of the Temple of Ptah at Memphis, Sais (renamed Egypt by the Hebrews and Greeks). This stone, itself, only dates back to the 8th century B.C.E. It was prepared by Sha-baka - the Ethiopian (Kushite) Pharoah of Egypt - founder of the Temple of Ptah. It was Pharoah Shabaka's attempt to preserve the words of his very much more ancient indigenous African ancestors, whose descendants are today called "Negroes, Bantus, Pygmies, Ni-lotes" and other such names. It is estimated (by Egyptologists) that the original script was written around 1,300 years before Moses (Moshe) - the messenger of Yahweh (Jehovah), 2575 years before the birth of the Christians' God - Jesus Christ, and 3,197 years before the Moslem (Muslim) Prophet of Allah - Mohamet. Why, then, is it told that the first time man was given only "TEN" of these one-hundred and forty-seven (147) "CONFESSIONS" - called "COMMANDMENTS" - was when God allegedly"gave them to Moses at Mt. Sinai?" Because each religion that followed the other in this re- gion co-opted most of the myths and traditional dogmas of the former - Judaism, through Moses, being no exception to this rule of historical tradition.

From the Nile Valley Africans High-cultures, commonly called "civilizations," mankind adopted that which is today called"re- ligion." But they all began in the "MYSTERIES." They all came from Alkebu-lan (the continent the Greeks and Romans renamed "AFRICA").

Ra, JuJu, Voodoo, Magic, Witchcraft, Shango, Ngai, Damballah Ouedo and other traditional Gods and religions of ancient Alkebu- lan came from the same source - the GREAT LAKES REGION.[56] This source reached its zenith in Sais (Egypt) - North Africa; in the Holy of Holies in Zimbabwe (renamed "Rhodesia" by British colonial slavemasters) - Monomotapa, South Africa; in the West African empires - Ghana, Melle (Mali),and Songhai (Songhay); and Kush (Ethiopia, formerly "Abyssinia" by Arab colonialist slavers); also Punt (today's Somalias), East Africa; thousands of years before the invention of the Hebrews (Jewish) "ADAM AND EVE" and the "GARDEN OF EDEN" myth.

All evidence point to the fact that mankind's first attempt at declaring that "there is a God" is when he began to worship the Sun - the God "RA," the first "God" of the indigenous Afri - cans(who are today called "NEGROES, NIGGERS, BANTUS, AFRICANS SOUTH OF THE SAHARAH, BLACK AFRICANS, PYGMIES, BUSHMEN, HOTTEN- TOTS, CRIME IN THE STREET, BENIGN NEGLECT," and many other such

71

degrading terms of the slave trading and colonial days when the
Africans were subdued by the Europeans under the pretext of
"PLANTING CHRISTIANITY IN AFRICA." It should be needless to say
that the same had happened to the Africans hundreds of years
before the arrival of the Christians from Europe, when the
Moslems from Arabia in the 6th Century C.E. with their jihads -
Holy Wars - scourged the lands of North and East Africa. The
Hebrews (Jews) can take no comfort from these exposures, as they
too aided the Christians and Moslems in the enslavement of the
Arican peoples; at least the Hebrews provided many of the
writers who morally justified the enslavement of the Africans
through their warped interpretations of the Hebrew Torah
(Christian Old Testament) - as evidence in the writings of the
6th century C.E. Babylonian Talmudic scholars (see quotations
in BLACK MAN OF THE NILE, by Y. ben-Jochannan; from R. Patti and
R. Graves; HEBREW MYTHS).

72

ST. AUGUSTINE: AFRICAN INFLUENCE IN CHRISTIANITY
(The "Christian Church Fathers")

Chapter Two

The death of the last and greatest of the indigenous African "Christian Church Fathers" — Saint Augustine, Bishop of Hippo (354-430 C.E.), North Africa, was the major event in Christendom's history which started the decline of power and control by the indigenous Africans in the Christian Church, especially the "North African Church" (the "Mother Church").

St. Augustine was born at Tagaste, Numidia, North Africa, 15 November 354 C.E., at the time Numidia was a Province of the Roman Empire.[1] Augustine's birth having occured exactly forty years after Emperor Constantine - "the Great"- became sole ruler of the Roman Empire of the West and adopted Christian symbols after having dropped his "Divine" role. Constantine -"the Great", as he was called, mounted the Roman Throne in the year 312 C.E.;[1a] more than one-hundred (100) years after the indigenous Africans ("Negroes"etc.) of the Empire of Kush (Ethiopia), East Africa, had already established Christianity as the <u>official religion</u> of their empire.[2]

St. Augustine's birth followed the martyrdom of one of the other two indigenous African "Church Fathers" - St. Cyprian, the Bishop of Carthage (249-258 C.E.). Cyprian was the African martyr that hollered these famous last words; "...Deo gratis..." (thanks be to God) upon being told that there was an order stating:

"It pleases that Thrascius Cyprian" (his full name)

73

"be beheaded with the sword."

This order was issued by Roman authorities, who were trying to stomp out Christianity during, and before Cyprian fled into hiding (underground) to continue his teachings of the ancient versions of the "Gospel of Christ"; not as it has been corrupted today. This was during the reign of Emperor Galerius, who later on issued an Imperial Edict granting tolerance to the Christian community. Mrs. Stewart Erskine (considered an "authority" on this phase of Christian Church history), in her book - THE VANQUISHED CITIES OF NORTHERN AFRICA, p. 80, with regards to the martyrdom, wrote that St. Cyprian faced death in honour as:

> "He died magnificently, giving twenty-five
> pieces of gold to the executioner."[3]

The same type of praises could have been heaped upon other great Africans* who made Christianity (although Europeanized) what it is today; such as Namphamo - the "first of the Christian martyrs." In conjunction with her "martyrdom" C.P. Groves in his book, THE PLANTING OF CHRISTIANITY IN AFRICA, P. 59, wrote:[4]

> A certain Namphamo, claimed as the first
> martyr, also came from Numidia, the name in
> this case being Punic. As from this point the
> story of the Church in Africa unfolds before
> us, we find a devotion under persecution not
> excelled elsewhere, and a fervent fidelity to
> the faith expressed in Puritan ideals that
> gave Montanism a second home in Africa. The
> names Tertullian, Cyprian and Augustine add
> an imperishable lustre to the history of the
> African Church.

Added with Namphamo were the second and third Christian martyrs, Perpetua and Felicita, both of whom were also indigenous Africans.*

At this point, it is necessary to introduce another of the in-

---

* Indigenous Africans, in this work, specifically refers to the ancestors of and present Africans who are today called "Negroes, Bantus, Hottentots, Pygmies, Bushmen,"etc.;even "Niggers" by some.

74

digenous Africans known as the three most important "Church Fathers" of Christendom, Tertullian. He was born in Carthage sometime during the year 155 C.E. In his era, he was revered as "...one of the most outstanding scholars in rhetoric, Latin,and Greek." His mastery of these disciplines led him into becoming the head of a Montanist community in his own homeland's capital city of Carthage. And it was his depth in, and love for, Latin which caused him to make it the official language of the Holy Roman Catholic Church (an outgrowth of the North African Church) and Christendom in general.[5]

Although listed last Tertullian, a contemporary of the most noted of the indigenous African emperors of the Roman Empire – Septimus Severus (146-211 C.E.), must be mentioned in the order in which he chronologically arrived in the history of Christendom.

Before dealing with the role of Tertullian in the makings of Christianity, it is necessary to project certain background material on how Christianity came to the northwest from northeast and east Africa as a power-block during the height of Roman imperialism and colonialism throughout most of North Africa.

In North Africa, just before the period of Christianity's legal entry into Rome – due to Constantine "the Great" conversion in the 4th century – there were many Hebrew (Jewish) "tribes" that are of indigenous African (the so-called "Negroes") origin. These African Jews, as all other Romanized-Africans of this era, were caught in a rebellion in Cyrene (Cyrenaica) during 115 C.E. against Roman imperialism and colonialism. This rebellion also marked the beginning of a mass jewish migration southward into Soudan(Sudar or West Africa) along the way of the City of Aer (Air) and into the

75

countries of Futa Jalon and Senegal (Sene-Gambia) which lie below
the parabolic curve of the Niger River's most northern reaches,
where the City of Tumbut (Timbuktu, Timbuctoo, etc.), Melle (Mali)
presently stands. These Jews were divided into two main groups
and took separate directions further southward into West and Central West Africa. One group joined the Fulanis of Futa Jalon –
from whom the present population of indigenous Africans of Bornu
and Kamen, in Nigeria, inherited their "Hebrew (Jewish) traditions."
This indigenous African Jewish penetration from North Africa into
the Soudan* even reached the borders of Lake Tchad (Chad) in Central Africa.[6]

The indigenous African tribes, of the Hebrew faith, of Cyrenaica had migrated there by way of Numidia before the defeat of
General Hannibal Barca and the conquest of Carthage by Rome in
202 B.C.E. Carthage, about 1000 B.C.E. was re-established by Phoenician mariners who had left the City of Tyre (around today's Middle East) under the leadership of Princess Elissar (Dido) of Phoenicia.[7] The place these mariners, the vast majority of whom were
male, first conquered and settled on North Africa's coastline is
today called Tunisia – previously Khart Hadas (the New Town) by
its original indigenous (so-called "Negro") African population.
These mariners, who later on amalgamated with the indigenous Africans of Khart Hadas and other regions around, also defeated
other indigenous Africans further west along the coast of North

---

* "Soudan" is a name given to the area of West Africa that was
physically colonized by France for over one-hundred years. A
semblance of political freedom came to the French oriented Africans,
the majority, in 1961 C. E. through political agitation.

76

Africa and established the City of Lixus - where presently the Kingdom of Morocco now stands. In Europe, along the Iberian Peninsula, these African-Asian peoples also established the City of Cardiz - which is today called "Southern Spain," formerly Iberia. It is said, however, that "the Phoenicians had already passed through the "Pillow of Hercules" - today's "Straight of Gibraltar", formerly called the "Straight of Tarikh" - taken from Gibra[1] Tarikh,[8] about 1100 B.C.E., approximately one hundred years before they settled with the Africans of Khart Hadas.

Most European and European-American writers have conceded that even though the thrust of Jewish involvement was in Egypt (more than three-hundred years before their alleged expulsion - Passover - about c1225-1232 B.C.E., with Moses, by Pharoah (King) Rameses II) thousands of them had already preceded the Phoenicians' migration of 1000 B.C.E. into the northwest regions of North Africa; but these same writers have utterly neglected to state that the Hebrews (Jews) amalgamated with the fellow Africans they met both in Egypt and points farther northwest, southwest, and east.

Approximately sixty-five years after the Cyrenaica rebellion in c115 C.E., and sometime before July 180 C.E., Christianity was introduced into Northwest Africa. This date is approximately true, because there was never any mention of Christians there before in any of the records of the Roman imperial government that colonized the area. The first mention of the Christians came about with the martyrdom of many of their numbers on 17 July 180 C.E. There is no record giving the exact number of the original group either, only of those tried and found guilty of:

> "...committing Christian acts against the
> Roman State...," etc.

were mentioned. They were five women and seven men - twelve in all. Amongst these martyrs was their twenty-two-year-old leader, the person responsible for the total action of the group. She was a married woman, and the mother of one child. This woman - Perpetua - was also of indigenous African birth. It is to be noted, however, that at this period in history Tertullian also made his presence felt as spiritual leader of all of Christendom; also that Christendom was still centered in North Africa, under indigenous African (the so-called "Negroes") control.

It must be remembered that the Christians of Carthage were indigenous Africans brought in from the neighboring state called "Numidia" as slaves for the Roman imperialists who were ruling Carthage and other parts of North Africa at the time. It is also to be noted that among these earliest of Christian slaves (of every color) were Perpetua's brother and the same Felicita mentioned before, of whom it was said:

> "Her ordeal caused the premature birth of her
> only child a few hours previous to her death as a
> martyr for Jesus Christ...," etc.

And in her honor a chapel named "St. Perpetua" was built. It still stands at what was the center of the ancient African City of Carthage - presently a part of Arab-controlled Republic of Tunisia. This chapel was constructed with stone pillars and other materials taken from runied structures that once adorned the glorious City of Carthage during the days of General Hannibal Barca - the African ("Negro") who once ruled all of the Iberian Peninsula, parts of Southern Gaul (France), and all of Northern Italy for more than twenty (20) long years with more than one hundred thousand indigenous African troops.

78

Strangely enough, the greatest of the indigenous Africans who became Emperor of the Roman Empire was charged by many European and European-American Christian Church historians of being "the emperor who ordered the persecution and execution of Perpetua and her followers," his name - Septimus Severus (146-211 C.E.).[9] But the truth is that Emperor Septimus Severus did not mount the throne of the Roman Empire until 193 C.E.; this he did subsequent to the murder of Emperor Marcus Aurelius'[9a] son - Marcus Aurelius Commodus Antonius - about 17 March 177-180 C.E. Septimus Severus, at the time of his elevation to the throne of the Empire of Rome, was Rome's greatest general, and a former civil magistrate. It is to be further noted that color was never a condition to his ascendency to the Roman throne, as only one Roman Governor had failed to accept this indigenous African role of imperial Rome. The dissident was Allinus - Governor of Britany (England, Scotland, Wales and Ireland). But Emperor Septimus Severus quickly did away with this problem, as he defeated and killed Clodius in 197 C.E. during the Battle of Lyons, France.

Septimus Severus' victory over Clodius placed an African ("Negro") in complete control of every nation along both sides of the Mediterranean Sea and every European nation along the Atlantic Ocean* up to, and including, Angloland (Britany). It also

----

* During this period the present "SOUTH ATLANTIC OCEAN" was called "ETHIOPIAN OCEAN." Only that which is today called "NORTH ATLANTIC OCEAN" was considered in this manner. The "ETHIOPIAN OCEAN" appeared on maps made by European chartists and cartographers until the latter part of the 18th Century C.E. See BLACK MAN OF THE NILE, by Yosef ben-Jochannan, pp. 266-268, for maps showing these conditions.

placed this African in charge of the entire Roman Empire at the time when the Roman military was being corrupted, due to the extensive employment of mercenaries. Monetary inflation, coupled with high prices and over-burdening taxes on all classes of the Roman peoples, also created chaos in the empire. These conditions brought into being the widespread uncontrollable money-lending and the serious decline in taxes, to the extent that the Imperial Exchecquer found it extremely difficult to collect the necessary taxes for the Imperial Treasury. During all of this turmoil the Roman State was being challenged by a "new religion" - "Christianity," which had crossed over from North Africa and was giving every indication of causing further disaffection from the already disrupted Roman army, as it was already causing full-scale conversions by too many of Rome's finest military officers - including her best generals. This "new religious force," in direct and open conflict with the existing official religion of the state, had even begun to gnaw away at the already disorganized Roman body politic. The seeds of all this had in fact started during the reign of Augustus Caesar (27 B.C.E. - 14 C.E.);[10] however, at which time a "new God" was born amongst the Hebrews (Jews), his name - "JESUS CHRIST."

The conditions already outlined, along with many more, forced Emperor Septimus Severus, as Emperor of Imperial Rome, to issue an edict in 202 C.E.. In this "edict" he forbade any new conversion to Judaism or Christianity, neither of which he intended to stomp out, but instead check. The "edict" has been purposefully overstated by religious bigots and over-zealous racist fanatics alike. Some even dared to charge that Emperor Septimus Severus and the other indigenous

80

Africans involved with the control of the Roman hierarchy was in itself the cause of the decline of the Roman Empire. But, to this racist contention the "renowned authority" in this area of North African and Church history, Jane Soames, in her book - THE COAST OF THE BARBARY, pp. 30-31, wrote:

> At the height of Roman power in North Africa, the population of Italy was actually declining and there was never any vast number of Roman colonists in the racial sense of the word. The Romans knew nothing of those modern emotions which are to us so powerful and omnipresent that we can hardly imagine a civilization from which they should be absent; she had neither colour prejudice nor religious intolerance in the days of the Republic. The Christian martyrs of the early church suffered because they were felt to be a menace to the State, propagating doctrines subversive to good order and discipline: they were regarded as the Communists of their day. But highly cultivated Roman opinion considered all religions to be essentially the diverse manifestations of one great truth, and had no conception of that white heat of missionizing zeal which would put whole populations of unbelievers to the sword or send men to the scaffold and the fire for the sake of a disputed theological definition.
> All that part of the make-up of men's minds came later, as did the acute sense of differentiation of race and consequent antagonism which may be summed up in the phrase "colour bar."

On the otherhand, many of today's religious fanatics continue to charge Emperor Septimus Severus of ordering :

> "...the martyrdom of Perpetua, Felicita and the other Christians on 17 July 180 C.E.,..." etc.;

and of course of:

> "...the persecution of the Christian Church."

But his distractors , to date, have failed to account for the fact that Septimus Severus did not become Emperor of Rome until 193 C.E., thirteen (13) long years after the reported persecution and martyrdom of his fellow indigenous Africans of the "new religion" -

81

Christianity. Some historians, not knowing that the alleged martyrs were themselves also indigenous Africans (blacks, "Negroes",
etc.) like the emperor himself, even dared to charge him with:

"...murdering the white Christians...,"

in their attempt to introduce colour prejudice and racism into
the history of a people who knew not what the term or feelings
were.

Why did Emperor Septimus Severus issue the "edict" barring
"further Roman conversion to Judaism and Chritianity?" For the
same reason any president, king, emperor or dictator and other
types of soverign,today suppress any religion which stands to
disrupt the orderly functions of the established government. For
the same reason that the Nation of Islam (nicknamed "Black Muslims")[11] - headed by the Prophet Elijah Mohammed - is being dis-
missed by the rulers of the United States of America as:

"...not amounting to a religion in the strict
sense of the word...," etc.;

and that Mohammed, its spiritual leader,is a:

"...false prophet, who is fooling the Negroes."

Also, for the same reason that Mohammed Ali (Cassius Clay) is not
considered a "minister of religion" by the Federal Courts of the
United States of America, as they consider other boxers who are
members of the European-American-style Christian clergy. Yet former repented murderers and thieves in other acceptable religions
(Judaism and Christianity) are accepted as having been:

"...called by God to His ministry."

The ministry, in this case, is mostly European-American-style
Judaeo-Christianity; even Moslems from Mecca are not recognized

82

in this context. It was, therefore, incumbent upon Emperor
Septimus Severus, as Emperor of Rome, to protect his empire.
Yes, even to the point of committing executions. For, is it
not true that every nation up to this very period in man's
history commit murder in the same fashion when they condemn
a suspected or convicted "traitor" to death and carry out said
"edict," which is much more sophisticatedly called:

"...judgment by a jury of your peers?"
Many whits have compared the Christians within the Roman
Empire, at this period, with the Communists of the United
States of American during the Senator Joseph McCarthy's[12] era:
and to a great degree even today.

It is also true that there were those who hated both Jews
and Christians within the Roman Empire. And, most certainly, they
wanted to destroy Judaism and Christianity. But one must also
remember that thousands of Christians went out of their way to be
martyred in order to:

"...win the blessings of Jesus Christ,"
whom they believed, during that period, was about to make his
"second coming." At least, that was the prevailing claim by the
leaders of the "new religion." It was in this type of atmosphere
that Emperor Septimus Severus began his rule. Because of it, he

made the Praetorian Guard universal and stopped the practice of
having only legionnaires stationed in Italy to fill vacancies as
they arose. In so doing, he also militarized every aspect of the
empire's civil administration with retired generals, to whom he
owed his ascendency to the throne. It was under these conditions
that Emperor Septimus Severus' contemporary, another of the African
"fathers of the Church" - Tertullian, assumed control of the
Christian minds of North Africa, the North African Church, and
influence over all of Christendom, especially within the Roman
Empire; but, excluding Egypt and Ethiopia.

Tertullian inherited the history of a Church which had
its African beginning with John Mark - evangelist, who did
his missionary work in Egypt, where he established many churches
in the City of Alexandria.[14] But it was really during the Episcopate of Demetrius of Alexandria (189-232 C.E.) that the North
African Church got its real beginning as a fully recognized
religious body. This, of course, does not mean that the
beginning of Christianity in Africa started at this juncture.
The reference to the Ethiopian convert in Acts viii, 26-40, of
the King James Version of the Christian "Holy Bible" proves
the contrary.

The North African Church had already established the world
renowned "Catechetical School of Alexandria" under the leadership

of an African named Pantaenus - its founder. It was at this center of Christendom and Christian scholarship that the **world's famous**
and most distinguished scholars of their time - Origen and Clement - served as bishops along with Pantaemus. It was also from
this center that another African of Egyptian birth left to found
the world's first monastery of hermatic living (the life of a hermit). He was called - "Anthony the Hermit of the Sahara," because
he withdrew to that area to meditate in a life of poverty after
abandoning his wealth to the Egyptian state.

Tertullian, born in Carthage about 155 C.E., was to become
important in Christendom as was his contemporary - the Emperor of
Rome, Septimus Severus, **in government.**   But, his was not to be
in the piously spiritual philosophy of his religion.His was the
socio-economic relationship of Christianity to man and his cultural involvement; and to civilization in general. In light of this
involvement,Tertullian wrote in one of his most famous works,
called DE ANIMA, the following:[15]

> Surely a glance at the wide world shows that
> it is daily being more cultivated and better
> peopled than before. All places are now accessible,
> well known, open to commerce. Delightful farms have
> now blotted out every trace of the dreadful wastes;
> cultivated fields have overcome woods; flocks and
> herds have driven out wild beasts; sandy spots are
> sown, rocks are planted; bogs are drained. Large
> cities now occupy land hardly tenanted before by
> cottages. Islands are no longer dreaded; houses,
> people, civil rule, civilization, are everywhere.

The man who wrote this had drawn the attention of Christians
everywhere; from their citadels in Egypt and Numidia, to his own
surroundings in Carthage. And, to his memory the honoured English
historian - Miss Stewart Erskine, wrote:[16]

The three great names that bring honour to the

> African Church are Tertullian, the first of the
> Church writers who made Latin the Language of
> Christianity; Cyprian, bishop and martyr; and
> Augustine, one of the most famous of the "Fathers
> of the Church."

Before his death, in 222 C.E., Tertullian had the honor of
seeing the North African Church grow from twenty-three bishops in
200 C.E. to approximately seventy, or eighty. But to really
appreciate this African's role in the Christian Church, one has to
refer to Professor C.P. Groves' remarks on page 70 of this book.[17]

Cyprian, like Tertullian, was born in Carthage of indigenous
African (so-called "Negro," "Bantu," etc.) parentage who were of
wealthy means. But Cyprian's exact date of birth is unknown. However, it is known that he was at least forty-six years old when
he had his "...heavenly birth..." (the phrase he used for explaining his decision to leave the world of a life of wealth for that
of religion and poverty).

Cyprian's "heavenly birth" proved no problem to him, as he
had held a professorship in philosophy at the University of Carthage and excelled in rhetoric. This background led him to become Bishop of Carthage in very little time subsequent to his religious transformation.

The ascension of Cyprian to a bishopric also led him to
his "earthly death." For it was during his reign as Bishop of
Carthage that the persecution of the Christians of North Africa
really got underway. It was equally true for all of Roman Europe.
The words of Mrs. Stewart Erskine best summed up his ending, when
she wrote:

> "... he died magnificently, giving twenty-five
> pieces of gold to the executioners."[18]

Cyprian was fully aware of the possibility that he would be martyred, as the "new religion" he had embraced became an irritant to the vast majority of the Africans of Carthage and their Roman overlords. He had already seen, and heard, Christians being thrown to the lions at the amphitheatres as the crowds clamored:

"...washed and saved!"

This exp ession having been originated by the Christians of Egypt and Numidia before it was adopted by the brethren of Carthage as a rallying cry; yet it was in other parts of the Roman Empire before its use in Carthage. But as he expected, their cries very soon thereafter changed to:

"...the Bishop to the Lions!"

Like any other man, this bishop was not interested in his own suicide, as he carried his teachings underground (n hiding), whence he continued to lead the outlawed Christian Assembly for years following. Cyprian, in his characteristic style - which was exclusively his, explained his plight and temporary safety, thusly:

"The white rose of the crown of labour might
be as fair as the red rose of martyrdom."

Cyprian was to cry out in a sense of relief from the agony of evading the law and never knowing just when his end would come at the hands of the Imperial Executioner, or by the claws and jugular-cutting teeth of the lions. Thus, his "Deo gratis" (thank God), in response to the command:

"...It pleases that Thrascius Cyprian be
beheaded with the sword."[19]

It was now 222 C.E., eleven years after the death of Emperor Septimus Severus and the elevation of his only son - Caracalla -

on the throne of the Roman Empire. It was also near the height of Emperor Caracalla's (212-217 C.E.) attempt to exterminate the Christians from the empire. This period marked an era of one of mankind's most brutal highpoints of genocide; where one group exterminated the other because of the need to protect an empire. It must be carefully stated, the extermination of the Christians was not because of their adherence to the "new religion," instead, because of the teachings of the religion that affected "law and order" as established by the Imperial Government of Rome. The Romans, at this period, would have exterminated any group, religious or secular, because of their being annoyed at a dying empire. Neither was it "race," as some historians have tried so hard to insinuate; nor was it "color," which was not a factor in the societies of the ancients.

The persecution of the Christians and Jews, irrespective of race or color, had reached its zenith. And Emperor Caracalla had succumbed totally to the bestiality of his colleagues in the Roman Senate and the army, who benefited materially from the confiscation of the personal and real properties of their martyred victims. Emperor Caracalla, himself, however, was also murdered by the same army officers on 8 April, 217 C.E. Sixty-seven years had passed. Rome was not ruled by emperors Maximianus and Diocletian (284-305 C.E.), who followed Caracalla and fifteen other to the Roman throne (Macrinus to Carus). Yet, the persecutors had continued for nineteen years after Diocletian's rise to power in the East, slowing down somewhat in 303 C.E. - just two short years before emperors Maximianus' and Diocletian's abdication in 313 C.E. The persecution of the Christians actually stopped in Rome, following the Emperor Galerius' May 305 or May 311 Imperial Edict - which granted tolerance to what had become a Romanized Christian Church. The same Emperor Galerius had tried to persuade Emperor Diocletian to declare a "...general persecution of the Christians" on 23 February, 303 C.E. This is added proof that the persecution and prosecution of the Jews and Christians were much more political than religious throughout the Roman Empire, this being true even during the greatest height of the persecutions under the Emperor Caracalla.

One year after the abdication of former Emperor Diocletian (284-305 C.E.) Emperor Constantine "the great" (306-337 C.E.) had become the uncontested ruler of the Roman Empire of the West. In 324 C.E. he had also become Emperor of the East, at which time he actually adopted Christianity and dropped all of the pretenses of his Divine Rights - the religious custom of his forerunners. Constantine "the great" followed his own conversion by converting his own army, through force; making them carry standards of the Christian Church - the so-called "new religion." Within a very few years later the "new religion" - North African Christianity, now Romanized European Christianity, had become the official religion of the entire reunited (East and West) Roman Empire. This was the religious and political picture of the Roman Empire when the greatest of the indigenous Africans that became one of Christendom's "Fathers of the Church"; a man, who was born in the city of Tagaste, Numidia, 15 November, 354 C.E.: his name, Augustine, later on called "Saint Augustine" (354-430 C.E.). Note that the nation of Numidia occupied an area of the territories now forming the nations of Algeria and Libya, North Africa.

In dealing with the state of the Roman Empire at the time

St. Augustine was old enough to become the Bishop of Hipp Regious, to the point where he had written the most profound philosophies on Christianity to date; the noted historian - Jane Soames, wrote:[20]

> The empire, essentially a federation of municipalities, tried unavailingly to prevent a movement which weakened and depopulated the cities; and at the same time delivered over the populace more and more completely into the hands of the great landlord, whose wealth depended upon their labour.
> It was in such a world, torn by civil strife and threatened by barbarian invasion under the splendid but fading shadow of Rome, that St. Augustine's genius flowered. The Church in Africa had produced great men before this day; the writings of Tertullian and St. Cyprian both testify to its keen intellectual vitality; but neither achieved his stature - the last and noblest product of Roman African civilization. We learn a great deal about that civilization from the CONFESSIONS, the product of a mentality strikingly sympathetic to the European mind, though bearing the imprint of its African origin.

The underscored words are to emphasize the value of St. Augustine's African background in all of his works, including the Confessions. Jane Soames continues in the next paragraph:

> St. Augustine is far more comprehensible to a European audience today than are most contemporary North African authors - a fact which is in striking disproof of modern racial theories, for it is community of philosophy which makes for affinity far more than the accident of birth.

Jane Soames could have hardly explained the question of racism surrounding St. Augustine's African (Negro) origin; as she most adequately cited the major importance in Augustine's being:

> "... for it is community of philosophy which makes for affinity far more than the accident of birth."

With respect to the "CONFESSIONS" mentioned by Jane Soames,

90

another historian - Mrs Stewart Erskine - wrote the following:[21]

> St Augustine's CONFESSIONS are the most fa-
> miliar and intimate documents, whether he is
> approaching God, to whom they were made, or man,
> for whose benefit they were written down. He
> conseals nothing and is extremely modern in his
> point of view.

This African (Black, "Negro," etc.), as "...the greatest of

the Church fathers," was also one of the greatest thinkers and

philosophers of all time. With reference to the greatness of St

Augustine, professor George H. Sabine wrote the following:[22]

> The most important Christian thinker of the age now under
> discussion was Ambrose's great convert and pupil, St Augustine.
> His philosophy was only in a slight degree systematic, but his
> mind had encompassed almost all the learning of ancient times,
> and through him, to a very large extent, it was transmitted to the
> Middle Ages. His writings were a mine of ideas in which later
> writers, Catholic and Protestant, have dug. It is not necessary
> to repeat all the points upon which he was in substantial agree-
> ment with Christian thought in general and which have already
> been mentioned in this chapter. His most characteristic idea is
> the conception of a Christian commonwealth as the culmination
> of man's spiritual development. Through his authority this
> conception became an ineradicable part of Christian thought,
> extending not only through the Middle Ages but far down into
> modern times. Protestants no less than Roman Catholic thinkers
> were controlled by St Augustine's ideas upon this subject.
> His great book, the *City of God*, was written to defend Chris-
> tianity against the pagan charge that it was responsible for the
> decline of Roman power and particularly for having caused the
> sack of the city by Alaric in 410. Incidentally, however, he
> developed nearly all his philosophical ideas, including his theory
> of the significance and goal of human history by which he sought
> to place the history of Rome in its proper perspective. This
> involved a reinstatement, from the Christian point of view, of
> the ancient idea that man is a citizen of two cities, the city of his
> birth and the city of God . . . on the one side stands the earthly
> city, the society that is founded on the earthly, appetitive, and
> possessive impulses of the lower human nature; on the other
> stands the city of God, the society that is founded in the hope of
> heavenly peace and spiritual salvation. The first is the kingdom
> of Satan, beginning its history from the disobedience of the angels
> and embodying itself especially in the pagan empires of Assyria
> and Rome. The other is the kingdom of Christ, which embodied
> itself first in the Hebrew nation and later in the Church and the
> Christianized empire. History is the dramatic story of the
> struggle between these two societies and of the ultimate mastery
> which must fall to the city of God. Only in the Heavenly City is
> peace possible; only the spiritual kingdom is permanent.

St Augustine's background began with his mother - Monica, a

Christian convert, and his non-Christian father - Patricius; both

of whom were not wealthy, but of aristocratic breeding. His father, being a minor State official, afforded Augustine - at the age of eleven - the chance to be sent to Madausos (the ancient Numidian city built by King Syphax)[23] for his education. In school he learned Greek, which he hated, and he did very poorly. The best of his subjects being Classical Latin - which he considered next in importance to his own language and Rhetoric. This, of course, was just the beginning of his formal education; as he was later on (in 370 C.E.) sent to Carthage to complete his advance studies. This later involvement required him to spend three years in very serious and exacting studies (370-373 C.E.). Four years later, Augustine won a prize for his dramatic poem, and wrote his first book - ON THE BEAUTIFUL AND THE FIT.

Having completed his schooling, Augustine further enjoyed the "better things of life." He also frequented the major houses of "...ill repute...," and paused to enjoy the gladiators at the various amphitheatres, with an occasional time for gambling. Of course, the houses of prostitution he frequented did not stop him from living in "common-law relationship" with a woman for a period of almost eleven years; who bore him a son by the name of "Adeodatus." Augustine made no attempt to marry this woman or legitimize his son in the manner most European and European-American-style Christians assume is the only moral way to Jesus Christ's acceptance; each forgetting that Jesus Christ supposedly said:

> "Suffer little children to come unto me, for such is the kingdom of heaven."

Yet some writers claimed that:

> "...he was very much attached to his son's mother."

In other words this mortal man, "...greatest of the Christian

Church Fathers," who was later made a "Saint" by his successors, lived what some of today's puritanical Christians and pious Jews will call a "dissipated" life in his youth - until he was at least twenty-eight years (354-382 C.E.) of age.

Augustine credited his piously aristocratic mother with being the person who was most responsible for his conversion to Christianity. Yet he spoke of his meeting with his mentor in Milan, whose name was Ambrose - later Saint Ambrose, as a major factor in his leaving Carthage for Italy without his mother's approval or knowledge. For this reason most historians credited Ambrose with being responsible for the conversion. At least Ambrose is due part of the credit, along with Augustine's mother Monica.

Augustine remained in Italy, living in Milan and Rome, where he was followed by his beloved mother - Monica, later Saint Monica. At the time of Monica's arrival in Italy, Augustine had already become a Christian believer and professor of Rhetoric, both of which pleased her emensely. After spending a period of time with her one and only son, Augustine, Monica prepared to return to her native Numidia. On her way back she was fatally stricken at Ostia, Rome's sea port, where she was subsequently laid in her final resting place. There is not too much more known about this indigenous African woman - mother of one of the world's greatest thinkers of all times. That which is known of her comes from the short biographical sketch provided by her son in his own attempt at giving a precise background of his early life he gave in his CONFESSIONS. Her "sainthood" must have rested upon her attempts to impose upon her son her newly-founded religious belief - North African Christianity. No other reason can be drawn from the ski py information available about her life.

Augustine returned to Carthage shortly after the untimely death of his mother. At this point in his life he had become devotedly attached and involved in Christian ethics and divine matters. To some extent it was due to the shock the sudden death of his mother , to whom he was dearly attached, had on him. From these experiences he developed his extraordinary desire for the permanent religious seclusion he took in the monastery of North Africa in later days; this of course does not diminish his other loves that made his final decision to follow said course, much of which will be detailed later on in this chapter.

Upon his return to North Africa, from Rome and Milan, Augustine's involvement in **spiritual matters was** so outstanding that he was literally forced to accept the "Bishopric of Hippo Regius." Augustine took command of the Bishopric in the year 395 C.E., as ordered by Pope Siricius (later on Saint - 384-399 C.E.).[24]

The elevation of Augustine to Bishop of Hippo Regius gave him extra time for added meditation and writing. From this vantage point he wrote extensively without resting between works. But, of all his major works it is the three major treatises - CONFESSIONS, ON CHRISTIAN DOCTRINES,and the HOLY CITY OF GOD which most scholars to this very day find to be agelessly profound. His moral, religious, political,and social fervor in them are still applicable to the present. A very short extract from his CONFESSIONS is shown on page 102 of this work; others to appear as required.[25]

What has been so far shown about St Augustine's life is pri-

94

marily his youthful background, also his religious conversion and
sudden acceleration into prominence as a theologian, philosopher,
and Bishop. But Augustine also had the misfortune of becoming
Bishop of Hippo Regious shortly before Gaiseric (or Genseric) led
his rampaging Vandals (Barbarians)[26] into North Africa from the
Iberian Peninsula (Spain). Gaiseric's invasion was in support of
General Bonifatius' disaffection from the Roman Empire in 429 C.E.;
when he unwisely declared himself ruler of the Roman province
under his command in North Africa. During this same period
Valentinian III was Emperor of the Western Roman Empire (425-455
C.E.). He was the son of Honorius' half-sister, Galla Placidie
(Galla Placidia), who was sole ruler. Honorius also was the former
general that defeated and murdered the Emperor Constantine near
Arles in 411 C.E. He was, at the time, commander of the army
under Emperor Constatius.

The Vandals' invitation to North Africa by General Bonifatius
was hastily accepted because they were being chased from Spain by
the Visigoths. The Visigoths had already conquered Gaul (France)
in 412 C.E. under the leadership of Athaulf, the brother-in-law of
Aleric, who subsequently died in Italy after sacking Rome on 14
or 24 August, 410 C.E. By 416 C.E., Vallia (416-419 C.E.), who
succeeded Athaulf had established the first "Barbarian Kingdom."
But a Royal Bloodbath had already started with Emperor Constantine's murder. Thus, in 423 C.E. Johannes (423-425 C.E.) had forced
himself into power and usurped the Roman purple on the death
of Honorius, at Ravenna, which he had made his capital in preference to Milan, and which his predecessors used. But in
425 C.E. Johannes' rule was hurriedly terminated, when he, too,

was murdered by troops sent from the Roman Empire of the East by Theodosius II.

Augustine's ebbing life had witnessed Rome's disintegration and the dawn of the Vandal's rule in North Africa. As such, he was obliged to comment on these historic events in most of his last works, which took on more of the political and socio-economic messages found in the writings of his fellow African forerunners - Tertullian and Cyprian (also "Saint" Cyprian).

Before Augustine died on 28 August 430 C.E. the Vandals had already ravaged North Africa for a period of three months (the year ending 430 and during the beginning of 431 C.E.). But, the extent of their barbarity was never excelled by any other group during the dawn of the Christian Era (C.E.), except during the period when the Christians themselves became the "new Barbarians;" as they too ravaged the Middle-East and North Africa[26] from Europe.

On the day St. Augustine died the curtain fell on the last and most noted of the truly "great Christian writers and philosophers." But the second half of the Fourth Century C.E. was to witness the revival of non-Christian writings - the so-called "pagan Latin literature" - which was no doubt as rich as the North African Christian Church literature it was replacing. The greatest significance was the fact that this period marked the return of things cultural to the populace, rather than to the middle and upper classes for whom "Latin literature" catered in its European-style Christian setting. Although the so-called "non-Christian literature" was much more invigorating, because of the emphases placed on it, it was never-the-less men like Boethuis (the class-

96

ical philosopher) who translated Aristotle's Egyptian-based "LOGIC" (which Aristotle stole from the Africans of Egypt) into Latin from its original Hieroglyph and Greek in order to write his "DE CONSO-LAITIONE PHILOSOPHAINE" while he languished in prision awaiting ex-ecution by Theodoric — the Osthrogoth — in 524 C.E. But Boethius' contemporaries were not at all like Augustine's — who lived in the Fourth Century C.E. with men such as the Galic poet Ausonius (Con-sul in 379 C.E.),and Claudius the Alexandrian (court poet of emper-. ors Honorius and Stilieho). Of course many European and European-American historians (religious and secular) tend to rate Pepys' and Jean Rousseau's biographies on the same level with that of Augustine's CONFESSIONS. Many of them also tried to rate the "Lat-in Fathers" — Lactantius (d.c. 325 C.E.); St Ambrose (340-397 C.E.), Bishop of Milan; St Jerome (340-420 C.E.) — who deserted Rome for Bethlehem, where he translated the Christian Bible from Greek to Latin (the Vulgate) , with the genius of St Augustine. However, in their attempts, they gave no comparative analysis to these men's writings with those of St Augustine's, thereby eliminating the logic of their own contentions.

The "Greek Fathers" — whom they tried to compare to the "Lat-in"(Roman) and "African Fathers" — were, Basil of Caesarea (330-379 C.E.); **his** brother Gregory of Nyasa (d.c. 394 C.E.); and Gregory of Mazianaus (329-389 C.E.). They were known as "...the three Cappadocians." Included were also John Chrysostom (329-389 C.E.) — Patriarch of Constantinople (381 C.E.); and Eusebius* (264-340 C.E.) — Orthodox Bishop of Caesarea (315 C.E.), noted for his

---

* Not to be confused with Arian Eusebius of Nicomedia.

"HISTORIA ECCLESIATICA" and other historical works.

Noting the "Latin" and "Greek Fathers" mentioned, historically none of them produced any major work on the level of St. Augustine's "CITY OF GOD," "ON CHRISTIAN DOCTRINES," or "CONFESSIONS"; not one of them even matched Augustine's "lesser works." Augustine's mentor, St. Ambrose of Tries (340-397 C.E.) - a former Roman Provincial Governor - who was later elected Archbishop of Milan (374 C.E.) before his baptismal, who was also responsible for making Emperor Theodosius do penance on the basis that:

> "...the ecclesiastical matters of a Bishop
> is superior to an emperor,"

was also chief architect of Stoic tradition, author of the "Duties of the Clergy" (according to Cicero's "DE OFFICIS") - the standard thesis on ethics before Augustine's works. **This** work, Ambrose's best, also failed to equal either the "HOLY CITY OF GOD," "CONFESSIONS,"   "ON CHRISTIAN DOCTRINES," or any other of the "lesser writings" of Augustine.

What Augustine's works had over all of the other "Church Fathers" was his deep love for the wretched and the poor, which he knew so well through his personal contacts as a young man when he visited houses of ill-repute, gladiators, gambling saloons, etc.; all of which when he converted he brought to the "School of Christian Theology" he founded. He also fathomed the inner secrets of neo-Platonism and Manichaeism - which he moderated by linking them with his understandings of indigenous African mythological and Ancestral Spirit Worship. The latter two are fundamentally indigenous African theology and moral principles which are today called "paganism" and "fetishism"
98

by Europeans and European-Americans. Many Africans and African-
Americas, sons and daughters of converted slaves to European and
European-American-style Christianity (European-Style), aided and
abetted by their Jewish (Hebrew) and Islamic cohorts, also
condemn these Africanisms in like manner.

There was another critical aspect of St. Augustine's philosophical thoughts, as experienced in his works, which must be
credited to the depth of his understanding of life and life's
practical application as seen in its translation into spirituality.
This is best observed in the relationship between St. Augustine
and his common-law son, Adeodatus, whom he took with him wherever
he went. Even in the year 384 C.E., when he was assigned a
Municipal Chair at Milan, he took his son with him; this was during the same period when his mother Monica visited him. When he
moved on to Rome, where he abandoned Manichaeism while under the
influence of his friend and mentor Abrose* (later saint), and
started to indulge in reading the neo-Platonists, he also carried
his son with him. In 388 C.E., when he set sail for his return
to Taghaste - Numidia, North Africa, he carried his son Adeodatus.
But tragedy struck St. Augustine heavily once more, as Adeodatus
suddenly died in 389 C.E. after a very short illness, a tragedy
that was later on to enrich Augustine's thoughts in his philo-
phical idealism and writings on Christian dogmas about "carnal intercourse, the deity of Jesus Christ, the sainthood and immaculate
conception of Mary" and the "sainthood of Joseph," etc.

* The common belief is that Ambrose was Augustine's teacher in
Christianity; everyone of said historians holding said position
overlooking the fact that Christianity was already common in the
area of Africa from where Augustine came to Milan and Rome. Also
that Augustine also contributed his first attempts at Christianity
to his mother.

The legacy St. Augustine left the entire world is included in that which is today called "GREAT WRITERS OF THE WESTERN WORLD," and other noted internationally accepted titles. Because of this genius, however, his indigenous African ("Negro, Bantu, Black," etc.) origin has been carefully camouflaged, suppressed, or otherwise made to appear that he was only born in North Africa, but, that he was a "Caucasian." Of course any African who was responsible for anything which "Western Society" based its origin and morality upon must have been anything other than a "Negro, Bantu African South of the Sahara," or plain old "Nigger." The extent of St Augustine's legacy, the genius of his indigenous African origin, includes the following works:

1. The DRAMATIC POEM; which he wrote for a poetry competition in 377 C.E.[27]

2. ON THE BEAUTIFUL AND THE FIT.[28]

3. AGAINST THE ACADEMICS, ON THE HAPPY LIFE.

4. ON ORDER.[29]

5. ON MUSIC.[30]

6. ON THE MORALS OF THE CATHOLIC CHURCH AND OF THE MANICHEANS.[31]

7. ON CHRISTIAN DOCTRINE.[32]

8. ON THE TRINITY.[33]

9. CITY OF GOD.[34]

10. RETRACTIONS.[35]

In the above listed works entitled "RETRACTIONS" - Augustine commented on all that he had already written under more than two-hundred and thirty-two (232) other separate titles; all of which did not include his "SERMONS" or "LETTERS, which he had hoped to publish in a separate series.

100

To fathom more into an understanding of the inner depths of St Augustine's thinking and philosophical pronouncements the following extracts are given. Thus he wrote on "...communion with the Gods:"[35]

> (VI) 13. And how Thou didst deliver me out of the bonds of desire, wherewith I was bound most straitly to carnal concupiscence, and out of the drudgery of worldly things, I will now declare, and confess unto Thy name, "O Lord, my helper and redeemer." Amid increasing anxiety, I was doing my wonted business, and daily sighing unto Thee. I attended Thy Church, whenever free from the business under the burden of which I groan.

On "carnal concupisence" cited in the above, he wrote:[36]

> But now, the more ardently I loved those whose healthful affections I heard of, that they had resigned themselves wholly to Thee to be cured, the more did I abhor myself, when compared with them. For many of my years (some twelve) had now run out with me since mine...," etc., etc., etc.

His disdain for his fellow indigenous Africans (Blacks, Negroes, etc.) of North Africa, who were forced into the service of the Emperor of Rome (North Africa being at the time a Province of Imperial Rome) brought forward the following:[37]

> 14. Upon a day then, Nebridius being absess (I recollect not why), lo, there came to see me and Alypius one Pontitianus, our countryman so far as being an African, in high office in the Emperor's court. What he could with us, I know not, but we sat down to converse, and it happen ed that upon a table for some game before us, he observed a book, took, opened it, and contrary to his expectation, found it the Apostle Paul; for he had thought it some of those books which I was wearing myself in teaching.

If there was any doubt of the indigenous African origin of St Augustine what-so-ever, Augustine left no doubt of such origin in his own words underscored for emphasis above. He made no effort what-so-ever to claim any European origin, and actually displayed utter contempt for fellow Africans in the service of the Romans.

101

On problems of his conversion from the indigenous African
traditional religion of his father, the religion of Numidia, to
Christianity, Augustine wrote:[38]

> ...when, upon the reading of Cicero's HOR-
> TENSIUS, I was stirred to an earnest love of
> wisdom; and still I was deferring to reject
> mere earthly felicity, and give myself to
> search out that whereof not the finding only,
> but the very search, was to be preferred to
> the treasures andd kingdoms of the world,
> though already found, and to the pleasures of
> the body, though spread around me at my will.
> But I wretched, most wretched, in the very
> commencement of my early youth, had begged
> chastity of Thee, and said, "Give me chastity
> and continency, only not yet." For I feared
> lest Thou shouldest hear me soon, and soon
> cure me of the disease of concupiscence, which
> I wished to have satisfied, rather than ex-
> tinguished. And I have wandered through crook-
> ed ways in a sacrilegious superstition, not in-
> deed assured thereof, but as preferring it to
> the others which I did not seek religiously,
> but opposed maliciously.

In his "disputations against the academicians" he wrote:[39]

> (IV) 7. Now was the day come wherein I was
> indeed to be freed of my Rhetoric Professor-
> ship, whereof in thought I was already freed.
> And it was done. Thou didst rescue my tongue
> when before thou hadst rescued my heart
> And I blessed Thee, rejoicing; retiring with
> all mine to the villa. What I there did in
> writing, which was now enlisted in Thy service,
> though still, in this breathing-time as it
> were, panting from the school of pride, my
> books may witness, as well what I debated
> with others, as what with myself alone, before
> Thee: what with Nebridius, who was absent, my
> epistles bear witness. And when shall I have
> time to rehearse all Thy great benefits towards
> us at that time, especially when hasting on to
> yet greater mercies? For my rememberance re-
> calls me, and pleasant is it to me, O Lord, to
> confess to Thee by what inward goads Thou tamedest
> and how thou hast evened me, lowering the
> mountains and hills of my high imaginations,
> straightening my crookedness, and smoothing my
> rough ways; and how Thou also subduedst the
> brother of my heart, Alypius, unto the Name of
> Thy Only Begotten, our Lord and Saviour Jesus

102

Christ, which he would not at first vouchsafe to have inserted in our writings. For rather would he have them savour of the lofty "cedars" of the Schools, which the Lord hath now broken down, than of the wholesome herbs of the Church, the antidote against serpents.

On Scripture and on Confession he wrote:[40]

II. And with a loud cry of my hear I cried out in the next verse, Oh in peace," Or for "The Self -Same!" Oh what said he,"I will lay me down and sleep," for who shall hinder us, where "cometh to pass that saying which is written Death is swallowed up in victory"? And Thou surpassingly art "the Self-Same," Who art not changed; and Thee is ret which forgetteth all toil, for there is none other with Thee, nor art we to seek those many other things, whichart not Thou art; but Thou Lord, alone has made me dwell in hope. I read, and kindled nor found I what to do to these deaf and dead of whom myself had been, a pestilent person, a bitter and blind bawler against those writings which are honied with the honey of heaven, and lightsome with Thine own light; and I was consumed with zeal at the enemies of this Scripture.

On the indentification of his teacher[41] he stated:

(V) 13. The Vintage Vacation ended, I gave notice to the Milanese to provide their scholars with another master to sell words to them; for that I had both made choice to serve Thee, and through my difficulty of breathing and pain in my chest was not equal to the professorship. And by letters I signified to Thy Prelate, the holy man Ambrose, my former errors and present desires, begging his advice what of Thy Scriptures I had best read, to become readier and fitter for receiving so great grace. He recommended Isaiah the Prophet: I believe because he above the rest is a more clear foreshewer of the Gospel and of the calling of the Gentiles. But I, not understanding the first lesson in him, and imagining the whole to be like it, laid it by, to be resumed when better practised in our Lord's own words.

As a master on the emptying of the soul, he wrote:[42]

Thou hast taught me good Father, that "to the pure, all things are pure," but that "it is evil unto the man that eateth with offence"; and that "every creature of Thine is good, and

nothing to be refused, which is received with
thanksgiving"; and that "meat commendeth us
not to God", and that "no man should judge us
in meat or drink," and that he which eateth,
let him not despise him that eateth not; and
let not him that eaeth not, judge him that
eateth. These things have I learned, thanks to
Thee, praise to Thee, my God, my Master, knock-
of my ears, enlightening my heart; deliver me
out of all temptation. I fear not......,etc.

Still holding to the Platonist philosophy and arguing for
same, he supported the position in the following manner:[43]

...If, the, Plato defined the wise man as one
who initiates, knows, loves this God, and who
is rendered blessed through fellowship with
Him in is own blessedness, why discuss with
the other philosophers? It is evident that none
come nearer to us than the Platonists. To them,
therefore, let that fabulous theology give palce
which delights the minds of men with crimes of
the gods; and that civil theology also, in which
impure demons, under the name of gods, have se-
duced the peoples of the earth given up to earthly pleasures, desiring to be honoured by the errors of men, and by filling the minds of their
worshippers with impure desires, exciting them
to make the representation of their crimes one
of the rites of their worship, whilst they themselves found in the spectators of these exhibi-
tions a most pleasing spectacle - a theology in
which, whatever was honourable in the temple,
was defiled by its mixture with obscenity of the
theatre, and whatever was base in the theatre
was vindicated by the abominations of the temples.

For those who could not accept the God of the "New Religion,"
Christianity, he wrote:[44]

Hath not God made foolish the wisdom of the
world? For after that, in the wisdom of God
the world by wisdom knew not God, it pleased
them by the foolishness of preaching to save
those that believe. For the Jews require a
sign, and the Greeks seek after wisdom; but
we preach One crucified unto the Jews a stumb-
ling -block unto the Greeks foolishness; but unto those which are called, both Jews and Greeks
etc., etc., etc.

Over the controversy of Methuselah's age he wrote:[45]

"...from this discrepancy between the Hebrew
books and our own arises the well-known question as to the age of Methuselah; for it is
computed that he lived for fourteen years after the deluge, though Scripture relates that
of all who were then upon the earth only the
eight souls in the ark escaped destruction of
the flood, and of these Methuselah was not
one. For according to our books, Methuselah,
before he begat the son whom he called Lamech, lived 167 years; then Lamech himself,
before his son Noah was born, lived 188 years,
which together make 355 years. Add to these
the age of Noah at the date of the deluge,
600 years, and this gives a total of 955 from
the birth of Methuselah to the year of the
flood. Now all the years of the life of Methuselah are computed to be 969; for when he
had lived 167 years, and had begotten his
son Lamech, he then lived after this 802
years, which makes a total, as we said, of
969 years. From this, if we deduct 955 years
from the birth of Methuselah to the flood,
there remains fourteen years, which is supposed to have lived after the flood. And therefore some suppose that, though he was not on
earth (in which it is agreed that every living
thing which could not naturally live in water
perished), he was for a time with his father,
who had been translated, and that he lived
there till the flood had passed away. This hy-
pothesis they adopt, that they may not cast a
slight on the trustworthiness of versions which
the Church has received into a position of high
authority, and because they believe that the
Jewish MSS, rather than our own are in error.
For they...,etc., etc., etc..

St. Augustine's keen mind, sharp as it is in the CONFESSIONS

and CITY OF GOD, reached its high point ON CHRISTIAN DOCTRINE.

Why? Because he seemed to have believed that his own writings were

Note: Augustine, like all of the members of his Church that followed him, who call themselves "Christian missionaries," have to be
right in everything they say and do. Here Augustine is seen con-
demning the same book and religion from whence even his God -
Jesus Christ; his God's mother - Mary; and his God's father -
Joseph,sprung. Is he saying that the Jews were in error, and that
he alone is correct. Or is he saying that not only this aspect of
the entire religion of the Hebrews is incorrect, but the entire
works. If either, then so must be Christianity, which has adopted
its foundation from the Hebrews religion.

105

'inspired by God.' In this regards Augustine is to be observed in the following:

> I.   There are two things on which all inter-
> pretation of Scripture depends: the mode of
> ascertaining the proper meaning, and the mode
> of making known the meaning when it is ascer-
> tained. We shall treat first of the mode of as-
> certaining, next of the mode of making known,
> the meaning - a great and arduous undertaking,
> and one that, if difficult to carry out, it is,
> I fear, presumptuous to enter upon. And pre-
> sumptuous it would undoubtedly be, if I were
> counting on my own strength; but since my hope
> of accomplishing the work rests on Him Who has
> already supplied me with many thoughts on this
> subject, I do not fear but that He will go on
> to supply what is yet wanting when once I have
> begun to use what He has already given. For a
> possession which is not diminished by being
> shared with others, if it is possessed and not
> shared, is not yet possessed as it ought to be
> possessed. The Lord saith, "Whosoever hath, to
> him shall be given." He will give, then, to
> those who have; that is to say, if they use
> freely and cheerfully what they have received,
> He will add to and perfect His gifts. The loaves
> in the miracle were only five and seven in numb-
> er the disciples began to divide them among the
> hungry people. But when once they began to dis-
> tribute them, though the wants of so many thou-
> sands were satisfied, they filled baskets with
> the fragment that were left. Now, just as the
> bread increased in the very act of breaking it,
> so those thoughts which the Lord has already
> vouchsafed to me with a view to undertaking this
> work will, as soon as I begin to impart them to
> others, be multiplied by His grace, so that, in
> this very work of distribution in which I have
> engaged, so far from incurring loss and poverty,
> I shall be made to rejoice in a marvellous in-
> crease of wealth.

He was very emphatic on the only way the Scriptures should be interpreted. On this he wrote:[46]

> 2.   All instruction is either about things or
> about signs; but things are learnt by means of
> signs. I now use the word "thing" in a strict
> sense to signify that which is never employed
> as a sign of anything else: for example, wood,
> stone, cattle and other things of that kind.
> Not, however, the wood which we read Moses
> cast into the bitter waters to make them sweet,

nor the stone which Jacob used as a pillow,
nor the ram which Abraham offered up in
place of his son, nor...," etc.

Of course he was as presumptive on the ineffability of God:[47]

6. Have I spoken to God, or uttered His praise,
in any worthy way? Nay, I feel that I have done
nothing more than desire to speak; and if I have
said anything, it is not what I desired to say.
How do I know this, except from the fact that God
is unspeakable? But what I have said, if it had
been unspeakable, could not have spoken. And so
God is not even to be called "unspeakable," because to say even this is to speak to Him. Thus
there arises a curious contradiction of words,
because of, it is not unspeakable if it can be
called unspeakable. And this opposition of words
is rather to be avoided by silence than to be explained away by speech. And yet God, although
nothing worthy of His greatness can be said of
Him, has condescended to accept the worship of
men's mouths, and has desired us through the medium of our own words to rejoice in His praise.
For on this principle it is that He is called
DEUS (God). For the sound of those two syllables
in itself conveys no true knowledge of His nature; but yet all who know Latin tongue are led,
when that sound reaches their ears, to think of
a nature supreme in excellence and eternal in
existence.

The question of what is "Sacred" or "Profane" literature has
been around with mankind for quite a long time. On this subject
Augustine wrote the following:[48]

22. But when unacquainted with other modes of
life than their own meet with the record of such
actions, unless they are restrained by authority,
they look upon them as sins, and do not consider
that their own customs either in regard to marriage, or feasts, or dress, or the other necessi-
ties and adornments of human life, appear sinful
to the people of other nations and other times.
And, distracted by this endless variety of customs, some who were half asleep (as I may say) —
that is, who were neither sunk in the deep sleep
of folly, nor were able to awake into the light
of wisdom — have thought that there was no such
thing as absolute right, but that every nation
took its own custom for right; and that, since
every nation has a different custom, and right
must remain unchangeable, it becomes manifest

107

that there is no such thing as right at all.
Such men did not perceive, to take only one
example, that the precept, "Whatsoever ye
would that men should do to you, do ye even
so to them," cannot be altered by any diver-
sity of national customs. And this precept,
when it is referred to the love of God, de-
stroys all vices; when to the love of one's
neighbour, puts an end to all crimes. For no
one is willing to defile his own dwelling; he
ought not, therefore, to defile the dwelling
of God, that is , himself. And no one wishes
an injury to be done him by another; be himself, therefore, ought not to do injury to
another.

On Divinely inspired authors and authority he wrote:[50]

9. Here, perhaps, some one inquires whether the authors whose divinely inspired writings
constitute the canon, which carries with it a
most wholesome authority, are to be considered
wise only, or eloquent as well. A question which
to me, and to those who think with me, is very
easily settled. For where I understand these
writers, it seems to me not only that nothing
can be wiser, but also that nothing can be more
eloquent. And I venture to affirm that all who
truly understand what these writers say, perceive
at the same time that it could not have been properly said in any other way.

Augustine's writings, as seen in this work , although only
a very limited amount of extracts from three of his most famous,
show much of the insight he revealed to his fellow Christians
which made them adopt his teachings as the basic concepts of
Christianity (as developed in the North African Church under indigenous Africans) from the Fourth through the present Twentieth
Century C.E.

For example: In speaking about, and against, the Manichees
Augustine called upon Scriptures - as he always did - to convince
his audience. Thus; in the CONFESSIONS, Book I, (III), 3. He
wrote:

Do the heaven and earth then contain thee, since

108

thou fillest them? Or dost thou fill them and
yet overflow, since they do not contain thee?
And whither, when the heaven and the earth are
filled, pourest thou forth the remainder of
Thyself? Or, hast thou no need that aught contain thee, who containest all things, since
what thou fillest thou fillest containing it?

One sees that even in questioning things Augustine was at
the same time emphasizing what he thought to be his "God's commands," with repect to the answers. This type of questionary-
directives have become the standard procedural escape for members
of the Christian clergy to this very date. And the clergy have
since employed it as a means of answering all questions for which
they do not have any hard and fast answers, especially for questions dealing with the origin of God Himself, or the realism of
Christ's "virgin birth."

Augustine not only taught his Christian brethren On Christian
Doctrines, he also taught them how to apply their own feelings and
propaganda of the faith in his Book IV of this same quoted title.
For example: In Chapter 30, subtitled - "THE PREACHER SHOULD COM-
MENCE HIS DISCOURSE WITH PRAYER TO GOD." But it was Augustine
alone who would do this best, as it is seen in sub-section 63 of
the above mentioned work:

> 63. But whether a man is going to address the
> people or to dictate what others will deliver or
> read to the people, he ought to pray God to put
> into his mouth a suitable discourse. For if Queen
> Esther prayed, when she was about to speak to the
> king touching the temporal welfare of her people,
> that God would put fit words into her mouth, how
> much more ought he to pray for the same blessing
> who labours in word and doctrine for the eternal

welfare of men? Those again, who are to deliver
what others compose for them ought, before they
receive their discourse, to pray for those who
are preparing it; and when they have received it,
they ought to pray both that they themselves may
deliver it well, and that those to whom the address it may give ear; and when the discourse
has a happy issue, they ought to render thanks to
Him from Whom they know such blessings come, so
that all the praise may be His "in whose hand are
both we and our words."

Typical of his technique, Augustine called upon the Book of

Esther, 4 : 16 (Septuagint) and Wisd. 7 : 16, for Scriptures that

would gain for himself what he obviously believed to be biblical

approval.

Even in recognizing his own limitations, Augustine made it

seem that through himself and his own teachings were the only ways

to salvation. This is best seen in the last Chapter in ON CHRIS-

TIAN DOCTRINES, Book IV:

64. This book has extended to a greater length
than I expected or desired. But the reader or
bearer who finds pleasure in it will not think it
long. He who thinks it to long, but is anxious to
know its contents, may read it in parts. He who
does not care to be acquainted with it need not
complain of its length. I, however, give thanks
to God that with what little ability I possess I
have in these four books striven to depict, not
the sort of man I am myself (for my defects are
very many), but the sort of man he ought to be
who desires to labour in sound, that is, in Christian doctrine, not for his own instruction only, but
for that of others also.

Much of the dogmatism in European and European-American-

style Christianity today (as seen) comes from the positions and

attitudes in Augustine's writings. However, it is frequently

Stated that :

"St Augustine's brilliance was due to his study
of the works of Homer, Socrates, Plato, Virgil,
Aristotle and other Greeks."

110

While it is true that Augustine ardently studied the works of the Greeks mentioned above, it is equally true that their works came down from the teachings they received from the indigenous Africans (the so-called "Negroes") of Egypt (Sais), Ethiopia (Kush) nad other indigenous Africans of the nations along the three branches of the Nile River (Blue Nile, White Nile, and Atbara River); also from North, West, East, and Central Africa (Alkebu-lan). This is best shown in Y. ben-Jochannan's, BLACK MAN OF THE NILE, Alkebulan Books, New York, 1970. All of these Africans were influenced by other indigenous Africans further south of Mediterranean North Africa, above and below the Equator. For example: Was it possible for Aristotle who was never known to have written a single book before he left his native Greece to suddenly write over one-thousand (1000) books after he joined Alexander "the great" in the invasion and conquest of Egypt in 332 B.C.E.?[51] And, was it possible that he, and the thousands of Greek students he imported into Egypt for the sole purpose of being taught by indigenous African teachers from the books and other documents of the Royal Libraries which Alexander captured and Ptolemy I (Gen'l. Soter) seized, did not claim most of the indigenous Africans ("Negroes", etc.) works as their own?[52] None of these two questions needs any lengthy explanation, for history has already detailed the fact that the Royal Library, which Aristotle and Ptolemy I renamed "Library of Alexandria," was used as a school for training in all disciplines all of the pre-Christian Greek students.[53] And, they made very certain that Egyptian and other indigenous African students were barred from further studies therein. Yet, the first teachers of these and former Greeks were all indigenous African priests of the "Mysteries." The Chief Priest of the school was Manetho - the African who divided Egyptian history into "pre-dynastic" and "dynastic" periods.[54] Moreover; was it not the universal custom for all invading armies, the Greeks in particular, to ravage their victims' women, loot their victims' treasuries and treasures - including all sorts of written documents, and sack their cities? The Greeks - like the Persians, Assyrians, and Hyksos that preceded them into Egypt (Sais) as conquerors - ravaged Northeast Africa, just as they ravaged everywhere else they had conquered, Europe not excluded.

This short departure from St. Augustine's legacy was very much necessary, in order that it be clearly understood that his works were not, to any great extent, influenced by those who are usually misnomered "Greek Philosophers" - per se. But, that "indigenous African Philosophers" of North Africa and along the entire 4,100 mile-long Nile River Valley (from Uganda to the Mediterranean Sea - formerly the Egyptian Sea or Sea of Sais) and throughout Africa were the originators of much of what is alluded to by "Western educators" as of Greek origins.[55] And that they, too, directly influenced him. Even those indigenous Africans, called "Mystics," with their Ju Ju and Obyah (Witchcraft), who were his contemporaries had their effects on him, and moulded much of his thinking and philosophical expressions in his writings.

To say that St. Augustine's expressions in any, or all, of his works were developed, only as a result of his studies under the "Latin Church Fathers," and in particular - St. Ambrose - after he completed his professorship in Milan, along with his readings of the Greek works - such as Virgil's AENAE, would be to ignore his earliest experiences with his father's religion in his native city

112

Tahgeste - Numidia, North Africa. It would be also ignoring St.
Augustine's own background as a young man in Carthage, North
Africa. And of course it would be willfully overlooking the depth
of his own involvement with his mother - Monica - and his son -
Adeodatus,* both of whose death stunned him most severely; all of
which he spoke about very strongly in his CONFESSIONS.[56]

It is impossible for Augustine not to have been more than
casually influenced by his indigenous African religious background
in his native North Africa; especially since he was already twenty-
eight (28) years (354-382 C.E.) old when he left Africa (Carthage)
for his one, and only, visit to Europe (Milan and Rome) to serve
as a professor. Not only was he affected by his indigneous African
High-Culture (civilization) in Numidia and Carthage; but his
constant reflections on "celibacy" throughout most of his writings
indicate the effects which his out-of-wedlock son's birth had on
him; the son being referred to is the one, and only, child Augustine
ever had - Adeodatus. This mortal man, irrespective of being
declared a "SAINT" by those who are in charge of making saints
after death (those who followed him by hundred of years within
the religion he helped to stabilize and to become the powerful
force it is today, even though his descendants are now barred from
many of its doors), was still haunted by his earlier life before
he entered Christendom - which he revealed with deepest remorse[57]
in his CONFESSIONS.

---

* As stated before; except for St. Augustine's CONFESSIONS there is
very little, if any, information available on his father, Patricius, his mother - Monica and his son - Adeodatus; the latter obviously never amounting to much in his own right - in the sense of
academics. For, it is also very obvious that Adeodatus died at a
very young age; this too is missing from Augustine's story.

To say that St. Augustine's early life, on the other hand, was a "sordid one," as so many have stated in hundreds of works dealing with "Sin" and "Righteousness," is a value judgment which only those whose particular "MORALS" and "RELIGIOUS CONVICTIONS" follow such directions; for it is obvious, or it should be, that none of his early youth indulgences were against the social mores or religious scruples of the majority of the people of Carthage before the dominance of that country's indigenous and traditional culture, which included religion and social mores, by the people of the "New Religion" - Christianity. The truth of the matter is best expressed in St. Augustine's own work; when he said that "...each nation has its own moral...," etc.

The fact that St. Augustine's father - Patricius - never saw it fitting to convert to the "New Religion" from Manichaeism also had to have its effect on him. It had to have certain adverse reactions on him, as his respect and deep love for his non-Christian father - Patricius - was as crucial as that for his mother - Monica - who was a convert from the same religion of his father - Manichaeism, to Christianity. Is it to be assumed that they did not carry over any of their beliefs from Manichaeism into Christianity? If so, then Christianity is also free from the carryovers from Hebrewism (otherwise called "Judaism" in modern times). The stranger fact, in this specific argument, is that St. Augustine nowhere mentioned any difficulty between his parents as a result of their differences in religious persuasions. And he did not indicate that either parent tried to convince the other of which was the RIGHT or WRONG way to religious conscience. One can then conclude, that there was individual tolerance and religious freedom throughout

114

Numidia and Carthage during St. Augustine's youthful days, both countries, at the time, being Roman Provinces.

What is so different in St. Augustine's writing in "ON CHRISTIAN DOCTRINES" from other indigenous Africans expressed in Voodoo, Ju Ju, Damballah Ouedo, and other traditional African religions, except for the God-head - "JESUS CHRIST," which makes Christianity "truth" and the others mentioned "lie?" The answer is, BELIEF; and sometimes this belief is manifested with gun powder and/or economic persuasion - as seen in Mr. Achebe's book, THINGS FALL APART - in the first Chapter of this work.

Christianity, like Judaism and Islam, is not static. It, too, adds to its own development from every culture and religion in which it comes into contact, all of which is evidence in St. Augustine's writings with respect to "Libations, Oracles, Greek Philosophers," etc. In Egypt (Sais) Christianity was basically indigenous-Egyptian in almost every aspect. As Christianity moved across North Africa to Numidia and Carthage (birthplaces of the African Christian "Fathers of the Church") the indigenous Africans there reformed and adopted much of its Egyptian format to suit Numidian and Carthagenian culture and religious customs. And as Christianity entered each European colonized nation, throughout Asia, the Americas and the islands of the world, it became the national religion through force and violence; yet Christianity was forced to adopt many of the local taboos in order to co-opt the local religion. This was done in the name of "JESUS CHRIST," yet with soldiers marching with guns as they sang "ONWARD CHRISTIAN SOL-DIERS, MARCHING UNTO WAR, WITH THE CROSS OF JESUS," etc., at the same time suppressing all other religions, forgetting their own oppression.

This type of behavior is not only common to Christian institutions; each and every other religious institution powerful enough to finance mercenaries or build its own armies, such as the ancient Hebrews (Jews) in the Bible (Torah, Old Testament) and Moslems (Muslims) - through their "JIHADS," have been willing, and did, enforce its will upon "UNBELIEVERS" (those who had other religions which their forerunners passed down to them); and they have done so all through history, stopping only when they too become too weak militarily. But, Christianity, which suffered a most horrible beginning, today has become the major religion of the people whose fortune or misfortune it is to control the most extensive arsenal of weapons of destruction the world has ever witnessed. The Christian nations have used such power to their own selfish gain, they are also able to control the less fortunate peoples of the entire world, along with Communism, in a manner which millions cannot call "Christ-like", or even, "the Christian way of life" as established in North Africa. This is still true, and it was especially so during the periods of imposed slavery when mankind purchased his brother in chains, and enforced colonialsim upon the indigenous African peoples of Africa, Asia, and the Americas. It was also true to some extent when most of the smaller national groupings in Europe were subjected to a similar type of treatment. These acts are considered part of the same Christian development that the African "Fathers of Christendom" - Tertullian, St. Cyprian, and St. Augustine, crystalized in the North African Church and influenced the European Church. To this there is not the slightest bit of "truth."

It is necessary, at this juncture, to examine St. Augustine's acceptance or rejection of the Greek and Latin "Church Fathers"

116

teaching, also of the so-called "Greek Philosophers."* In so
doing, one must pay very careful attention to the exception Augustine took to Cicero's mannerism in refuting the Stoics. For
example: In Chapter 9, para. 1, he wrote:

> And this he" (Cicero) "attempts to accom-
> plish by denying there is any knowledge of
> future things and maintains with all his might
> that there is no such knowledge either in God
> or man, and that there is no predictions of
> events. Thus, he both denies the foreknowledge
> of God and attempts by vain arguments and by
> opposing to himself certain oracles very easy
> to be refuted, to overthrow all prophecy, even
> such as is clearer than the light (though even
> these oracles are not refuted by him).

Besides differing with Cicero, one finds Augustine holding
steadfast to the Manichaeans belief in "oracles;" a carry over
from his early indigenous religion which he was born into in his
native Numidia, North Africa. Yet, he also condemmed Cicero for
believing in the Greek God - JUPITER, as he questioned Cicero's
quoting the following Homeric verses from the ODYSSEY, Book XVIII,
pp. 136-137:

> Such are the minds of men, as is the light
> which Father Love, himself doth pour illustrious
> o'er the fruithful earth.

"Indigenous African Religions" and "Western Religions" broad-
ly cite certain basic characteristics common to all religions. Yet

---

* In BLACK MAN OF THE NILE, by Yosef ben-Jochannan, Alkebu-lan
Books, New York, 1970, an entire Chapter deals with the indigenous African origin of the so-called "Greek Philosophers" and
"Greek Philosophy." That work is the foundation of this work.
Where this work begins the other stopped. There the entire historical chronology of how that which is being called "Greek Philosophy" came about from the indigenous Africans along the Nile
Valley. The contributions of the Africans to Europe and the rest
of the world, before the origin of "Adam and Eve", are told in
very simple terms; yet an academic posture is maintained.

they are regarded as "paganism" by the current practitioners of Christianity, Islam, and Judaism when applied to Africa and the indigenous African peoples. This is also noted in St. Augustine's defense of "Christian oracles," as he condemns the Greeks' "Paganism" - that which he chose to call "Greek mythology." But, in his zeal, he then, like others now, failed to take note that the "mythology" in the so-called "Western Religions" - Judaism and Christianity," sometimes Islam, stemmed from the original source; the source in Africa where the Greeks received their fundamentals in philosophy.

What is an "oracle" anyway? In common parlance, it is no more or less a fortune teller than any local "Gypsy mystic" one sees around the nieghborhood giving out numbers for the local bookies (horse players). They were supposed then, as they are now, to be able to "prophecy the future." Of course, the best ones were those who belonged to the religion of the person they had served. In the case of St. Augustine, it was the "oracles" that damned the Greek Gods and blessed the Hebrew and Christian Gods. The Moslem God, Al'lah, not having been created by Mohamet during Augustine's lifetime, due to Mohamet's lateness of birth - with respect to Augustine's - many centuries after, 570 C.E., made it impossible for Augustine to accept Al'lah in this light.

Augustine further answered a question when he asked of Cicero in Chapter Nine, 4th paragraph, the following:

---

* The third part of what is today called "WESTERN RELIGION" - Islam - did not exist during St. Augustine's lifetime (354-430 C.E.). Augustine died more than one hundred and ninety-one (191) years before Mohamet founded his religion at the Oasis of Yathrib in Medina, Arabia, in 622 C.E. (or AH. 1). For further details see Chapter Four following.

118

> Neither let us be afraid, lest after all,
> we do not by will that which we do by will,
> because He (Jesus Christ)* whose foreknow-
> ledge is infallible, foreknew that we would
> do it. He was this which Cicero was afraid
> of, and therefore opposed foreknowledge.
> The Stoics also maintained that all things
> do not come to pass by necessity, although
> they contended that all things happen ac-
> cording to destiny. What is it, then, that
> Cicero feared in the prescience of future
> things?

Like most of his contemporaries of Christendom, his prede-

cessors and followers, Augustine also despised scientists. At

least, he verbally scorned them into oblivion.

One can see in Augustine's writings the utter contempt he

held for Cicero's position was not motivated by hatred for the

man, but for the position Cicero took on things spiritual; which

if they disagreed with Augustine's point of view with respect to

his own God - Jesus Christ, he had to condemn; Augustine's at-

titude in this regard was still the common attitude of modern

Christian clergymen and laymen. This is best seen when one reads

the following comments by Augustine, in his CITY OF GOD, Book

XIX, Chapter 14:

> But as this divine Master inculcates two
> precepts - the love of God and the love of
> our neighbor - and as in these precepts a
> man finds three things he has to love - God,
> himself and his neighbors - and that he who
> loves God loves himself thereby, it follows
> that he must endeavour to get his neighbor
> to love God, since he is ordered to love
> his neighbor as himself.

This was part of the genius of St Augustine, just as it was

with his two other indigenous African predecessors - Tertullian

and St Cyprian. They, too, never indulged in character assassi-

* Words shown in brackets by the author of this work.

nation of their opponents, but of their works. Yet, it cannot be said that they were not dogmatically "Christian fanatics." They had to be, because they had become the authorities and philosophers on "CHRISTIAN DOCTRINES", and of CHRISTENDOM itself. Expecting them to have done otherwise would be tantamount to expecting the present Pope in Rome to accept that Judaism or Islam would get you into heaven as easily as Roman Catholicism, or at least by way of Protestantism. To expect that a Grand Rabbi or a Chief Iman would accept the reverse in the case of Christianity would be equally as absurd.

> And, therefore, although our righteous father[58]
> had slaves and administered their domestic affairs
> so as to distinguish both the condition of slaves
> and the heirship of sons in regard to the blessings
> of this life, yet, in regard to the worship of God
> (Jesus Christ*) in whom we hope for eternal bless-
> ings, they took an equally loving overnight of all
> members of their household.[59]

The above comment followed Chapter 15 - the last sentence of St. Augustine's book, HOLY CITY OF GOD, Book XIX; in which he also wrote the following:

> And therefore the apostle admonishes slaves to
> be subject to their masters and to serve them
> heartily and with good will, so that, if they can-
> not be freed by their masters, they may themselves
> make their slavery in some sort free, by serving
> not in crafty fear, but in faithful love, until
> all unrighteousness pass away, and all principal-
> ity and every human power be brought to nothing,
> and God be all in all.

St. Augustine's compassionate feelings for the slaves he was speaking of did not make him react differently than he responded to Cicero's position on "prophecy" or the "oracles." He still

---

* Words in brackets by the author of this volume.

looked, in this brutal relationship between man to man, on with
a sense of tranquility for the slaves, that is, if they maintained "law and order", and were obedient to their masters and to
Jesus Christ. This type of logic still permeates the thinking of
modern Christians, as it prevails in European-style Christian
ethics and practices within the so-called "Christian nations of
the world" and other smaller communities, a kind of a ...DONT
ROCK THE BOAT, JESUS WILL TAKE CARE OF IT ALL...philosophy. In
these areas,St Augustine's philosophical, moral,and spiritual
thoughts in his writings reflected the Romanized - African upper
middle class background from whence he came. This was especially
true, because of the following reasons: (a) It must be remembered
that he was already twenty-eight years of age before he began any
serious devotion to the "New Religion" - Christianity; (b) That
his father - Patricius, was a minor official in the Provincial
(colonial) Government of their native Numidia, a position which
Augustine condemned other Africans for holding in the Romans empire; (c) That he had grown up within a system, which normally
accepted and benefited immensely from the proceeds of slavery; (d)
And, that the North African Christian Church, itself, had become
engaged in slavery - to the extent that many of its highest officials benefited to the point of becoming some of the wealthiest
slave masters. These precedents led to the acceptance of slavery
as an economic base for European and European-American "Christian"
governments approximately 1,030 years after Augustine's death -
when Pope Martin V[th] accepted from Prince Henry(the so-called"nav-
igator") of Portugal the first five slaves kidnapped on the West
coast of Africa, and gold dust stolen from the same place by his

121

fellow European "Christians." This conduct of European-style
Christian depravity that enhanced Augustine's followers'coffers,
both secularly and religiously, was yet to be the basis for the
expansion of slavery, as it became the major source of Christendom's financial empire 535 years later; at which time the Right
Reverend Bishop Bartolome de LasCasas (1474-1566 C.E.) got King
Charles I of Spain[59a] and Pope Clement VII (Giulio de Medici)*
to endorse the inauguration of the infamous chattel slave trade
that introduced the genocidal depopulation of the entire continent of Africa (Alkebu-lan) and the forced migration of millions
of Africans to the "New World" (the Caribbeans and the Americas),
which to a great extent continues on today.

Since Augustine did not condemn slavery in his teachings; his
silence gave comfort later on to the Reverend John Hawkins - Captain of the notorious slave ship, "JESUS (Christ) de LOBIC,* to
murder and enslave Africans in the name of Christianity and civilization. But slavery was also ordained by the Hebrews (Jews)
against the Amalakites, Hittites, Moabites, and others before they
finally committed genocide against them, just as the European
Christians sang their religious war chants, "ONWARD CHRISTIAN
SOLDIERS MARCHING ON TO WAR...," etc., in memory of the "CROSS
OF JESUS" they carried as they enslaved the Muslims (Moslems)
during the various "CRUSADE," justifying their barbarous actions
on what they claim was a "CALL FROM GOD (Jesus Christ) TO SAVE
THE WORLD."

Augustine's moralization of "...salvation through Christ..."

* Eric Williams, DOCUMENTS OF WEST INDIAN HISTORY, 1492-1655
(PNM Publishing Co., Ltd., Port-of-Spain, Trinidad, W.I.).

122

should the slaves accept 'law and order' by the State-Church,
equally their masters, was grounded in the following passages of
the Hebrew and Christian "Holy Scriptures," which were supposedly
written by "Holy men inspired by God," meaning of course only males
of the Hebrew, Christian, and,maybe,of the Moslem religions. Thus,
Exodus, Chapter 21, Verses 1 - 25, etc., as noted in the LAWS CON-
CERNING SLAVERY:

21 "Now these are the ordinances which you shall set before them. 2 When you buy a Hebrew slave, he shall serve six years, and in the seventh he shall go out free, for nothing. 3 If he comes in single, he shall go out single; if he comes in married, then his wife shall go out with him. 4 If his master gives him a wife and she bears him sons or daughters, the wife and her children shall be her master's and he shall go out alone. 5 But if the slave plainly says, 'I love my master, my wife, and my children; I will not go out free,' 6 then his master shall bring him to God, and he shall bring him to the door or the doorpost; and his master shall bore his ear through with an awl; and he shall serve him for life.
7 "When a man sells his daughter as a slave, she shall not go out as the male slaves do. 8 If she does not please her master, who has designated her for himself, then he shall let her be redeemed; he shall have no right to sell her to a foreign people, since he has dealt faithlessly with her. 9 If he designates her for his son, he shall deal with her as with a daughter. 10 If he takes another wife to himself, he shall not diminish her food, her clothing, or her marital rights. 11 And if he does not do these three things for her, she shall go out for nothing, without payment of money.
12 "Whoever strikes a man so that he dies shall be put to death. 13 But if he did not lie in wait for him, but God let him fall into his hand, then I will appoint for you a place to which he may flee. 14 But if a man willfully attacks another to kill him treacherously, you shall take him from my altar, that he may die.
15 "Whoever strikes his father or his mother shall be put to death.
16 "Whoever steals a man, whether he sells him or is found in possession of him, shall be put to death.
17 "Whoever curses his father or his mother shall be put to death.
18 "When men quarrel and one strikes the other with a stone or with his fist and the man does not die but keeps his bed, 19 then if the man rises again and walks abroad with his staff, he that struck him shall be clear; only he shall pay for the loss of his time, and shall have him thoroughly healed.
20 "When a man strikes his slave, male or female, with a rod and the slave dies under his hand, he shall be punished. 21 But if the slave survives a day or two, he is not to be punished; for the slave is his money. 22 "When men strive together, and hurt a woman with child, so that there is a miscarriage, and yet no harm follows, the one who hurt her shall be fined, according as the woman's husband shall lay upon him; and he shall pay as the judges determine. 23 If any harm follows, then you shall give life for life, 24 eye for eye, tooth for tooth, hand for hand, foot for foot, 25 burn for burn, wound for wound, stripe for stripe.

Augustine's writings on this subject (then) was in reality
only a refinement of the moral and spiritual justification for
his contemporaries to follow; as he, being the Christian "Father
of the Church" at the time, could not accept that the "Holy Scriptures" (VULGATE Bible) were unjust. As such, he completely appeased
the slavemasters, Jewish and Christians alike, to the fullest
extent of his ability, as seen in the last sentence of his CITY OF
GOD, Book XIX, Chapter 20. He wrote:

123

> For the true blessings of the soul are not
> enjoyed; for that is no true wisdom which does
> not direct all its prudent observations, manly
> actions, virtuous self restraint and just ar-
> rangements to that end in which God (Jesus
> Christ)* shall be all and all in a secure
> eternity and perfect peace.

One must understand, however, that St. Augustine (an indigenous African, a so-called "Negro," etc.) did not acquiesce
to racial, religious, or national identification as the means by
which a specific group was most fitted for enslavement - as do
the Calvinists, Latter Day Saints (Mormons), and other White Protestant, Roman Catholic, and Jewish (Hebrew) sects in the southern,
southeastern and soutwestern sections of Africa; also others of
these contemporaries in the United States of America. He saw the
institution of slavery when every type of humanity was enslaved by
slavemasters who were as varied as their slaves, which included
Europeans, Asians, and Africans as masters and slaves. As a matter
of fact, Augustine's homeland was a part of the "COAST OF THE BAR-
BARY," Jane Soames' book, of like name, so correctly described.
Later on Christian writers of all types - including the Roman
Catholic Christian Missionary Raymond Lull of the world famous
"LULL REPORTS"[59b] (who did everything within his power to become
a martyr for Christendom) also came and lived to stem the tide of
Islam. It was also a place where the vast majority of the slaves
came, from as far off as Angloland (England or Britain), and were
of European origin (Caucasian, or White).

In dealing with political matters St. Augustine severely criti-
cized Cicero's work, "DE REPUBLICA," in which Cicero supported

---

* Words in brackets by the author of this volume.

Scipio Afer's (Africanus, or Scipio the African) definition of just what is the vital fabric of any republic. As such, one finds St. Augustine writing the following remarks in his CITY OF GOD, Book XIX, Chapter 21:

CHAP. 21. *Whether there ever was a Roman republic answering to the definitions of Scipio in Cicero's dialogue*

This, then, is the place where I should fulfill the promise gave in the second book of this work,[1] and explain, as briefly and clearly as possible that, if we are to accept the definitions laid down by Scipio in Cicero's *De Republica*, there never was a Roman republic; for he briefly defines a republic as the weal of the people. And if this definition be true, there never was a Roman republic, for the people's weal was never attained among the Romans. For the people, according to his definition, is an assemblage associated by a common acknowledgment of right and by a community of interests. And what he means by a common acknowledgment of right he explains at large, showing that a republic cannot be administered without justice. Where, therefore, there is no true justice there can be no right. For that which is done by right is justly done, and what is unjustly done cannot be done by right. For the unjust inventions of men are neither to be considered nor spoken of as rights; for even they themselves say that right is that which flows from the fountain of justice, and deny the definition which is commonly given by those who misconceive the matter, that right is that which is useful to the stronger party. Thus, where there is not true justice there can be no assemblage of men associated by a common acknowledgment of right, and therefore there can be no people, as defined by Scipio or Cicero; and if no people, then no weal of the people, but only of some promiscuous multitude unworthy of the name of people. Consequently, if the republic is the weal of the people, and there is no people if it be not associated by a common acknowledgment of right, and if there is no right where there is no justice, then most certainly it follows that there is no republic where there is no justice. Further, justice is that virtue which gives every one his due. Where, then, is the justice of man, when he deserts the true God and yields himself to impure demons? Is this to give every one his due? Or is he who keeps back a piece of ground from the purchaser, and gives it to a man who has no right to it, unjust, while he who keeps back himself from the God who made him, and serves wicked spirits, is just?

Augustine's writings in the CITY OF GOD and ON CHRISTIAN DOCTRINES showed that he had such contempt for man's society on earth that he felt it necessary at all times to ignore the material for the spiritual. He, therefore, wrote in condemnation of all that did not, in his estimation, meet prevailing biblical (the Vulgate) and philosophical prophecy, which he based upon Christian values —as he understood them.

In Chapter 37 of ON CHRISTIAN DOCTRINES, Book III, St. Augustine, from this writers observation, outlined the spiritual values upon which he condemned the failure of man to develop what he believed to be a "...true republic...." Thus, in outlining what he called "The Seventh Rule of Tichonius;" he wrote:

55. The seventh rule of Tichonius and the last, is about *the devil and his body*. For he is the head of the wicked, who are in a sense his body, and destined to go with him into the punishment of everlasting fire, just as Christ is the head of the Church, which is His body, destined to be with Him in His eternal kingdom and glory. Accordingly, as the first rule, which is called *of the Lord and His body*, directs us, when Scripture speaks of one and the same person, to take pains to understand which part of the statement applies to the head and which to the body; so this last rule shows us that statements are sometimes made about the devil, whose truth is not so evident in regard to himself as in regard to his body; and his body is made up not only of those who are manifestly out of the way, but of those also who, though they really belong to him, are for a time mixed up with the Church, until they depart from this life, or until the chaff is separated from the wheat at the last great winnowing. For example, what is said in Isaiah, "How he is fallen from heaven, Lucifer, son of the morning!" [1] and the other statements of the context which, under the figure of the king of Babylon, are made about the same person, are of course to be understood of the devil; and yet the statement which is made in the same place, "He is ground down on the earth, who sendeth to all nations," [2] does not altogether fitly apply to the head himself. For, although the devil sends his angels to all nations, yet it is his body, not himself, that is ground down on the earth, except that he himself is in his body, which is beaten small like the dust which the wind blows from the face of the earth.

In Book IV, of the above work, Chapter 2, however, He refuted his own position by suggesting that it is right to use falsehoods in defense of Christianity. Of course, he did not mention the word "Christianity" specifically, being that he was a master of the art of rhetoric, which he relied upon very heavily in his analysis. For example, on the issue of "rhetoric" Augustine wrote:

CHAP. 1. *This work not intended as a treatise on rhetoric*

1. THIS work of mine, which is entitled *On Christian Doctrine*, was at the commencement divided into two parts. For, after a preface, in which I answered by anticipation those who were likely to take exception to the work, I said, "There are two things on which all interpretation of Scripture depends: the mode of ascertaining the proper meaning, and the mode of making known the meaning when it is ascertained. I shall treat first of the mode of ascertaining, next of the mode of making known, the meaning." [1] As, then, I have already said a great deal about the mode of ascertaining the meaning, and have given three books to this one part of the subject, I shall only say a few things about the mode of making known the meaning, in order if possible to bring them all within the compass of one book, and so finish the whole work in four books.

2. In the first place, then, I wish by this preamble to put a stop to the expectations of readers who may think that I am about to lay down rules of rhetoric such as I have learnt, and taught too, in the secular schools, and to warn them that they need not look for any such from me. Not that I think such rules of no use, but that whatever use they have is to be learnt elsewhere; and if any good man should happen to have leisure for learning them, he is not to ask me to teach them either in this work or any other.

Augustine continued from this point to speak of the age one had to acquire before he could become a skill master in "rhetoric" in Chapter 3, and culminated it with the duties of said orator as a Christian teacher in Chapter 4. As usual, he had to add his own personal values of Christian purity for this skill also - as he elaborated on the necessity for "...The Sacred writers eloquence with wisdom." One can only wonder if this master of "rhetoric" and poetic spirituality recognized himself for the genius he was. If not, these writings certainly betrayed his inner self in this direction.

Augustine's assuredness about Christianity and the world to come, "HEAVEN," brings to memory the following remarks in the Hebrew Scriptures, as stated in the Torah (Five Books of Moses), Exodus (Second Book), Chapter 14, Verses 13 and 14:

> And Moses said unto the people: "Fear ye not, stand still, and see the salvation of the Lord, which He will work for you today; for whereas ye have seen the Egyptians today, ye shall see them again no more forever. The Lord will fight for you, and ye shall hold your peace."

The "SIX-DAY WAR" in June, 1967 C.E., between the Asian population that presently occupy and control Egypt and the European and European-American population that occupy and control Israel is a far cry from the prophecy stated. These two new foreign encroachments, probably, would have caused St. Augustine very serious consternation if he were alive today; as he would have realized that many of the prophecies he held to be infallible with regards to Israel and Egypt were in fact the opposite. He would have noted that neither Hebrews (Jews) nor Egyptians (Moslems) are presently indigenous to either nation (Israel or Palestine and Egypt or Sais).

The Vulgate Bible - the official Latin "Old" and "New Testament" from which St. Augustine based his authority on Christianity - was only one of the many Latin versions during the period after Latin was made the official language of the Roman Catholic Church by Tertullian (one of the indigenous African "Fathers of the Church"). It was also from this version that most of the common vernacular versions that followed were made. During this period Latin was the language of the entire Roman Empire; but Christians in Ethiopia (the first Christian nation in history) spoke Gheez (or Geez) - then the national language of Ethiopia, which is today only used for the purpose of religious ceremonies; it too has been replaced by the new national language of Ethiopia, AMHERIC, in secular matters. It must be also noted, that the Greek Christians used Greek - the language in which the first Christian Bible, the SEPTUAGINT, was written.* The oldest body of Christians in the world, as an institution, the Copts of Egypt, wrote Koptic or Coptic.

When Christians, today, begin to understand that the original Text of the Vulgate Bible followed many Greek and Coptic versions, which before them followed many other Hebrew and Aramaic Versions of the Torah (Five Books of Moses, the Christians Old Testament), hopefully, they will begin to question just how much of the current allegedly "original stories" within any of them are truly valid or truthful. The Vulgate version, however, is the only version in which St. Augustine and St. Ambrose, along with the other "Church Fathers, labored. Therefore, that which seems to be discrepancies in St. Augustine's works, with respect to the present versions of the Christian "Holy Bible, are really for the most

---

* This does not mean that the first Christian writings were in Greek. The oldest Christian writings known to date were in Koptic (Coptic), the language of the Egyptian Church of North Africa - the Koptic Church.

128

part conflicting interpretations by contemporary translators who have digressed from the original Vulgate version[60] (Text) which Augustine followed.

In conjunction with the latter remarks, the following work by another of the indigenous Africans, known to the world as the "Fathers of the Church," Caecilius Cyprianus (St Cyprian), while Bishop of Carthage (249-258 C.E.), was written:[61]

> *The pitiful condition of the lapsed—the result of general laxity* (4–6).
> 4. These heavenly crowns of the martyrs, these spiritual triumphs of the confessors, these outstanding exploits of our brethren cannot, alas, remove one cause of sorrow: that the Enemy's violence and slaughter has wrought havoc amongst us and has torn away something from our very heart and cast it to the ground. What shall I do, dear brethren, in face of this? My mind tosses this way and that—what shall I say? How shall I say it? Tears and not words can alone express the grief which so deep a wound in our body calls for, which the great gaps in our once numerous flock evoke from our hearts. Who could be so callous, so stony-hearted, who so unmindful of brotherly love, as to remain dry-eyed in the presence of so many of his own kin who are broken now, shadows of their former selves, dishevelled, in the trappings of grief? Will he not burst into tears at sight of them, before finding words for his sorrow? Believe me, my brothers, I share your distress, and can find no comfort in my own escape and safety; for the shepherd feels the wounds of his flock more than they do. My heart bleeds with each one of you, I share the weight of your sorrow and distress. I mourn with those that mourn, I weep with those that weep, with the fallen I feel I have fallen myself. My limbs too were struck by the arrows of the lurking foe, his angry sword pierced my body too. When persecution rages, the mind of none escapes free and unscathed: when my brethren fell, my heart was struck and I fell at their side.

The above quotation is an English translation by Maurice Bevenot, S.J., from the Latin original of "THE LAPSED." He also translated St. Cyprian's "THE UNITY OF THE CATHOLIC CHURCH," of

which the following is taken:⁶²

THE UNITY OF THE CATHOLIC CHURCH

The devil's wiles must be unmasked and overcome by obedience
to Christ's commands (1–2).

1. Our Lord solemnly warns us: '*You are the salt of the*
earth,' and bids us in our love of good to be not only
simple but prudent as well. Accordingly, dearest brethren,
what else ought we to do but be on our guard and watch
vigilantly, in order to know the snares of our crafty foe
and to avoid them? Otherwise, after putting on Christ
who is the Wisdom of God the Father, we may be found
to have failed in wisdom for the care of our souls. It is not
persecution alone that we ought to fear, nor those forces
that in open warfare range abroad to overthrow and defeat
the servants of God. It is easy enough to be on one's guard
when the danger is obvious; one can stir up one's courage
for the fight when the Enemy shows himself in his true
colours. There is more need to fear and beware of the
Enemy when he creeps up secretly, when he beguiles us
by a show of peace and steals forward by those hidden
approaches which have earned him the name of the
'Serpent.' Such is ever his craft: lurking in the dark, he
ensnares men by trickery. That was how at the very
beginning of the world he deceived and by lying words of
flattery beguiled the unguarded credulity of a simple soul;
that was how he tried to tempt Our Lord Himself, ap-
proaching Him in disguise, as though he could once more
creep upon his victim and deceive Him. But he was
recognized and beaten back, and he was defeated precisely
through being detected and unmasked.

2. Here we are given an example how to break company
with the 'old man,' how to follow in the steps of Christ
to victory, so that we may not carelessly stumble again
into the snare of death, but being alive to the danger, hold
fast to the immortality given us. And how can we hold
fast to immortality unless we observe those commandments of Christ by which death is defeated and conquered?
He Himself assures us: '*If thou wilt attain to life, keep the*
commandments'; and again: '*If ye do what I command you, I*
call you no longer servants but friends.' He says that it is
those who so act that are strong and firm; it is *they* that
are founded in massive security upon a rock, *they* that
are established in unshakable solidity, proof against all the
storms and hurricanes of the world. '*Him that heareth my*

130

words and doeth them,' He says, 'I will liken to the wise man who built his house upon the rock. The rain fell, the floods rose, the winds came and they crashed against that house: but it fell not. For it was founded upon the rock.'

We must therefore carry out His words: whatsoever He taught and did, that must we learn and do ourselves. Indeed how can a man say he believes in Christ if he does not do what Christ commanded him to do? Or how shall a man who when under command will not keep faith, hope to receive the reward of faith? He who does not keep to the true way of salvation will inevitably falter and stray; caught up by some gust of error, he will be tossed about like windswept dust; walk as he may, he will make no advance towards his salvation.

Cyprian continued in Chapters 3 to 5 to warn against "heresy and schism;" noting that "...Christ founded the Church on Peter."[63] One can see the very distinct differences between St.Cyprian and St Augustine, also Tertullian's, works in the following extracts taken from one of the latter's masterpieces, THE TREATISE AGAINST HERMOGENES;" as translated into English from the original Latin Text by J. H. Waszink. In describing Hermogenes,[64] Tertullian wrote:

FOREWORD. WHO IS HERMOGENES?

Ch. 1] When[1] dealing with heretics, to shorten the discussion, we follow the practice of laying down against them a peremptory rule based on the lateness ⟨of their appearance⟩. For in as far as the rule of truth is earlier, reporting as it did ⟨, among other things,⟩ the occurrence in the future of heresies, just so far can all later doctrines *a priori* be regarded as heresies, as it is their future existence which was announced by the older rule of truth. 2. Now the doctrine of Hermogenes is such a new doctrine. He is, briefly, a man who up to the present is living in the world, and, moreover, a born heretic; he is, further, a turbulent man, who takes loquacity for eloquence, regards impudence as staunchness of character, and considers the slandering of individuals the normal task of a good conscience. Apart from this, he exercises the art of painting, a thing forbidden ⟨by the Law⟩, and marries continuously: he defends the Law of God in the interest of his lust, and despises it in the interest of his art. He is a falsifier in two respects, with his cautery and with his pen, and an adulterator in every respect, with regard both to his preaching and to the flesh. ⟨Nor is this surprising⟩: to begin with, the contagion coming from marrying people produces a bad smell, and, secondly, the Apostle's Hermogenes did not stick to the rule of faith either.

3. But let us forget the man—it is his doctrine which I have to look into. He does not seem to acknowledge another Lord, but he makes a different being of Him whom he acknowledges in a different way; nay, since He will not have it that it was out of nothing that He made all things, he takes from Him everything which constitutes His divinity. 4. Thus he turned away from the Christians to the philosophers, from the Church to the Academy and the Porch, and from there he took the idea of putting matter on the same level with the Lord—for in his opinion matter, too, has always existed, being neither born nor created, without any beginning or end, and it is from matter that the Lord afterwards made all things.

In the following two chapters Tertullian outlined Hermogenes' main position, as he saw them. Chapter 2 alone is cited here:[65]

THE BASIC ARGUMENTS OF HERMOGENES

Ch. 2] To this first and utterly lightless shade this very bad painter has given colour by means of the following arguments. His fundamental thesis is that the Lord made all things either out of Himself, or out of nothing, or out of something, in order that, upon demonstrating that He could neither have made them out of Himself nor out of nothing, he may consequently affirm the remaining possibility—that He made them out of something; and, next, that that something was matter.

2. He says that He could not have made ⟨all things⟩ out of Himself, because whatever things the Lord had made out of Himself would have been parts of Him; but that He cannot be divided into parts, since, being the Lord, He is indivisible and unchangeable and always the same. Further, if He had made something out of Himself, that something

would have been part of Himself; but everything, both that which was made and which He was to make, must be considered imperfect, because it would be made of a part and because He would make it of a part. 3. Or if, being whole, He had made the whole, He must have been whole and not whole at the same time, since it would have befitted Him to be both whole, in order to make Himself, and not whole, in order that He might be made out of Himself. Now this is extremely difficult, for if He existed, He could not be made, but would exist ⟨already⟩, whereas if He did not exist, He could not ⟨in that case⟩ make anything because He would be nothing. But He who always exists, ⟨so he asserts,⟩ does not come into existence but exists for ever and ever. So ⟨he concludes that⟩ He did not make all things out of Himself, since He was not of such a condition that He could have made them out of Himself.

4. Further, that He could not have made them out of nothing is asserted by him on the following argument: He defines the Lord as a good, even a very good, being, whose desire to make good and very good things is as strong as He is ⟨good and very good⟩; nay, He desires and makes nothing that is not good and very good. Therefore, good and very good things only should have been made by Him, in accordance with His condition. It is found, however, that evil things as well have been made by Him—certainly not by His decision and His will, for then He would not have made anything unfitting or unworthy of Himself. Now that which He thus did not make by His own decision must be understood to have been made from the faultiness of something, which without a doubt means that it originated from matter.

In defense of his Christian teachings, and to protect the reputation of the Vulgate Bible of the Christian Church used during his reign as "Father of the Church," Tertullian wrote the rest of his entire treatise. The following extract is from Chapter 4. In Chapter 5 through 45 he used quotations from every book in the Latin Vulgate Bible Text to refute Hermogenes. He wrote:[66]

a) Matter as Equal to God

Ch. 4] At this point I shall finally begin to discuss matter, that, according to Hermogenes, God makes disposi-

133

tion of it, when at the same time it is presented as equally unborn, equally unmade, equally eternal, with neither beginning nor end. For what other essential property of God is there than eternity? What other essence has eternity than ever to have existed and to go on existing forever because of its privilege of being without a beginning and without an end? 2. If this is the special property of God, it must belong to God alone, since it is His special property—for clearly if it should be assigned to some other being as well, it will no longer be the special property of God, but a property shared with that being to which it is also assigned. 3. For *though there be that are called gods* in name, *whether in heaven or in earth, yet for us there is but one God, the Father, of whom are all things;* and therefore it is still more necessary that in our conviction that should belong to God alone which is the special property of God, and which, as I have said, ⟨if shared with another being,⟩ would be no longer His special property, since it would ⟨then⟩ belong to another being ⟨as well⟩. Now, if God is this (i.e. One), it must necessarily be a unique property that it may belong to One. 4. Or what will be unique and singular, if not that to which nothing equal can be produced? What will be principal, if not that which is above all things and before all things and from which all things have originated?

5. It is by having these qualities alone that He is God, and by having them alone, that He is One. If another being should possess them as well, then there will be as many gods as there are beings which possess the qualities proper to God. Thus it is that Hermogenes brings in two gods—he introduces matter as equal to God. 6. But God must be One, because that is God which is supreme; but nothing can be supreme save that which is unique; but nothing can be unique if something can be put on a level with it; but matter will be put on a level with God, when it is authoritatively declared to be eternal.

Tertullian closed his treatise on Hermogenes in the same dramatic fashion in which he opened it. In the closing one also sees the same brashness which made him stand out so differently from St. Augustine and St. Cyprian. For whereas his other two indigenous African successors, "Fathers of the Church," were solely theologians concerned primarily with "soul" and its "heavenly

134

entry," also "law and order in the Church"; he, on the other hand, was engaged with challenging individuals (including the **hierarchy** of the Church in Rome and North Africa) who dared to differ with what he felt was "truth" in relationship to his own religious tenets in respect to the role of the Church and social action as against its heavenly goals of sending people to heaven. He wrote:[67]

EPILOGUE

4. And thus, in as far as it has been established that matter did not exist (also for the reason that it cannot have been such as it is represented), in so far is it proved that all things were made by God out of nothing. I would add only that by delineating a condition of matter quite like his own—irregular, confused, turbulent, with a disordered, rash, and violent motion—Hermogenes has put on exhibition a sample of his art: he has painted his own portrait.

There are many books listed in the bibliography **that** this author used in preparing this chapter which should also prove to be extremely helpful to anyone who wishes to pursue in greater details the indigenous African "Fathers of the Church" works. There are many other translations from the original Latin Texts into several languages; the most common being in French, English, and German.

Like St. Augustine, there is not very much written about St. Cyprian and Tertullian lives before they became the spiritual leaders of the North African Christian Church and all of Christendom in general. There is not much about their personal lives during their reign as philosophers of their religion either. Were it not for their brief sketchy background of themselves, as stated in their works, nothing of their non-Christian lives as indi-

135

genous Africans with their own traditional African religions
would have been known. Of course, there were many who dared to
make certain assumptions about their lives, but without any success whatsoever.

One can only wonder why Tertullian was not made a "Saint!"
He certainly did as much for Christianity and Christendom to make
them what they are today as did the other two indigenous African
(so-called "Negroes," etc.) "Fathers of the Church" - St. Cyprian
and St. Augustine. Added to all of this, he was an activist, more
than a philosopher; a kind of a 16th Century C.E. Catholic priest
- Martin Luther - and the 20the Century C.E. Protestant minister -
Dr. Martin Luther King, Jr., conglomerate. Tertullian matched his
Christian idealism with physical action; whereas the others sat
back and philosphized On Christian Doctrine and Ethics. Maybe
someday this African, Dr. Martin Luther King, Jr., also, shall be
made a "Saint" in his Church. However, the lack of such confirmation does not in anyway whatsoever lessen his greatness. This is
more so true, when one considers that the greatest pacifist of
modern times - Mohandas ("the Sacred One") Karamchand Ghandi -
will never become a "Saint," solely because he was not a Christian
confessant. It would have been unlikely, however, that Cyprian
and Augustine would have made "sainthood" in the racist world of
the 20th Century C.E., especially when considering that they were
indigenous Africans (who are today called by such names as "Negroes,
Bantus, Africans South of the Sahara, Hottentots, Bushmen, Pygmines
Coons," and a host of other derogative superlatives to the African
people), even though totally Judaeo-Christian in their every action
One could suspect that there are very few "Christian Churches" in t
136

United States of America where they would have been tolerated, much less welcomed. Yet, they were the originators of most of the basic tenets which all of Christendom today believe.

The only reason that the three indigenous African Popes of the Roman Catholic Church have not been examined here should be obvious; if not, it is because they have done nothing outstanding in the history of Christendom, like most of their fellow Popes who were not outstanding leaders.

MOSES: AFRICAN INFLUENCE
ON JUDAISM
Chapter   Three

To speak of an "ALMIGHTY GOD" in the context used by Jews,
Christians, and Moslems is impossible without going back to the
roots of said belief. In so doing, one has to **delve** beyond the
origin of Judaism (the Hebrew religion and peoples) - the parent
of the three religions mentioned, Christianity - the child, and
Islam - the grandchild. All eyes have to be centered on the
indigenous African religions of the Nile Valley from whence all
three derived, religions which are today called the "EGYPTIAN
RELIGION" and/or "MYSTERIES." But, in order to delve into the
depths of the study of traditional African religions of Egypt and
other lands along the banks of the more than 4,100 miles length
of the Nile River, one needs a complete set of volumes on this
subject alone. Never-the-less, a few basic citations of the main
African religion upon which Judaism, Christianity, and Islam -
the so-called "WESTERN RELIGIONS"- rest are hereby entered into
and examined.

For example: The concept of the making of **man (creation)** by
"ONE" - the Sun-God RA, who was sometimes identified with the
God OSIRIS, was in fact dealing with a monotheistic God even
though polytheism seemed to be the basic foundation of the African religions of Sais (later called "EGYPT" by the Hebrews, Greeks
and Romans). Yet one sees, in the BOOK OF THE DEAD - as translated from **Hieroglyph** to English by Sir E. A. Wallis-Budge, Chapter clxxxii, 1.15, Osiris shown as the only God who could make man
138

inherit "everlasting and eternal life;" also that he alone had
the power to :

>   "... cause men and women to be born again...."

The same God, OSIRIS, was responsible to represent "ONE" -
the "SUPREME BEING," as He "...loved life and hated death...;"
this having been shown in the following extract from Chapter cliv.
of the BOOK OF THE DEAD:

> "...Homage to thee, O my divine father Osiris,
> thou hast thy being with thy members. Thou didst
> not decay, thou didst not turn into worms, thou
> didst not rot away, thou didst not become cor-
> ruption, thou didst not putrefy.... I shall not
> decay, I shall not rot, I shall not putrefy....
> I shall have my being, I shall live, I shall
> germinate, I shall wake up in peace.... My body
> shall be established, and it shall neither fall
> into ruin nor be destroyed off this earth.

The above prayer was by Pharoah Thotmes III (1504-1550 B.C.
E.) to the God Osiris. One can see the basic values of death and
its treatment from this episode and its corruption in the Hebrew
which followed many hundreds of years later.

In the book, FIRST STEPS IN EGYPTIAN, p. 179ff, the author
- Sir E. A Wallis-Budge, "ONE" is identified through the Gods -
RA and OSIRIS - as the "SOUL OF RA"   in the
"...body of God." But, "ONE's" identity as an absolute fact of
the truest manifestation of the "SUPREME BEING" - the "GOD OVER
ALL OTHER GODS" - the one and only "GOD ALMIGHTY" - is best noted
in the following extract from the BOOK OF THE DEAD, Chapter clxxxi:

> "...Homage to thee, O governor of Amentet, Un-
> nfer, the lord of Ta-tchesert, O thou who risest
> like Ra! Verily I come to see thee and to rejoice
> as thy beauties. His disk is thy disk, his rays
> are thy rays; his crown is thy crown; his majesty

---

*   Hieroglpyh whence the English translation derived. See
BOOK OF THE DEAD: also OSIRIS.

```
                is they majesty; his beauty risings are thy
                risings: his beauty is thy beauty; the awe
                which is his is the awe which is thine; his
                odour is thy odour; his hall is thy hall; his
                seat is thy............etc., etc., etc.
```

The indigenous Africans' of Egypt (Black people from Central

East Africa's Great Lakes) religious belief in "ONE" was cited as

follows by C.P.Tiele in the ENCYCLOPEDIA BRITANNICA, Vol. XX,

p. 367:

> "...the adoration of one God above all others
> as the specific tribal god or as the lord over
> a particular people, a national or relative mon-
> otheism, like that of the ancient Israelites,
> the worship of an absolute sovereign exacts
> passive obedience. This practical monotheism is
> totally different from the theoretical monothe-
> ism, to which the Aryans, with their monistic
> speculative idea of the godhead, are much nearer.

However, it must be also noted that Professor Tiele was not deal-

ing with the Africans of Egypt (Egyptians), but the Haribu (He-

brews, today called erroneously "Jews") - who had already left

Egypt (Sais) and established their own national culture and re-

ligion upon the principles they learnt while they were in Egypt,

and in fact, what they were born under. At least, their ancesotrs

were in fact native-born Africans of Egypt, of the Hebrew faith.

Nevertheless Professor Tiele, in his own work, HISTOIRE COMPARÉ

DES ANCIENNES RELIGIONS, Paris, 1882, stated that there were two

contradictory and irreconcilable phenomena in the Africans'of

Egypt religious philosophy:

> 1. A lively sentiment of spirituality of God
>   united to the coarsest materialistic re-
>   presentations of different divinities.
>
> 2. A sentiment, not less lively, of the unity
>   of God, united to an extremely great mul-
>   tiplicity of divine persons.

Between the declaration in Max Muller's work, HIBBERT LEC-

TURES, p.285, in which he indicated that the quality of the "ONE"
- as the creator of heaven and earth - was only a "...phase of
religious thought" among the ancient Nile Valley Africans of
Egypt, and that of professor C. P. Tiele, already shown above;
yet, the facts remain somewhere in the explanation given by prof-
fessor J. Liebman's book, EGYPTIAN RELIGION, Leipzig, 1884, in
which he held the following:

> "When we, for instance, take the Indo-Europeans,
> what do we find there? The Sanskrit word DEVA is
> identical with the Latin DEUS, and the northern
> TIVI, TIVAR:; as now the word in Latin and north-
> ern language signifies God it must also in San-
> skrit from the beginning have had the same signifi-
> cation. That is to say, the Arians, or Indo-Euro-
> peans, must have combined the idea of God with
> this word, as early as when they still lived to-
> gether in their original home. Because, if the
> word in their pre-historic home had had another
> more primitive signification, the wonder would
> have happened, that the word had accidentally
> gone through the same development of significa-
> tion with all these people after their separation.
> As this is quite improbable, the word must have
> had the signification of God in the original Indo-
> European language. One could go even further...,"
> etc., etc., etc.

Although professor Liebman's theory was very extensive, this
short extract from the whole should be sufficient for the purpose
intended herein. Yet, professor Liebman was dealing primarily
with the meaning of the Egyptian verb "nuter," which is the Latin
word "Dieu" and Sanskrit "deva," with respect to the manner in
which the meaning of the word "nuter" 𓇳𓏏𓂋𓊹 or its variant
form 𓏏𓂋𓇳 changed as it was integrated into each
of the languages that adopted its usage, the same having taken
place within the Hebrew (Jewish) YAHWEH or English GOD.

These concepts were not new when the first of the Haribu (Hebrews) - as they were then called - entered Sais (Egypt) with

Abraham and his family (around c1640 B.C.E.)- as shown in the
Book of Genesis, Chapter 13, Verses 1:18. They were in existence
a very long period before the building of the first major pyramid
of Saqqara by Pharoah Djoser (whom the Greeks called **"Zozer"**) and
the other major works, those by pharoah Khufu (whom the Greeks
called "Cheops" or "Kheops"), Mycerenius, and Khafra (whom the Greeks
called "Chephren"), in a period covering from 3,100 to 2,258 B.C.E.,
more than 618 years the last one was built before the birth of
the first Haribu (Hebrew or Jew), Abram (Avram or Abraham) was
born, more than 1,500 years before the concept of "Adam and Eve"
was developed by the Hebrews. Therefore, one can safely say that mon
otheism" was indeed the prime factor in the religion of the
African of the Nile Valley, especially in the Egyptian "Mystery
System" thousands of years before the existence of the Hebrew God
YAHWEH (Jehovah),and of course thousands more before the creation
of the Christian and Moslem Gods - Jesus Christ and Allah. "Immortality" was also a very basic concept within the same system,
during the same period, giving rise to the "NETHER WORLD" described so adequately in the BOOK OF THE DEAD. The "Book of the Dead"
being the name given the works of the ancient indigenous Africans
of Egypt (the Egyptians and other Nile Valley Africans) outline
and recording of man's "life after death", which the ancient Haribu copied and distorted under the name of the "HEREAFTER."

It is suggested that a copy of each of the following works -
BOOK OF THE DEAD ; OSIRIS; THE GODS OF THE EGYPTIANS; and, THE
FIRST BOOK OF EGYPT- become part of the collection of each reader's library; especially with respect to the origin of the basic
religious concepts most Jews, Christians,and Moslems still believe

originated with the so-called "inspired men of God" theory still
being expounded by "men of the cloth." These works are translated from original Coffin and Pyramid Texts in Hieroglyphs into
English by scholars called "Egyptologists." However, another of
the major works needed in the set is MAN AND HIS GODS; also the
works of Count C. Volney - RUINS OF EMPIRES; and that of Professor George G. M James - STOLEN LEGACY.

With the above background and understanding from whence the
concept of "monotheism" first came, one can readily enter the
following discussion with much greater insight and appreciation
for the role the indigenous Africans (called "Negroes," etc.) and
their traditional religions had, and still have, in Judaism (or
Hebrewism) - the religion the African Haribus adopted from their
brother and sister Africans of the traditional religion of the
worship of "ONE" or "RA," as represented by the God - OSIRIS.

> Three main regions and three main kinds of
> wandering and imperfectly settled people there
> were in those remote days of the first civili-
> zation in Sumeria and early Egypt. Away in the
> forests of Europe were the blond Nordic peoples,
> hunters and herdsmen, a lowly race. The primi-
> tive civilizations saw very little of this race
> before 1500 B.C.

The above quotation is taken from H. G. Wells, A SHORT HIS-
TORY OF THE WORLD. It should aid somewhat in beginning this chapter.
Hopefully, it will further open people's mind to the point where
they can avoid the pitfall C. P. Snow reflected in his comment on
Sir Charles Darwin's book, THE NEXT MILLION YEARS. Sir Charles
(the grandson of the Victorian scientist bearing the same name)
dealt in his works with evidence that denies "any justification
for race prejudice," and stated that in "the not too distant future
the non-White peoples will wrest economic and military power from

the Whites." To this C. P. Snow wrote:[2]

> It means, incidentally, that the racial dis-
> crimination which has been the least credit-
> able feature of the period of White hegemony
> is not only wicked; it is worse than wicked,
> it is criminally foolish.

Strangely enough the New York Times periodical of April,
1969, C.E. quoted the same C. P. Snow as having backed the position
of a "chosen people" above other peoples for the "Jewish race."
This of course refutes the above position he held with respect to
Sir Charles Darwin Jr's statements in his book quoted above. But
it would seem that C. P. Snow's remarks, in this respect, are to
be given no extraordinary attention. Why? Because there are still
Jews today of almost every ethnic group in Europe, Africa, Asia,
the Americas, and most of the habitable islands of the world. There
are Yemenite and Cochin Jews from Yemen and India (Asia), most of
whom are in the State of Israel currently. The Beta Israel, commonly called "Falasha" (Falasa), in Ethiopia, East Africa (some of
whom are in Israel - a very small amount), are the blackest, and
most ancient in Hebrew (Jewish) traditions. The Swedes and Nor-
wegians of the European Jews, on the otherhand, are the whitest.
In the "Western Hemisphere," the so-called "New World," the United
States of America included, all of these types of Jews are in existence, plus various other combinations of them. Therefore, from
this extraordinarily wide spectrum of colors and ethnic groupings
one finds the conglomerate which is today called the "Jewish
people."[4] And, if they were ever a "separate race" at anytime in
the ancient past, they are not now.

This chapter continues in a high degree with the "truth" or
"falsehood" of the "Story of Moses," not from the standpoint of

144

his ever existing at all, but as to his indigenous African origin,
and the origin of the message he is alleged to have brought to
mankind after the Pesach (Passover) from Western to Eastern Egypt
(Mt. Sinai).

With regards to Moses origin the SECOND BOOK OF MOSES (Exo-
dust), Chapter 2, Verses 16:19 states:

> But Moses fled from Pharaoh, and
> stayed in the land of Mid'i-an; and he
> sat down by a well. 16 Now the priest
> of Mid'i-an had seven daughters; and
> they came and drew water, and filled
> the troughs to water their father's
> flock. 17 The shepherds came and
> drove them away; but Moses stood up
> and helped them, and watered their
> flock. 18 When they came to their
> father Reü'el, he said, "How is it that
> you have come so soon today?" 19 They
> said, "An Egyptian delivered us out
> of the hand of the shepherds, and even
> drew water for us and watered the
> flock." ♣

"...an Egyptian delivered us out of the hand of the Sheherds"
etc., is the above declaration. Not a Jew. It should be obvious
to anyone that the priest of Mid'ian's daughters recognized Moses
as an indigenous African - "an Egyptian" - "a Negro" - "a Bantu."
They recognized him the same as they would have recognized any
other Jew in Africa at this period in history. This verse, among
many other verses, substantiates the indigenous African characteristics of the Haribus (Hebrews or Jews), proving at the same
instance, that there was no more difference in the physical make-
up of the Jews than any other indigenous African of any different
religious conviction along the entire Nile Valley civilizations
(from present day Uganda to the Mediterranean Sea). Also, that
they were not stigmatized as they were in Eastern Europe over two
thousand years later, by having to wear special garments or
other means of identification that would have made them
stand out from the general population; this was at a time
when the Jews were not permitted to register as Caucasions
anywhere in Europe. Of course, there were no "Semites"
and "Hamites" invented at that period with Moses by certain ethno-

145

logists, this profession having not existed, neither its racism, nor its religious bigotry.

The identification of the type of Africans Moses was born among is stated in Herodotus, HISTORIES, Book II; Thus:

"The Colchians, Egyptians and Ethiopians have thick lips, broad nose, wooly hair, and they are burnt of skin."

Herodotus' words were needed in those days, for ancient man had not yet developed (neither did he have) the sophistication whereby he could see two or three "races" of mankind coming out of the same "Adam and Eve;" no more than he could have seen the different "races" evolving from the same "apelike" Mister and Mrs Zinzathropus boisie* of Kenya, East Africa, more than 1,750,000 years ago. They were not as sophisticatedly racist as yet.

Religious history reveals that the Jews lived in Egypt for approximately a little more than 400 years (somewhere between c1640 and 1232 B.C.E.) before Moses (Moshe) led them towards the "Promised Land" during the reign of Rameses II sometime between 1298-1232 B.C.E. That from the time their tiny numbers, seventy to be exact, entered with the first of their fathers - Abraham , they were all welcomed and enjoyed all of the privileges afford- ed all other people in Egypt, depending upon their classes. And, as such, many Jews, as many of the other indigenous Africans, be- came high government officials within many pharoahs'(kings) cab- inet, most noted of them was Joseph - who became "Prime Minis- ter during the reign of Pharoah Horenheb or Kamose. That Moses, himself, was brought up as a member of the Royal Family of Pha-

* See BLACK MAN OF THE NILE, by Yosef ben-Jochannan, Alkebu-lan Books, New York, 1970, chapter dealing with fossil-man.

roah Pep I's first daughter. This is true, because Moses was supposedly eighty (80) to ninety (90) years of age (depending on which version of which bible one is reading at the time) when he fled from Western Egypt towards Eastern Egypt (Mt. Sinai) sometime between 1298 and 1232 B.C.E.[4a]

It is extremely important to note that there are no records that the Jews, prior to any mention of Moses, brought into Sais (which they called "Egypt" in their mythology about the sons of Jacob and Isaac) any scrolls or books whatsoever. There are no records that they had any homeland where they had established a government, institutions of higher learning or an organized religion before they entered Sais (Egypt) from their nomadic life in the Asian desert. The first record of them in Egypt speaks of their small settlement around the Nile Delta on the Mediterranean Sea, near the cities where there was a flourishing boat building industry - approximately c1640 to 1630 B.C.E.,[4b] the vast majority of them residing around the seaport of Aswan.

From this earliest background of the original Haribus (Jews) that allegedly "gave the world" that which is today called "Judaism," rested upon traditional African values established thousands of years by indigenous Nile Valley Africans (the so-called "Negroes," and others), from Uganda in Central East Africa to the Egyptian Sea (now the Mediterranean) in North Africa before the birth of the first Jew, Abraham, for their philosophical concepts. The entire spiritual and moral foundations of "Judaism" today and yesteryear are based upon the so-called "TEN COMMANDMENTS" in the FIVE BOOKS OF MOSES (Torah). Yet, all of these "Commandments" and the lesser ones - which most people do not know exist - are

147

almost exact copies of laws and religious philosophical concepts
which the African Jews, as they were by that time, lived under
during their more than four hundred (400) years in Egypt and other
parts of North Africa. Because of this background the indigenous
African identity is purposely excluded from Judaism, as presently
being taught in synagogues and schools within the United States of
America. To make certain this image of a non-African beginning of
the Jews is perpetuated, and the following terms are created:
"AFRICANS SOUTH OF THE SAHARA, NEGROES, BLACK AFRICANS, SEMITIC
AFRICANS, HEMITIC AFRICANS, TROPICAL AFRICANS, CAUCASOID AFRICANS,
HOTTENTOTS, PYGMIES," and a host of other Africans which are too
numerous to try and list here. These terms, and others, were added to satisfy the political, cultural, religious and psychologi-
cal separation of many sections of Africa (Alkebu-lan)*, from its
northern limits and much of its eastern territories. Therefore,
one hears of "Egypt, Libya, Tunisia, Morocco, Algeria, Ethiopia,
and Africa." Of course, the average person who digests this type
of semantical experimentation of racist scholars becomes imbued
with the opinion that Africa is separate from the countries listed
before the "...and Africa." With the fait accompli of North Africa
and East Africa removed from the balance of the continent of Africa
set in the minds of people everywhere an established fact, as
taught in "Western" educational institutions, it was then very
easy for the educators to remove the indigenous Africans, Blacks
(also called "Negroes," even "coloureds" sometimes), from ever
having anything whatsoever to do with these areas of Africa until
their allegedly first entrance as "...slaves from Nubia." Yet,

---

* See page 266 of Yosef ben-Jochannan's book, BLACK MAN OF THE
NILE, for the names Africa was called by the ancients.
148

the same Nubia (Sudan) being referred to is where the major
cataracts - one through six - are located, known as "UPPER EGYPT."
This is the location where most of the greatest structures of Nile
Valley-Man High-Culture (civilization) were erected. Also; it is
through the same Nubia that the Nile River and its tributaries
flow before it reaches Egypt (Lower Egypt). The same Nile River
routes the ancient indigenous Africans travelled from its source
in Central Africa (Uganda) when they built their earliest High-
Cultures (civilizations) to the point of their zeniths in Egypt,
Nubia, Kush (Ethiopia), Punt (the Somalia area of East Africa),
Numidia, Libya, Khart Haddas (Carthage or New Town), and other
areas in North and East Africa. Before that time, however, other
Africans had travelled and reached architectural, engineering,
scientific, philosophical, and religious greatness, and to the Zenith of their culture, in southern Africa - ZIMBABWE (the Portuguese called it Zimboae, the British called it Rhodesia) in the
largest African land-based empire - MONOMOTAPA (the entire area
of southern Africa, from the Zambesie River to the Cape of Good
Hope (the Portuguese "Cabo de Tormentos").

Moses and Judaism, like Jesus Christ and Christianity (the
daughter of Judaism), had their origins in the Nile Valley civilizations. And of course Islam, with her God - Allah (the grand-
daughter of Judaism, and daughter of Christianity) cannot escape
its indigenous African origin, even if the Ka'aba[*5a] should be
abandoned by the Moslems of the Holy City of Mecca.

In support of the statements already made in reference to

---

* A "black stone" - a piece of a fallen meteor found in Ethiopia
and carried into Arabia when the Ethiopians of East Africa ruled
the Arabian Peninsula hundreds of years before Islam was founded.

Moses, the following facts are re-emphasized:...Moses, his brother
Aaron and his sister Mirriam were all indigenous Africans of Egypt.
Biblical history states that they were born in Egypt, North Africa,
during the reign of Pepi I, Pharoah of Egypt, which began in 1381
B.C.E. and continued for twenty (20) years after (1298 B.C.E.).[5]
Not only these few Jews were indigenous Africans, but almost every
last Jew fleeing from western Egypt to the "Promised Land" in
Eastern Egypt - Mount Sinai - were indigenous Africans. Those who
are today called "Negroes"(and the likes)are descendants of the
same people. The source of these facts can be found in the Hebrew
Torah (the FIVE BOOKS OF MOSES), the Christian Holy Bible (all
versions of it) and the Moslem Koran, among other major scholarly
works on the subject, all of which could be found throughout this
and other works. Thus it is written:

> And there was a famine in the land: And Abraham
> (Avram) went down into Egypt (Africa)*to so-
> journ there; for the famine was grievous in the
> land..., etc.**

Sir E. A. Wallis-Budge, Professor James H. Breasted, Professor George G. M. James, Josephus, and a host of other outstanding
Egyptologists, all elaborated extensively on the life of the indigenous African Jews in ancient Egypt before their flight from
Pharoah (King) Rameses II,sometime between 1298 and 1232 B.C.E.,[5]
as shown in the chronology of BLACK MAN OF THE NILE, pp. 101 and
113.

Though not using the name Jews or Hebrews (Haribus), most
modern historians dealing with this period in Egyptian history

---

* Words in bracket by author for particular emphasis on this point.
** See Genesis, Chapter 12, Verse 10 of the Hebrew Torah.

wrote of "Semitic peoples" that entered Egypt around the year
1400 B.C.E.[5a] Yet, none of these writers could find any records,
other than the Hebrew Torah (FIVE BOOKS OF MOSES), to validate
any historical evidence related to the "PASS OVER." This is not
to say that many Jews were, or were not, slaves in Egypt; or that
they did, or did not, labour in the building of one or more of
the minor and least important of the pyramids. But, if they did,
it was not because of their "religion" or "ethnic" groupings because
the Egyptians, as well as other ancient peoples of that era in
history, were unaware of "race hatred" or "color prejudice," also
"religious bigotry," in any form common to Twentieth (20th) Century C.E. thinking. This may be, of course, difficult for most
Americans to accept, irrespective of race, creed or color, since
Americans have never known a period in their history (since they
stole the country   from the indigenous peoples they call "Indians") when racism and religious bigotry were not part and par-
cel of the basic structural fabric of the government of the United
States of America and the private sectors, otherwise called "free
enterprise." As such, most Americans seem unable to understand
how any other civilization, past or present, could have developed a society free of religious bigotry and racial hatred.

Whereas, "race," for whatever the word means today, had no
bearing on ancient Egyptian society; "religion" did. Not only was
"religion" a factor with foreigners, but amongst various indigenous pharoahs (kings). For example: The boy pharoah, Tut-ankh-amen
(Tut, as he is affectionately known), changed the worship of the
Theban Period God - AMEN. Pharoah Akhnaten (Akhanaten, Iknaten,
etc.), Tut's father-in-law, had changed it to the God - ATEN.[5b]

151

However, at no time was there a war or any period of persecution in Egypt because of "religious intolerance." But, it is in"religious tolerance" that the story of the indigenous Africans influence in Judaism, past and present, is written; thus, the Pass Over drama; showing the Africans of the religion of the God - AMEN of Egypt as devils, and the African Jews of the God - YAHWEH as "God's choosen people."*

Some additional insights may be gained by a review of the life of Moses, according to the ancient Hebrew biblical history, which was adopted by the Christians and Moslems. It would seem that "...Moses was born of the tribe of Levi," at a period when the indigenous African Hebrews were already enslaved by fellow Africans of another religion in Egypt, North Africa.[5b]

Moses was saved through his miraculous discovery by the princess' maid, supposedly his own sister, who seized him from "... floating down the Nile River in a bulrush basket." His mother was supposedly, to have hid him in the basket to save his life, since the Pharoah, Rameses I, was killing all of the Hebrew males born throughout the Kingdom of Egypt, etc.[6]

The princess gave Moses to a woman, who was in fact his own mother,[7] to nurse him; she was paid by the princess for her services to her own child.

His name, Moses, meant "drawn out from the water," according to the Egyptian princess - who allegedly had no name, but she

---

* In this term, "choosen people," the seeds of religious bigotry and avid racism were planted. For what were the "choosen people" persecuted or prosecuted? This was written at a period in man's history when the foundation of bigotry was being established for the first time in human history. All of the Gods of that time "choosen people" were to suit their own prejudice and racism.

gave him his name.[8]

Moses murdered his fellow Egyptian, who was not of the Hebrew faith; this supposedly happened before he had received the "TEN COMMANDMENTS"[9] at Mount Sinai.

There is no record that he did anything to free "his people" up to the time that he murdered his fellow Egyptian; nor that he ever gave up his life of luxury from the support his mother received from the princess for his support, all of which was stated to have come from the daughter of the pharoah, Pepi I (his first daughter),[10] the same girl who saw him floating down the Nile River in the "bulrush basket."

It was only when Moses had to flee Pharoah Ramese II's anger because he had murdered Rameses representative - the soldier, did Moses begin to plan the "EXODUS" of his fellow indigenous Egypans of the Hebrew Faith from Western to Eastern Egypt (from the Aswan end of the Nile River Delta to Mount Sinai).[11]

Here, Moses is seen fleeing one of the same laws he was supposed to have received from God (Yahweh, Jehovah) along with the "TEN COMMANDMENTS." It is obvious that the same God of the Hebrews (Yahweh), or some other God, must have given the same "TEN COMMANDMENTS" to the other Egyptians of the religion of the God RA before He handed it out to Moses on Mount Sinai, because Moses was running to escape being prosecuted for violating the law that states:

THOU SHALT NOT KILL

Similarly, the "Commandment" which stated to the Hebrews:

THOU SHALT LOVE THY NEIGHBOUR AS THYSELF

was also violated by Moses when he killed his fellow indigenous African brother of Sais (Egypt).

153

There are hundreds of source materials which reveal evidence
that substantiate the indigenous African origin of the other nine
"Commandments";[11a] such data not only prove their African origin,
but in most cases the author of each document or law.

Genesis, Chapter 3, Verses 7 and 8, the "Lord" (God, or Yahweh) is shown aiding and abetting Moses to steal his neighbor's
property, as Jehovah promised Moses the "Caanite, Hittite, Amerite,
Jebusite, Perizzites land flowing with milk and honey."[11b] What
was the difference between these invasions Moses and his fellow
Hebrews were planning to commit, and they later committed, and those
made by the pharoahs of Egypt against other peoples and lands on
the suggestions and approval of the God, RA, of Egypt (Sais)? The
Jews (Hebrews) were only taking a page from the history they learned
while they were still indigenous Africans in Egypt. As a matter
of fact, they were still in Egypt when the "Lord" - Yahweh - supposedly approved their colonialist invasion and confiscation (liberation) of other peoples' lands. He had already parceled out
these lands to the other peoples and nations who, obviously, must
have assumed them to be their own, since He (the "Lord") had given
them the lands they were occupying before He had conspired with
Moses to liquidate them (commit genocide) for the benefit of
his newly "chosen people" - the Haribus (Hebrews or Jews).

The parallel of the story, where Moses and his brother Aaron
confronted Pharoah Rameses II and said:

> Thus sayeth the Lord, the God of Israel: Let my
> people go, that they may hold a feast unto Me
> in the wilderness.[12]

is being echoed in the cries of African-Americans everywhere in
the Americas today. Up until this day the Blacks in America still
154

sing "Let my people go;[22a] but many substitute "...from Jim Crow's
land" for "Pharoah's land" with as much, or possibly more, fervor
than did the African Hebrews (Jews) of Egypt during Moses' era
when they sang their songs of liberation from their fellow Africans.
Strange as it may seem, the first people to sing this song were
the African-Americans - there being no record whatsoever to the
contrary.

Pharoah Rameses II is made to look like a raving maniac, a
kind of an ancient Adolf Hitler of the "Egyptian race." The
Egyptians, of course, were supposed to have had no ancestral connection with the ancient indigenous African Haribus (Jews). This
was not true, because the ancient African Haribus of Egypt, the
females, gave birth to hundreds of thousands of offspring. This
condition the Hebrews could not avoid, that is, providing they
were in fact slaves of their fellow Africans that worshipped the
God Ra. It is common knowledge what happens to the women of an
enslaved people, the Haribus (Hebrews or Jews) being no exception
to this rule. If the Haribus were of a "separate race," "Semitic"
or otherwise, when they entered Egypt, they certainly were not any
such thing when they were forced out of Egypt four hundred (400)
years later. One must remember that their last few years were
spent in the worse form of bondage under the other Africans who
worshipped the God Ra - according to the Second Book of Moses,
EXODUS. This story is corroborated by the fact that they were
only "seventy" when they entered Egypt, according to the
FIRST BOOK OF MOSES, Genesis, Chapter 46, Verses 1 through 27.
_____
* Prior to the "Negro Spritual" by the name, "LET MY PEOPLE GO,"
there was no other song by that name recorded in Jewish history.

These indigenous Africans, today called "Negroes, Bantus ,"
etc.; the originators of the Pyramid and Coffin Texts, the BOOK
OF THE DEAD, the Memphite Drama,and other such works, by the
thousands, in religious and secular proses, had already spoken
of a monotheistic God in the person of RA (the Sun God), the God
that existed before Moses and Abraham, even before Adam and Eve.
They had developed in each municipality a series of Gods for each
situation; but the greatest of all Gods, RA, commanded the same
role of having minor Gods, as did the Jews, Christians, and Moslem Gods; each saying:

> I AM A JEALOUS GOD, THOU SHALT HAVE NO
> OTHER GOD BEFORE ME.

This "COMMANDMENT," as it is presently called, needs no clarification. It is no different from the Commandment which was rendered
to the indigenous African peoples of Egypt in the Mysteries by the
God RA.*

In the Passover drama scene, it was not the indigenous Jews
alone who journeyed from the City of RAMSES to Succoth with their
fellow African - Moses; they were:

> "...about six hundred thousand men on foot, beside
> children. And a mixed multitude went up also with
> them; and flocks and herds, even very much cattle.[13]

> And the Lord said unto Moses and Aaron: "This is
> my ordinance of the passover; there shall non-Hebrew
> (alien) eat thereof; but every man's servant that is
> bought for money, when thou hast circumcised him,
> then shall he eat.[14]

It seems rather strange that the indigenous African Jews,
including the "mixed multitude," should be fleeing Egypt because

---

A second point is that the African-Americans (Blacks, "Negroes,"
etc.) are from the same African background of the original Haribus
and Egyptians - formerly known as the "PEOPLES OF THE NILE VALLEY,"
even before the birth of the first Haribu - Abraham. This song is
as much the property of Black Jews as it is White Jews.
*   See pages 57 and 58 of this volume for the HYMN OF ADORATION TO
THE GOD OSIRIS;also Note 55, Chapter I,at the rear of this volume.
156

they were being held as slaves by fellow Africans; when, in the same book, EXODUS, Chapter 12, Verses 37 - 51, the Jews are speaking about their own "slaves" which they stopped and bought in Egypt. Note, also, that they did not allow "non-Jews" amongst them:

"...to eat of the meat until they were circumcised" (made Jews).[14a] This meant two things; (a) the indigenous African Jews forced their non-Jewish religious Egyptian-African brothers and sisters to convert to Judaism if they wanted to "...eat of the meat" and enjoy whatever else the Jews were having; (b) they (African Jews - Negroes, etc.) had, themselves, become slave owners. This is not to say that the practise of slavery by the indigenous African Jews was any better or any worse than the non-Jewish Africans. It is saying, however, that mankind seems only to worry about SELF; self as an individual person, family, tribe, nation or group of allied nations; even the biblical people - the "choosen people" - were guilty of this type of human failure.

Before going further, one has to remember that Moses and all of the other African Jews from Egypt mentioned in the Passover drama were preceded in Egypt by the first Jew, Abraham, who was a Chaldean (Chaldees) from the City of Ur. Along with Abraham were:

"...Sarah, his wife and Lot his brother's son,
and all their substance that they had gathered,
and the souls they had gotten in Haran...,"[15]etc.

But the mass migration by the predecessors of Moses actually took place with the entrance of Joseph into the indigenous Africans' land (Egypt, and possibly parts of Libya and Numidia), according to the Book of Genesis. Thus; it is written:

"...Then Joseph went in and told Pharoah; saying:

157

> 'My father and my brethren and their flocks and
> their herds, and all that they have are come out
> of the land Canaan; and behold, they are in the
> land Goshen. And from his brethren he selected
> five men, and presented them unto Pharoah. And
> Pharoah said unto his brethren: 'What is your
> occupation?' And they said unto Pharoah: 'Thy
> servants are shepherds, we and our fathers both.'
> And they said unto Pharoah: 'In thy land we come
> unto sojurn, for there is no pasture for thy ser-
> vants' flocks; for the famine is sad in the land
> of Canaan....'" (Genesis, Chapter 41, Verses 1 -
> 4).

The story drew to its ending with Joseph introducing his father,

Jacob, to receive the Pharoah's grant of " a hundred and thirty

years..." of sojourning (Genesis, Chapter 41, Verse 9). It ended

with the following:

> And Joseph placed his father and his brethren,
> and gave them a possession in the land of Egypt,
> in the best of the land, the land of Rameses" (I),*
> as Pharoah commanded. And Joseph sustained his
> father, and his brethren and all his father's
> household, with bread, according to the want of
> their children.**

There are many factors about the entrance of the Asian Hari-

bus (Jews) from Canaan (approximately where Phoenicia was located)

into the Africans' homeland,[14b] which was never emphasized, be-

cause of their complementary nature in regards to their African

hosts.

Thus it should be noted:

(a) During this period the Jews, formerly called Hebrews,

from Asia were a starving lot; just as the Irish who fled Ireland

to the United States of America during the Irish Potato Famine

(c1848-1890 C.E.). The Africans, who gave food, water, shelter,

---

* Word in brackets by the author of this volume.
** Genesis, Chapter 41, Verses 11 and 12.

and land to these very unfortunate nomads from Asia had to be of
very highly religious character. Obviously, they were "godly" in
every sense that the word is presently used today; at least as
far as charity is concerned.

(b) There is no indication that those lowly Asian Jews had
any formalized education of a standard in any way comparable with
that which the indigenous Africans of Egypt had developed. Neither
is there any evidence that they had a set code of ethics and morals
that were contrary, or in support, of those they met in the African
land – Egypt. None of them appeared to have had any talent which was
beyond the basic needs of a nomadic people; at best they were shep-
herds when they entered Egypt.

(c) It had to be Pharoah Rameses I or Pharoah Khamose ruling
at the time of Joseph's entry into Egypt (Sais). For, if the Jews
(Asian and African) spent four-hundred (400) years in Egypt, which
ended during the reign of Pharoah Rameses II (1298-1232 B.C.E.),
their date of entrance had to be about c1232 + 400 = 1632 B.C.E.
Strangely enough, this was about the same period when the Hyksos
(Shepherd Kings) invaded Egypt from around the same area the Asian
Jews allegedly came - Canaan,[15a] in c1675 B.C.E.

(d) The Africans accepted their Asian brothers and sisters,
the Haribus, as equals, and integrated them into Egyptian society
according to their social and economic classes. Thus, from the
first day of their entry in Africa they were amalgamated and integrated with Egyptians.

Up to this period the Asian Jews had not established a government anywhere, other than tribal groupings. The major pyramids
were already built by the Pharoahs Khufu (renamed "Cheops" by the

159

Greeks), Khafra (renamed Chephren by the Greeks) and Mycerinus -
a period covering 2680 - 2258 B.C.E., the IInd through IVᵗʰ Dynasties; as such, the Jews could not have slaved on the building
of the Sphinx of Ghizeh or any of the major pyramid structures in
Egypt prior to c1632 B.C.E. It must be also noted that Imhotep,*
the architect, prime minister and first physician (called "God of
Medicine"), and Pharoah Djoser (called "Zozer" by the Greeks) had
built the first Step Pyramid at Saqqara in 3100 B.C.E.

None of these Asian Jews were Caucasians, or even of Caucasian origin; therefore no blonds, redheads or brunnettes one sees
today as Jews are in any sense authentically Jews moreso than the
black, yellow, and brown one sees from Africa and Asia.

There are many more important analyses that could be drawn
from this biblical story, but such is beyond the scope of this
work. There are, of course, many thousands of works on the subject,
which go into in-depth detailing, many of which are listed in the
bibliography at the rear of this volume.

The newcomers prospered or suffered like any other Egyptian
in this African land. Their first generation to be born in Egypt
was treated like any other African, as there were no racial, religious or national segregation noted at that time in any part
of Africa (Alkebu-lan).

Here in Africa, for the first time, the Asian Jews, now Egyptian nationals, had begun their first introduction into the "Nether
World" (the world of the great beyond), religious scriptures -"The

---

* If Imhotep was a physician more than two-thousand (2000) years
before the birth of Hipocrates; why is Hipocrates called "the
father of medicine" instead of the "father of European medicine?"
Note that Imhotep is called "Aescupalius in the so-called "Hipocrates Oath"; in which he is the God of Medicine.

Pyramid Texts," "Monotheism" - the worship of "One God above all other Gods" - the worship of the major God, RA (the Sun), and "Coffin Texts" (also of the "Nether World") - the story of life beyond and after death - the "Hereafter."

At this juncture the basic philosophical concept which supposedly distinguish "heathens" and "pagans" from Jews, Christians, and Moslems comes into sharply conflicting ideologies between writers on both sides of the issue. Yet, not one can be proven to be any better than the others. Then; what is there in "paganism" and "heathenism" which Jews, Christians, and Moslems no longer practise that make them feel superior to those who still observe such religious tenets, which everyone copied from the Great Lakes and Nile Valley indigenous Africans religious theories?

Is there any difference between the ancient Asian Jews conversion to the indigenous African Mysteries found in Egypt than the African-Americans conversion to European and European-American-style Christianity, other than the fact that the small band of Asian Jews entered Africa of their own free will; and whereas the African-Americans' ancestors were captured and kidnapped in Africa and forced to migrate into slavery in the Americas? In both cases neither had much choice as to which religion they would follow. Yet, the indigenous Africans, from every section of Africa (Alkebu-lan) entered the Americas with substantial roots in their religions, which is more than the Asian Jews could have said for themselves when they first entered Egypt. However, like the Asian Jews, the indigenous Africans, who were enslaved in the Caribbeans and the Americas, particularly in the United States of America, furthered their religion in places where they were allowed to

161

practise their own indigenous faiths. For example, the Yoruba religion of Cuba, Haiti, Brazil,and other parts of the Caribbean Islands and South America is as highly developed as its Jewish, Moslem,and Christian counterparts in these same areas.

In the Americas and Europe the indigenous Africans were forced to adopt Judaeo-Christianity and Islamic standards; whereas in Africa (Egypt) it was the Asians and Europeans having to adopt to the Mysteries and other indigenous African traditional religious standards, mythology,and taboos. There should be no conflict or reason for shame over these revelations by any"ethnic" or religious group, as it would have been impossible for the few Asian Jews in Egypt, who had become Egyptian nationals even before their first generation was born in that African land, not to have become Africanized like the Africans in America under similar conditions not to have become European-Americanized. Only those who feel some sense of "racial", "ethnic" or "religious" superiority may find reason to resent the comparisons being made herein; though not being able to refute the facts, never-the-less. Yet, such protest could be understood - though not tolerated, because of the "Tarzan and Jane" Hollywood movie image or the "Stanley and Livingstone Darkest Africa" stereotype "Negrophobia," both still attached to things African by those who control, to a great extent, the written and spoken word.

The whole concept of a "God" or "Gods" came out of the Nile Valley African civilizations thousands upon thousands of years before Sumner (the Kingdom of Hamurabi) was established along the banks of the Tigris and Euphrates rivers. That was more than thousands of years before Abraham - the first Hebrew (Jew) - was born

162

in the City of Ur, Chaldea. This concept, which had gone through very extensive changes and revisions for thousands of years before the arrival of the Asian Jews, all seventy-seven (77) of them, in Africa, was in its zenith when Abraham, Isaac, Jacob, and Joseph entered the land at the end of the Nile River - Sais, which they later called "Egypt."

The indigenous Africans of Egypt had already become proficient in the sciences that allowed them to; (a) embalm their dead; (b) name the bodies in the celestial universe; (c) name their God and minor Gods; (d) develop agriculture; (e) establish a Solar Calendar in 4,100 B.C.E.;[16] (f) develop a fertility control tampon recipe;[17] (g) build temples to the Gods - including the world wonder, the Sphinx of Gezeh (Giza); (h) develop engineering; (i) develop medicine - including internal surgery;[18] (j) develop pharmacology and many other disciplines too numerous to try and outline or define at this time. They even wrote poetry and short stories during said period along with their historical achievements in the sciences. All of this the small group of half-starving Asian Jews met, and were exposed too, from the first day they entered Africa out of the Asian desert, where they were nomads. At no time in their history is there any record of them being exposed to such knowledge before their encounter with the indigenous Africans of the Nile Valley, who had settled in Sais, Egypt, for the thousands of years before the Jews came. This, then appears to be the beginning of what is today called "Judaism, Judaeo-Christianity, Christianity" and "Islam." It is also at this juncture that all of the concepts, be they material or spiritual, which are in any manner connected to either of these generally labelled "WESTERN RELIG-

163

IONS"[19] originated.

These facts are primarily revealed in order that a better understanding of _truth_ and _fiction_ in that which is today called "holy" and "unholy" scriptures can be revealed. They are, of course, extended to include the "paganism" that exist in Judaism, Christianity,and Islam. The reason for not showing this relationship in other major religions is due to the fact that they are not labeled "WESTERN RELIGIONS," even though most of them have been, to a large extent, responsible for the three religions so designated.

For example, one finds that the "PROVERBS" in the Judaeo-Christian "Holy Books", allegedy "written by inspired men of God" (the Hebrew God, Yahweh or Jehovah), were"written by King Solomon of Israel." But, is it not a fact that most of the same "Proverbs," as they have been called, if not all, are to be found in a collection of poetry and songs by an indigenous African - Pharoah (King) Amen-em-ope (1405-1370 B.C.E.), who lived more than three-hundred (300) years before the reign of King Solomon (976-936 B.C.E.). A few examples of that which is called the "PROVERBS" are given for your comparison with the original source - "THE TEACHINGS OF AMEN-EM-OPE." Note that there are many English versions and translations of the alleged "PROVERBS OF KING SOLOMON." All of them, however, relate to the same meaning as the following"

THE COMPARATIVE WORKS

The Teachings of Amen-em-ope Pharoah of Egypt (1405-1370)	The so-called"Proverbs"of King Solomon of Israel (976-936)
Give thine ear, and hear what I say, And apply thine heart to apprehend;	Incline thine ear, and hear my words, And apply thine heart to **apprehend;**

164

It is good for thee to
place them in thine
heart,
Let the rest in the cas-
ket of the belly.
That they may act as a
peg upon thy tongue.
*****

Consider these thirty
chapters;
They delight, they in-
struct.
Knowledge how to answer
him that speaketh,
And how to carry back a
report to one that
sent it.
*****

Beware of robbing the
poor,
And of oppressing the
afflicted.
*****

Associate not with a pas-
sionate man,
Nor approach him for con-
versations;
Leap not to cleave to
such a one,
That the terror carry thee
not away.
*****

A scribe who is skillful
in his business
Findeth himself worthy to
be a courtier.
*****

For it is pleasant if thou
keep them in thy belly,
That they may be fixed upon
thy lips.
*****

Have I not written for thee
thirty sayings,
Of counsels and knowledge!
That thou mayest make known
truth to him that speaketh.
*****

Rob not the poor for he is
poor,
Neither oppress the lowly in
the gate.
*****

Associate not with a passion-
ate man,
Nor go with a wrathful man,
Lest thou learn his ways,
And get a snare to thy soul.
*****

A man who is skillful in his
in his business
Shall stand before kings.
*****

The plagiarism on Solomon's part cannot be overlooked; as
he too often copied Amen-em-ope's work in too many instances word
for word. For added comparisons one only needs to secure books
on this subject listed in the bibliography of this work.[19a]

The above revelation is minor by comparison to the fact that the entire "TEN COMMANDMENTS", which Moses is reported to have received on Mt Sinai, are just "Ten" of the more than one-hundred and forty-seven (147) laws the indigenous Africans had written before the first Haribu (Jew), Abraham, entered Sais (Egypt), and still were in use when, and after, Moses left western Egypt for Mt. Sinai during the EXODUS drama spoken of in the Torah. This can be best observed in the excerpts from the "NEGATIVE CONFESSIONS" on pages 69 and 70, Chapter I, of this volume. Strangely enough, wherever the "Ten Commandments" are being taught they are presented as a development that was void of any indigenous African origin or involvement. This is best demonstrated in the following comments over the failure of educational institutions in the United States of America to take into account a greater degree of European American Jewish heritage; yet, from similar sources the struggle against African-American heritage within the same educational institutions are being resisted very fiercely. But the following article should be sufficient proof as to why African-American history, not "Negro history," is of importance to every American - irrespective of race, creed, national origin, sex or color, etc.

THE NEW YORK TIMES, SUNDAY, MAY 18, 1969

A Study Says Textbooks Err on History of Jews

By IRVING SPIEGEL

The American Jewish Committee reported yesterday that a study of history and social studies textbooks used in junior and senior high schools throughout the country had shown "many errors and misconceptions" about Jews and a disregard of their achievements.

The findings of the study, prepared by researchers with extensive academic backgrounds, was made public by Bertram H. Gold, executive vice president of the committee, at its 63d annual meeting at the Waldorf-Astoria Hotel.

The major portion of the study was devoted to a detailed examination of 45 textbooks and other instructional material in wide use throughout the country.

Texts, Mr. Gold said, were assessed on the basis of their handling of Biblical and post-

Biblical times, the Middle Ages, the modern era and the establishment of Israel as a nation, the Nazi period, and contributions by Jews to American society.

The study listed a textbook entitled "A History of the United States," by Alden and Magenia, published by the American Book Company in 1960.

"There is no listing for the Jews in the index, no mention of the presence of Jews among the early settlers in the United States . . . no mention of any Jewish contribution," the report said.

Another book, "The American Story" by Gavian and Hamm, D. C. Heath and Company, Boston, 1959, the study said, makes no mention of the "large Jewish migration to this country and its contribution" or of "Hitler's persecution of the Jews."

"There is very little information on Israel, except to mention its existence," the study found.

Also cited was "A Global History of Man," by Leften S.

****

A Disregard for Achievements Is Shown in High Schools' Materials, Panel Finds

Stavrianos, Allyn and Bacon, Inc., Boston, 1962.

History of Hebrews

"The text devotes half of a sentence to the fact that six million Jews were murdered during World War II. This is referred to as one of the costs of the war," the study said.

According to the study, "The World Story," by Bruun and Haines, D. C. Heath and Company, Boston, 1963, in relating the history of the early Hebrews, concludes with the following statement:

"Their [the prophets'] teachings, together with the earlier records of the Hebrews, were later put together to form the Old Testament of the Christian Bible."

The committee's study said that "the fact that the Christians later adopted the Old Testament as the first part of their Bible is of no particular

****

relevance in a discussion of the early Hebrews and their religion," adding that "Abraham, Moses, the prophets are all ignored in this text."

This textbook, the study said, makes no mention of "Jewish suffering during the Crusades and at the hands of the Spanish Inquisition."

"As usual, the Jews of the Middle Ages are completely ignored," the report said.

The study assailed a New York State Grade Seven curriculum book entitled "New York's Golden Age." It "contains horrible stereotypes of Jews and caricatures of the lowest caliber," said the report, which cited a chapter entitled "Of a Friday in the Jewish Quarter of New York."

In a summation of the study's conclusion, Mr. Gold asserted that "the presence of Jews in the world from Biblical to modern times is frequently disregarded" and that "many histories of the United States show a conspicuous absence of references to anti-Semitism, bigotry, ethnic and minority groups, discrimination and prejudice."

****

The co-option of the "sacred scriptures" (writings) by various religious groups was common among the ancients. This practise came down through the adaptation of the basic tenets from the indigenous Nile Valley Africans "Mystery System" into Judaism. Christendom extended it when it made Judaism its foundation. From this historical background it re-entered the various indigenous African traditional religions through colonialism and imperialism. In the Americas, including the Caribbean Islands, the indigenous African religions the enslaved Africans brought with them from West, Central, North, South, and East Africa were overshadowed. But, in this co-optation the African-Americans were able to retain much of their ancient heritage through Judaism and Christianity, otherwise called "Judaeo-Christianity." In contemporary times they have been able to make Islam meet local traditional African-American standards, also.

167

The African-American expanded Judaism and Christianity
through their special suffering during slavery. European-style
Judaism and Christianity were both embraced by means of their co-
option into that which is today still being called "NEGRO SPIRIT-
UALS." Thus, one of them, the ever popular "MOSES IN THE PROMISED
LAND," invokes all sorts of arguments as to whom it belongs.[20]
The African-Americans, who brought the song into prominence,
claimed its authorship as a song which they created and used in
their attempt to console themselves while in servitude of their
European and European-American (White)* Christian and Jewish
slave masters; on the other hand the White Jews **considered** that
its authorship was theirs, on the ground that Moses was a fellow
Jew (Hebrew) who led the Jewish (Hebrew) people out of bondage
from Pharoah Rameses II's Egypt, forgetting, of course, the fact
that they were themselves Black Jews when they were in Egypt for
four-hundred (400) years. Or is one to assume that after four-
hundred years of slavery in Egypt (under the rule of the indigenous
Black people of the Nile Valley) the Hebrews (Jews), if they were
of a special "race" other than the Egyptian Africans, would have
left Egypt a **pure** whatever-they-were when their little band of
less than one-hundred (100) entered with Abraham, Jacob, and
Joseph?

The two positions in this argument completely overlooked that
Moses was an indigenous African, at the same time a Haribu (Hebrew
or Jew);[21] a sort of Marcus Garvey[22] and Theodor Herzl,[23] or Dr.
Martin Luther King, Jr.,[24] combined. To the Moslems and Christians
regardless of race, sex, color or nationality, Moses is also theirs

---

* Many do not know that there are thousands of Black Jews in the
United States of America, the vast majority in the New York area.

168

Hopefully, one can also see in this argument why it is so difficult for so many to appreciate whatever the indigenous Africans
have done for, or to, that which is called "WESTERN RELIGIONS."
Since they were chattel slaves, and still remain mentally so,
White America (Jews, Christian, Moslems,and others) persistently
deny Black America (Jews, Christians,and Muslims and all others)
recognition for their contributions to this Greek-centric Anglo-
Saxon Judaeo-Christian oriented society,[25]the United States of America.

One has to understand the significance of the social factors which make a European-American (White) Jew reject the possibility of his, or her, indigenous African ancestry.[26] Because,
just as their fellow European-American Christians and Moslems,
they too consider themselves "Caucasians" (White) first, and Jewish after.[27] If it were the opposite, the Commandment, "THOU SHALL
LOVE THY NEIGHBOR AS THYSELF" (not White ones only)[28] would take
precedence when an African-American (Jewish, Christian, Muslim,
or traditional religion) move into one of their buildings. But,
this is not easy to do, for the European-American Jews are for
all purposes European in culture; as such they react as any other
person of European origin to the Black-White confrontation in
progress in the United States of America. To follow this fact,
and then say that the "White Jewish problem" in America is similar to that of the Black Jews is totally ironic; and it is much
more so in the case of the Black Christians, Muslims,and African
religious traditionalists. Therefore, current groups of African-
Americans have found it necessary to target White Jews (also a
minority, but only in a religious sense, not racially, for they
have for generations registered as "Caucasians", not "Semites,

169

in the United States of American and elsewhere in the "New World," as well as in Europe)[29] as they do White Christians.

Many White Jews in the United States of America took the lead in the so-called "civil rights movement" through sheer co-incidence. This involvement did not begin with any temple, synagogue or related organization, but through the efforts of two people - the Spingarm brothers,[30] who happened to be Jews. These two men, being responsible for the creation of the "Niagra Movement," now defunct, the forerunner of the "National Association for the Advancement of Colored People" (N.A.A.C.P.) in c1906 C.E., took turns in controlling this organization through the following roles: Joe as "Chairman of the Board of Directors," and Arthur as President until 1966 C.E.[31] This organization has always remained under the financial control of European-Americans, and has always reflected the views of what so-called "Liberal" White America thinks Black America wants, and must have.[32] Of course, White America (Jews and Gentiles alike) is not to be blamed for protecting its own financial and social interests in orgnizations such as the National Alsociation for the Advancement of Colored people and the Urban League. This is still true, even to the point where their money controls those "Negroes" whom one sees in the forefront of such movements. Why? Because the "Negro Leaders" White America selects for Black America have for generation after generation said just what White American always wanted to hear.[33] What White America heard about Black America, from their "Negro Leaders," satisfied their economic, social, and religious philosophies, the White Jews being no exception. Of course this type of involvement had its effects upon the obliga-

170

tions to which all Jews of all colors are bound in the Torah (Five Books of Moses) and its compliments.[34]

Instead of helping its Black American co-religionist neighbors, the Black Israelites,* Talmudic Jews demanded to be their leader, and to some extent it won. This was possible only because certain Jewish religious leaders involved themselves individually in the "civil rights movement" as Jews rather than as European-Americans (Caucasians or White people). It was, therefore, very common to witness donations for said movements in the name of Jewish religious and philanthropic institutions, and of course by individual rabbis and their parishioners, each making it known that such financial aid was coming from Jewish sources. It was, also, only natural that wherever a man placed his money there he went to protect or to manage it, or at least to make his voice heard about how it is to be disbursed. It was, also, only natural that the White Jews would have conducted themselves in the same manner as other European-Americans have done thus far in the "civil rights movement."

As African-American militancy[35] increased and Black leadership separated from "Negro leadership," it was equally natural that the comfortable middle-class minded and oriented White (Jews and Gentiles) controlled "Negro leaders" and their non-African-American community-based organizations[36] would have come under attack. It was, also, natural that White donors would have also come under attack because of their group identification; especially when said groups have been for generations associated with the

---

* The so-called "Black Jews" prefer to be called "ISRAELITES." They will answer, however, to "Black," but never to "NEGRO." This is very important in dealing with African-American "Jews."

ownership and leadership of the so-called "respectable" type
"Negro organizations"; none of which had any locally-based
people (for whom they were allegedly founded) involved in the
power structure of said movements - their Board of Directors.

The fact that so very few Americans in the "civil rights
movement," of every grouping, know that there are people called
"Jews," who are not of European origin, in itself creates severe problems for the Talmudic (White) Jewish community, which
failed to address the Black-White Jewish problem that arose over
the issue of "community control." This is not only true for the
Talmudists, it also affects the Falashas and their fellow African-
American (Black) Israelite (Jewish) community, both groups having suffered all sorts of rebuff from their fellow African-
American Christian and Muslim believers, and also from traditionalist African religious observers. This is so, because they
believe that the Black Israelites relationship with their White
counterparts is a sort of an "Uncle Tom" and "Aunt Tomasina"
comedy.[37] This is especially true when "Negro Christians" of
national fame convert to Talmudic Judaism and extensive publicity follows, unlike when "White Christians" of similar social
standing do likewise. Sammy Davis' the "Negro" singer, comedian,
dancer, movie star, and stage actor)[38] conversion was such an
example of note.

Judaism, as a "race-culture," is as preposterous as a Roman
Catholic or Moslem race. M. Fishberg in his noted work, THE JEW,[39]
dealt with this issue extensively. Whereas Joel A. Rogers,* in his

---

* Isolated by "Negro" and White historians for generations because he dared to make researches into the background of many
"pure Whites" and expose their "Negro ancestry." J.A. Rogers' works
today, now that he is dead, are required readings in many colleges.
172

book, SEX AND RACE, Vol I, stated the following:[40]

WÈRE THE JEWS ORIGINALLY NEGROES?

EUROPEAN painters and sculptors by their use of white models to typify Biblical characters have falsified tremendously the physiognomy of the ancient Jews. We are familiar with the scores of portraits offered to us as Christ. But do good Christians ever stop to think what he really looked like? Josephus, first century historian, described him as dark skinned and simple in appearance, in the Halosis, suppressed portion of his work.

Solomon, too, is portrayed as a white man, though in the Songs attributed to him he speaks of himself as "black but comely." After visiting most of the leading galleries of Europe and America, the only realistic painting of an Eastern crowd that I have ever seen is "Christ and Barabbas" by Verlat in the Royal Museum of Antwerp where the mob is clamoring for Barabbas in preference to Christ. Solomon, too, is always painted white. The only picture I have ever seen of him as a Negro was in a certain luxurious palace of Cytherea in Paris.

Mention was made of the biblical theory that Negroes became black because Noah, supposedly white, cursed the sons of Ham. But the earliest Jews were in all probability, Negroes. Abraham, their ancestor, is said to have come from Chaldea and the ancient Chaldeans were black. "The Chaldees," says Higgins, "were originally Negroes." As was said, too, relics of prehistoric Negroes have been discovered in this region. It is even possible that the Jews originated, not in Asia, but in Africa. Gerald Massey has advanced considerable argument in proof of that theory.

Whatever was the original color of the Jews they lived for more than four centuries among the Negroid Egyptians. Their supposed oppressor, the Pharaoh, Mernepthah, shows marked Negroid traits.

The Black Israelites (Jews), more than 99% of whom must live in the same slums where African-American Christians and Moslems, as well as other Black African-American traditionalist religious groups, reside, find themselves totally dependent upon the outside Talmudic (European-American) Jewish community for their religious regalias, food, clothing, literature and all other wherewithal necessary to maintain a proper religious home and community, and of course religious center of worship (synagouge or temple). The main cause for this dependency is plain old economics. A factor which Talmudic community European-American Jewery no longer have to worry about, since they manufacture what they need in most of

---

* See BLACK MAN OF THE NILE, by Yosef ben-Jochannan, for chronology of Pharoah Mernepthah rule over the Haribus (Jews).

these lines. They also kill and preserve the meat they eat; even though non-Jews do handle Kosher foods and meats prior to, and after, their preparation, a condition which the Beta Israel (Children of the House of Israel), also called Black Jews and/or Falasha, of Ethiopia, East Africa, would never tolerate.[41]

When speaking about the "Falashas" (Falasa)[42] of Gondar Province in northern Ethiopia, East Africa, it must be remembered that very few of them reside in the United States of America. That the vast majority of the African-American Jewish community claimed their origin from them, which is no less valid than the European and European-American Jews claim of their origin from Hebrews that once occupied the "Promise Land" more than three-thousand years ago.[43] However, that which is most significant in this matter is the infrequent contacts currently between the two African Hebrew (Jewish) groups. Again, one must face up to the hard realities of the time that cause this separation, capital (money). The result of said capital need is that there is 85 to 90% more contact between the European-American (White) Jews and their fellow African (Black) Jews (Falashas) than between African-American (Black) Israelites (Jews). The net gain is on the side of the White Jews, who through such organizations as Hadassah and others, religiously oriented and philanthropic, sponsor "Falasha" youngsters to visit and live in Kibutzim*[44] in Israel. This means that the Falashas contacts with European and European-American Jewry are on the rise; whereas, in the case of their own direct descendants, the Black Israelites (Jews) in America, such contacts are on the decline, in some cases almost non-existent.

* Communal farms and other such oriented economic projects.

174

What do these new contacts between Falashas and their White
Jewish brothers and sisters of Talmudic Judaism in the United
States of America mean to their poorer Black fellow American
Jews (Israelites)? It has many varied meanings; the worst of which
is the fact that the White Jews can turn their head toward northern
Ethiopia to help the Black Jews there; yet the same group of
White Jews remain blind to the needs of the Black Jewish communities throughout the United States of America, all of whom are in
front of their own White Jewish community backyard.[45] One could
have readily seen the same pattern of behaviour in the civil war
debate between the supporters of the central government of Nigeria
and those who supported the breakaway Eastern Province that renamed itself "Biafra."[46] In this issue there seemed to have
been complete agreement and harmony by the powers that be within
the hierarchy of European-American(White) Judaism, Christendom
(Roman Catholicism and Protestantism), and other White sects
against the alleged "crime of genocide the Nigerian race is committing against the Ibo race of Biafra."[47] This same combination
of men and women "of good will" have failed miserably to marshal
their forces of red-blooded patriotic European-Americans, "new
left" and "old left" - including "old" and "new" right, against
genocide and slavery in the ancient Empire of Monomotapa (called
disgracefully the "Republic of South Africa) by their fellow Whites.
They, having conveniently forgotten that the land called "Union of
South Africa," now "Republic of South Africa," was also, and still
is, the empire that once included what is today called "Mozambique,
Angola (Ngola), and Rhodesia (Zimbabwe);[48] and secession there is
not encouraged by them. Moreover, they have also failed to see

the starving African-Americans, their own fellow Black Jews and
Black Christians - also Black Muslims, of the "Biafras" within
the United States of America.[49] They seem only to become aware
of the American-type "Biafras" whenever their synagogues, temples,
churches, and other real and personal estates go up in flames from
riots by their own Black "Ibos" of the Harlems of America, all
of which result in capital losses of at least 20% or more of the
face value of their insured investments in such real and personal
properties in the "Biafran" communities in the so-called "Black
ghettoes." Of course, this figure does not take into account the
high non-taxable profit from said real estate investments which
they had already extricated from the Black (Jewish, Muslim, Christian, and others) communities of the Harlem-type "Biafras" for generation after generation without ever investing one solitary dol-
lar in the rebuilding of said communities. Yet, said profits can
turn up in Israel, Rome, England, Ireland, and all other countries
in Europe, but never in Africa. And when African-Americans (Blacks,
Jews, Christians, Muslims, and others) suggest that monies be sent
to their fellow Africans in Africa all sorts of window-dressing
"Negro Leaders" could be found to condemn said activities as "racist in kind." This type of behavior was best dramatized when said
"Negro Leaders" were hailed before the American public to decry
"Black Studies programs" and "KiSwahili" language courses; at the
same time these "Negro Leaders" conveniently forgot to challenge
other area studies and the teaching of "Hebrew, Galic, Italian,
German, and many other languages. They should have noted that there
are less people who use these languages than those using Swahili.
Of course these "Negro Leaders" proved their own need to take
176

"Black Studies," since they do not know that there are more than fourteen (14) African nations, with more than one-hundred million Africans in which KiSwahili is spoken; and in one (the Republic of Tanzania, with a population of more than ten times that of Israel) Swahili is the "Official National Language." And of course they should have known that Judaism had its literary beginnings in Africa - along the banks of the Blue and White Nile - in Egypt and Ethiopia.* These facts are to be remembered, if this chapter is to be meaningful at present.

The American Black Israelites (Black Jews), wanting to be as their brother and sister African Israelites (Black Jews, Falashas, Beta Israel), experienced that they cannot have their "animal sacrifices" on Pesach (Passover), Yom Kippur (Day of Atonement), and Rosh Hashana (New Year); neither Mikvahs (ritual baths for cleansing); nor the exclusion of non-Jews from their communities after "Sundown" (night fall). Equally forbidden is their raising of "the first male lamb from its mother for the sacrifice"; and maintain the separateness of the Kahen (Cohen) - priest - and Levi (theologians and scribes) from the rest of their faithful. They cannot bake their matzah (unleavened bread) on stones from the heat of the sun;[50] instead, they found that they too must follow the customs of their European and European-American Talmudic Jewish brothers and sisters of the faith - who have also abandoned most of these traditions within the Torah (Five Books of Moses) for "modern" European and European-American culture and Judaeo-Christianity - including its racism and religious bigotry.

How can the Black Jews in the United States of America follow the Third Book of Moses, where it is commanded:[51]

* See Genesis and Exodus (First and Second Books of The Hebrew Torah (the Christian Old Testament) for documentation of this fact.

177

3 "If a man's offering is a sacrifice of peace offering, if he offers an animal from the herd, male or female, he shall offer it without blemish before the LORD. 2And he shall lay his hand upon the head of his offering and kill it at the door of the tent of meeting; and Aaron's sons the priests shall throw the blood against the altar round about. 3And from the sacrifice of the peace offering, as an offering by fire to the LORD, he shall offer the fat covering the entrails and all the fat that is on the entrails, 4 and the two kidneys with the fat that is on them at the loins, and the appendage of the liver which he shall take away with the kidneys. 5 Then Aaron's sons shall burn it on the altar upon the burnt offering, which is upon the wood on the fire; it is an offering by fire, a pleasing odor to the LORD.

6 "If his offering for a sacrifice of peace offering to the LORD is an animal from the flock, male or female, he shall offer it without blemish. 7 If he offers a lamb for his offering, then he shall offer it before the LORD, 8 laying his hand upon the head of his offering and killing it before the tent of meeting; and Aaron's sons shall throw its blood against the altar round about. 9 Then from the sacrifice of the peace offering as an offering by fire to the LORD he shall offer its fat, the fat tail entire, taking it away close by the backbone, and the fat that covers the entrails, and all the fat that is on the entrails, 10 and the two kidneys with the fat that is on them at the loins, and the appendage of the liver which he shall take away with the kidneys. 11And the priest shall burn it on the altar as food offered by fire to the LORD.

12 "If his offering is a goat, then he shall offer it before the LORD, 13 and lay his hand upon its head, and kill it before the tent of meeting; and the sons of Aaron shall throw its blood against the altar round about. 14 Then he shall offer from it, as his offering for an offering by fire to the LORD, the fat covering the entrails, and all the fat that is on the entrails, 15 and the two kidneys with the fat that is on them at the loins, and the appendage of the liver which he shall take away with the kidneys. 16And the priest shall burn them on the altar as food offered by fire for a pleasing odor. All fat is the LORD's. 17 It shall be a perpetual statute throughout your generations, in all your dwelling places, that you eat neither fat nor blood."

They cannot fulfill their obligations of "burnt offering" either; as the God of Abraham, Isaac, and Jacob commanded[52] - according to the following recordings in their fellow Black Jews, Moses, Torah:

4 And the LORD said to Moses, 2 "Say to the people of Israel, If any one sins unwittingly in any of the things which the LORD has commanded not to be done, and does any one of them, 3 if it is the anointed priest who sins, thus bringing guilt on the people, then let him offer for the sin which he has committed a young bull without blemish to the LORD for a sin offering. 4 He shall bring the bull to the door of the tent of meeting before the LORD, and lay his hand on the head of the bull, and kill the bull before the LORD. 5And the anointed priest shall take some of the blood of the bull and bring it to the tent of meeting; 6 and the priest shall dip his finger in the blood and sprinkle part of the blood seven times before the LORD in front of the veil of the sanctuary. 7And the priest shall put some of the blood on the horns of the altar of fragrant incense before the LORD which is in the tent of meeting, and the rest of the blood of the bull he shall pour out at the base of the altar of burnt offering which is at the door of the tent of meeting. 8And all the fat of the bull of the sin offering he shall take from it, the fat that covers the entrails and all the fat that is on the entrails, 9 and the two kidneys with the fat that is on them at the loins, and the appendage of the liver which he shall take away with the kidneys 10 (just as these are taken from the ox of the sacrifice of the peace offerings), and the priest shall burn them upon the altar of burnt offering. 11 But the skin of the bull and all its flesh, with its head, its legs, its entrails, and its dung, 12 the whole bull he shall carry forth outside the camp to a clean place, where the ashes are poured out, and shall burn it on a fire of wood; where the ashes are poured out it shall be burned.

These ancient traditions, which are still "commanded" of Jews (Black, White, Yellow, Red, Brown, and others) everywhere, are still being followed by the Falashas. They should have held the same significance among the Black Israelites (African-American Jews) in the United States of America, who have surrendered traditional African Hebrewism (Judaism) for the economic convenience of European-American-type Talumudic Judaism.

As the Falashas "eat meat with milk together," but do not "boil the meat in its mother's milk," so should have the African-American Israelites maintained their custom and not succumbed to the Europeanization of this basic law in the Torah and adopt the Talmudic interpretation of European and European-American Jews of not eating "meat with milk," a prohibition that is no where entered in any of the Five Books of Moses. The nearest prohibition of its kind in the Book of Leviticus (Third Book of Moses) bares heavily on the difference between the Talmud and Talmudic Judaism of Europe and the United States of America against traditional Torah Hebrewism of East Africa.[53]

The major problem of the African-American Israelites, who have aligned themselves with the traditional Hebrews of Ethiopia on a religious basis, also for political reasons, is the inability of their being able to finance any meaningful exchange programs between themselves and their fellow religious brothers and sisters at home in East Africa. If they could borrow money for this type of operation they fear that the programs would be co-opted by the lenders, who would be more than likely European-American Jews; as it is believed that the White Jews would not cooperate in any project which will tend to make known the existence of Black Jews throughout the "Western World," which this project would certainly accomplish.

Religion and economics by necessity are partners, equally as much as religion and government. Because of the marriage between these two most powerful forces over the behavior of mankind, the vast majority of those who differ with either must be ready to take on the other. Black Hebrewism finds itself outside of the marriage between government and religion; therefore, it is also never there when the BRISK (circumcision) of the new born is performed. If it is not present with the cutting of the cake, it cannot compete. If it cannot compete, it must either join the bride or bridegroom, or slowly die. Sorry to say that the latter is the present course taken by the Black Hebrews in the United States of America. White Talmudic Judaism can save it. But, why should this be? What is there to be gained by the Talmudists by so doing? Black Judaism does not offer any aid to the present State of Israel – neither cultural, spiritual or economic; nor does it support Talmudic Judaism in the United States of America in its current alarm against what it chooses to call "Negro anti-Semitism"; which anyone is subject to be called if he or she disagrees with any action taken by the State of Israel, or any Jewish organization or person trying to continue domination over "Negro organizations" or individuals, especially in the so-called "civil rights movement."

The isolation and refusal of the Black "Jews" to make themselves heard in the present struggle for African-American culture and identity in the United States of America will yet prove to be the death-knell of Black Judaism – as it hides away and hopes to emerge smelling like a rose – untouched and unscared. The "Black Jews" will be remembered by other Black Americans (Christians, Muslims, and traditional African religions such as Voodoo, Damballah Ouedo, etc.) who now need the help of every Black Israelite today, but receive it not. Black Israelites are too busy proving their "Hebrewness" (which needs no proof to anyone but themselves) to their "White Israelite" brothers and sisters; as such the struggle passes them by.

Today, when leaders of the African-American (Black) Muslim, Christian, and traditional African religious communities are speaking out against injustices directed against Black people in general, the Black Israelites remain conspicuously silent by their absence from the arena of conflict. This is even true when the interest of the Black Israelites in the United States of America is directly threatened. Why should this be? Are there no young leaders amongst them who feel the need for Black "Jewish" involvement in the present enertia of social and economic events of the day? These are but two of the very pertinent questions being asked of the Black Israelites (Jews) in the United States of America, especially those in New York City, New York, and in other major cities of the northeastern part of this nation.

The impact of Black Judaism on the overall Black community should, and could, have been one of leadership. This opportunity was theirs, as it was the Nation of Islam (the so-called "Black Muslims"), but their "chosen people's"[54] obsession and attitude (similar to that of their sister and brother White Jews) have stopped them from freely intermingling with their fellow Blacks of other religions, solely on the basis of their own religious intolerance and bigotry. The net result is that the vast majority within the Black community is shocked to even hear that there are Black Jews in the United States of America, except the occasional Sammy Davis type converts, and naturally, the same charge that:
"...the Jews killed Christ...," etc.[55]
is leveled at them by their Black Christian and Muslim neighbors,

just as it is among the Whites, when they find out. Of course, Black Jews cannot claim "anti-Semitism" in such cases, as do their White counterparts. Why? Because European-American (White) Jews can be "Semitic" (Shemitic) or "Caucasian" (White) whenever, or where-ever, the situation warrants. On the otherhand, African-American (Black) Jews are ruled out from "Semitism" in "Western" circles, meaning that they are not considered to be the descendants of Noah's eldest son - Shem.[56] But, strangely enough, the First Book of Moses (Genesis) disagrees with those who will prefer to make Judaism a racist sect to satisfy their own personal Anglo-Saxon and/or Greek-centric prejudice. Thus, it is written:[57]

10 These are the generations of the sons of Noah, Shem, Ham, and Ja'pheth; sons were born to them after the flood.
2 The sons of Ja'pheth: Gō'mer, Ma'gog, Mad'ai, Ja'van, Tu'bal, Me'shech, and Ti'ras. 3 The sons of Gō'mer: Ash'ke·naz, Ri'phath, and Tō·gär'mah. 4 The sons of Ja'van: E·li'shah, Tär'shish, Kit'tim, and Do'dà-nim. 5 From these the coastland peoples spread. These are the sons of Ja'pheth[n] in their lands, each with his own language, by their families, in their nations.
6 The sons of Ham: Cush, Egypt, Put, and Canaan. 7 The sons of Cush: Se'ba, Hav'i·lah, Sab'tah, Rä'a·mah, and Sab'te·ca. The sons of Raamah: Sheba and De'dan. 8 Cush became the father of Nimrod; he was the first on earth to be a mighty man. 9 He was a mighty hunter before the LORD; therefore it is said, "Like Nimrod a mighty hunter before the LORD." 10 The beginning of his kingdom was Ba'bel,

E'rech, and Ac'cad, all of them in the land of Shi'när. 11 From that land he went into Assyria, and built Nin'e·veh, Re·hō'both-Ir, Ca'läh, and 12 Re'sen between Nin'e·veh and Ca'läh; that is the great city. 13 Egypt became the father of Lu'dim, An'a·mim, Le·ha'bim, Naph'tu·him, 14 Path·ru'sim, Cas·lu'him (whence came the Philistines). and Caph'tō·rim.
15 Canaan became the father of Si'don his first-born, and Heth, 16 and the Jeb'u·sites, the Am'ō·rites, the Gir'gà·shites, 17 the Hi'vites, the Ark'ites, the Si'nites, 18 the Ar'và·dites, the Zem'à·rites, and the Ha'mà·thites. Afterward the families of the Canaanites spread abroad. 19And the territory of the Canaanites extended from Si'don, in the direction of Ge'rär, as far as Gä'zà, and in the direction of Sod'ōm, Gō·mor'räh, Ad'mäh, and Ze·boi'im, as far as La'shà. 20 These are the sons of Ham, by their families, their languages, their lands, and their nations.

Who is that brilliant that he, or she, can now, after more than three-thousand years, separate the sons of Ham from those of Shem, if the above recorded history from the Torah is "true." Here it is seen that there was a merger of the three families of the "sons of Noah." That"Cush"(Kush or Ethiopia) and"Egypt" (Sais) are as much a part of the Hebrew peoples as those of Palestine (Israel or Canaan), having the same grandparents. The Hebrew (Jewish) Torah ends this story in support of the contention being put forward herein. Thus:[58]

> 32 These are the families of the sons of Noah,
> according to their genealogies, in their nations;
> and from these the nations spread abroad on the
> earth after the flood.

If the Kushites (Ethiopians, sons of Cush or Kush), Egyptians (sons of Egypt), and the Punts (Somalians, sons of Punt or
Put) are the grand-descendants of Ham, and Ham is the "second
son of Noah, then it stands to reason that the Africans, at least
of Egypt, Ethiopia and the Somalias, are as much Jewish as the
Talmudic Jews of Europe, Israel and the Americas - the so-called
"sons of Shem" or "Semites."

It must be remembered that the marriage between Moses and
his "Cushite wife", which most White Jews would prefer not to remember, it would seem, also deny the theory of a separate "Semitic race" resulting from his offsprings.[59] Thus, it is written
in one of the Five Books of Moses (Torah):

12 Miriam and Aaron spoke against Moses because of the Cushite woman whom he had married, for he had married a Cushite woman; 2 and they said, "Has the LORD indeed spoken only through Moses? Has he not spoken through us also?" And the LORD heard it. 3 Now the man Moses was very meek, more than all men that were on the face of the earth. 4And suddenly the LORD said to Moses and to Aaron and Miriam, "Come out, you three, to the tent of meeting." And the three of them came out. 5And the LORD came down in a pillar of cloud, servant Moses; he is entrusted with all my house. 8 With him I speak mouth to mouth, clearly, and not in dark speech; and he beholds the form of the LORD. Why then were you not afraid to speak against my servant Moses?" 9 And the anger of the LORD was kindled against them, and he departed; 10 and when the cloud removed from over the tent, behold, Miriam was leprous, as white as snow. And Aaron turned towards Miriam, and behold, she was leprous. 11And Aaron said to Moses, "Oh, my lord, do not punish us because we have done foolishly and have sinned. 12 Let her not be as one dead, of whom the flesh is half consumed when he comes out of his mother's womb." 13And Moses cried to the LORD, "Heal her, O God, I beseech thee." 14 But the LORD said to Moses, "If her father had but spit in her face, should she not be shamed and stood at the door of the tent, and called Aaron and Miriam; and they both came forward. 6And he said, "Hear my words: If there is a prophet among you, I the LORD make myself known to him in a vision, I speak with him in a dream. 7 Not so with my seven days? Let her be shut up outside the camp seven days, and after that she may be brought in again." 15 So Miriam was shut up outside the camp seven days; and the people did not set out on the march till Miriam was brought in again. 16After that the people set out from Hazeroth, and encamped in the wilderness of Par'an.

Professor Elliot Smith in his book, HUMAN HISTORY, supports
the above biblical chapter in the following remarks:[59a]

"Every kind of intermingling has taken place

183

between the original groups of the Negro, Hamitic and Semitic peoples."

Furthermore, is it to be assumed that the children of Moses with his Cushite (Ethiopian) wife did not continue the genealogical heritage of their mother's father and mother - descendants of Ham? Or the line of their father's father and mother - descendants of Shem? According to this genealogical background, these major biblical characters were all close relatives to each other up to the time when Moses was alleged to have made the Passover (Pesach) from the western Nile Delta to Sinai in the East, allegedly by the way of the Red Sea. They were all African Hebrews (Haribus) in Egypt (Sais) at the period of THE EXODUS.

Much of the religious history which one generally refers for clarification is based upon the Hebrew Torah - the Law (11,1,1, 11), the Oral Law (folklore, traditonal mythology, etc.) is meant. This body of Laws started as a set of explnations and expansions of a much more ancient body of written Laws. Each of them was supposed to have been "received by Moses from (his) God on Mount Sinai." Were they not the men of the "The Great Synagogue," all 120 of them - composed of prophets and teachers during the time of Ezra, who actually wrote the Torah (Five Books of Moses)? As such, one should recall the episode dealing with "...Jehovah giving the Law." Thus, the Great Synagogue scholars wrote:

> "Moses received the Law at Mount Sinai and committed it to Joshua...,"

who then passed it on to the elders; the elders passed it on to the prophets; and the prophets finally handed it on to the "Great Synagogue." From this basic foundation "Rabbinic Literature" and "Rabbinic Judaism" got their start. This occurred a few hundred

184

years before the event of Helenistic Judaism[60] - as shown in the Second Book of Maccabees, which indicates an origin of Second Century B.C.E. Pharisaic kinds of piety. However, out of the Great Synagouge came the three major principles of its order: (1) Raise up many deciples, (2) Build a protective fence around the Law, **and (3), Be** deliberate in all your judgments. But, Simeon ("the just"), a member of the Great Synagouge during its decline, stated that its main function was to make certain that everyone knew the "three main things" that were responsible for the world: "The Law," meaning the "Ten Commandments, "the Temple Service," and "the Deeds of loving kindness."

The question of authority among "the sages" of early Judaism arose long before European-style Talmudic Judaism, however. This could be best seen in the debate that took place between the factions of Judaism led by Beth Hillel and Beth Shammai over what could or could not be done on "Festival Days." For example, In <u>Eduyoth</u>, it is said that:

> "The school of Shammai adopted the more lenient;
> and the school of Shammai the more stringent,
> on the issue of whether or not an egg laid on a
> Festival Day may be eaten."

The school of Shammai also held that:

> "...a man may not divorce his wife unless he was
> found unchastity in her."

The school of Hillel held that:

> "...he may divorce her even if she spoiled a
> dish for him."

These two schools of Rabbinical scholars were almost diametrically opposed to each other's interpretation on almost every rule or law in the Torah (Five Books of Moses), the Oral Law and the Written Law.

185

Another prime example of how the observance of Jewish Law
and Customs has changed is seen in Rabban Johanan ben-Zakkai's[61]
changing the carrying of the:

> "...Lulab for seven days in the Temple, but in the
> provinces one day only..."

before the destruction of the Temple to only:

> "...seven days in memory of the Temple...."

But the rebuilding of the Temple was completed in 70 C.E., at
which time he had reconstituted the Sanhedrin, at Jebneh, with
changes as he saw fit. Is one to assume that Rabban Johanan remembered everything in the Torah that was destroyed by the Romans,
along with the Temple?[62] Or, that the scholars he used did not
enter their own opinions as to what they felt were ncessary to
be changed and/or updated?

Any further examples of how European-American-style Judaism
grew in terms of its literature, dogmas, and taboos would not change
the present Black and White Jewish situation within these communities of the United States of America. These citations are primarily
to show that Judaism has always had its deviationists that continuously disagreed with the many teachings in the Torah, and later on
the Talmud (an interpretation of the Torah, called "official") -
which itself suffered many revisions. They also support the reasons
why African-American Judaism need not follow the same standards
established by European-American Judaism; as there is no standard
interpretation of Judaism that applies to all of the Jews of the
world except the Basic Five Books of Moses(Torah), and these are,
and were, subjected to many translations and interpretations - including the Babylonian to European Talmuds. Even in Israel today those

who call themselves "Orthodox Jews" cannot agree with others on certain interpretations of religious law to meet Twentieth Century C.E. living conditions.

The dispute between factions in Judaism took on racial overtones many thousands of years later. This was only natural, because the European Rabbinate was as much a part of European co-colonial expansionists' thinking as was their fellow Europeans of the Christian clergy. With colonial expansion racism also spread. In this regards M. Fishburg was moved to write in his book, THE JEW,[63] the following:

> The white Jews keep aloof and do not associate with their (black) co-religionists. Such persons also have a Jewish physiognomy, which is so specific that one would be inclined to believe that they are of mixed blood, were they not so cruelly maltreated by their white co-religionists and treated as black Jews.

"Such persons" were the Black (Cochin) Jews of India, who very much fit the description of the "Jewish people" cited by Ratzel in his book, HISTORY OF MANKIND.[64] He wrote:

> The entire Semitic and Hamitic population of Africa has ... a mulatto character which extends to the Semites outside of Africa.

The reverse of the Black-White confrontations in Judaism is further cited in Suyuti's, HISTORY OF THE CALYPHS.[65] With respect to the false prophet "Moses." He wrote:

> A Negro who pretended to the gift of prophecy was brought before al-Mamun (the Caliph) and said: 'I am Moses, the son of Imram,' and al-Mamun said to him, 'Verily, Moses the son of Imram drew forth his hand from his bosom white, therefore, draw forth thy hand white that I may believe thee.'

The above analogy cited in Suyuti's book has been found in many recordings with reference to Noah and the Ark drama in the First Book of Moses - Genesis, Chapter 9, Verses 20-28, where references

187

are made to "...Ham...staring at his uncle's nakedness...,"
etc. This Calvinistic theory, as stated before in this work, is
that"...the curse placed on Ham by God..." (Yahweh, Ywh or Yvh)**
in which "...Ham turned from white...," supposedly, "...to black."
Of course the Semitic and Hamitic dialogue that manipulates the
present racist thinking in Judaism, Christianity, and Islam is
very carefully avoided by the Calvinist Christian sects of late.
At this juncture one should refer to Note 64 of this Chapter, page
188 for Ratzel's contention on this major point; for in it lies
the explanation for much of the current indifference existing
between White Jews and Black American Jews ("Negro" Jews excluded).*
Behind this background one should also comprehend the current
drama being staged by the refusal of the European-American (White)
Rabbinates to recognize any of the African-American (Black) Rabbinates, which in reality should not be of surprise to anyone, since
such action on their part appears to be nothing more, or less, than
what happened in their own intra-sectual inability to set their own
house in order. The Rabbinates' squabble has, therefore, also
produced wings and sects in Judaism entitled..."ORTHODOX, CONSER-
VATIVE, REFORM, RECONSTRUCTION, JEWISH SCIENCE," etc.

Is Judaism (European, European-American, African, African-American, Asian, Asian-American, etc.) pluralistic or monistic in its development as it stands today? This question is of major significance.
From the evidence so far revealed, it is without any doubt whatsoever pluralistic in origin and development. In this regard, it has,

---

* Among the Black Jews, or Israelites, the term "NEGRO" has always
been rejected; it is, to them, degrading and contemptible.
** The Hebrew, not "Jewish," word for God. Generally the word
"Adoni" is substituted for Yahweh in Hebrew religious services,
except in very special passages of the Torah.

from its African beginnings and development in Sais (Egypt), even through its Hellenistic (European) transformation and re-identification with Greek mythology and dominant Christian influences, changed. It also made changes due to its accommodation of the slave-trading experiences it had with European-style Christianity. There were other major changes caused by the "Spanish Inquisition"[66] and Nazi genocide.[67] Of course, in its present semi-power structure status here in the United States of America, it continues the maintenance of its pluralistic experiences. But, as much as anyone may try to show the "Europeanness" or "Caucasianness" of Jewish pluralism, just so much its "Africanness" or Blackness," "Asianness," or Brownness" will equally come to the surface. The latter point is best highlighted in the following citation by Sir T. W. Arnold:[68]

> "According to Mohammedan tradition Moses was a
> black man as may be seen from the following pass-
> age in the Koran, 'Now draw thy hand close to thy
> side; it shall come forth white but unhurt' –
> another sign (XX,23). 'Then he drew forth his hand
> and lo! it was white to the beholders. The nobles
> of Pharoah said, "Verily this is an expert enchant-
> er." (VII, 105-06.'"

The social, political, and economic status of the Black Jews in the United States of America is in fact below that of their fellow African-Americans of the Christian faith, and to a greater extent of their fellow Black brothers and sisters of the Nation of Islam (misnomered "Black Muslims"). In the case of the African-Americans in the Nation of Islam, their social status has been greatly enhanced, because of their successful efforts toward economic independence within the capitalistic structure of the United States of America, while others await an economic revolution for the establishment of socialism. This they have done through

189

an alignment with the existing forces that are willing to back what is today called "BLACK CAPITALISM" and the "BLACK CAPITALIST SCHOOL OF THOUGHT," currently being adopted among certain former "civil rights" organization leaders, most of them who formerly looked for social acceptance of Blacks, whom they called "Negroes," as the solution to the Black Man's problems, forgetting that it is money (capital) which makes the United States of America move, no Judaism, Christianity, or Judaeo-Christianity - all of which one tends to fool himself in believing.

Was it not Terentius Afer (Terrance the African), an ex-slave, who wrote the classic statement:

"Homo sum humanii nihil a me alienum puto."
(I am a man and nothing human is alien to me)

Was he not the one the ancients called..."the greatest of the Latin stylists?" Was he not the only one of his era who had written six plays? And like General Hannibal Barca (a fellow indigenous African Black man who crossed the northern half of the Italian Peninsula with 100,000 indigenous African troops for twenty long years), he too is not mentioned in textbooks of the United States of America as being of indigenous African origin; nor was he described as having "woolly hair, thick lips, and a jet black complexion" - as indicated on the legal tender (coins)[69] used in Carthage during Hannibal's era. In fact, was it not the mother of Clitus Afer (Clitus the African) Dropsica, whose son Alexander "the great" made King of Bactria, who nursed Alexander as an infant, but was not shown as a Black woman; nor her son as a Black man.*[70]

---

* The name "Clitus Niger" (Clitus of the Niger) was erroneously recorded by certain Western historians as "Clitus the Negro"; but they have utterly failed to justify the use of the word "Negro."

190

The above revelations were not upset by the fact that an
Ethiopian empress, who allegedly gave birth to a"White child" and
blamed the statue of the Virgin Mary for it, stating that she

"...happened to look at the" (White) "statue during
the time of my conception...,[71]

as so many "Western" educators have used this piece of African
mythology as an indication of the ...."Ethiopians desire to be
White, and **have rejected all possibilities of their "Negro heritage."**
This type of propaganda, malicious and vindictive as it obviously is, still serves to create the required conflict between many
Ethiopians and other Africans, also African-Americans, over the
issue.

The reasons for race and religious bigotry probably will never end. Because of this, maybe it is best not to expect to see a
Jewish community in the United States of America which would be
any less corrupt by racial and religious bigotry than any **other**
European-American (White) community or institution. For this culture, the United States of America, appears to be incapable of
working towards the Commandment that recite:

"Thou shall love thy neighbour as thyself,"[72]

muchless achieving it. These suppositions are not imaginary; they
are as real as the fact that Pietro Olonzo Nino, captain of Cristobal Colon's flag-ship Santa Maria, was the first known African
to arrive in the "New World" (the Americas). Because they are so
real,mankind in the United States of America finds itself unable
to live harmoniously in intra-group relationships, much **less groups.**
The suppression of such historical facts are indicative of the
reason why Black Jews (Israelites) must still live separated from
their White counterparts; the Black Muslims from the White Moslems,

191

and Black Christians, also, from their White brethren. Even the
Ethical Culture Society, Bahai, Jehovah Witnesses, Unitarians,
and other professed "liberal" religious institutions are totally
dominated in their leadership by European-Americans (Whites),
but have just enough Blacks in choice positions, mostly public
relations, where they can be seen and very little heard from,
and with no real power, which is more often than not called "to-
kenism." But the less sophisticated Black brothers and sisters,
the so-called "irresponsibles," still call it "Uncle Tomism" and
"house Nigger action."[73]

The role of the Black Rabbinate today is one of ostracism,
however. It is neither "Uncle Tomish" nor "house Niggerish"; because it has failed to do or say anything whatsoever during this
challenging phase of the "Black Experience "[74] taking place all
over the United States of America, and all other areas of the
world, today. The end result is that Black Christians and Muslims
feel that their Black Israelite (Jewish) brothers and sisters are
waiting perched on their fence to see how this "cultural revolution" will end - with the intent of joining the "winner " or "sur-
vivor," of which there may not be any.

It is extremely pathetic that there is no Black Jewish leadership in the clergy, or the laity, which could have become a
sort of mediator between Black Christian and Muslim communities
and the White Jewish community over the inflammatory issue of
"community control in the Black neighborhoods."[75] For it is in
reality the issue of "community control in Black communities,"
the same as it is in White communities, that brings on the over-
reactionary cry of "Negro anti-Semitism."[76] This is not to say

192

that to the less informed and frightened European-American Jews
that the over-emphasized..."anti-Jewish feelings among Negroes"
is not on the upswing, of which some Jews hysterically claimed
has reached"proportions of Hitler's Nazi Germany." But, when the
righteous outcry has subsided, maybe everyone will stop to consider that within European-American-style Christianity, itself,
the basic elements of "anti-Semitism" can be found grounded in
the Easter Services and birthed in the Passion Drama of Good Friday.[77] It is during this period of each succeeding year that the
rehearsal about the

"...the Jews killed Christ"[78]

is most echoed. And, of course, no one should expect Black Christians, who were forced by armed violence centuries ago into European and European-American (White)-style and type Christian control culture and religion, to be less "anti-Semitic" than their
former European and European-American slavemasters' descendants
and teachers;[79] this is no less reasonable than to expect White
Jews to be less racist or religiously bigoted against Black people
than their White Christian and Moslem brothers and sisters.

Strangely enough, "anti-Semitism can be easily charged to many
Africa-American (Black) Jewish groups here in the United States of
America. This is, providing that only European and European-American (White) Jews are to be designated by the mythological term "Semitic" (the descendants of the mythical "SHEM"), a term which tends
to indicate all of the descendants of Noah were not related to the
same original Haribu (Jew, Hebrew) - Abraham.[80] If, on the otherhand, the African-American Jews (Israelites) prove incapable of
breaking out from their own "wall around the Law, [81] then Black

193

Israelism (Judaism) in the United States of America is doomed to a much more miserable future than it appears to be heading towards at present.[82]

This work will of necessity provoke all sorts of angry denounciations, maybe; but, would the facts to countervail this be forth-coming also? One must now ask: Is it not time for the African-American (Black) Israelites to make themselves known, seen, and felt in the Black peoples struggle for survival as African people?

This writer could not think of any better words in which to close this Chapter than those in the first paragraph of Chapter One in the BOOK OF JUDAISM,[83] as follows:

THE FACT OF THE COVENANT

God's initial covenant with Abraham was with the head of a family, and the Jewish people was conceived as the ever-increasing number of his descendants. Hence to this day, the convert to Judaism is not only accepted into the faith; the ritual prescribes that he be adopted into the family as a child of Abraham. The covenant with Moses is a new and wider one, with a people as a whole. This is symbolized by the "new name" by which God makes Himself known.

194

BILAL: AFRICAN INFLUENCE
ON ISLAM

(Chapter Four)

Within the past ten years, or more, there has been a definite increase of African-Americans converting to Islam and Islamic-type religions. In so doing, many have begun referring to themselves as ...."ASIATIC BLACK PEOPLE." Without entering into the political or social aspects of this declaration it must be noted, however, that the term "Asiatic" is in itself semantically a European colonialist word, having the same stereotype connotations as the word "Nigger."[1] The correct nomenclature should be "ASIAN;" which is the name established by the people indigenous to the continent they called "ASIA."[2]

Those African-Americans (Blacks) who recently rushed to claim Islam and "Arabic heritage" in their struggle to rid themselves of"Judaeo-Christian religious enslavement"[2a] obviously indicate a complete lack of knowledge of the history of the Jihads (Holy Wars) Islam brought to Africa from the year 640 C.E. (18AH), and in East Africa from the 12th century C.E. Included in this sordid epoch was the Arabs rape of western and central Africa in the 18th and 19th centuries.[3] They have forgotten, if they ever knew, that chattel slavery of a type unheard of before in the history of Africa was first introduced by Islamic Arabs from the Arabian Peninsula[4] over two-hundred (200) years before the equally notorious European Christian slavers in the early 16th century C.E. And, that Africans,by the millions, were captured, kidnapped,and shipped off like cattle to Saudi-Arabia and Persia to become slaves for their

Arabian and Persian Moslem (Muslim) overlords and slavemasters.[5]
Is the history of slavery by the Arabs against the indigenous
African peoples of the entire central and southeastern coastline
of Africa (which the Arabs and Persians renamed "ZENJABAR" –
during their invasions and colonizations of the area) to be
ignored? Truly all of this took place before the arrival of the
first Europeans, the Portuguese, in the area of the late half of
the 15th century C.E. in search of food and trade. But the period
of this part of the Arab history of atrocity against the Africans
cannot be overlooked, or ignored. Not for one moment. This
cannot be, for the height of this drama was the fact of the
Islamic Arabs' imposition of slavery on the African people. Yet
the descendants of the same African people, who are the new converts to Islam, want each and every Black man, woman, and child
to embrace one of their former slavemasters' religion in their
flight from their present day "slavemasters." The Kongo (Congo),
originally BoKongo and ManiKongo, was introduced to chattel slavery
by the Moslem Arabs. This act weakened the Congolese peoples to
the point that it was possible for colonizers Henry Morton Stanley
and King Leopold II of Belgium (two of the world's worst masters
of genocide) to use the excuse of "...Arab slavery in the Congo..."
before the lilly-white Berlin Conference of 1884-1885 C.E. to
justify their own establishment of a much more brutal system of
depopulation against these African peoples – such as the world
had never witnessed before, and has never seen since.[7] This was a
period of the extermination of the Africans by Europeans and
European-Americans that made Adolph Hitler's Nazi Germany's
record of genocide against the Jews of Europe a minor act by
comparison.
196

Like Judaism and Christianity (the grandmother and mother of Islam), Africans were involved in Islam's creation, nevertheless. But, the Moslem Arabs, also, have been for some time recently teaching a sort of religious history in which the indigenous Africans find themselves omitted from the historical role they played in Islam's origin. They are also excluded from the highest posts of the administration of Islam in Mecca, which they had traditionally held from the beginning of Islam with the Prophet Mohamet, and Hadzart Bilal ibn Rahab* - "the first treasurer and head of the Nation of Islam," besides being "the first Muezzin."

Islam was to be no better than Judaism and Christianity, as its modern administrators attempted to eliminate its indigenous African founders from the eyes and ears of the faithful, and the world in general. But history, written history, once more acted in her own equating way, and mannerism, as it clamoured, once again, for Islam's indigenous African originators.[8]

If one is to read of the greatest pilgrimage (hajj) ever made to Mecca, the Moslems' (Muslims) Holy City, it would be discovered that, here too, it was an indigenous African, his name - Mansa (King, Sultan, Emperor, or Kan Kan, etc.) Musa, the most noted monarch of one of Africa's greatest West Coast nations - the Melle (Mali) Empire (138-1488 C.E., or 616-866AH).[9] But one would probably ask: Why did this African Emperor pay such homage to an Asian religion and God, Islam and Allah? The answer lies in the origin of Islam, itself, in Arabia during the turn of the 7th century of the Christian Era (C.E.), as cited in the following paragraph.

Around the year 610 or 612 C.E. (12 or 14 BH) a wealthy Arab merchant (formerly an impoverished camel driver), named Mohamet,

---

* Bilal was born in Ethiopia, East Africa, where he was captured by Arab slavers and carried off to Mecca before the birth of Islam in 622 C.E., or AH-1 ("The Year of the Hejira").

claimed to have spoken to "...an angel of Allah" (the Moslems'
or Muslims' God).[10] This mythological "revelation," like those
which the prophets and biblical actors of Judaism and Christianity were also reported to have experienced, was to develop into
the most powerful colonial **expeditions to conquer the world**
and its peoples.[11] But among those who felt the wrath of this "new
religion" first were the ones it destroyed most; namely, the indigenous Africans of the area the Arab invaders and zealous religious missionaries labelled "Bilal-as-Sudan" (the land of the
Blacks).[12] Let it be, then, made very clear, at this juncture,
that this Arabic name referred to the entire continent of Africa
(Alkebu-lan) and not the exclusively called "French Soudan, as
the Arabs had names for every regional area of Bilal-as-Sudan;
such as "al-Mhagred" for the Northwest, and "Zenj Bar" for the
East Coast.[13]

What is the African background behind this "new religious
force"? Who were some of its indigenous African co-founders? Why
was it necessary for them to abandon Judaism, Christianity, traditional indigenous African religions or other indigenous Asian
religions of the Arabian Peninsula for this "new faith"? These
are but a few of the major questions one would ask in order to
become **intelligently knowledgeable** of the vast majority of its
faithful, the same as it is with the faithful of Judaism and
Christianity. This is presently true, because Islam (the name of
the "new religion") is absent of the day-to-day practical religious applications necessary and required in the indigenous religions of most of the African peoples who have succumbed to its
teachings for one reason or another.

198

The name of the Ethiopian ("Abyssinian," according to the Arabs), Hadzart Bilal ibn Rahab, who was serving in Arabia as a slave when "...Mohamet got his call..." may not mean much to most non-Moslems or Muslims.* Yet, this African (who is only listed as "Bilal" in the Moslems' Holy Book, the Qur'an or Koran) was the very first Muezzin (High Priest,or Caller of the Faithful) and Treasurer of Islam (Mohammedan Empire). He was, also, the first "soul" (man) Mohamet is said to have converted, while Mohamet himself was still a camel driver and hardly anyone wanted to listen to him and his "...strange teachings and foreign ideologies."[14]

Bilal's first contact with Mohamet followed his own capture in his native East Africa, Ethiopia (Abyssinia) - according to the Arabs' own history of his enslavement in Mecca, Arabia. His slave-master was Omeyya, whom he was forced to kill later on. But Bilal was only one of the many hundreds of thousands of indigenous Africans from the East Coast of Africa (Zenj Bar) that were held in slavery in Arabia and Persia during the year 600 C.E. (22 BH)** when he became acquainted with the "camel driver" - Mohamet, who was later on to marry a very wealthy widow and gain recognition of the faithful as "...the only Prophet sent by Allah"(God) "since Abraham and Jesus Christ."[15] It is to be noted that Moses, as in the Hebrew religion, is not listed as a Prophet in Islam.

Bilal, the former African slave, was responsible for the creation of much of what Moslems, past and present, believe about "Paradise" (Heaven), also of many of their first original prayers and doctrines. For example: He was the one who established the

*The conflict over the use of the words "Moslem" and "Muslim" is as heated as between"African-American" and "Afro-American" today.
* BH = Before the Hegira. AH = After the Hegira.

concept of the "TABA," the wonderful "TREE OF LIFE," which takes:

> "the swiftest horse in Islam at least 150 years to cross its shade" (branch span).

The..."Tree of Life"..., Bilal said:

> "...is laden with every kind of the best things to eat, and bends its branches at the slightest request of the righteous."16

What is beginning to unfold here - perhaps another St. Augustine? In point of fact it is the life of a philosopher and diviner, a man whose vision of the "Nether World" ("Next Life," or "Paradise") offers to every depressed and lowly outcast male of Islam the greatest hopes for - "...food, the better life, freedom from want..."; and most of all, "...carnal love" infinitum (forever).

The last, "carnal intercourse," the greatest offer Islam's "Paradise" (equal to the Christians' "Heaven" and Hebrews' "Hereafter") holds for its faithful males, is just the opposite of St. Augustine's (the greatest Christian moralist) doctrine on the issue. For St. Augustine saw "virtuosity" through the male and female's physical "virginity" before marriage as being a prerequisite for entering the Kingdom of Heaven of his God - Jesus Christ. He saw "carnal love" as a slave's necessity for procreation, and nothing more. And he associated "carnal intercourse" for the sheer pleasure it gives with the "major sins."17 Unlike St. Augustine, however, Bilal saw "carnal love" as the height of gratification on earth; and its reward in heaven - Paradise - he assured for the faithful males of Islam, only. Thus, a basic difference between the "Heaven" of the Christians and the "Paradise" of the Moslems he had established, which remains moot in Judaism's "Hereafter."

Bilal promised the faithful "Hur-al-Oyum" (Black-eyed daughters of Paradise; African virgins), who were the prize of the en-

200

tire Arabian world. But the earthly "Black-eyed daughters," during and before Mohamet and Bilal's lifetime, had already become
the mothers of many Sultans (Kings and Emperors) of Arabia, just
as many of them are today. Bilal wrote the following about them:

> They have beautiful, well-rounded bodies,
> fresh with the eternal youth and virginity
> that is constantly renewed.18

One can clearly see that Bilal (the former Ethiopian Koptic
Christian) may have been manipulating the same people (Arabs and
Persians) who had once held him in contempt as an "African slave."
For he knew their greatest weakness at that era, their appearent-
ly unquenchable thirst for the indigenous African "Black-eyed
daughters." Thus, one sees this African diviner, philosopher, and
assistant-prophet completing his carnal paradise with the offer
of:

> "...seventy-two of these lustily beautiful
> creatures" (Black-eyed daughters) " are given
> to every" (Male) "believer, who himself will
> possess eternal youth and vigor."

It is quite obvious that Bilal's outline above was intended to
take care of the "seventy-two virgins", who will have their virginity ever renewed each time they completed carnal intercourse.[19]
It should be, also, obvious at this point, if it was not observed
before, that SEX WORSHIP was a basic part of Arabic culture, as
it was throughout the Middle East (Fertile Crescent) - including
Greece and Turkey in Europe. Notably, Jews and Christians also
practised SEX WORSHIP in their early religious history.

It would be hypocritically prudent for "modern" Christian and
Jewish males to say that they would not have heeded the offer of
Bilal and joined up with Mohamet, had they lived in Arabia during

201

that period, when Islam was being born. Divorce statistics of these United States of America and every other European and European-American **society should** prove Bilal's offer quite contemporary. Not only divorce records, but the so-called "census" figures on "illegitimate births" in the United States of America of the 1960's and any other year among White Jews, **Christians,**[20] and all others, will prove Bilal's "Heaven" a welcome blessing from God; any God.

There were many other philosophically interesting aspects to Bilal. One stemmed from the persecution he suffered along with Mohamet and other faithful when their religion was being steered through its infancy, all of which occured at the period when the officials in Mecca still considered Mohamet the "lowly camel driver." They had been placed repeatedly in the open and parching hot sun of the Arabian Desert, inside the vicinity of Mecca - which was later to become "the Moslems' most Holy City, to suffer the agony of third-degree sunburns. At times, their heads were held back, so that their eyes could be exposed to the sun's rays. After this, they were **wetted down** - just **enough** to keep them alive for the next sunbake.[21] These were only a few of the many methods of torture to which they were subjected.

The punishment the Prophet Mohamet and his small band of Koreish people, of whom he was one, along with Bilal and other ex-slaves, suffered, was due to their attempt to convert their fellow men from the "...worship of idols..." and the acceptance of the foreign ideology of a worship of "One God" whom the authorities could not 'see, feel or hear.' It must be remembered, however, that "idol worship" is only charged to non-Moslems, non-Jews, and

202

non-Christians, all of whom are also classified as "pagans." Of course the "idols" being worshipped in all three of the so-called "Western Religions" (Judaism, Christianity,and Islam) are not considered by their adherents to serve the purpose of "worship"; theirs being only "symbols of the faith." This answer is good, however, only to the person who is being served by such an explanation; for the leaders of the three "Western Religions'" **followers** often charge each other with "practicing idolotry,"[22] among other "sins."

Sir William Muir, in his book, LIFE OF MOHAMET, London, 1894, wrote the following about Bilal's strength in the "new religion" (Islam) he developed and helped to create and expand "...in the name of Allah:"

> They were seized and imprisoned, or they were
> exposed to the scorching gravel of the valley,
> to the intense glare of the midday sun. The tor-
> ment was increased by intolerable thirst until
> the wretched sufferers hardly knew what was said.
> If under the torture they reviled Mohamet and
> acknowledged the idols of Mecca, they were re-
> freshed with draughts of water and taken to their
> homes. Bilal alone escaped the shame of recanta-
> tion. He would not yeild. In the depths of his
> anguish the persecutors could force from him but
> one cry: 'Abad! Abad! (One, only one God).

The persecution of Bilal and the small, but fanatical, group of followers of Allah, through the leadership of their Prophet Mohamet, aided Islam to become a religion which for the rest of its history cherished the "sword" and its bearer - the soldier. This experience was to make Bilal promise the soldiers of the - Islam :

> "...If a believer" (a soldier) "died in battle,
> he goes straight into the midst of the Hur-al-Oyum."[23]

It must be noted, also, that the soldiers and other male survivors

of "...battle in the cause of Allah..." were allowed the spoils
of war; which included BLACK, BLOND, GRAY, YELLOW, BLUE, and
BROWN-EYED daughters of the planet Earth. The only exception in
the surviving soldiers' booty was that they got earthly virgins
as well as non-virgins. And their earthly booty could be virgins
only once in a lifetime; whereas, the perished martyrs (soldiers
for the cause of Allah) received the "...replenishing virgins."

Another aspect of Bilal's life that influenced every Moslem's
way of life, religious belief and morality, was his calling of
the faithful, which was his role as the first Muzzin, each and
every morning at six o'clock for "...the worship of Allah." He
would cry out:

> Great is the Lord! Great is the Lord! I bear
> witness that there is no God but the Lord! I
> bear witness that Mohamet is the Prophet of God.
> Come unto prayer! Come unto salvation! God is
> great! God is great! There is no God but the
> Lord! Prayer is better than sleep! Prayer is
> better than sleep!

The above is called, the "AZAN" (Call to Prayer). To date, this
Prayer ranks as "the most beautiful of the rites " of the Moslem
religion (Islam). This custom is also known to most of the faithful as a "Command from Allah," when in fact it was only an act of
a one time lowly, tall and skinny, frizzled-hair indigenous Black
man (African) of Ethiopia, East Africa, who felt that:

> ...a man has to rise at sun up to thank Allah (God)
> for his resting in the long night and his awakening
> in the morning.

It was a custom that was new to the original followers of Mohamet,
but not Bilal. He came from a civilization in Ethiopia where it
was an established "divine rule" for the worshippers of Koptic
(Coptic) Christianity, Judaism, and other indigenous traditional

204

African religions that demanded it[23a] – including the "MYSTERIES
SUN and FIRE GODS."

Bilal's Azan (Call to Prayer) indicates, to some extent, the
depth of his zealousness in the need to profess his faith in Al'-
lah.

For the Prophet Mohamet, Bilal had another Azan, which begins
as follows:

"To prayer! Oh Apostle (or Prophet) of Allah.
But it was Bilal alone who led the Prophet and all of his
faithful in prayer to Allah. This he did, even during the period
when Mohamet became the most revered personage within the Arabian
Peninsula and the Persian world;[24] which he continued long after
Mohamet's death.

Along with his duties as Muezzin and Treasurer of Islam, Mohamet also left Bilal to take charge of all foreign diplomats and
other visiting dignitaries that came to Mecca.* The fact is that
Bilal administered Islam all through Mohamet's lifetime – as the
"select Prophet of Allah." Bilal also continued to lead Islam after Mohamet's death, even though the official religious title of
leadership went to Mohamet's most faithful and trusted general,
Abu Bekr. For Mohamet, while lying on his death bed, had beseech-
ed Bilal to become his successor, Bilal having yielded to Abu
Bekr. It was not strange, then, that Omar "the Great," the successor to Abu Bekr, also continued the aging Bilal as leader-in-
fact, while he, like Mohamet and Abu Bekr, conducted the expan-
_____
* Besides being the Holy City of the Islamic World, Mecca was also the capital of the entire Islamic Empire, from whence all secular power emanated through Bilal to minor officials.

sion of Islam through colonialism; which they accomplished at the
end of the sword and prayers to Allah.

To prove that Bilal was the one and only final power in Islam
after Mohamet's death, once the Caliph Omer "the Great" made General Khobab (another of Mohamet's contemporaries and most famous
of his generals) set himself on the throne. After he was seated
on the throne Omar told the general:

> There is but one man in this entire empire that
> is more worthy of the honour than you, Khobab, and
> that is our leader, Bilal.

This incident took place as a result of very serious wounds General Khobab had sustained during a battle for the expansion of
Islam, which he was displaying to Omar. Khobab had been praising
Omar for being the one person that represented Islam in the name
of the Prophet Mohamet and the God Allah - for whom he would freely surrender his own life.[25]

"Bilal is the third part of Islam" echoed the words of Omar
"the Great."[26] Quite a compliment to a man by a nation whose citizen had already spanned three continents - viz., Asia, Africa
and Europe. The insulting words:

> I will have nothing to do with this black slave...[27]

was yet to follow this compliment. But, who dared speak in this
manner of the only man alive that was responsible for the creation
of Islam itself besides Mohamet the Prophet? Most certainly, it
was not a Moslem. It was Prince Constantine, the Christian general in the service, and Chief of Staff of the Syrian army. But the
man he had insulted was the same person with whom he had to negotiate for peace, Syria having lost to the newly created Islamic Empire, and was about to be taken over by Omar "the Great's"

206

aide - General Amru. The terms of the peace, for which Syria
had sued, was to be worked out between a priest Prince Constantine had dispatched with General Amru, who would have introduced
him to Omar "the Great." But Omar, who refused to take any action
dealing with the administration of the Nation of Islam (Islamic
Empire) without Bilal's approval, insisted upon Bilal returning
with Constantine's representative (the priest). However, Prince
Constantine's priest had already tried every method at his command to avoid taking back Bilal with him, having known of Constantine's prejudice against Africans, and especially since a
large percentage of the soldiers that defeated Constantine's men
(under his personal command) were indigenous Africans in the service of the Arabians. Prince Constantine was yet to live and regret the insulting remark he made about "the second highest" human
being in Islamic history - Bilal, "second only to Mohamet the Prophet, himself alone." The exact **price Prince Constantine paid**
was shared by all of Syria's indigenous Christian population; as
Bilal, with whom Constantine was forced to negotiate the peace
treaty, imposed extremely severe economic and political penalties
on Syria; all with the approval of General Amru.[28]

Prince Constantine's rejection of Bilal, because of his black
color, was typical of European Christian behaviour by the turn of
the seventh century C.E. ,as Europeans had already taken over the
North African Church from its indigenous African (Black, "Negro")
leadership. And by this period, the Christian "fathers of the
Church" - St.Cyprian, Tertullian,and St.Augustine, who made Christianity the viable religion it had become, were already forgotten
as indigenous African figures. Christianity had become a 'European

religion.' Its universal (catholic) message was, by now, a thing of the past. But its younger rival, Islam, had become the "new universal religion" of the time. Disillusionment among the ranks of the Christians had already set in, and mass conversions to Islam had become a problem. Christendom was corrupted. It had too much of the "paganism" it once charged Rome of indulging in sinfully. And one of its prize stars, Prince Constantine, was forced to bow before the same "Black slave" (Bilal) he once refused to see, because of Bilal's color.

One can best summarize the life of Bilal with the remarks of a man whom history has credited with knowing enough to be classified "an authority on the subject." In this regards, a book entitled, LIFE AND LETTERS OF LAFCADIO HEARN, by Bisland, does the honour very well. On page 281, Volume I, Lafcadio is quoted:[29]

> "Bilal, the black Abyssinian, whose voice was the mightiest and sweetest in Islam. In those first days Bilal was persecuted as the slave of the persecuted Prophet of God. And in the 'Gulistan' it is told how he suffered. But after our Lord had departed into the chamber of Allah and the tawny horsemen of the desert had ridden from Mecca even to the gates of India, conquering and to conquer, and the young crescent of Islam, slender as a sword, had waxed into a vast moon of glory that filled the world, Bilal still lived with a wonderful health of years given unto the people of his race. But he sang only for the Caliph. And the Caliph was Omar. So one day it came to pass that the people of Damascus whither Omar had travelled on a visit begged the Caliph saying: 'O Commander of the Faithful, we pray thee that thou ask Bilal to sing the call to prayer for us even as it was taught him by our Lord Mohammed.' Now Bilal was nearly a century old, but his voice was deep and sweet as ever. And they aided him to ascend the minaret.

In dealing with the above comments by Lafcadio, one can see how it was possible for this indigenous African "great" to command as much respect as he did among the followers of Islam in his more than one-hundred (100) years of living. The fact is that Bilal lived through the entire Seventh Century C.E., having been born in the year 600 C.E. (BH22). The proof of Bilal's birth came from the following remarks by Lafcadio:

> Now Bilal was nearly a century old, but his voice
> was deep and sweet as ever.

It is rather peculiar that so many European authors have mentioned in their works the "racial" origin of Bilal, many who have failed to do likewise for similar indigenous Africans (Black, or "Negro") like St. Cyprian, Tertullian, and St. Augustine (all three "fathers of the Christian Church"). Could it be that European and European-American writers have no trouble in giving Africans credit in matters not directly connected with Europe and European-American beginnings? Or, is it to be understood that as long as Christianity remains a purely European or European-American (White) dominated religion, as presently operated and taught to be, the indigenous Africans (Blacks, or "Negroes") can be shown in their rightful place in any other religion? Of course, Judaism is also considered off-limits to any suggestion of indigenous African involvement, even though its entire religious, educational, and cultural experiences began in Africa (Egypt)[30] by indigenous Africans, Moses being the prime example.

The comparative life of St. Augustine (354-430 C.E., or BH 268-192) and that of Hadzart Bilal ibn Rahab (Bilal for short, c600-701, or BH 22 - AH 79), are in themselves proof that "Africa South of the Sahara" has produced as many scholarly indigenous Africans as "Africa North of the Sahara." But, who will see Bilal as the "Saint" and "Prophet" he was, rather than the "black face" he bore? Today, not even most of the European and European-American Moslems, misnomered "Black Muslims," would rate Bilal as such. Yet one can readily see that it was Bilal who was in fact the actual

brain behind the Prophet Mohamet's "...call by an angel of Allah."
St. Augustine, at least, got credit for being above mortal man, as
he was "beatified" by his disciples who revered him. Islam, not
having the convenience and machinery for creating "saints,"could
not so honour Bilal. Instead, to millions of Moslems,Bilal was
solely remembered as the first Muezzin - "caller of the faithful to pray."

Bilal was Islam itself. He gave it its "Paradise." He made
its rewards interesting enough to make Christians and Jews,
alike, leave their own religion and convert to Islam. He made
Mohamet the Prophet.[31] He managed Islam's treasury and built its
capital resources.

Bilal and Malcom X (al hajj Malik Shabazz) had a lot in common, so far as loyalty to a leader was concerned.[31a] In the case
of Mr. X,the Prophet he praised without question or personal interest was the Black Muslims (Nation of Islam) leader and Prophet -
Elijah Mohammed. For Bilal, it was the founder of Islam himself -
the "Holy Prophet Mohamet." But it was Bilal who established the
fundamentals of Islam; whereas, Malcom X only repeated that which
the Prophet Elijah Mohammed dictated as "...the laws" of his own
"Nation of Islam" for "...Asiatic Black men and women."[32]

History speaks of Mohamet* the Prophet of Allah and the letters he sent to the Emperor Heraclitus of Byzantium (champion of
Christendom) and King Karadh of Persia (champion of Zarathustraism
or Zoroasterism) demanding that both :

---

* It is to be noted that the Prophet of the Moslems, other than
the "Black Muslims of the United States of America, name is spelled
"MOHAMET;" not MOHAMMED. Only one person in the Moslem religion
is entitled to bear that name in that spelling, Mohamet himself.

210

"...acknowledge the One True God and serve Him."
At the same time these letters were delivered, Emperor Heraclitus
was restoring order in Syria as civil strife had already beset
the Byzantium Empire. This was during the Persian-Byzantium Battle of Mineveh in 627 C.E. (AH 5). At such time the Emperor
Herclitus had routed Chosores II; the defeat of Chosroes had
made it possible for his son, Kavadh, to overthrow his own father one year later (628 C.E., or AH 6).[33]

No mention of Heraclitus' reaction to the letters is known to
have been recorded anywhere by historians. However, there is an
abundance of materials on Kavadh tearing up his letter when he
received it at Cestiphon, and in utter anger, chasing the messenger that brought it.[34]

Who was this man that dared to challenge the world's two most
powerful monarchs during the year 629 C.E.(7AH of the Moslem Calendar)? His name, MOHAMET ("the Praiser"). Born in Mecca, or Medina, in the year 571 C.E. (BH51), he began his career as a "camel
driver," but removed himself from poverty by marrying a rich widow
whose husband was a prominent merchant of Mecca. He was an Arab
of the Quraish people* who inhabited Western Arabia at the time
of his birth. But it must be carefully mentioned that although
Mohamet's parents and other members of his immediate family were
very poor, they were at the same time very well respected, and of
very high influence among the Quraish people. As stated previously, wealth brought Mohamet leisure which in turn brought on a lust
for the mysteries of the unknown (mysticism), which he honoured
_____
* Most "Western" historians use the word "tribe" in this case. By
itself the term is correct; never-the-less its present connotation
is derogatory and is considered very offensive to Africans and Asians.

until his death at the age of sixty-one (61) in the year 632 C.E. (AH 10).

Why was Bilal so influential **on this man** who had been worshiping El Ka'aba.* How did he counteract the worship of El Ka'aba, **whom** the people of Arabia worshiped along with the Goddess Al'lat? This was extremely important, since Mohamet's family worshiped both El'Kaba and Al'lat.** The answer could be said to be "faith," that is,if one is prone to be a mystic. If not, then, the logical answer could be history. None of these answers are complete without further information and documentary support. All that is available is that they did meet. And that Bilal did lead the Prophet Mohamet in the interpretation of what Mohamet felt he believed.[35] He was very much like the Hebrew (Haribu or Jew) Joseph to the Pharoah (king) of the Mysteries of Egypt, North Africa, mentioned in the Book Of Genesis (First Book of Moses).

With the unquenchable appetite Mohamet had for poetry, of which the Qu'ran (Koran) is full, he had to create an angelic communication to justify their origin.as coming from Al'lah. This was no different than the "Ten Commandments" Moses learned in the Negative Confesssion of the Coffin Texts while a student in Sais (Egypt), which he is said to have presented the Hebrew (Jewish) people as the "...original set of Laws..." given to him "...by Yaweh (Jehovah, God) on Mount Sinai." And it does not surpass

---

*A black stone's remains from a meteorite that was imported into Arabia by the Africans of Ethiopia (Abyssinians) when they ruled Arabia and Persia, and all the way into India - to the Ganges.

**Note that the name "AL'LAT" was the origin of the later word "AL'LAH," or "SUPREME GOD."

212

Jesus Christ being placed into "his mother's (Mary) womb by an angel of God..." without the benefit of carnal intercourse with his father (Joseph), bearing in mind that there are no records which indicate anything like artificial insemination was known to the physicians of those days, and not overlooking the fact that Mary and Joseph were married for quite a long period before her "immaculate conception." In such cases, as these, one can only say that:

> All Faith is false, all Faith is True:
> Truth is the shattered mirrors strewn
> in myriad bits; while each believes
> his little bit the whole to own.*

It could be further stated that "truth" is what one wants to believe, and religion is the "crutch to sustain such belief."[35]

The "YEAR OF THE HEGIRA" 9622 C.E. or A.H. 1) was the year the Prophet Mohamet, Bilal, Abu Bekr, and their small band of faithful and fanatical followers had to flee Mecca and take refuge at the "PALM OASIS OF YATHRIB" in Medina.[36] History cited this fact as the reason why Medina became the Moslems' "SECOND HOLY CITY." This period, and date, marked the beginning of the "Year One" (1) of the Moslem Calendar. Thus A.H. 1 - "The Year One after the Hegira," or 622 C.E. At this period in history the Prophet Mohamet was already fifty-two (52) years of age. It also marked the date of the birth of the Moslems' religion, which is officially called "ISLAM." For the continent of Alkebu-lan (Africa), it was the beginning of an era which witnessed the ravaging of her peoples and territories as she had never experienced before. Africa witnessed the Arab-Moslems and their compatriots from all over the Islamic world, at that time, burning

---

* See page following dedication of this work for authorship and translator.

213

her most precious documents of thousands of years duration along the Nile Valley, the raising of her many structures that marked the beginning of man's greatest architectural and engineering achievements, and the ravaging of her "black-eyed daughters" along her Eastern, Northern, and Western sea coasts, and of course in her Center years later. Most of all, it was the beginning of an era when the entire world shook, just as it had been shaken at the birth of Judaism and Christianity. Once again mankind was subjected to another holocaust under the banner of another "ONE AND ONLY TRUE PROPHET OF GOD." In this case it was Mohamet - the former "camel driver" of the Koerish people of Arabia. He was no more, and no less, a prophet than those that preceded him in Judaism and Christianity.

The date 611 C.E. (B.H. 11), eleven years before the Hegira and the fortieth year of Mohamet's birth, seemed to have been the most logical date when Mohamet really shook the world. This was the year in which he was reported to have received "prophetic" and "messianic" visions and soul-seizures, which were so common to the Hebrew prophets he apparently modeled himself to emulate; whom Bilal taught him of.

629 C.E., or A.H. 7, was the year Mohamet returned to Mecca from Medina, where he was forced to run and hide. It marked the date when the treaty agreement between Mohamet's government he had formed with Bilal in their six years of exile at the Oasis of Yathrib, in Medina, and the government he had fled in Mecca. Between these two dates (622 - 629 C.E. or A.H. 1 - 7), however, the government in Mecca witnessed a mass conversion of its citizens from the worship of the Goddess Al'lat and El Ka'aba (the black stone meteorite from Ethiopia, East Africa). These

214

established religions for centuries' duration had represented the
moral and religious fabrics of the government in Mecca. They were
also major sources of revenue for the treasury of the government
in Mecca, as millions of the faithful of both religions came
each year to pay homage and pilgrimage to the Goddess Al'lat and
the El Ka'aba, which represented very large sums of monies coming
into the treasury each year. When the people turned to Mohamet and
his "new religion," Islam, it forced the priests in Mecca out
of business first, then ruined the economy of the city. This
was the basic reason why those with vested interests in the city's
economy, along with the priests of the established religion, had
to kill Mohamet and all of his followers of the "new religion,"
if they could.

Mohamet triumphantly returned to Mecca. He and his faithful followers of Islam (the "new religion") adopted Mecca as their
"HOLY CITY." They also adopted El Ka'aba (the Black Stone meteorite
from Ethiopia). But they completely rejected paying any further
tribute to the Goddess Al'lat, who was replaced by the God Al'lah.
This marked the end of a hectic era which saw a "...lowly camel
driver..." move up to be a "...wealthy man, mystic, and prophet."
Mohamet had successfully challenged the mightiest monarchs of his
time. Among those powerful monarchs were Karadh, King of Persia;
Constantine, Emperor of Byzantium; and Tai-Tsung, Emperor of China;
all who received Mohamet's letter demanding that they get rid of
their own "...State religion and gods, and accept the worship of
the One and only True God, Al'lah," whose prophet was Mohamet
himself. Most "Western"historians generally fail to mention that
the Emperor of Ethiopia also received one of the letters sent by
Mohamet. Like Moses and the other sages of the Hebrew and Christian

215

religions, whose techniques he aped, Mohamet also took unto himself an assortment of wives from every corner of the known world
at that period.[37] This man, who was once declared "...an obscure
bandit..." in 622 C.E. (AH 1), had also learned the secret of
"marriage of convenience," which accounts for his marriages to women
of various lands his soldiers conquered in the "name of Allah." This
procedure was successful enough to gain Mohamet the right
to construct a Mosque (Moslems' place of worship) in Canton,
China - the oldest in existence throughout the world today. Mohamet, although not successful in his attempt to set fear in Emperor Tai-Tsung, nevertheless, his messengers were allowed to
build their Mosque with financial support from the emperor.

Mohamet and Bilal proceeded from this juncture in their prophetic mission and lives to leave the world a book of religious
instructions which Mohamet claimed was:

> Divinely inspired through (his) communication with
> Allah (God).*[38]

Mohamet's "...Divine inspiration..." followed similar "in-
spirations" by Abraham and Moses of the Hebrews, Jesus Christ of
the Christians, and thousands of other prophets and Gods before
and after them, and Mohamet. In line with Mohamet's "...Divine
inspiration" the world renowned historian, H. G. Wells, in his
book, A SHORT HISTORY OF THE WORLD, wrote the following:

> Yet when the manifest defects of Mohammed's life and writings
> have been allowed for, there remains in Islam, this faith he
> imposed upon the Arabs, much power and inspiration. One is
> its uncompromising monotheism; its simple enthusiastic faith
> in the rule and fatherhood of God and its freedom from theological
> complications. Another is its complete detachment from the
> sacrificial priest and the temple. It is an entirely prophetic
> religion, proof against any possibility of relapse toward blood
> sacrifices. In the Koran the limited and ceremonial nature of
> the pilgrimage to Mecca is stated beyond the possibility of dis-
> pute, and every precaution was taken by Mohammed to prevent

---

* Words in brackets by the author of this work for clarity.

216

the deification of himself after his death. And a third element of strength lay in the insistence of Islam upon the perfect brotherhood and equality before God of all believers, whatever their colour, origin or status.

These are the things that made Islam a power in human affairs. It has been said that the true founder of the empire of Islam was not so much Mohammed as his friend and helper Abu Bekr. If Mohammed, with his shifty character, was the mind and imagination of primitive Islam, Abu Bekr was its conscience and its will. Whenever Mohammed wavered Abu Bekr sustained him. And when Mohammed died, Abu Bekr became Caliph (successor), and with the faith that moves mountains he set himself simply and sanely to organize the subjugation of the whole world to Allah.

This was the Prophet Mohamet and the faith that the indigenous African from Ethiopia (Abyssinia), Hadzart Bilal ibn Rahab, helped to become what they are in history today; yet, Wells failed to mention Bilal. But Bilal's image suffered not, as Omar "the Great" so aptly said:

Bilal is the third part of Islam. Al'lah is the first, and Mohamet the second.

There were, of course, other great men who helped to build Islam and to spread "... the words of Al'lah." They came from Asia, Africa, and Europe. But, these were the indiegnous Africans whom so many millions have carefully forgotten, or just plainly elected to ignore. This is primarily due to the fact the black color of the Africans' skin has become the sole criterion for excluding them (this major segment of mankind) from the history of Islam. Yet it was the Africans, and others of African ancestry, who were most instrumental in Islam's creation.

Among the many great Black men of African ancestry who aided in the development of Islam and to spread the name of Al'lah and the "Holy One - Mohamet," was a man of an Arab-Asian father and a Sudanese-African mother - Shakla, his name Ibrahim Al Mahdi, also nicknamed "Al-Thinnin (the Dragon)." Of this man the Arab historian Ibn Khalikan (1211 1282 C.E. or A.H. 588-659) wrote:

This prince had great talent as a singer and an able hand on musical instruments; he was also

217

> an agreeable companion at parties of pleasure.
> Being of dark complexion, which he inherited from
> his mother, Shikla, or Shakla - who was an Afric-
> an Black - he received the name At-Thinnin (the
> Dragon).
> Ibrahim was a man of great merit and a persfect
> scholar, with an open heart and a generaous hand;
> his like had never been seen among the sons of the
> Caliphs, none of whom spoke with more propriety
> and elegance, or composed verses with greater abil-
> ity....
> He was proclaimed Caliph of Bagdad ... under the
> title of Al-Mubark - the Blessed.

Unlike Bilal, Abu Bekr, Omar "the Great," Khobad, and other

faithful who served Mohamet, the Prophet, when Islam was still

in its infancy, Al-Mahdi met an Islamic Empire with borders ex-

tending to the Northwest Coast of Africa and the Southwest of

Europe along the Atlantic Ocean. At the East it stretched all the

way to India, after touching the shores of the Indian Ocean.

What was the family background of Ibrahim Al-Mahdi? He was

the son of King Shah Efrend of Southern Persia and Shakla (men-

tioned above in the quotation) - an African slave girl whom the

Caliph Mansour had captured and placed in the harem that was at-

tended by his favorite wife, Monyyah, according to the Arab hist-

orian - Abou'l Mahasim. Shah Efrend was Caliph of Bagdad and a

member of the family of the Prophet Mohamet. Mohamet's grandfath-

er was the brother of Ibrahim's great-great-grandfather; a distant

kinship, which made Ibrahim and his owm offsprings superior to all

others in the eyes of the faithful. Al-Mahdi's father's son, a

half brother named Haroun Al-Raschid, was the renowned star that

was immortalized in the world famous "ARABIAN NIGHTS' ENTERTAIN-

MENT."

Born at a time when only slaves were allowed to entertain, by

singing in public places, Ibrahim A-Mahdi broke tradition with his

poetry he read and the songs he sang in any public place he could
get the chance. He included in his repertoire many of the songs
and much of the poetry of the Koran. Such genius on Ibrahim's part
influenced his father, who had become Caliph (King) of Bagdad
shortly after Ibrahim's birth, to the point where he sanctioned
his son's singing in private gatherings among the aristocrats.
Ibrahims' reputation as a singer travelled throughout the Moslem
world, and influenced the highest and the lowest of Islam.

Ibrahim and his half-brother, Haroun, dressed up in all sorts
of disguises and frequented many places which were off-limits for
people of their status. This relationship was later disrupted when
Ibrahim was sent off to Syria to be that country's ruler. The
estrangement ended shortly when he was recalled by Haroun to make
a joint hajj (pilgrimage) with him to Mecca. Haroun, who was now
the Caliph of Bagdad, had suffered immensely from the separation
between himself and Ibrahim, therefore the recall.

Ibrahim became Caliph of Bagdad subsequent to some bloody
palace coup and other intrigues of which he was not personally involved. His half-brother, Haroun, suddenly died. At that time
Ibrahim was only thirty-six years old (790-826 C.E. or A.H. 168-
204). Haroun's son, Emin, had become Caliph of Bagdad before
his uncle Ibrahim. But Emin, a spendthrift like his uncle Ibrahim,
found his uncle a willing accomplice in frequenting gaudy places
of entertainment and ill repute. Emin's brother, Mamoun, murdered
him and then married the daughter of Riza (of the enemy anti-
Abbasides) in a wedding that cost more than $5,000,000. Mamoun
later on named his wife to succeed him. Mamoun then left his
throne for an expedition. While Mamoun was away the Abbasides

seized the throne, for fear of Riza's daughter (the Princess)
and her people would have seized it themselves. Ibrahim's brother,
Mansour, was offered the throne, which he promptly refused, fear-
ing that he too would have suffered the same fate of Emin. Ibrahim was then besought to take the throne, which he consented after
refusing it at least three different times.

Ibrahim Al-Mahdi's elevation to Caliph of Bagdad brought him
face to face with all of the cultural and political problems of
his era, being that he was at this time the ruler of Islam - "the
new religion" (the most powerful empire on earth). He tried to meet
his obligations head on by first trying to eliminate poverty among
his people, rather than seeking to expand Islam, as all others
before him did. But he soon fell back into his insatiable love for
freedom and music - to which he had reduced his poetry. Thus, he
allowed favorites in the palace to run ministries of which they
had neither knowledge nor experience whatsoever, except that they
were loyal Moslems; all of which resulted in draining the treasury
to the point where "the soldiers of Allah" (the Moslems' God) could
not be paid their salaries.

Ibrahim's soldiers were in revolt. One of his chief generals,
Sehl, had turned traitor, leaving Ibrahim without defense to face
his well financed and fully militarily supplied nephew, Mamoun, who
was set on a course of recapturing the throne of Bagdad -
whence his wife and daughter were overthrown during his absence.
Facing this situation with no possible solution in sight Ibrahim -
lonely and a deserted man - fled for his life. Ibrahim was captured
as he tried to escape the city disguised as a poor old woman. He
was trapped because of his betrayal by a group of slaves, one of
whom Ibrahim had so sincerely tried to help when he first became
220

Caliph. The slave-woman that recognized him had revealed his disguise to Mamoun's soldiers. She pointed him out in order to receive the ransom offered by Mamoun; not because of loyalty. Arrested and jailed, Ibrahim was held for months awaiting Mamoun's (who had retaken the throne) decision. Mamoun's delay was due to the popularity of Ibrahim among the rich and poor people of Bagdad. If Mamoun had taken a chance on putting him to death, it could have caused civil war in Bagdad. One has to remember that Mamoun, himself, was not too very well liked by the vast majority of the people because he killed his own brother before he was overthrown, and also, becuase Ibrahim was Mamoun's uncle. Any attempt at killing Ibrahim would have made Mamoun a double killer on the throne, a condition which the people may not have accepted at that time. Ibrahim's wife was allowed to commence pleading his case successfully enough for Ibrahim, later, to complete his own defense. In defending himself, which he selected to do in the best manner he knew, through his poetry and songs which were later to become basic verses in the Koran (Moslems' Bible), he wrote the following:

> Prince of Believers, may Al'lah grant thee His mercy and benedictions!

The chained and shackled Ibrahim cried out while he knelt on the floor in front of his nephew, Mamoun. To this poetic plea Mamoun replied:

> I reject thy salutation as Al'lah will reject and excommunicate all traitors as thou.

In his poetic command of his language, even though facing a heartless Caliph, Mamoun, Ibrahim again responded:

> Gentle Sire, Sovereign power excludes hate. Those who pardon approach nearer to Al'lah.

Mamoun again rejected Ibrahims' pleading, saying:

> There are two in whose rights I must surely condemn thee...

221

This he said, while pointing toward his two sons with his head bowed in sorrow.

This drama, as detailed above, continued to the climax where Ibrahim's poetry touched Mamoun when he countered:

> Commander of the Faithful if it were only a
> question of politics or the state, this step
> would be wise, but Al'lah permits your Majesty
> to be merciful without danger because he has
> given the power that defies all attacks.

Touched by it all, Mamoun commanded his Grand Vizier to free his uncle Ibrahim and to fit him with all he needed for a long journey. The fitting included twelve camels loaded down with gifts from Mamoun and well wishers of the palace. He was also given a royal escort to accompany him to his old palace. All who aided Ibrahim when he was attempting to escape from Mamoun were forgiven; and instead of being punished, they were rewarded with gifts for so doing. The slave woman, who turned in Ibrahim, feared the worst. She was ordered, by Mamoun, to receive "one-hundred lashes," and to be imprisoned for the rest of her natural life." As he passed sentence upon her the Caliph, Mamoun, said:

> ...you had neither child nor husband, hence your
> wrong was not due to need.

Her wrong, he saw, was for the ransom, not to help in securing the throne for him - Mamoun.

Was Mamoun really the pious Caliph he was pretending to be? Not at all so. He hounded his uncle - Ibrahim - by having him constantly reminded by paid traitors who would ask Ibrahim:

> Art thou not the Black* Caliph Ibrahim...?

Ibrahim, in his poetic brilliance, would respond:

> Though I be a slave, my soul - through its noble
> nature is free. Yes, my body is black and
> mind clear.

---

* Some European-American historians have changed the work "black" to "Negro." However, the word "Negro" was unknown to the Arabs of the period in question; the Portuguese had not yet created it.

The insults to the greatest poet Arabia and the Islamic world have ever produced continued to the point where his nephew, the Caliph Mamoun, once piously noted:

> Uncle a jest of mine has put you in a serious mood. Blackness of skin cannot degrade an ingenious mind, or lessen the worth of the scholar of the wit. Let darkness claim the color of your body; I claim as mine your fair and candid soul.

For those who claim that:

"...color prejudice has never been a problem in Islam,"

Mamoun's words should dispel such notion. For even Bilal, Islam's "second highest personality," second only to the Prophet Mohamet, was discriminated against by the Arabs because of his BLACK SKIN. The color question had become universal very early during the Christian Era; at which time Europeans were wrestling control of the world and Christendom from the North Africans and the Arabs, all of which started shortly after the death of St Augustine (the African "father of the Church") in 430 C.E. (AH 192). It will be further seen, in the following quotations, that RACE and COLOR PREJUDICE were already prevalent in Islam before Ibrahim Al-Mahdi's birth.

The prose that won total repect for Ibrahim by his nephew, the Caliph of Bagdad - Mamoun, follows:

> Stream, flowing lightly and freely, someone has hindered thy course, and thy waters no longer flow free;
> Bird, which once flew freely in air, thou art a captive afar from the path that leads to the source.

A few of Ibrahim's greatest works of prose and poetry follow two comments on himself by others. The first by the nobleman and religious sage - Ahmed Daoud; and the other by the Arab historian and master astronomer - Mohammed:

First

Up to the time of hearing Prince Ibrahim I had
denied the effect that song could produce and
more than once I had expressed this opinion before the Caliph, himself, but after hearing him,
I felt myself forced to stop any criticism.

Second

For several years I have been one of those
previléged to attend the private affairs of the
Caliphs Mamoun and Moutassem, and this is what
I have noticed: as soon as the voice of Ibrahim
was heard, the people in the palace, and especially the valets, slaves, and laborers would
drop their work to listen to him. As soon as
another commenced to sing they would resume
their tasks without wishing to listen.

The following are sone of the works of poetry and songs the

aged Ibrahim Al-Mahdi wrote while at the palace court of his ne-

phew Mamoun - Caliph of Bagdad. Quoting another poet, he wrote:

Though I be a slave my soul, through its noble
nature, is free; though my body be black, my mind
is fair.

The following is a song he composed for his nephew, Mamoun,

in the presence of other royalty:

In describing the beauty of my beloved, I dream
of the pure gold in the coins of the ancient
Egyptians,
Of the pearl in its shell in the depths of the
sea, which is the dispair of the fisher,
Or of the exquisite fineness of the gold that
the gilder puts on the leaves of a book.

Al-Madhi, angered by his lover - Dinak, composed the follow-

ing poetry and song:

Cursed creature, thou art the mistress of the human race.
Wouldst thou have all the men in the world as love-
ers?
In mixing thou the fat with the lean, dost not thy
rise with disgust?

Ibrahim's poetry became a part of Islam's religious works.

224

The Caliphs (Divine Ones) of Bagdad, from the time of Ibrahim's nephew, Mamoun's rule,"made Al-Mahdi's songs and poetry required readings for (many) religious and secular functions." This custom became standard practice in many other Moslem countries.[39]

Ibrahim's defiance of the written rule, which prohibited **members** of the royal family of Moslem courts from singing in public places as entertainers, brought forward many serious challengers to his own reputation as "Islam's greatest singer and poet." One such competitor was his chief rival - Ishak, whose father - Moussoli - also competed at the court for the honour and large fortune it had begun to earn its performers.

Ishak and his father, Moussoli, performed with great distinction and acclaim throughout Islam. But Ibrahim's greater popularity came as the result of his diversion from the traditional style in his religious compositions, methods of recitation, also his uniqueness in religious singing. This creativity made Ibrahim catch the ears of everyone who had the opportunity to listen to his concerts.

The extent to which Ibrahim carried his creative genius and freedom from traditions in his art was shown in the two lines of one of the songs he composed while he was still Caliph of Bagdad:

> I am the Caliph (King) and the son of a king
> What it pleases me to sing, I sing.

It is quite elementary to question if Ibrahim sang whatever he felt like singing when he was forced to abdicate his throne to his returning nephew, Mamoun, for whom he had worked when he wrote his greatest poetry.

One must concede that Ibrahim had all kinds of reasons to

produce excellent works; whereas his competitors, Ishak and Moussoli, did not. He was always being pushed by one incident that
resulted from the time when he was Caliph, which required him to
compose poems and songs to combat them - while at the same instance not revealing his interference in politics. Any such
dedication on the part of his nephew, the Caliph Mamoun, would
have meant the difference between life and death for Ibrahim.

Once showing his superiority over his greatest rival - Ishak,
Ibrahim challenged him to a contest of religious singing and playing of instruments. Ibrahim began by singing in the traditional
religious chant and strumming on a string instrument, knowing all
very well that the contest would appear extremely close. But as the
tension rose he upped the wager; and of course Ishak and his
backers responded. Ibrahim, immediately after began singing in
a tone similar to the range of his instrument, then one octave
higher; then changing completely to a "chord grave," and ended at
a "bass octave." He had covered a range of four octaves, which
was the equivalent of three registers - tenor, baritone and bass.
The contest was over before Ishak had a chance to open his mouth
again. He and his backers knowing very well that with all the
effort and courage he could have drawn upon, he would not be able
to do any of the unusual feats of his competitor. This was the
end to the competitions between Ibrahim and all of his former
rivals.

While in his sixtieth year Ibrahim was able to turn to political poems and songs, a far cry from religion and love. This turn
was due to his aged life, at which time he had become obsessed with
the distress of war and poverty. However, the invasion of Syria by
Theophilus of Greece in 850 C.E. (AH228) gave him the excuse he
226

needed. The following poem he wrote in protest to the war was the first he composed and presented to the reigning Caliph. In it he included all of his genius in the first line, as he invoked his religious calling:

> "Al'lah, love, pity and compassion, hatred and ex-
>   treme patriotism."

This poem, and song, which he sang in his presentation to the Caliph's court,became the firey song that rallied his people against the invading Greeks. He wrote:

> Oh, anger of Al'lah, thou hast seen this horrible
>   spectacle, avenge, therefore the female victims.
> As to the men, they have found a glorious death,
>   perhaps a just punishment for their sins.
> But what of the innocent women and children?

Once again a song had whipped a nation of people into sufficient frenzy that it helped to overwhelm the enemy; this time it was the Babassies against the high-tailing Greeks.

The end of Ibrahim's career should have been in all its glory. But this man of African origin had a fellow poet call him "AT-THINNIN" (The Dragon) in one of his poems, a fact Ibrahim could not forget. He knew that it was his black color and huge frame which brought on the unkind comment. Yet, he could not overcome it.

The end of Ibrahim Al-Mahdi's career began closing in as he confessed his misgivings over the amount of wasteful things he had done in his lifetime, and the fact that he allowed himself to become Caliph. This brought on a request from a close friend who suggested that he burn all of his manuscripts that dealt with the useless parts of his youthful career. To this, Ibrahim responded with all the force his failing voice could summon:

227

> Fool thou art, what should I do with Charayah.
> Ought I to burn her too? She knows all my songs
>   by heart.

"Charayah" was Ibrahim's lifetime friend and disciple. She
had nourished him all through his victories and his defeats. She
was the inspiration for many of his poems on love he
wrote during all of his youthful life.

> In the art of Sound, Ibrahim was one of the most
> instructed men of his time. In singing, in rhythm,
> and in playing the stringed instrument, he excelled
> over all. The religious prejudices of his day and his
> royal birth at no time left him free to develop his
> rare gifts.

The above comment is the manner in which the noted Arab historian, Isfahani, spoke of Ibrahim Al-Mahdi (Islam's greatest
songster, poet and Caliph of Bagdad) in his masterful work, HA-
HANI'S BOOK OF SONGS.

All of the other outstanding Arabs of African descent and the
indigenous Africans who influenced Islamic religion and culture
are too numerous to mention in this work, as they could not possibly
receive the proper treatment necessary to detail their contributions. Never-the-less, a few of the most outstanding are hereby
noted as follow:

Ibn Suraidj, who introduced the Persian Lute into Islamic religious music in Mecca, was "Islam's Master Essayist." He was a
friend of the Caliph and composer of elegies in honour of him.
G. Palgrave in his book, ESSAYS ON THE EASTERN QUESTION, best
described Ibn Suraidj in the following remarks:[40]

> Ebn Soreyj, the Mario of Hejaz singers;
> his dusky and irregular features half-hidden
> by a veil betray his mulatto origin; he is
> known everywhere as the first musician; the
> sprightliest born-singer; and the ugliest
> face of the day.

Ibn Suraidj died during the year 724 C.E. (AH 102). His date
of birth is obscure. For further details on him, one should read
the ENCYCLOPEDIA OF ISLAM.[41]

Next was the man called "LORD OF THE GOLDEN AGE OF ARAB (Islamic) LITERATURE" - Al-Jahiz (778-868 C.E. or AH 156-246). He
was also acclaimed:

> The most genial writer of the age, if not Arabic
> literature, and the founder of the Arab prose
> style, was the grandson of a black*slave, Amr Ben
> Bahr; known as Al-Jahiz ("the Goggle-Eyed").

The above quotation on Al-Jahiz was taken from H. A. R. Gibbs,'
ARABIC LITERATURE.

According to P. K. Hitti's, HISTORY OF THE ARABS, Al-Jahiz was
described in the following manner:[43]

> An early representative of the zoological and
> anthropological sciences was Abu-Uthman ibn Bahr
> al-Jahiz... whose Kitab-al-Hawaya... contains
> germs of later theories of evolution, adaptation,
> and animal psychology. Al-Jahiz knew how to obtain
> ammonia from animal offal by dry distillation. His
> influence over later zoologists... is manifest.
> But the influence of Al-Jahiz as a radical theolog-
> ian and a man of letters is greater. He...was one
> of the most productive and frequently quoted schol-
> ars in Arabic literature. His originality, wit,
> satire, and learning, made him widely known.

Al-Jahiz was a native of Barza, Asia Minor, where he was a
student of the noted Arab professor (of African descent) and an-
Nassam, Mu'tazlite. Under this man Al-Jahiz studied science, philosophy, and psychology. He also rose to found his own school
which is still called today..."THE JAHIZITE PHILOSOPHY." From this
humble beginning he was to produce the following major literary
works of world fame:

---

* Gibbs used the word "NEGRO" here. This is incorrect; the Arabs
of this period did not know of this word, which is European in
origin. It was manufactured by the Portuguese in 17th Cty. C.E.

THE MERIT OF THE TURKS.
THE SUPERIORITY OF SPEECH OVER SILENCE.
IN PRAISE OF MERCHANTS AND DISPRAISE OF OFFICIALS.
THE SUPERIORITY IN THE GLORY OF THE BLACK RACE
    OVER THE WHITE.
THE BOOK OF ELOQUENCE AND RHETORIC.
THE BOOK OF ANIMALS, Vols. I - VII.

Many "Western" writers consider the last seven volumes of Ibrahim

work to be his greatest contribution to world literature. This is,

of course, subject to individual acceptance and interest. Quite

a few of his other works are considered to be equally great,

or greater, depending upon the critic.

In his book, KITAB al-SUDAN WAL'BIDAN (The Superiority in Glory

of the Black*Race over the White) Al-Jahiz wrote the following:[44]

> Loqman, whose writings are well-known and who
> was called "The Wise" by Mohamet in the Koran were
> followed by others. There were also Said ibn Jubair,
> a very pious man, highly esteemed for his profound
> knowledge of the traditions of the Prophet, Mohamet;
> the Ethiopian, Bilal, of whom Caliph Omar, said that
> he, alone was worth a third of all Islam; Afga, the
> first to die in the Holy Wars of the Prophet; El-
> Migdad, the first to fight in the Holy War as a horse-
> man; El Wanshi, who killed the false prophet, Musaili-
> ma; and Julaibib, who died in battle after valiantly
> killing seven men, and who was buried with the Pro-
> phet's own hand.
> There were also Faraj, the barber-surgeon, who was
> so just that he was often called by the judges for
> counsel; and El-Haiqutan, the poet. When the White
> poet, Jarir, saw El-Haiqutan in a white robe on a
> feast day, he remarked, "He looks like the penis of
> a donkey wrapped in white paper." El-Haiqutan re-
> plied to him in a poem in which he said, "Though my
> hair is wooly and my skin black as coal I am gener-
> ous and my honour shines. My color does not prevent
> my being valiant with my sword in battle. Know, you
> who would boast of your petty glory that the race of
> Blacks is more glorious than your race because the
> Ethiopian Emperor after meeting the Whites, accepted
> Islam instead...."

Al-Jahiz was writing in reference to Loqman (Lochman) - "The

---

* Note that the direct translation of the word with reference to
people of African origin in Arabic is "BLACK;" not "Negro;" as so
many European-American writers continue to use.

230

Wise," who was mentioned by the Prophet Mohamet in the Koran with Zenj (Zengh) and other indigenous Africans whom he felt surpassed any European of which he heard.

Al-Jahiz continued later on in the same work by noting the following:[46]

> We (Africans or Blacks) have conquered the country of the Arabs as far as Mecca and have governed them. We defeated Dhu Nowas (Jewish ruler of Yemen) and killed all the Himyarite princes, but you, White people, have never conquered our country. Our people, the Zenghs (Blacks of Africa's East Coast) revolted forty times in the Euphrates, driving the inhabitants from their homes and making Obollah a bath of blood.
>
> Everyone knows that the Blacks are amongst the most generous of mortals - a quality that is found only among noble characters. Blacks are distinguished amongst other peoples by their natural gift for rythmic dancing and the best artists on the drum, all of this without any special training. They are also the best singers.
>
> Their language is the easiest to pronounce. They are eloquent, are able to express themselves in a lively manner, and have no stutterers. It happens sometimes that Black orators speak before their kings from morning till sunset without need for a pause.
>
> Blacks are physically stronger than no matter what other people. A single one of them can lift stones of greater weight and carry burdens such as several Whites could not lift nor carry between them.
>
> They are brave, strong, and generous as witness their nobility and general lack of wickedness. They are always gay, smiling, and optimistic, all of which are signs of their honesty and frank nature. There are, however, those who interpret these qualities as marks of a feeble mind or a calculating one. But this would be equivalent to saying that the most intelligent people and the most gifted are the most avaricious and the most callous.
>
> The Blacks say to the Arabs, 'A sign of your barbarity is that when you were pagans you considered us your equals as regards the women of your race. After your conversion to Islam, however, you thought otherwise. Despite this the deserts swarm with the number of our men who married your women and who became chiefs and defended you against your enemies.

Note that the Loqman mentioned on page 226 was called "Aesop" by the Greeks and other Europeans. He was a native of Ethiopia, East Africa, and was called "The man black as coal." He spent most of his life in Sais (Egypt), where he died. He visited Greece for a a very short period of time.

You even have sayings in your language which
vaunt the deeds of our kings - deeds which you
often placed above your own, this you would not
have done had you not considered them superior
to your own.

J. A. Rogers, in his book, WORLD'S GREAT MEN OF COLOR, Vol.

II, stated that:

The Negro,* Akym ibn Akym, was more eloquent than
Eli-Ajjaj. It is from him that the Syrians learnt
the sciences and also from El Montagi ibn Nabham,
who was a native of Negroland*and had a pierced ear.
He had come to the Arabian desert as a child and
left it with a complete knowledge of Arabic.

With reference to Mohamet's (the Prophet) Black wife, he wrote

with regards to comments about her made by Bilal:

The Blacks can be also proud of the fact that the
single dead person over whom the Prophet every pray-
ed was their ruler, the Emperor of Ethiopia. And
whilst the Prophet was in Medina and the tomb of the
Emperor in Ethiopia. It was also this Ethiopian ruler
who married Omm Habiba, daughter of Abu Sofyan, to the
Prophet.
We, say the Africans frighten the enemy by our blackness even as night is more fearful than day. Wooly hair,
too, is the finest and strongest. Black is superior.
Black cows are considered the best and to have the most
durable hides for leather. The same is equally true of
black donkeys. Black sheep gives the creamiest milk.
Mountains and stones are harder the blacker they are.
The black lion is irresistible. Black dates are the
sweetest....Black ebony is the most solid and the most
durable of woods. The blackest hair is the most beautiful and in Paradise everyone will have black hair. The
pupils of the eye, too, are black and are they not the
most precious part of the human body?

He went ahead to desribe the Prophet Mohamet's **Black**

(African) ancestry, as he wrote:

The ten sons of Abd el Mottalib (the grandfather
of Mohamet) were all black and strong; so was Ab-
dallah ibn Abbas, Mohamet's cousin. The members of
the family of Abu Talib (a relation of Mohamet and

---

* The words "NEGRO" and "NEGROLAND" were frequently used by Rogers,
himself of African origin - from Jamaica in the Caribbeans.

the father of the Sultan Ali), were all more or
less black in color.

He went on to identify the Black peoples of the world. He said:

> The Blacks also have the sweetest breath and
> the greatest amount of saliva being in this re-
> spect like the dog as compared with other animals.
> As we said the Blacks are more numerous than the
> Whites since they are made up of Ethiopians, the
> Fezzans, Berbers, Copts, Nubians, Faghwans, the
> people of Meroe, Ceylon, India, Quamar and Indo-
> China.
> The isles between Africa and China are all
> peopled with Blacks, that is Ceylon, Kalah, Zabig.
> Most of the Arabs also are as black as we, the
> Africans are, and cannot be counted amongst the
> Whites. As for the Hindus they are even darker
> than the Arab....
> The Copts (natives of Egypt) are also a black
> race. Abraham wished to have a child by one of
> their race and thus Ishmael, the ancestor of the
> Arabs, was born. The Prophet Mohamet also had a
> child by Mary the Copt.
> If a black skin is thought unsightly what then
> must be said of the French, the Greeks, and the
> Slavs with their thin, red, straight hair and
> beard? The paleness of their eyelids and their
> lips appear to us, Africans, very ugly.... God
> did not make us black in order that we should be
> ugly; our color comes from the sun. The proof of
> this is that among the Arabs are also black tribes
> as the Beni Solaim ibn Mansour. These Greek slaves
> whose offsprings in the third generation become as
> black as the Beni Solaim because of the climate.

Al-Jahiz compared the role of the Europeans in his country,

during his lifetime,with the Africans as he continued:

> One hardly ever finds a Greek or a Khorassan
> in a position of trust in a bank. When the bank-
> ers of Basra (Jahiz' birthplace) saw the excel-
> lent affairs that Faraj Abu Kub, a Black, had ne-
> gotiated for his master, each of them took an
> African assistant. Caliph (Sultan) Abdelmalik
> ibn Merwan often said, "El Adgham is a master
> among all the Orientals. This El Adgham is also
> mentioned by Abdullah ibn Khazim, who calls him,
> 'An Ethiopian, a black son of Ethiopia.
> This concludes our essay on the Glory of the
> Black Race.

J. A. Rogers, WORLD'S GREAT MEN OF COLOR, page 95, Volume I,
states the following about Al-Jahiz and the use of the word"Negro."

It must also be noted that when Jahiz refers
to Negroes* he is speaking principally of those
in Africa and the first generation of Africans
living in Arabia, and that when he speaks of
whites he is also including Arabian-born mulattoes.
An Arab, near-white, or mulattoe, and even black,
was inclined to look down on the incoming blacks
from Africa and to consider them inferior much as
a Northern Negro is inclined to consider himself
superior to a Southern one or a white or a black
city-dweller does someone from the country.

Note that "Western" historians use the word "NEGRO" wherever

"African" now appears in the above quotation. The English text,

translated from the original Arabic work by Al-Jahiz, to which

Rogers refers, may satisfy Rogers and many other "Negro" writers,

and of course European-Americans (Whites), but the word "Negro"

was never used by anyone during the period in history when Al-Jahiz

lived. It never entered the language of Islam, Arabic, until the

late part of the 17th Century C.E., at which time the Arabs made

contact with the Portuguese originators of the word in West Africa.

The Portuguese had established their "NEGROLAND" and its "NEGRO"

people. The area they labeled "Negroland" the indigenous Africans

called "SONGHAY" (Songhai) Empire, and the vast majority of people

therein - Mende ("Mandingoes").

These concepts of the racial question in Arabia (Islam), as

presented by Al-Jahiz, Islam, are used against the Africans and

their descendants today by the same people whom the Africans ("Blacks

once considered their "inferior." It should be readily understood

that color prejudice is not the monopoly of Judaism, Christianity

or Islam, nor is it the exclusive property of Europeans and

European-Americans (Whites). One should readily see that the

---

* Since the word "NEGRO" was not in use during the time of Al-
Jahiz, it was impossible for him to have used it. Wherever it
would have occurred in this text, English translation, the proper
word has been substituted by the author of this volume.

234

once "lowly Europeans" (Whites) are now the masters of the once "high Africans"(Blacks). Also, that just as the Europeans were once excluded from history, or entered in a degrading manner by the ancients of Arabia, they too now join the ranks of the inquisitors and exclude the Africans or enter them in inferior references.

The relationship of the color question in Islam, with regards to the Blacks, was as much religious as it was racial and cultural; this should be obvious.

The identification of the Ethiopians (indigenous Black East Africans) in Al-Jahiz' works certainly refutes the general racist attempts by many European and European-American (White) educators and general informants who have tried to make the Ethiopians everything-else but Blacks (indigenous Africans), whom they too once called "NEGROES." It is also very significant to note that the same "educators" have translated the word "SUDAN," or "SUD," to mean "NEGRO," when in fact it meant "Africa" or "African" in the context of the Arabic usage. This, of course, was an attempt at still maintaining the racist concept that North Africa could not be "Negroid," but "Semitic" or "Hamitic." Yet the indigenous Africans of North Africa existed before the first Jew - Abraham, as well as before "Shem" and "Ham" of the mythical Noah's Ark drama. One can understand this, because Islam has been conceded to be a "Black," or "Negro," religion, because only a very small percentage of Europeans remain faithful to it, and very few European-Americans tolerate it in the United States of America. On the other hand it seems that Judaism and Christianity must be protected from becoming corrupted with "Negroes" - their originators, in

235

order that the lily "white lamb of the shepherd" (the blonde Jesus Christ painted by Michaelangelo) would never become the 'black sheep of the family;' and that no black-skinned angel would ever integrate or amalgamate the present Caucasian heaven being presented to Christians and Jews alike. Of course Ethiopian and Sudanese peoples are today called "black-skinned Caucasians"[47] along with many millions of other so-called "Negroes" in order to claim East and North African history and heritage for the "white-skinned Caucasians" of Europe and the Americas. The technique behind **this** **is** **the** attempt by the Whites to co-opt Zinjanthropus boisie, Boskop man, and others of the earliest human-like fossils unearthed in Africa.* This they hoped would have established the "white-skinned Caucasians" as the original people of the so-called "GARDEN OF EDEN" spoken of in the "Western Religions" (Judaism, Christianity, and Islam) being set straight with respect to their indigenous African origins in this work.

Al-Jahiz' statement, which most affected the above issue, is **once more** quoted:

> The Africans have the sweetest breath and the
> greatest amount of saliva being in this respect
> like the dog as compared with other animals. As
> we said Blacks are more numerous than the Whites
> since they are made up of Ethiopians, the Fezzans,
> Berbers, Copts, Nubians, Tagh-wans, the people of
> Black Ceylon, India, Quamae and Indo-China.[48]

This, in fact, was a commonplace identification of the indig-enous Africans and other peoples of the "Black Race" by members of said "race" before the colonial **and imperialist Europeans**

---

* See Y. ben-Jochannan, BLACK MAN OF THE NILE, Alkebu-lan Books, New York, 1970, Chapter on earliest fossil-man with respect to the co-option of Zinjanthropus boisie, Boskop man, etc., for a complete analysis.

and European-Americans re-classified them after the conquest of
the East (parts of Africa and Asia) by the Portuguese and the
West (the Caribbean Islands and the Americas) by the Spaniards,
and the extension of these two conquests by other European colonial nations from the late 15th through 19th centuries C.E.,
who planted European-style Christianity as the spiritual support
for their colonial expansion and the institution of chattel slavery.

In further identifying the "Black Race" Al-Jahiz wrote:

> The isles between Africa (Sudan)*and China are
> all peopled with Blacks, that is Ceylon, Kalah,
> Zabig. Most of the Arabs also are as black as we,
> the Africans are, and cannot be counted among the
> Whites. As for the Hindus (indians of India)*they
> are even darker (blacker)*than the Arabs.

Al-Jahiz' description and identification of the Prophet Mohamet placed him, Mohamet, in the family of the "Black Race." In
this regards Al-Jahiz wrote:

> The ten sons of Abd el Mottalib (the grandfather
> of Mohamet)*were all black and strong, so was Abdul-
> lah ibn Abbas, Mohamet's cousin. The members of the
> family of Abu Talib (a relation of Mohamet and the
> father of the Sultan, Ali)*were all more or less
> black in color.

What Al-Jahiz has revealed about the Prophet Mohamet's family
is a seldom mentioned historical fact about him. Even the Prophet
Elijah Mohammed's Nation of Islam (Black Muslims) of the United
States of America maintains Islam's exclusive "Asian origin."[49]
Also, that its originators were all "Asiatic Black Men." But Al-
Jahiz, who was born, educated and lived there in Arabia, refutes
these theories, and many more. This is best seen in his remarks

---

* Words in brackets, by the author of this volume, indicating the
errors in the translation of the original Arabic text to English
and/or emphasize the missing words.

with respect to Lockman (Loqman, whom the Greeks called "Aesop") and others,[59] and of course his identification of the Prophet Mohamet:

> Black ebony is the most solid and most durable
> of woods. The black hair is the most beautiful
> and in Paradise, everyone will have black hair.

The above comment by Al-Jahiz is repeated, as it was considered the most common description of the major writers of Asia of the Islamic peoples of his ear. This was no more a racist view than the expression in Michaelangelo's "everyone in heaven is blonde with golden hair and blue eyes" pictures. This is best expressed in Michaelangelo's painting of "THE LAST SUPPER" (Pesach) and other religious scenes of solely blonde angels in an all-white Christian heaven flying around an equally blonde Jesus Christ and his blonde family - Joseph (his father) and Mary (his mother). Jesus' brother, James, being carefully concealed or omitted from the scene, however.

On the conquest of the Blacks (Ethiopians in this case) over others, Al-Jahiz wrote:

> We (the Blacks) have conquered the country of
> the Arabs as far as Mecca and governed them. We
> defeated Dhu Nowas (the Jewish King of Yemen) and
> killed all of the Himyarite princes, but you,
> White people, have never conquered our country.
> Our people, the Zenghs (Blacks of East Africa)
> revolted forty times in the Euphrates, driving
> the inhabitants from their homes and making
> Obollah a bath of blood.

It is to be noted that the Blacks of Ethiopia (indigenous Africans whom many call "Blacks" or "Negroes," sometimes "Hamitic" or "Semitic") once set up their kingdom called "ELAM" in ancient Persia; and that they also conquered all of Arabia, most of Persia, and parts of India.

238

This historical record reveals that a Jew was once the ruler of Yemen, an Arab country across the Red Sea from Ethiopia. And that religious tolerance, not intolerance, was the pattern of living among the Blacks, even of Arabia. It also states that the Jews of that era were not "Caucasians" in any sense of the word, as so many modern European-American and European (Jews and Christians) historians have constantly inferred.

One can readily see why the Yemenite and Ethiopian (Falasha, or Beta Israel) Hebrews ("Jews") have maintained the oldest and most authentically ancient traditions (orthodox) of ancient Judaism. These traditions, of course, are expected to give way to European and European-American Talmudic Judaism, which is presently Germanized and Anglocized to meet current religious interpretations that are most suitable to the religious power-structure in the present European-American (White) dominated government of the modern state of Israel. This type of reflection is nonetheless true for any group of people who may have become similarly involved in the same historical circumstances as did the White Jews, and of course, those who are Black, Brown, Red, Yellow, and whatever-else. All of these colors are apparent among the Hebrew (misnomered "Jews") tribes which are still in existence and scattered all over the Planet - EARTH.

It would have been humanly impossible for the Jews (Semites, not Caucasians) to remain "racially pure" from the indigenous Africans (the so-called "Negroes," etc.) or their fellow Asians - the Arabs (once also called "Semites," now "Hamites."). This is providing the Jews were of a distinctly different "race" of people before they entered Africa (Sais, which they called Egypt). Of course, some people refer to the Jews, Irish, Italian, Ethiopians, Australians, etc., as "races," the word "race" having become in itself an enigma. Why? Because some of the same people who are classified as "Semites" and "Hamites" conveniently at times become "Caucasians" and "Whites." Even "Negroes" become "Hamites" and "Semites" and other names different to the slave nomenclature when everyone, or anyone, within the group do something of major significance. And of course "Blacks," such as St. Maurice of Aganon, Patron Saint of the Roman Catholic Church of Germany, lose their color in the religious shuffle along with St. Benedict the Moor, St. Cyprian, St. Augustine, St. Martin de Pores, St. Monica (St. Augustine's mother), St. Felicita, St. Perpetua, St. Nymphamo and the entire entourage of "saints" of Alkebu-lan (Africa according to the Greeks and Romans). This is true, to the point where it is still being averred that "...Pope Paul VI cannonized the first Negro saints of Africa when he visited Uganda...," etc.; thus overlooking the fact, or ignoring same, that the first martyrs - "Saints" of Christendom were indigenous Africans (Felicita Nymphamo and Perpetua)*- so-called "Negroes."

No one, with any sense of justice, can say that there is no need to mention that the indigenous Africans (who were responsible for the beginning of Judaism, Christianity and Islam) were of any particular color than any other persons involved. This would be ideal. But life, reality, and idealism are not synonymous with the terms "Negro" and "slavery." Yet "Negro" has been made synonymous with "inferiority." But its creators - European and European-American historians, "educators," etc., have failed

* These three are mentioned above with the other indigenous African (Black, Negro, etc.) "Saints."
240

effort (as always) to justify its application to people of African origin, and indicate offense when such is rejected by the African community of peoples. Therefore, it is beyond bare necessity to point out, at least, the major contributions by Black peoples (the so-called "Negroes, Bantus, Hottentots, Pygmies, Bushmen, Africans South of the Sahar, etc.) in all manner of human achievements, religion included.

Semantically speaking - there is an assumption in the American-English language that any human name without the adjective "Negro" is understood to be "Caucasian." Thus, "the Negro Minister, Dr. King, Jr.," instead of "the Reverend Dr. King, Jr. Why not then, "The Negro Muzzin and co-founder of Islam, Bilal?" Certainly not, because he was born in Ethiopia, East Africa. Therefore, he is supposed to have been a "black Caucasian" or something other than a plain old "Negro" one can meet any day in the Harlems of the United States of American, West Africa or the Caribbean Islands.

One reads about the chronology of events in the life of Mohamet. But, it is very rarely mentioned that in the year 615 C.E. or BH 7 his followers had to flee Mecca for Ethiopia, East Africa - a period of six short years before the Hegira (622 C.E. or AH 1). The same conspicuous absence from history is made of the fact that Mohamet also sent one of the letters mentioned before in this text and chapter to the Emperor of Ethiopia in 629 C.E. (AH 7) demanding that the emperors of the world drop their respective Gods "... and worship the one and only true God - Al-lah" as proclaimed by his Prophet - Mohamet himself.

A CHRONOLOGY OF THE LIFE AND DEATH OF MOHAMET

*BH 53 (569 C.E.) Death of Mohamet's father, just a few months before Mohamet's birth.

BH 52 (570 C.E.) Birth of Mohamet at Mecca, or Medina.

BH 46 (576 C.E.) Mohamet's mother - Aminah - died. Mohamet an orphan at age six (6).

BH 27 (595 C.E.) Mohamet married the wealthy widow of a merchant of Mecca - Khadija.

BH 12 (610 C.E.) "Mohamet receives his Call from the Archangel, Saint Gabriel."

BH 7 (615 C.E.) Flight of Mohamet and his followers to Ethiopia, East Africa. Some exclude Mohamet from this event; other writers declare he was with this group.

BH 3 (619 C.E.) Death of Mohamet's wife, Khadija.

BH 2 (620 C.E.) Mohamet's "Night Journey on the clouds from Mecca to Jerusalem aboard the Seventh Heaven," according to Moslem Holy Scripture.

**AH 1 (622 C.E.) The Hijra (or Year of the Hegira). The beginning of the "Moslem Era" and Calendar.

AH 2 (624 C.E.) Battle of Badr (Moslems massacre of the Quraysh (Quarish) people ("tribe").

AH 3 (625 C.E.) Moslems massacred in the Battle of Uhud.

AH 4 (626 C.E.) Black Jews (the "Tribe of Al-Nadhir) exterminated by the Moslems. No more than twelve of their number remained, but they were expelled from Arabia.

AH 5 (627 C.E.) Meccans defeated in their attempt to seize Medina and capture Mohamet and his followers - "The War of the Ditch."

AH 6 (628 C.E.) Mohamet and his "Soldiers of Al'lah" massacre the Black Jews of Aurayza. All women and children cold into slavery, except those taken as members for harems in Arabia and Persia. More than 700 men murdered. Only one (1) reported saved, because of his conversion to Islam.

AH 7 (629 C.E.) Mohamet sends his letters demanding that every head of state surrender themselves to "the only true Prophet of Al'lah," and to "Al'lah's Holy Words." Letters were sent to the emperors of Byzantium, Ethiopia, Yemen, China, and many others.

AH 9 (631 C.E.) Arabian states accepted Islam in the face of being liquidated by Mohamet's "army of Al'lah." The Year of Embassies."

AH 10 (532 C.E.) The farewell pilgrimage by Mohamet to his most trusted followers on the way to his death in Mecca, March 632 C.E., or AH 10. The last

---

* BH - Before the Hegira (The year Mohomet was forced to flee to Mecca and hide out at the Oasis of Yathrib in Medina). **AH = After the Hegira.

last day of life of the Prophet of Al'lah - Mohamet -
on the Planet Earth, June 8, AH 10 or 632 C.E.

THE EXORDIUM

Praise be to Al'lah, Lord of Creation,
    The compassionate and Merciful,
King of the Judgment Day!
You alone we worship, and to you alone our prayer
    for help is rendered.
Guide us along the straight path, The path of
    those you have favored,
Not those who have suffered your wrath.
Nor of those who have drifted astray.
Praise be to Al'lah, Lord of Creation.

The above prayer, "The Exordium," is to be said before reading any passage in "The Recital" - which means "KORAN" or "QUR'AN"
in Arabic (generally the Moslem Bible or Holy Bible).

The following are the Goddesses of Islam who became the...
"DAUGHTERS OF AL'LAH":

Al - lat, the Sun Goddess.

Al - Manat, the Goddess of Venus.

Al - Uzzah, the Fortune Goddess.

The major interpretations of the Koran used in this work are
taken from the standard authoritative commentaries by Al-Beidhawi,
Al-Jalaheim, and Al-Zamakhshari, three of the most outstanding Islamic scholars of the Koran. It is to be noted, however, that there
are other established interpretations in use by a number of Arab
schools, each having its own authority. Yet, this is the one which
has been endorsed by authorities in Mecca.

AL'LAH ALONE KNOW WHAT HE MEANT WHEN HE WROTE THESE
                    WORDS

The above quotation is typical of the response Islamic scholars give for the undeciphered Arabic script at the beginning of
certain verses of the Koran. This is the same manner in which this

243

chapter comes to its closing.

No one knows whether Mohamet, Jesus Christ, or Abraham was a
"TRUE PROPHET." Maybe the only "True Prophet" was a "pagan," or
perhaps one of the present African-Americans - who, like the prophets of old named above, is being ignored and rejected before
his acceptance, by his own people.

WHO? OR WHAT? MAKES A "PROPHET"?

KING, MOHAMMED, DIVINE, MATTHEWS, AND GARVEY: RELIGIOUS
NEW DIMENSIONS

Chapter Five

On April 4, 1968, the Reverend Dr. Martin Luther King, Jr.,
was shot down in cold blood by an assassin's bullets. This tragedy shocked the entire world in a similar manner to the assassination of Mahatma ("The Holy One") Mohandas Karamchand Ghandi - the man from whom the late Dr King, Jr., modeled his own
"non-violent philosophy." Dr. King's tragic death immediately set
off a chain reaction to the violence that struck him down. In
many of the African-American (Black) communities throughout the
United States of America, the reaction followed a line of mass
destruction to real and personal properties in which the rioters
had no ownership. This vengeance found its way against the absentee-
owned retail stores and tenement houses which these communities
have for generations held in contempt because of perceived mal-
practices that arise from their administration.

Somehow, Dr. King's short, but very active, career has been
solely associated with the struggle for "constitutional rights" -
the so-called "non-violent civil rights movement," a career which
took on another perspective when he was awarded the coveted "Noble
Peace Prize" on March 10, 1964, by the Parliament of the Kingdom
of Sweden for his work in the "non-violent movement" towards world
peace in the United States of America. But Dr. King's overall pro-
fessional life - from 1955 when he joined with Rosa Parks and
others in the "Montgomery (Alabama) Bus Boycott" - had another and
most neglected phase, that is, his revolutionization of the role
of a redundant and most repressive clergy (Jewish, Christian, Mos-

245

lem, and others) of the United States of America. In short, he removed "Soul saving" from the sanctum sanctorum of million-dollar churches, mosques, and synagogues to the people in the streets of the urban and rural communities which support them. He crossed religious-denomination barriers and classifications and ignored ethnic and national origins through action. He did not resort to meaningless rhetoric from pious pulpits on high - the usual decadence to which organized religion has sunk. He identified the goals of European-American Christianity (with which he was associated), thereby leading the multitudinous poor (the forgotten people of Judaism, Christianity, and Islam) whom his fellow clergymen were supposed to lead and serve, but whom they so miserably failed.

Dr. King's life in religion as a moving force for change, by an African-American was not unique. It was a life that enjoyed a limited sense of respect from those who controlled society during his lifetime, and now, and in all of its ramifications. Whereas, others who have struggled very much in the same manner, before his birth and after his assassination, have not met with the same type of approval he received by the "White Power Structure." The following people were, or are, just a few of the Black men who (in their own way) did as much: the late Father Divine, Honorable Marcus Moziah Garvey, and Sweet Daddy Grace. Those who are still alive include: Rabbi Wentworth Matthews and the "Honorable Prophet Elijah Mohammed." These men, both passed and alive, have done as much, or more, for millions of African-Americans to change the direction of their lives. The "Universalism" that was Dr. King's, through his endorsement of "White liberal" co-religionists and

246

their powerful religious propaganda machinery, not to mention
their allies within the government of the United States of
America, made him the international figure of "...change
through non-violent means." This does not, in any way whatsoever
take away from the greatness that was Dr. Martin Luther King,
Jr.'s; it only cites the main beneficiaries of his struggles –
the so-called "White liberals" of the United States of America.

The rythmic chanting voice of the Reverend Dr. King, Jr.,
with all of its African-American (Black) Baptist and Voodoo
stylistic delivery which came from a heritage of hundreds of years
of "westernizing" traditional African religious background,
integrated with European-American-type Christianity, was made
still on that infamous day in 1968 by the bullets from the gun of
the confessed assassin – James Earl Ray.[1]

The Reverend Dr. Martin Luther King, Jr., the Christian
reformer and martyr, had recently, before his murder, appealed to
his religious contemporaries of the clergy in the United States
of America in so many ways similar to the indigenous African
(Black, "Negro," etc.) "Church Fathers" (St. Cyprian, Tertullian,
and St. Augustine) of Christendom's appeal to early "Christian
Rome" to change its irreligious ways. But will Dr. King be
beatified for his Christ-like life? Not at all; he did not belong
to the correct "Christian sect." Yet, to the Africans (Black
peoples everywhere) his "SOUL HAS ENTERED THE ANCESTRAL SPIRIT
WORLD." Amongst European-Americans and African-Americans it may
have "entered into heaven to await judgment day." This must do,
for there is no precedent set for the beatification of the dead
among the Baptists, so that Dr. King, Jr., could be beatified

247

like other "Black saints," such as the South American St. Martin de Pores. But unlike St. Martin de Pores, whose major claim to beatification was said to be for "...chasing rats out of his country..."[2] (a kind of a St. Patrick of Ireland chasing the "snakes out of Ireland" myth), Dr. King Jr.'s beatification would be for "keeping things cool among the Blacks for the benefit of the White liberals."

To equate the Reverend Dr. Martin Luther King, Jr. with St. Augustine, to some, would be almost sacreligious. But the fact still remains that Dr. King was more actively engaged among the common flock than the greatest of Christendom's "fathers of the Christian Church" - St. Cyprian, Tertullian, and St. Augustine. These three indigenous African Christian "Church Fathers," of the North African Church which the Romans copied, were Christendom's greatest academicians and philosophers during their life, and remain so after their death. They set the "moral" and "spiritual" course for other Christians like the Reverend Dr. King, Jr. to follow, but Dr. King applied them for the first time in human history.

The Reverend Dr. King, Jr. went beyond the revolution within Christendom, further than his namesake - Martin Luther, the European Catholic Christian reformer of the Middle Ages. Dr. King, Jr. led the multitudes; and this he did irrespective of race, creed, color, sex, nationality, and other divisive classifications - something never before accomplished by the "Church Fathers," or his namesake, Martin Luther.

248

St. Martin de Pores' beatification was for his fighting against the inhuman slave trade which so many Christian (Roman Catholic and Protestant) and Jewish members of the laity and clergy of his country (and other parts of the "New World") controlled, or otherwise supported. The "slave trade" that was started by the Right Reverend Bishop Bartoleme de Las Casas in 1506 C.E. on the Island of Hispaniola (formerly called Hayte by the indigenous people - the so-called "Caribs" . Note that this island is presently divided into the Republic of Santo Domingo, and the Republic of Haiti) .

Dr. King's indigenous African predecessors - St. Cyprian, Tertullian, and St. Augustine - addressed themselves to philosophical Christianity. They saw no salvation for any man "...unless by the way of Jesus Christ,"[4] a criterion which the overwhelming majority of Christian leaders still confirm. Herein one sees another major dimension added to Christianity by another son of Africa (Alkebu-lan). And, of course, to all other religions. It was the Dr.'s ability to employ within Christianity in the United States of America that which is "God-like" in mankind, irrespective of religious creed. He most certainly employed this principle when he adopted the physical and spiritual techniques of a Hindu - who was designated a "pagan" by Christians, Jews, and Moslems alike, even though his life was the model for millions who cherish the "non-violent activist movements," at least those who say that they do, around the world today.

---

* Alkebu-lan was the original name for the continent the Romans and Greeks renamed "AFRICA." See BLACK MAN OF THE NILE, by Y. ben-Jochannan, Alkebu-lan Books, New York, 1970, for further information in this area of African history.

Were the things - the type of "Christian Doctrines" preached by St. Cyprian, Tertullian, and St. Augustine - what moved the Reverend Dr. Martin Luther King, Jr.? Or was it the humanistic traditions within the African-American subculture that expanded within the United States of America - of which Voodoo, Ju Ju, Obyah, and other traditionally indigenous African religions are component parts?

Most Jewish, Christian, and Islamic confessants would deny even the possibility of any indigenous African heritage in Dr. King's religious life. This is because they have associated the origin of Judaism (Hebrewism), Christianity, and Islam solely with Europeanism and Caucasianism, and of course capitalism - in simpler terms with "WHITE SUPREMACY." Yet, in the Reverend Dr. King's public appearances and speeches (mass meetings) before so-called "liberal" and "humanistic," as well as "philanthropic" societies, anyone familiar with the African-American (so-called "Negro") Church, Synagogue or Mosque could hear the carry-over of the indigenous Africans and their descendants in the "Western Hemisphere." African chants that entered the United States of America by means of the enslaved Africans (Blacks, not "Negroes") that were transferred from the sugar plantations and cotton fields of the Caribbean Islands (called the "West Indies" by the Spanish colonists from the days of Cristobal Colon, 1492 C.E.) from c1619 or 1620 C.E. For it was there in the Caribbeans that "CAESO" (kah-ee-so) or "Carry-so" became "Calypso," just as it was here in the United States of America that "Voodoo chants" and other indigenous African spiritualism was misnomered "NEGRO* SPIRITUALS."

* "Negroes" were never imported from Africa (Alkebu-lan) - Africans were. Africans cannot produce "Negroes," just as Europeans did not produce "Pale Face Trash" or "Honkies." These derogatory names were invented by certain men to maintain their own personal racism as a means by which to keep all Americans divided for their own benefit.

250

It is convenient, besides being ignorant, for anyone to assume that the Europeans and European-Americans were able to denude the indigenous Africans of all traces of their religious heritage they brought from Africa and then totally superimpose "pure" European-style Judaeo-Christianity without one thought of their Africanism (Voodoo, Obyah, Ngai, Limbo, Damballah Ouedo, etc.) remaining.

"Steal away, Steal away" the "Negro Spiritual" cries out. "Hide away, Hurry, Hide away, master (massa he come) is coming," it says. "Ah say, God be with you, yeah, ah say God be with - yeah, yeah, till we meet again! Ah say...," etc. In each of these one sees the Voodooistic African background asserting itself against the dry and soulless European-American Welch-style Christian presentation with its English perfectivity. Thus, "...God will be with you until it is possible for us to meet again." The Reverend Dr. Martin Luther King, Jr., as any other "Soul Preacher," would say:

> "Yeah, Ah been up to the mountain top - Ah say, I been up to the mountain top...," etc.

In the "yeah," as in the "Ah say," the SOUL of the African Voodooism finds itself being released. But does the "yeah" indicate some sort of vocabulary deficiency as many "Western" educators imply? The Reverend Dr. Martin Luther King, Jr.'s doctoral degree was earned from one of the most respected, academically that is, institutions of higher learning in the United States of America - BOSTON UNIVERSITY, Boston, Massachusetts.

Unfortunately, there are no musical sounds to come from these words in this chpater, and many who read them may never have the opporutnity of witnessing an African-American minister of the gospel - one who "received his calling" without any formal education in a European-American (White) type Christian seminary[5] - performing in an "Old Fashion Revival,"Bringing The Message of

251

Jesus Christ." The showmanship, at least the physical expressions
of the minister, alone, creates the necessary environment and setting for the transmigration (metaphysical) experience in which the
entire congregation (mostly women and children) becomes enraptured.
In this ceremony one can also see, mentally that is, the Oba or
Nana (priest) as he praises the God - Oledamare and his Orishas
(minor Gods). Then the congregation breaks loose in a trance-like
suspense, dancing in praises on high to their maker - Jesus Christ,
in this case as it would be, were they in Africa. In the same vain
one sees the houngan (Priest) and Mambo (priestess) as they shake
their asson (rattle) during the Voodoo ceremonies of the Caribbean
Islands' adaptation, of their fellow Africans, of the Yoruba religion of Nigeria, West Africa.[6]

From the earliest beginning of Voodoo's entry into the African Methodist Episcopal Church[7] all other forms of African-American
European-style Christian sects were equally affected. Besides
Christian ministers, and other personnel within the clergy, this
heritage found its way through conversions from Judaeo-Christianity
to Islam. To speak of Islam in this context should not offend
anyone, especially those who know the history of this religion
from the Arabian Peninsula African origins. However, the truth is,
very few of the newly converted Blacks to Islam understand this
context. Why? Because their new type of "Islam" also looks to Mecca,
but, only in the sense of respect for the original philosopher and
Prophet - Mohamet, to whom the original branch of Islam owes its
birth. Nevertheless, many have forgotten that Islam also owes its
birth to an indigenous African from Ethiopia -"Hadzart Bilal ibn
Rahab, the second greatest man in the history of Islam, second
only to Mohamet the Prophet."

252

The "Islam" being spoken of at this time is officially called —
"The Nation of Islam"— colloquially "The Black Muslims," the latter
name being the one Professor Eric C. Lincoln placed upon the faithful in his study of them that appeared in his book bearing the
same name.[7a]

"The latest Prophet," said to be the son of a Baptist preacher,
Wali Poole, and his wife — Marie, both of Sandersville, Georgia,
formerly called himself — Elijah Poole, presently renamed...
"The Prophet, The Honourable Elijah Mohammed, The Messenger, The
Lamb," and a host of other names his flock assigned to him. The
fact that this "Prophet" did not have, nor does he now possess,
any endorsement from Mecca, or any other center of International
Brotherhood of Islamic Peoples, is meaningless to his followers,
who sincerely believe that their new Prophet "...has been sent
by Al'lah to save the lost Negroes, and to complete the work left
undone by Mohamet"; who came to complete the work left undone by
Jesus Christ; who came to complete the work left undone by the
hundreds of religionists of the Nile Valley and Euphrates Valley,
all of which passed through Egypt by way of the Nile River (Blue
and White) and by indigenous Africans (whose descendants are today
called "Niggers, "Bantus," and other such insulting names) along
the Nile who came from the interior of East-Central Africa, with
what is known today as the "MYSTERY SYSTEM." This they did before
their descendant — Moses — could find the necessary Laws called
today "THE TEN COMMANDMENTS," which Moses took from the more than
one hundred and forty-seven (147) "NEGATIVE CONFESSIONS" already
shown in earlier pages of this volume, all of which took place
before Moses arrived at Mount Sinai with the indigenous African-
Hebrews.

The story of how Elijah Mohammed - "Prophet, Sheperd, Lamb, Messenger," or such, can be best seen in its fullest account in Professor Eric C. Lincoln's extensive first-hand inside revelations on the Nation of Islam, and need not be detailed further in this volume. However, an independent analysis of its connection through traditional heritage of its indigenous African background shall be emphasized, stressed, etc. This may not be the best acceptable explanation for most brothers and sisters connected thereto or friendly to those who claim to be "...Asiatic Black men and women." In so doing, and saying, however, they also claim that "... Islam was always here." They have denied their own origin from Alkebu-lan (Africa), and ignored every bit of anthropolgical evidence of mankind's earliest origin in the Olduvai Gorge area of Tanzania, East Africa.

The question, as to which God, or which religion, came first finds no support in this volume. What does find its way to the surface of investigation is an analysis of the many ways in which the African-American (Black) Nation of Islam still holds on to Voodooism, Judaism, Obyah, Magic, and many other indigneous African traditional religious beliefs within Islam itself, which are today still called "paganism." All of these traditional beliefs have been imported into the United States of America originally from West Africa by way of the Caribbean peoples of African origin; while much of these beliefs most African-Americans would now reject in preference for the religion their masters forced upon them.

The vast majority of the Nation of Islam's faithful are from traditionally African-American and African-Caribbean "Save Soul" and "FIRE AND DAMNATION" Baptist, Methodist, Church of God in Christ, and other such "Soul Shaking" religious experiences - which are most common in other indigenous groups such as Voodoo
254

and Judaeo-Christianity. Of course they are some who may say they
came from sects which are more "sophisticatedly" called "High
Churches," such as the Roman Cathlic Church, Presbyterian Church,
Anglican (Church of England), Lutheran Church, Moravian Church,
and others of the same intellectualized academically-based religious
institutions where the absence of "Soul" is compensated by philosophical Christianity. The other African-Americans in these sects
also came by way of the African Methodist Episcopal Church (A.M.E.).
They followdd such greats as Harriet Tubman - the fearless African-
American liberator of the slave period, the Reverend Nat Turner and
the Reverend Denmark Vesey - revolutionists who tried to free their
people from the slavemasters (Christians as well as Jews). These
Africans (not "Negroes") were forced to join this branch of African-
American Christianity during the period when no branch (sect) of
European-American-style (White) religions - Jewish, Christian or
Moslem - would accept in their membership any person of "non-
European" or "non-White pigment" to worship any God. From this
background of rejection the Africans (as they still refer to them-
selves) founded the "African Methodist Episcopal Church," with the
Right Reverend Bishop Richard Allen as its first leader. This is the
background and heritage of all subsequent African-American experiences in Christianity and other interrelated religions for
generation after generation. This was true until the turn of the
Twentieth Century, C.E., before indigenous African Jews (Israelites,
Falashas, Beta Israel) and Moslems began entering the United States
of American from the Caribbean and Africa as students and seamen.

Father Divine, called by many "...the most colorful figure
of the Great Depression Years" (1929-1942 C.E.), was an African-
American of extremely brilliant imagination. He came along on the

255

scene when Black America had a void in its political and economic leadership. Not only Black America, however, but the entire world was caught in the "Great Depression" of the Herbert Hoover era, an era of economic, as well as cultural and religious depravity, which was yet to become "...his period of greatness...", according to those who still remain faithful.

Looking back on the past compels one to ask: What forces did Father Divine employ to convince so many thousands of people of every ethnic group, religion, nationality, sex, age, and color to join what he elected to call his "Heavens?" The answer is as varied as there are people who question and who answer. But one dimension seems always to be overlooked, that is, his own religious background.

Father Divine was commonly known to be a "Mystic." But, he wore no turban, nor gazed into no crystal ball as people seemed to envision whenever the words "Father Divine" were mentioned. This "Mystic" was always impeccably dressed in a businessman's suit whenever he was seen in public or private audiences. Therefore, the old stereotype notion of mysticism generally associated with the Middle East or the Far East, and other far-off lands in the Pacific Ocean and the Mediterranean Sea was eliminated.

Employing a page from Voodooism, "Father" – as he was affectionately called by his faithful followers, would grant periodic receptions to each member of his flock. Each visit was limited to a maximum of "one minute." This limitation was also extended to strangers who frequented his "Heavens."[8] Herein was a major degree of the "mystery."

Imagine hearing about a man during your own lifetime whom

256

thousands have proclaimed to be "God", himself. If you became curious or in any other way interested to find out the truth or fiction of your imagination, and you somehow heard that you could go and see "God" in person for yourself - What would you do? This sense of curiosity alone widened the "mystery" around "Father," and thousands of all colors of people came to stare at the face of this African-American (Black) God - "Father (Peace) Divine."

Father Divine would stare back at his audience from a throne set above the elevation of all others within the main room which also served as a dining room, lecture hall, etc., as the latter still does now that he has gone to the "Great Beyond"; where his faithful maintain "...He sits and waits to Judge."[9]

Strangely enough, the type of Voodooistic Judaeo-Christianity developed in Father Divine's "Heavens" was forced to take on more subtle means of expression than the African-American Baptist background of "Father" himself. Why? Because of the disproportionately large following of European-American (White) faithful the movement attracted. As such, the usual tabourine beating, piano-pounding chants, and the entering into Voodooistic religious trances gave away to Father's modified African-American-style of European-type Christianity with its own sense of religious fervor in which its European-American brothers and sisters could feel most comfortable and participate fully. Since the vast majority of the faithful were at least in their late forties, except the very youthful in their teens, leaving very few between, their type of watered-down "Save Soul" Baptist imitations were possible.

"Brothers" and "Sisters" were not fraternal and sororial in terms of the same set of values normally used in the American-

English language. These terms were in essence of their physical meaning; as celibacy was the rule rather than choice within "Fat er's" movement, especially in the "Heavens." Of course this caus the dissolution of countless marriages, as evidence by the many wives and husbands who suddenly found physical sexual intercours with their spouse to be:

CONTRARY TO THE DESIRE OF GOD - FATHER DIVINE.

Therefore, this Voodooistic-Judaeo-Christian based religion debunked the First Book of Moses (Genesis)[10]- where it says the fo lowing:

> 16 To the woman He said,
> "I will greatly multiply your pain in childbearing;
> in pain shall you shall bring forth children,
> yet your desire shall be for your husband,
> and he shall rule over you."

Law suits resulted, and in many of the actions Father Divine was mentioned as being the root-cause of the disaffection. Many others followers when once faithful followers became disenchanted and wanted to reclaim their life's savings, which they had surrendered voluntarily as a prerequisite for entrance to any of th many "Heavens" thoughout the United States of America. Amazingly many very wealthy individuals surrendered their total fortune to this movement. And, of course, they also surrendered their mind, body, and soul to "Father."

What kept this "God" going? What "Black Magic" was there that made him "Father" which moved poor people? This, the unbelievers asked. And to this, thousands of answers were readily given. But none seemed to fit the bill as well as...

THE SECRECY OF SUSPENSION

which one finds so readily in "Black Magic," "Black Magic," as used i

258

this sense - within its religious sophistication, and in all of
its beauty as practised and developed in West Africa. As "suspension;" not of fear, but of great expectation; of hope, and not
dispair; of a guranteed communion with God - Himself (Father Divine), and not of an unkown "God" where one must take his (or
her) chance that heaven's gate may not open to him, therefore
no chance to "...sit at the right hand of God the Father Almighty
...," etc., according to the Christian religion's Text to this
effect.[11] A God whom you could not touch as an ordinary follower,
but you could stare upon whenever you are fortunate enough to have
Him leave His Main Heaven in New York City, New York, or in Philadelphia, Pensylvania, where it had to be moved because of litiga-
tions between "Father" and the "People of the State of New York."[12]

These typically traditional Africanistic rites, where the Oba,
Nana, Manteng,and other High-Priests - the direct representatives
of God, Oledamare, on earth - are not to be touched or even spoken
too in public was instituted by this African-American, "Father
Divine," who mastered Voodooism. When one adds to this the mythi-
al concepts built into the story of Jesus Christ and his Jewish
(Hebrew) origin, along with those the Jews took from the Africans
of Egypt and mixed with Greek mythology, there should be no reason
why one should not see just what was "Mystical" about Father Divine - who took all of these myths and then added his own.

As one moves from the "Mystic Divine" to the much more "sophisticated" Rabbi Wentworth Matthews -"Dean of African-American
(Black) Jews (Israelites - as they prefer to be called) - one
enters into a most sensitive area of concern. This area becomes
delicately balanced, not because of the truths and untruths sur-

259

rounding the faithful, but because of the general charges of
"anti-Semitism" of which one must become so conscious of late
when dealing with **"Jewish" matters.** However, this revelation will
continue, in spite of this latter condition. Why? Because the confrontation between Black and White Jews (Hebrews-all) is a fact
like that between White and Black Christians.

For as long as there were European and European-American
(White) Jews in the United States of America (up until the turn of
the early Twentieth Century C.E.) it was believed that no people
of indigenous African origin - the so-called "Negroes" - were Jews.
Very few Americans, of any color, knew that there were thousands
of Black Jews called "Falashas" in Ethiopia, East Africa. These
Jews, "Hebrews" as they prefer to be called, are properly designated "BETA ISRAEL" (Children of the House of Israel, **correctly —**
House of Israel) - the name they call themselves. The knowledge
of the existence of these African Jews brought to the surface the
presence of the West African - Rabbi Wentworth **Matthews, craving**
to find out more about the religion of the European Hebrews - as
practised. In so doing he also found that there were no schools
in the United States of America on this subject, Hebrewism, where
he could matriculate about this vitally important religion of his
forefathers; but, that there was one in Germany, of which he grasp-
ed the opportunity and enrolled. Completing his Rabbinical training, European-style, in 1928 C.E., the Rabbi returned to the United
States of America and founded the "COMMANDMENT KEEPERS CONGREGATION"
of traditional Hebrewism on the order of the Ethiopian Hebrews,
with headquarters above a pharmacy located in a tenement building
at the northeast corner of Lenox Avenue and 128th Street, Harlem,

260

New York City, New York. This institution has since moved to 123rd Street, at the northwest corner of Mount Morris Park West, Harlem.

Because Rabbi Mathews did **not** secure Rabbinical credentials from a particular European or European-American Yeshiva acceptable to European-American (White) Jews, which is not required by the Torah to become a Rabbi, he found himself excluded from European-American-style Talmudic Judaism; this also holds **true for the** members of his congregation; and every sect of White Judaism maintain the exclusion - Orthodox, Conservative, Reform, Reconstuction,[13] and the very new group that calls itself "Jewish Science." Yet there are Rabbis by the dozens from Eastern Europe (White ones, that is) who have no credentials what-so-ever, only the endorsement of another Rabbi - all that is required, and they are acceptable to at least one,or more,of the Jewish sects already mentioned. If one should say that the BLACKNESS of Rabbi Matthews' skin has anything to do with his rejection as a Rabbi by his White-skinned Jewish equivalents,all sorts of "anti-Semitic" charges would ensue, of course. But one must wonder why, afer forty-one (41) long years (1928-1970 C.E.) there is not one solitary black-skinned African-American Rabbi in a European-American synagouge or temple, or even an African-American congregation with the necessary credentials acceptable to any of the European-American (White) Talmudic groups. This is of course, not neglecting the fact that many attempts have been made by Rabbi Matthews and a number of other Black Rabbis for affiliation with the White Jewish community.   Is it not true, that because of the White Jews cultural and "racial" influences and allignment with their White Christian brethren from Europe, they are not free to challenge the effect of the admittance of Black Jews.

261

In very plain, and very simple, language: Are the White Jews of
the United States of America not subjected to the same economic,
social, and political pressures within this society as all other
White Americans like themselves, and in like manner respond? Regardless of defenses, the fact still remains that Black Jews (Israelites) in the United States of America are no better off among
White American Jews than their Black Christian brothers and sisters are among White Christians - their co-religionists. The "racism" that affects the entire United States of America, including
its colonies (called "possessions" and "territories") affect its White
Jews equally as it affect White Christians, Moslems, and other religionists that are of European (Caucasian) origin.

The teachings of Rabbi Wentworth Matthews follow strictly the
Five Books of Moses, commonly referred too as the "Hebrew" or "Jewish" Torah. And, of course, he also teaches the other major works
included in an Israelite's life. Like the Beta Israel (Falashas),
however, the Talmud [14] (which is only an interpretation of the Torah by various schools of Jewish "scholars," and not necessarily
accepted by every other Jewish communities) does not receive the official sanction equal to the Torah, from Rabbi Matthews. There are other Jews,
including the Karraites living in Israel, who also have not accepted the Talmud, on the grounds that "no man has the right to make
a standard   interpretation of the words of God." The acceptance
of the Talmud, or its rejection, does not make one set of Jews
Kosher and the other un-Kosher. Never-the-less, the Black Jews' experiences in the United States of America, the Caribbeans, and Africa do not warrant the use of the Talmud. On the other hand, it is
quite understandable to see why the White Jews, also because of

262

their experiences in Europe and the United States of America, need the Talmud. But, it must be also remembered that there is no law or requirement for Jews to have a Talmud, or to read from one as if it was the laws by the Prophets with respect to the TORAH (Five Books of Moses); for Moses knew not any TALMUD. Therefore, neither Moses, Isaac, Jacob, nor Jehovah (Yahweh) acknowledged the Talmud. But, they did acknowledge the Torah, according to the Hebrew (Jewish) teachings.

If one can understand that the "Falashas" (African Jews of Ethiopia, East Africa) would not have a HANUKAH (Feast or Festival of Lights) like the European and European-American Jews, because of their separation from what is today the "White" (or Caucasian) Jews centuries before "Queen Esther's (Hadas'sah) struggles to save the Jewish people from King Haman" (the Ag'agite),[15] then one should equally understand why the Falashas and other African, or African-American Israelites (Jews) may have, or may have, or may not have, Holy Days which are familiar or unfamiliar to their European and European-American counterparts.

The net result of the estrangement between independent African-American Hebrews (Israelites, or Jews) and their fellow European or European-American Jews developed into two separate forms of Judaism. However, the division is much wider and more diverse than it is between Black and White Christians. Therefore, a White Jew can not easily enter a Black Jewish synagogue (House of Worship) and still follow the rituals in order of their performance, just as a Black Jew will be at a loss when he enters a White Jewish syna-

gogue. Yet, to a great extent this is also true among White
sects of Judaism - Orthodox, Reform, Conservative, Reconstruction,
etc.[16] On the other hand, there are many basic similarities
that stem from Hebrewism's (Judaism) indigenous African origin
common among both groups; but apart from this, their differences
are much wider and more uncommon than those between the sects of
White Orthodoxy and Reconstructionalism; all of which involve the
effects of "racism" and "color prejudice" that gnaws away at the
United States of American like a cancerous growth , which Gunnar
Myrdal called "AN AMERICAN DILEMMA" in his book of like name.

The course of Black Judaism* in the United States of America
is further affected by economic considerations. But Black Judaism
is exclusive of the one or two Sammy Davises who convert to European-American (White) Talmudic Judaism under the label of "NEGRO
JEWS";*the latter term being contemptible. Black Judaism, as Black
Christianity and Black Islam, due to fundamental economic necessi-
ties and social rejection had to become "race conscious," though
not necessarily "racist." Unfortunately most European-Americans
(Whites) cannot distinguish between the two terms when African-
Americans endeavour to honor the former; yet the Whites practice
the reverse, and teach the Blacks its operations. For this is
very much a part of the social structure of the "AMERICAN DREAM,"
ugly as it may appear.

The occasional converted "Negro" from Christianity to European
American Talmudic Judaism is generally a personality that is
economically well off. Because of the economic advantage over

---

* African-American (Black) Hebrews prefer to be calle "ISRAELITES,
"Black Jews" and "Black Judaism" are sometimes accepted; but when-
ever speaking to any of these religionists of the Hebrew Faith,
"NEGRO JEWS" are never to be mentioned - it is insulting to them.

264

the Black Jews (Israelites),as a result the "Negro Jews" remain almost non-vocal within whatever sect of White Judaism they have selected - none of their members being represented on the decision and policy-making bodies of their respective House of Worship. The net result is that the controllers of Talmudic Judaism, the White Jews, have so far assumed that "Black Judaism" should be **contented** with the mere privilige of association with it; but nothing could be further from the truth. This is contrary to the position taken by more than ninety-nine percent (99%) of the total African-American Hebrew (Israelite) communities throughout the United States of America,[17] a position that is endorsed by all of the African-American (Black) Rabbis.

The African-American Rabbinate, all of which in one degree or another, branched off from Rabbi Wentworth Matthews and his COMMANDMENT KEEPERS' CONGREGATION in Harlem, New York City, New York. This historic fact apply equally to the handful of Black Jews who broke away from Rabbi Bevins' synagogue and affiliated themselves with a European-American Talmudic group - under the name of "HATZAAD HARISHON," and in so doing,also accepting the slavemasters'"NEGRO JEWS" nomenclature. This group, suddenly, finds the source from whence they originally sprung untenable; thereby they rejoice in their newly found role as trailblazers from Black Judaism to "Negro Judaism." Their longer history of the awareness of Hebrew life, which they were first introduced to in the Black Israelite communities, affords them power and prestige over the Sammy Davises, since most, if not all, of them are conversant in the present form of Hebrew (Sfardic) spoken in Israel today as the official language of that nation. The "Negro in the window" type

affiliation brought forward from these "Negro Jews" on March 10,
1968, a published condemnation of what they elected to call "Negro anti-Semitism,"[18] but not a single word of protest about, or
against, 'Jewish anti-Blackism.' On the other hand the Black Israelites (Jews), from whence the "Negro Jews" originated, felt
no obligation on their part to publish any such denounciation,
realizing very well that individuals within each group (Blacks and
Whites), of Jews and non-Jews, have been equally guilty of "racism, religious bigotry," and all other such cultural patterns of
behavior that have become so vitally important to the "AMERICAN
DREAM." Of course so-called "liberal minded" hopefuls would con
test these findings; but secular and religious United States of
America itself daily reveals such inequalities, as shown in the
following extracts"

THE NEW YORK TIMES. SUNDAY, MAY 18. 1969

Protestant Churches Divided on Their Urban Crisis Programs

The emergence of James Forman as a leader of a campaign to make churches and synagogues pay $500-million in "reparations" to black Americans for past injustices has brought into focus sharp differences among Protestant church leaders over ways of dealing with the poor.

On one side are churchmen who would make unrestricted grants to organizations of poor people, including militant ones; on the other are those who prefer to maintain control over their funds in church programs of service to the poor.

In the last year several Protestant denominations have started special "crisis in the nation" programs emphasizing the direct transfer of money to groups of the poor.

Many administrators of these programs complain bitterly, however, that the amounts allotted are insufficient to have any measurable effect on the poverty program. They also report that the well-publicized programs, many of which were spurred by the assassination of the Rev. Dr. Martin Luther King Jr., appear to have spent far less than was indicated in the original announcements.

Under the subtitle, MOST PROGRAMS TRADITIONAL, the following
was cited:

Traditional programs, representing the overwhelming bulk of expenditures in programs for the poor, have taken the service-oriented approach of urban "missions," hospitals, education projects and other plans developed by church personnel. Church officials who have

266

The constant lack of religious institutions initiated programs is indicated above. Furthermore, it is shown that the
churches and synagogues only move in objectively meaningful ways
when they are proded by the so-called "Black militants," or by
"race riots."

On the summary of what these religious institutions were in
fact actually doing the article's subtitle, SURVEY UNDER WAY,
highlighted the following:

These programs brought about their own problems, as shown by
the following, under the subtitle, TENSION OVER PROGRAMS:

As tension grew factions arose, as seen in the subtitle, VIEWS
IT DISPUTED:

As the so-called "Black Power Movements" have been either maligned or over-played by the mass communication media, so it has
done to the religiously controlled programs, as shown under the
subtitle, PUBLICITY MISLEADING:

Mr. Modeste agreed that initial press releases had given the impression that the fund would amount to $3-million a year for a three-year period. In 1968, grants to 101 organizations totaled $1.6-million, and about $700,000 has been distributed so far in 1969.

The church's total budget is $14-million. It provides more than $1.7-million for "experimental and specialized services," a category characterized by Mr. Modeste as an extension of old-style methods for involving churches in service-oriented social programs.

"The church will have to reorganize its whole structure," said Mr. Modeste, "to eliminate these traditional services and start putting significant money into the kinds of projects we are involved in."

But, Mr. Modeste's words were rebutted as follows:

Most black churchmen interviewed described the Episcopal program as the best in a slow field. They conclude that the churches have used words such as "emergency" and "priority" to pay lip service to a need for a massive commitment of funds.

"The churches are beginning from a position that does not recognize the dimensions of the problem," said the Rev. Dr Charles S. Spivey, executive director of the Department of Racial Justice of the National Council of Churches. "That's what white racism is all about."

The involvement of the African-Americans (Blacks) in this
chapter of their life is not isolated to them. The indigenous
Africans influence in the so-called "WESTERN RELIGIONS" in the
Americas, especially European-American-style Christianity, was
also fostered by other well-known African-American personalities.
Two of the major personalities referred to were: PROPHET (Bishop)
"SWEET DADDY" GRACE - who founded "The Church Of All Nations And
All People" back in the 1930's; and PROPHET JONES - founder of
the "Universal Church For All People." There was a host of other mino
"prophets" and "prophetesses."[20] Of course millions of Americans
considered them "charlatans, imposters, infidels," and hundreds
of other such names they felt appropriate to the issue. But these
"diviners" and "prophets" asked in turn:

WHO, OR WHAT, HAS THE AUTHORITY TO MAKE PROPHETS?
Their logical answer, to their own question, follow this line of
reasoning:

268

'The same type of God or Gods who made the diviners and prophets that preceded them in the
Mysteries of the Nile Valley religions of the
Sun God Ra, which the Hebrews, Christians and
Moslems adopted and put in their "Holy Scriptures"(Torah, New Testament, Koran), also made
them prophets.'

The followers, faithful, of these prophets reminded their

critics that:

'...man established prophets, heaven, and sainthood, and the standards for same; just as man established the story of Adam and Eve, and the physical birth of Jesus Christ through a virgin - for
a mother who got pregnant by an angel from heaven.'

Since the Apostle's Creed of Christendom still begins with:

"I BELIEVE IN GOD THE FATHER ALMIGHTY, MAKER OF
HEAVEN AND EARTH," etc.; (not) 'I KNOW'...,etc.

Then people can feel free to adulate their own God in any manner

most desirable to themselves. Mankind may equally reject the pos-

sibility of the existence of a God, or at least give it different

dimensions; as such it is still the same "I believe" which the

African-American followers of modern "prophets, prophetesses,"

and "diviners," used as their authority.

The indigenous Africans and many of their relations in the

Americas and the Caribbeans want to know if the "I Believe" in

Voodooism, JuJuism, "Black Magic," and other solely traditional

African religions is not as authoritative as the "I Believe" in

the so-called "WESTERN RELIGIONS" (Judaism, Christianity, and Is-

lam). The answer, naturally, has not been forth-coming, verbally

that is. But the silent gentlemen's agreement within two of the

so-called"Western Religions" - Judaism and Christianity - that

dominate other religious thoughts in the Americas and the Carib-

beans, supported by the active cooperation of the established governments, make the "Western" (European and European-American, White) "**I believe**" official. Certainly "official," but only in the sense that any distraction by any other group equally having an "I Believe" different to that of Judaeo-Christian teachings must suffer all forms of pressures, should such "I Believe" become known to the general public. In simple words, every society, the United States of America included, either adopt or allow to practise one or more religions and reject others not catering to the State-culture in power. When this is done, the preferred religions become adjuncts of each government's structure. The end result is a marriage between religion and government. In some countries the marriage is with the official sanction and **license** of the State; in others - such as the United States of America - it is a common-law relationship. In the United States of America the bride is Judaeo-Christianity. At the wedding, between Judaeo-Christianity and Capitalism ("Americanism), Islam is not an officially invited guest, nor member of the family, even though tolerated when she crashes the marriage ceremonies. Voodoo, **Buddhism,** Black Magic, Shintoism,and all other religions which are not popular within the European and European-American experience also have been excluded from the wedding and marriage of the"Western Religions" (the brides) to the governments of the Americas (the groom). This is best displayed on January 9th of each fourth year when a president of the United States of America is to be innagurated. As the "groom" is sworn in the "bride" performs the cere-

---

* "TRADITIONAL AFRICAN RELIGIONS" is the proper expression for the various religions of Africa which are uncommon to the knowledge of all who now call them "paganism, animism, fetishism" and other names assigned African religions by the slave masters.

mony. Her swearing-in book, the "HOLY SCRIPTURE" of Judaism and
Christianity, upon which the "groom" must place his left hand,
while raising the right to take the oath to the "bride's" crea-
ors - Jehovah and Jesus Christ. Even Islam, the outside lover,
the other part of the "bride" - "Western Religions," does openly
show her affection for the "groom" on that day of the wedding
ceremonies. Of course Voodooism, Budhism, "Black Magic," Shintoism and all other non-approved religions (the harlots) are not
even invited as guests, the marriage couple being too fearful
that their "heathen ways" may contaminate the sacred rites that
was handed down by Jehovah and Jesus Christ with one of their
"bad omens" (witches or bitches brew). But as the merriment begins Voodooism is let through the back door or side window, of
course avoiding the eyes of the lookers on - the fanatical followers of the "bride," to prepare the 'LIBATIONS' - more commonly
known as toastings (alcoholic beverages).

    King, Mohammed, Matthews and Divine affected Judaism, Chris-
tianity and Islam - the so-called "WESTERN RELIGIONS" - to the
point where their marriage and/or harlotry to the government of
the United States of America must be overhauled with deepest se-
riousness and meaningful changes for the benifit of the African-
Africans (Blacks). The extent to which these African-Americans
have made the rulers, or leaders, in charge of what Jews, Christians and Moslems believe, cannot be estimated in any particular
definitive statistical methodology. However, the continued social
unrest, which is presently at it highest pitch since the passing
from the African-American (Black) political scene of such notables
as Marcus Moziah Garvey, William E. B. DuBois, El hajj Malik Sha-

bazz (Malcom X, or Malcom Little), Carlos Cooks, Arthur Reed, and a host of others before them, have had tremendous impact on what is today called "...the cultural revolution..." among the youth (African - Black, and European - White) of the United States of America's total involvement on the college and high school campuses.

Marcus Moziah Garvey, once the best known Black man in the world (1917-1928 C.E.) and founder of the "UNIVERSAL NEGRO IM-PROVEMENT ASSOCIATION, Inc." (U.N.I.A.) - can be seen as the original personality who projected the "Black Revolution" in the direction it is presently taking with respect to religion all of which began in the early 1900's (1918-1924 C.E.), which the Reverend Dr. Martin Luther King, Jr. later brought to its zenith in the 1960's C.E. For it was the late Marcus Moziah Garvey who first demanded, at the turn of the Twentieth Century C.E., that:

> BLACK PEOPLE OVER THE WORLD MUST WORSHIP A GOD
> OF THEIR OWN LIKENESS - ONE BLACK AS THEY ARE

Mr. Garvey's demand was institutionalized when he established the AFRICAN ORTHODOX CHURCH as an adjunct of the U.N.I.A., and when he set up George Alexander McGuire as "Archbishop and Primate" of that institution.[21] In so doing, Mr. Garvey followed and introduced a "nappy haired (woolly haired), black and thick-lipped Jesus Christ" to the more than five million (5,000,000) exclusively Black membership of the African Orthodox Church throughout the Americas, the Caribbeans, Canada, and Africa. This image of a "BLACK GOD" was adopted from the Ethiopian Coptic (Koptic) Church picture of Jesus Christ which became the standard picture of Jesus Christ in many African-American churches - which once would

272

not have had, and could not imagine, a Jesus Christ other than
the WHITE BLONDE NORTHERN ITALIAN of Caucasian (European) origin
Michaelangelo painted for Roman Christendom.[22]*

Songs that were originally created by European-Americans for
the presentation of a lily-White man's Christian heaven were re-
worded by the theologians of the African Orthodox Church to suit
a Black man's Christian heaven. No more was it necessary for a
Black man's heart to be "...white as snow..."[23] to "...enter the
gates of heaven" as required in a European-American Christian
Hymanl. They also created their own songs for their own hymnals.
The "ONWARD CHRISTIAN SOLDIERS" were not the same European or
European-American (White) soldiers of the first through sixth
"CHRISTIAN CRUSADES" of the attempted annexation against Moslem
lands. It was given a new meaning: Thus they were the "liberation
soldiers" of Africa from the membership of the U.N.I.A. But the
African Orthodox Churchs' newly-founded Christian hymnals had
to take a back seat to the U.N.I.A.'s greater slogan that repre-
sented the TRI-COLOR FLAG OF AFRICA - the Red, the Black, and the
Green- which Mr. Garvey established in 1918 C.E. as"the National
Flag of Black peoples;" as he stated:

> AFRICA FOR THE AFRICANS, THOSE AT HOME, AND THOSE
> ABROAD.

The first part, "AFRICA FOR THE AFRICANS," was originated
by the late Dr. Edward Wilmot Blyden (a Black man who was one of
the original Pan-African advocates before the turn of the
Twentieth Century. C.E. Dr. Blyden was born in the Danish

----

* See extract 26 on page 277, entitled,...THE IMAGE OF GOD.

Virgin Islands, presently the United States Virgin Islands - since
1918 C.E.. After leaving there, he became President of the College of Liberia, West Africa; also Ambassador to the Court of St.
James, Great Britain, for his government. He was the author of
many basic books on African religions, Christianity, and Islam).

In the PHILOSOPHY AND OPINIONS OF MARCUS GARVEY, edited and
published through his second wife - Amy Jacques Garvey, Mr. Garvey
stated the basic tenets that formulated his religious belief
under various sub-titles; as follows:[24]

PRESENT DAY CIVILIZATION

We are circumvented today by environments more dangerous
than those which circumvented other peoples in any other age. We
are face to face with environments in a civilization that is highly
developed; a civilization that is competing with itself for its own
destruction; a civilization that cannot last, because it has no
spiritual foundation; a civilization that is vicious, crafty, dishonest,
immoral, irreligious and corrupt.

We see a small percentage of the world's populace feeling happy
and contented with this civilization that man has evolved, and we
see the masses of the human race on the other hand dissatisfied and
discontented with the civilization of today—the arrangement of
human society. Those masses are determined to destroy the systems
that hold up such a society and prop such a civilization.

As by indication, the fall will come. A fall that will cause the
universal wreck of the civilization that we now see, and in this
civilization the Negro is called upon to play his part. He is called
upon to evolve a national ideal, based upon freedom, human liberty
and true democracy.

With respect to the rights of the Black man to inherit the
earth, he said the following:

DIVINE APPORTIONMENT OF EARTH

God Almighty created all men equal, whether they be white,
yellow or black, and for any race to admit that it cannot do what
others have done, is to hurl an insult at the Almighty who created
all races equal, in the beginning.

The white man has no right of way to this green earth, neither
the yellow man. All of us were created lords of the creation, and
whether we be white, yellow, brown or black Nature intended a
place for each and every one.

If Europe is for the white man, if Asia is for brown and yellow
men, then surely Africa is for the black man. The great white man
has fought for the preservation of Europe, the great yellow and

274

brown races are fighting for the preservation of Asia, and four hundred million Negroes shall shed, if needs be, the last drop of their blood for the redemption of Africa and the emancipation of the race everywhere.

In order to articulate as much as he did on the subject of religion, especially with references to Christianity, Mr Garvey assumed the role of a philosopher, as seen in the following:[25]

PURPOSE OF CREATION

The man or woman who has no confidence in self is an unfortunate being, and is really a misfit in creation.

God Almighty created each and every one of us for a place in the world, and for the least of us to think that we were created only to be what we are and not what we can make ourselves, is to impute an improper motive to the Creator for creating us.

God Almighty created us all to be free. That the Negro race became a race of slaves was not the fault of God Almighty, the Divine Master, it was the fault of the race.

Sloth, neglect, indifference caused us to be slaves.

Confidence, conviction, action will cause us to be free men today.

If there was anything Mr. Garvey loved as much as his own life, it was his "race." He wrote the following in conjunction with his belief:

PURITY OF RACE

I believe in a pure black race just as how all self-respecting whites believe in a pure white race, as far as that can be.

I am conscious of the fact that slavery brought upon us the curse of many colors within the Negro race, but that is no reason why we of ourselves should perpetuate the evil; hence instead of encouraging a wholesale bastardy in the race, we feel that we should now set out to create a race type and standard of our own which could not, in the future, be stigmatized by bastardy, but could be recognized and respected as the true race type anteceding even our own time.

Since Mr. Garvey was not a believer in non-violence as a way to the freedom of the Black man, he also saw his God —Jesus Christ, as a "War Lord:"

GOD AS A WAR LORD

God is a bold Sovereign—A Warrior Lord. The God we worship and adore is a God of War as well as a God of Peace. He does not allow anything to interfere with his power and authority.

The greatest battle ever fought was not between the Kaiser of

> Germany on the one hand and the Allied Powers on the other, it was
> between Almighty God on the one hand and Lucifer the Archangel
> on the other.
>
> When Lucifer challenged God's power in Heaven and marshalled
> his forces on the plains of Paradise, the God we worship and adore
> also marshalled His forces, His Archangels, His Cherubims and
> His Seraphims, and in battle array He placed Himself before them
> with the royal standard of Heaven.

Mr. Garvey had to adopt the use of the word "NEGRO" when he first organized the U.N.I.A., because Blacks at that time were too much brainwashed with that word to accept their blackness. It is for this reason that he spoke of a "Negro God:"[26]

THE IMAGE OF GOD

> If the white man has the idea of a white God, let him worship his
> God as he desires. If the yellow man's God is of his race let him
> worship his God as he sees fit. We, as Negroes, have found a new
> ideal. Whilst our God has no color, yet it is human to see every-
> thing through one's own spectacles, and since the white people have
> seen their God through white spectacles, we have only now started
> out (late though it be) to see our God through our own spectacles.
> The God of Isaac and the God of Jacob let Him exist for the race
> that believes in the God of Isaac and the God of Jacob. We Negroes
> believe in the God of Ethiopia, the everlasting God—God the
> Father, God the Son and God the Holy Ghost, the One God of all
> ages. That is the God in whom we believe, but we shall worship
> Him through the spectacles of Ethiopia.

Mr Garvey tied his Christianity to the everyday activities common in Voodooism. In keeping with an eye on the age-old indigenous African tradition, he also tied the African Orthodox Church to the politics of Africa, Ethiopia in particular, when he ordered that it "Be Resolved; That the Anthem, "ETHIOPIA, THOU LAND OF OUR FATHERS...," etc., shall be the Anthem of the "NEGRO RACE." The following stanzas are taken from the:

THE UNIVERSAL ETHIOPIAN ANTHEM

I

Ethiopia, thou land of our fathers,
Thou land where the gods loved to be,
As storm cloud at night suddenly gathers
Our armies come rushing to thee.
We must in the fight be victorious
When swords are thrust outward to gleam;
For us will the vict'ry be glorious
When led by the red, black and green.

Chorus

Advance, advance to victory,
Let Africa be free;
Advance to meet the foe
With the might
Of the red, the black and the green.

II

Ethiopia, the tyrant's falling,
Who smote thee upon thy knees,
And thy children are lustily calling
From over the distant seas.

Jehovah, the Great One has heard us,
Has noted our sighs and our tears,
With His spirit of Love he has stirred us
To be One through the coming years.
CHORUS—Advance, advance, etc.

III

O Jehovah, thou God of the ages
Grant unto our sons that lead
The wisdom Thou gave to Thy sages
When Israel was sore in need.
Thy voice thro' the dim past has spoken,
Ethiopia shall stretch forth her hand,
By Thee shall all fetters be broken,
And Heav'n bless our dear fatherland.
CHORUS—Advance, advance, etc. ✱

In describing Christianity, Mr Garvey wrote the following:[28]

CHRISTIANITY

A form of religion practised by the millions, but as misunderstood and unreal to the majority as gravitation is to the untutored savage. We profess to live in the atmosphere of Christianity, yet our acts are as barbarous as if we never knew Christ. He taught us to love, yet we hate; to forgive, yet we revenge; to be merciful, yet we condemn and punish, and still we are Christians.

If hell is what we are taught it is, then there will be more Christians there than days in all creation. To be a true Christian one must be like Christ and practice Christianity, not as the Bishop does, but as he says, for if our lives were to be patterned after the other fellow's all of us, Bishop, Priest and Layman would ultimately meet around the furnace of hell, and none of us, because of our sins, would see salvation.

Further analysis of the philosophical concepts by the "Black Moses" (a name Mr. Garvey was afeectionately called) would be superfluous to one's understanding of the Africans' mind in religion, if it has not caught on by now. However, it must be understood, that Marcus Moziah Garvey was the only Black man that ever lived

---

* From a poem by the late Burrell and Ford, U.I.A. members.

within continental United States of America who truly challenged European-American-style Christianity with any success, all others having formed European-style Christian-like religions with the same blonde Jesus Christ and family, or converted to other religions which are closely connected to the same origin such as Judaism and Islam, all of them maintaining a blonde or other than Black "SUPREME GOD."

One must also remember that Mr. Garvey came from a "Maroon" background on the Island of Jamaica, in the Caribbean "West Indies," where he was born on 17 August, 1887 C.E., to Marcus and Sarah Garvey, Sr. Mr. Garvey, senior, was not a man of African or European-style Christianity; instead he held to his Voodoo-type African worship - which was typical of the Africans (Maroons) who fought the British and won their right to independence on one end of the island early in 1739 C.E.[29] The conflict in parental religious devotion affected young Garvey, Jr. to the point where at such an early age he questioned Christianity's exclusively "WHITE" colonialist control and its direct relationship to the British Imperialist administrators of the British colony - Jamaica.[30]

There should be no doubt that the "Black Moses" did changed the course of normal acceptance of millions of Blacks from a "White Jesus Christ" and "Heaven" as depicted by Michaelangelo and the Roman Catholic Church of Rome. If no one else, his millions of followers and their admirers were affected; they in turn influenced thousands, or millions, of their offspring and friends.[31] The result of Mr. Garvey's teachings resulted in a Malcolm X, Roy Innis, Stokely Carmichael, and a host of other "modern Black militants" who now control the "Black liberation movement," at least

278

those who still consider Africa as the final solution of the Black man's struggle in the world.

The legacy of Voodooism inherited by so-called "Western Religions" should not surprise anyone more than the legacy Christianity inherited from Judaism, or the legacy Islam inherited from both Judaism and Christianity, and of course, the legacy all of them inherited from the traditionally-African religions of the Nile Valley cultures that reached their zenith in Sais (Egypt). What is strange about all of this, however, is that most "Western (White) educators" continue writing volumes after volumes on the more than four hundred (400) long years the Hebrew (Jewish) peoples spent in North Africa, Egypt in particular; yet, they seem to expect that the Jews were able to remain immune to any cultural impact of their host country, Egypt, and its indigenous people - the Egyptians (the so-called "Negroes, Bantus, Blacks, Niggers, Africans South of the Sahara, Pygmies, Hottentots, Bushmen, and a host of other such nomenclatures).

How can anyone remain rational when discussing the merits of his or her religion against another to which someone else belongs? Very easily so, by remembering the first fundamental law of all religions - the "I BELIEVE," as against the "I KNOW." The "I BELIEVE" should make it possible for an open-minded discussion dealing with religious differences among intelligent people, that is, people who are willing to listen to the opinions of others and respect them. Respecting or understanding the other person's words does not necessarily mean accepting them. Therefore, the removal of the unusual fear which usually accompanies comparative analysis of religions and religious institutions can be accomplished. Unfortunately, most people are afraid to openly discuss religion or its institutions and administrators, unless such discussion is complimentary to that which he or she believes. Some reduce this further to a particular sect's position within the same religion; and as such they have no religious tolerance for any religious sect but their own.

Many critics of religion have pointed out that:

> ...the differences within an individual religion are much more insoluble than the differences between various religions.

For example: It seems to be easier to create a lasting friendship between a Moslem sect and a Christian sect than between a Roman Catholic sect and a Protestant sect the same between Baptist and Methodist. The inter-relationship between an individual religion - vis-a-vis - Orthodox Judaism and Reform, Suni Moslem and Ismali - is equally as strong as those listed already. Because of these facts, no other reason being necessary, one should more readily understand why it is difficult for anyone in the U.S. professing either of the so-called "WESTERN RELIGIONS" (Judaism, Christainity,and Islam) to accept their own non-Western origin, much-less their acceptance of Voodooism as being a basic part of their present religious behavioural pattern.

Never-the-less Voodooism, like Obyah, Judaism, Black Magic,and any other form of indigenous African, American (so-called "Indian) or Asian religion [32] - will survive as long as there is religious belief. Why? Because the basic qualities which are inherent in any one religion can be found in all others. Thus, (a) the main justification of religion is fear of the unknown; (b) the sec-

ond is _egotism_. Yet, both of these values are combined into a
common understanding called "FAITH." This "_faith_" allows no questioning about its source - "GOD." However, without the availabil-
ity of further investigation into anything that is subject to
changing developments the end result of compounding intolerance
becomes almost inescapably catastrophic. The cycle becomes more
and more frustrating as the dogma of non-dissension becomes a
part of a particular group dynamics. Thus, the foundation of prejudice that is predicated upon hearsay and faith, rather than
upon investigated factual data, certainly is typical of today's
versions of that which is called "WESTERN RELIGIONS."

King, Mohammed, Divine, Matthews, and Garvey have made their
mark on religion in the United States of America, Mohammed and
Matthews being the only survivors of the group. Mohammed leading
his _Nation of Islam_ towards an independent _Muslim Nation_ confined to the United States of America; whereas, Matthews leading
toward the day when Israel should be ready to open its arms to its
Black sisters and brothers of the African-American (Black) _Isra-
elite community on an equal basis_, the same as it does for its
European and European-American Jewish communities.

With regard to the Prophet and Messenger - Elijah Mohammed,
the mere thought of a non-Judaeo-Christian state or nation of
lily-White European-Americans within the structure of the gov-
vernment of the United States of America is inconceivable to the
"powers that be" - much less one controlled by African-Americans of
Islamic persuasions. This statement is not meant to be an endorsement or condemnation of the "...all Black State" or "States" proposition of the Nation of Islam for the "Black Nationalists move-

ments". It is, on the other hand, a statement of current expressions among European-Americans with regards to the so-called "Black-White confrontation" one hears so much about lately. This empasse crosses religious lines among the European-Americans (Whites) communities; whereas it has a religious factor as well as a secular one amongst the African-American communities. For example, European-American Jews are not against an "...all Black state..." because of their Judaism, but because of their common European (White, Caucasian) heritage with the vast majority of their fellow European-Americans (Whites) of the Christian, Moslem, and other faiths. On the other hand, the "All Black State" to which Prophet Elijah Mohammed alludes is one to be controlled by himself and others within his Nation of Islam - a theocratic state which is contrary to the "...socialist oriented society" spoken of by most of the current non-Garvey type Black Nationalists groups. The secret is the economic and religious outlook of the Nation of Islam, which cannot tolerate an Al'lah-less type non-capitalist society, whether ruled by Whites or Blacks. In this respect the Nation of Islam is a true friend of the economic system of the European-American power structure in the United States of America. As such, it protects it from others, be they Black or White whose desire it is to remove and replace it with any other economic system other than another form of capitalism. Yet, the common goal remains at least:

One independent Black State within the Union of
the United States of America,

a far cry from the independently settled :

Africa for the Africans, those at home, and those
abroad...

282

proposition of the Black Nationalist followers of the school of
Marcus Moziah Garvey and the U.N.I.A., along with the teachings
of its adjunct - the African Orthodox Church.[33]

As one looks at history, Garvey's protest can be very well
identified in the following excerpt from the lesson in the age-
old African-American*Spiritual:"[34]

> Joshua fit de battle of Jericho,
> Jericho, Jericho,
> Joshua fit de battle of Jericho,
> And the walls came tumbling down.

This "Spiritual" is a far cry from the solace the "Negro"
sophisticates of today find in European-America-style Christianity
as they win a few more social niceties from a segregated Christian community in White America. As such, the following excerpt
from a later African Spiritual shows the new resignation of surrender to the European Christian God - Jesus Christ - and the
appeasement of standard middle-class "Negro Church" ideology and
theology:[35]

> My God is a rock in a weary land,
> My God is a rock in a weary land,
> Shelter in the time of storm.

Here one sees a tired and beaten "Negro" who has lost all
hope of victory over slavery. And as another "Spiritual" says:

> Ah aint gona study war no mo, Ah aint gona study war
> no mo, no mo, no mo, ...etc.[36]

By 1928 C.E. the "Negro" was completely defeated once more.
The gains he had made, whatever they were, he could no longer
see any relevance in them. He had lost the African ministers -
Nat Turner and Denmark Vesey, and a few   the "Negro Ministers"

---

* "NEGROES" were not imported from Africa to the "Western Hemis-
pher " or "New World;" Africans were. Thus, instead of "Negro Spirituals," it should be AFRICAN or AFRICAN-AMERICA SPIRITUALS, if
at all it is Spiritual, rather than Voodoo Chants from Africa.

as his fire and damnation-preaching leaders who tried to adopt
the European and European-American crusaders "<u>Onward Christian
Soldiers</u>"[37] anthem, and applied it to the African-American Christian converts against their European-American Christian and Jewish slavemasters. But there were no more Benjamin T. Tanner[38]
to lead them into their own Christian Church of social action
the "Black Church" having become a social centre for Sunday
School services and soul-searching, dancing, prancing, and wailing. His fighting courage, which he had displayed in "...<u>de
battle of Jericho</u>..." spiritual, was dead, and his later found
hero and savior -Marcus Moziah Garvey (Black Moses) had been already deported back to his native Jamaica in the Caribbean.[39]

Father Divine had become the new spiritual guide to many
thousands, possibly millions.* At the same time another "diviner,"
Prophetess Mother Horne,[40] was also making a bid for recognition
as the major religious leader of another European-American-style
African-American based Christian community from her headquarters
on the east side of Lenox Avenue, between 129th and 130th Streets,
Harlem, New York City, New York.

Divine's "<u>Peace Mission Movement</u>" and other "<u>Holiness</u>" Christian sects - such as Bishop Ida Robinson's "Mt. Sinai Holy Church"[41]
of Philadelphia, Pensylvania, and the Holiness churches of Chicago
moved the "...<u>good old Spiritualist</u>..." Voodoo type African-American parishoners toward the cultist tradition spoken of by the
biblical Daniel in the Hebrew Torah (Five Books of Moses).

Who was this "New God" - Father Divine?[42] About his origin

---

* No one really knew the wealth or numerical strength of the Divine movement except those within control of it.

very little statistical data seems to be available, except for his role as founder of the "Peace Mission Movement." But Major J. Divine (the name he originally called himself) had made for millions a "Heaven", and changed European-American-style Chris- tian traditions for even many more from 1919 C.E., when he became the shepherd of his own religiously-based economic movement. This movement actually had its origin at Sayville, New Jersey where Divine bought a moderate-sized cottage from a German-American couple. In so doing, they were disregarding the prevailing "Cau- casian only" covenant that governed their house, a type of gentle- men's agreement which is still common in real estate deeds through- out the United States of America, even though the nation's Supreme Court has since ruled them "unconstitutional."

With his first wife, Penninah, Divine **moved into the mo-** destly furnished cottage and immediately thereafter established an employment agency that was "...free of charge to all without regards to race, creed, color, or sex." Soon after the Divines be- gan clothing and feeding the destitutes who could not find any sort of gainful employment, and also giving them lodging. By 1930, in the midst of the "Great Depression," Father Divine and Mother Divine - his wife, had begun preaching their sermons of "Godli- ness, Purity, and Redemption." Reverend Divine had become the "Most Worshipful Father Divine," and the cottage had become the first of a series of "Heavens" for the multitude who could raise sufficient funds to pay their way to reach it. But the restric- tions established by Father had also begun to set the pattern for what was later on to come. It started with prohibitions against intoxicating beverages, but none on foods. These "Dietary Laws,"

285

similar in many of its aspects to those of the Hebrew Torah (Book of Leviticus), could be found in the "NEW DAY" - the sacred teachings of Father. The "New Day" was Father's weekly publication that carried the messages and other news of his Kingdom. It took the place of the Christians' Holy Bible, which was barred to all of the faithful - as there was to be no other "Holy Scriptures" than that which Father placed in the "New Day." Yet the "New Day" carried advertisements for all of the businesses Father had acquired.

"Thank You Father" - had replaced the need for prayer to Jehovah, Jesus Christ or Al'lah. These words were only to be mentioned and "...the afflicted would be cured." For, to the faithful Father was "God Himself on Earth" - who could "never die." To them "illness" was "...due to sin against the teachings of Father," and "...death his punishment."[43] In these two conditions Father was substituted for Jehovah, Jesus Christ and Al'lah.

The movement came to the "Big City" (New York) in 1932 C.E., the toughest year of "The Great Depression." Father was received by his New York faithful in Harlem amidst these clamouring words:

THE REAL GOD IS THE ONE THAT FEEDS US[44]

But "the real God," Father Divine, met a former fish peddler who had turned "Prophet" - one Elder Lightfoot Solomon Micheaux[45] - also grabbing to get hold of the vacuum the 1927 C.E. deportation of Marcus Moziah Garvey (Black Moses)* had created in the Harlems of the United States of America. Micheaux, whom his faithful fol-

---

* Mr. Garvey was deported after serving two years of a four-year sentence for "Mail Fraud" on trumped-up charges by the U.S.A.

286

lowers used to call the "HAPPY I AM PROPHET,"[46] was contending
for the crown Divine had also set his eyes upon; along with Bishop "Sweet Daddy Grace"[47] and Prophetess Mother Rosa Artimus Horne
(the former seamstress) - whose followers called "Pray for me
Priestess."[48]

Being a woman in an African-American (Black) world made it
virtually impossible for Mother Horne to amass the fortunes of
either of her male competition for the crown of African-American
spiritual leader. This left the contest to Divine and Grace. Bishop
"Sweet Daddy Grace" was an immigrant to the United States of America; and of African-European origin from the Cape Verde Islands
off West Africa's coastline. It is believed that "...he entered the United States of America around the early 1920's" and
remained until his death in 1960 C.E. It must be noted, however,
that his followers, who are now led by one Bishop McCullough,
have refused to accept his death - claiming that:

"...He has risen into heaven;"[47]
an adoptation from their original European-American style Christian background. Daddy Grace (a former cook on many American rail-
way systems) had established the "United House of Prayer for all
People" with almost as many branches as Divine's Peace Missions.
But unlike Divine, Grace made Washington, D.C., his headquarters.
Its location, to him, represented the symbol of his high prestige
of office, which he said was equal to that - at least on Earth -
of the President of the United States of America, but higher in
heaven, being "God" himself.

These religious dimensions were similarly expressed in another
aspect, as pronounced in the protest of the major African-American

287

writers during the 1930's, when Ralph Ellison wrote his "INVISIBLE MAN";[48] Richard Wright his "BLACK BOY," and "NATIVE SON,"[49] only to be followed by Langston Hughes' "SIMPLE."[50] The 1930's witnessed a revival of African-American culture and spiritual awareness that were exhibited by Phyllis Wheatly[51] in the 1700's; Harriet Tubman[52] in the 1800's; W.E.B. DuBois[53] and M.M. Garvey[54] in the 1900's. These rebirths did not remain on the shores of continental North America - the United States of America in particular, for they are still seen in Rio de Janiero's (Brazil) Black communities; throughout the island of Haiti and Santo Domingo; among the African-Cubanos of Cuba; the African-Puerto Ricanos of Puerto Rico - with her two Black towns, Carolina and Louisa;[55] also, in Jamaica, and Trinidad, where their exponents are best seen in the CAIESAU - which has since become the world's famous "CALYPSO."

In the United States of America's VIRGIN ISLANDS, St. Croix, St. Thomas, and St. John (formerly Danish Virgin Islands until 1918 C.E.), it took the form of "OBYAH" (Obiah). In Puerto Rico, Cuba, and Santo Domingo it became "BRUJA." In Haiti, Guadeloupe, and Martinique it is called "VOODOO." And in the United States of America it is still being called "WITCHCRAFT" and "BLACK MAGIC." Put them all together and they spell the same thing they did for thousands of years before they arrived in these parts, logically and simply, the "MYSTERY SYSTEM" that the indigenous Africans of the Nile Valley and other parts of Africa (Alkebu-lan) developed, when all others mentioned, so far as this entire volume is concerned, were either non-existent or unknown in recorded history, this of course includes Greece and her first known - HOMER.

The Black man had established for himself a form of religion
288

that was neither African, Asian or European in origin, but AFRI-
CAN-AMERICAN. African-American in the sense that it was a combination of all three cultural involvements he had been subjected to,
withstanding them, under his enslavement by the Europeans, then
the European-Americans (Whites), and that which he had retained
from his own culture of his Mother Land - Africa (Alkebu-lan). All
of this, he developed to its zenith while sojourning here on this
continent, especially the United States of America. He had reached
the point where Bishop "SWEET DADDY GRACE" could tell his fellow
African-American faithful:

> ...never mind about God. Salvation is by Grace only.
> Grace has given God a vacation; and since God is on
> vacation, don't worry about him....If you sin against
> God, Grace can save you, but if you sin against Grace,
> God cannot save you.[56]

With all that has been brought forward within the lights so
far, it must be also maintained, and admitted, that many writers
disagree with the view that the it was not the African-Americans'
disaffection from European-American-type Christianity that caused
them to return to their original African religious base. One may
be able to agree with such a position on its face value, but not
in its historical reality, which is so obvious throughout the
Black communities of the Americas, especially if one is anthro-
pologically attuned to the culture and religion of said people.

There was another uniquely phenomenal religious movement that
developed during the 1930's under the leadership of an African-
American named Cherry - called endearingly "PROPHET F.S. CHERRY."
His group practised basic Christianity, European-American-style,
but they adopted the Jewish Talmud in preference to the KING JAMES'
NEW TESTAMENT of the Christian Holy Bible. "THE CHURCH OF GOD," the

name of the new religious institution, was to have its parishoners

adopt the name of "BLACK JEWS." Prophet Cherry, a self-educated

man, and former merchant marine turned Minister or Rabbi, claimed

that:

> ...the so-called white Jew is a fraud. [57]

He insisted that the:

> ...Black man is the original man created by God -
> Jehovah (Yvah).

That:

> ...the enslavement of the Africans was predicted
> in the Hebrew Torah; (also) their emancipation.

Christmas and Easter were tabooed

> ...because Christ was never killed by man; nor was
> he born of a Virgin birth....

according to his faithful followers. Saturday was maintained as

"the true Sabbath" (Holy Day), not Sunday. Hebrew was compulsory

for each and every member to know, in order that

> ...ancient Hebrew manuscripts could be read in the
> original language of the Torah.

Death and funerals were paid very little attention, in keeping

with the

> ...let the dead bury the dead and the living be of
> the living...,[58]

paraphrasing of the Hebrew regulations on this subject according

to the Torah. But the Torah (Hebrew Holy Bible, equivalent of the

Christian Old Testament) was not the final authority. It was only

the reference book of the sect. Strangely enough, they did not

claim any special lineage with the world's oldest Hebrew (Jewish)

peoples, who also have black pigment - the Beta Israel (Falashas,

or Black Jews) of Ethiopia, East Africa; nor the Yemenites (form-

erly of Yemen and Arabia, Asia) who now live in the State of Is-

290

rael.[59]

The African-Americans' move toward separation have stymied the smaller, but more sophisticated assimilationists among themselves. These "NEGROES," as they still prefer to be called, insist that...

> Jesus Christ has no color... (therefore) ...He was an integrationist.

The separatists retort to as much of what they **can** tie to their indigenous African traditionalism; whereas the assimilationists **clung** to their High Episcopalianism and other similarly sophisticated religous involvement that **will** give them the feeling that they are equally European-American style Christians as their White communicants. For this the integrationists would prefer death than have a religion that is indigenous to Africa, and have no White members; this they also reject for another reason, that is, in order to retain the blonde Caucasian image of a Jesus Christ - their God - painted by the Italian, Michaelangelo, for a White (European) Christendom and heaven; yet they will, in the face of this truth, maintain that....

> JESUS CHRIST HAS NO COLOR.

If he "...has no color" he should not appear in any form whatsoever in paintings and other material presentation, especially in a Christian church.

Sunday morning 11 May, 1969, was highlighted by a small group of well-meaning African-Americans, who challenged the method of participation the well-healed European-American Christian "liberals" of Riverside Church, at 120th Street and Riverside Drive, Harlem, New York City, New York, and their handful of middle-class

291

aspiring "Negro" parishioners who mostly live in the blackest
section of the Harlems of the City of New York, but could no
longer involve themselves with the same Baptist or soul-saving
religious institutions of which they were members of before they
found their middle-class status. As they sat in their pews the
sermon began, only to be interrupted by a group of Black Americans
under the leadership of one James Forman, of the NATIONAL BLACK
ECONOMIC DEVELOPMENT CONFERENCE. Mr. Forman led his followers
down the main aisle of the plush church in the direction of the
altar, where the minister was already beginning one of his usual
intellectual "liberal Christian" services common in such sophisticated middle-class churches - where the poorest people of the
community in which the church is based are intellectually mentioned,
but in practice ignored. As the opening song was being sung, Mr.
Forman began to read from what was later identified as the "BLACK
MANIFESTO," which he felt the religious institutions (of all
denominations and sects) of the United States of America were duty
bound to meet because of their role in colonialism, slavery, and
big business. Extracts from the Black Manifesto follow:[60]

"We are demanding $5,000,000,000 to be spent in the following way:"

"1. We call for the establishment of a southern bank to help
our brothers and sisters who have to leave their land because of
racist pressures for people who want to establish cooperative
farms, but who have no funds..." "We call for $200,000,000 for
implementation of this program."

"2. We call for the establishment of four major publishing
and printing industries in the United States to be funded with ten
million dollars each. These publishing houses are to be located
in Detroit, Atlanta, Los Angeles and New York...."

"3. We call for the establishment of four of the most
advanced scientific and futuristic audio-visual network to be located
in Detroit, Chicago, Cleveland and Washington, D.C....."

"4. We call for a research skills center which will provide research on the problems of Black people. This center must be funded with no less than 30 million dollars.

"5. We call for the establishment of a training center for the teaching of skills in community organizations, photography, movie making, television making and repair, radio building and repair and all other skills needed in communications. This training center shall be funded with no less than ten million dollars.

"6. We recognize the role of the National Welfare Rights Organization and we intend to work with them. We call for ten million dollars to assist in the organization of welfare recipients, etc.

"7. We call for $20,000,000 to establish a National Black Labor Strike and Defense Fund. This is necessary for the protection of Black workers and their families who are fighting racist working conditions in this country.

"8. We call for the establishment of the International Black Appeal (IBA)..." "...$20,000,000." "The IBA is charged with three functions and shall be headed by James Forman:

    a) Raising money for the program of the National Black Economic Development Conference.

    b) The development of cooperatives in African countries and support of African Liberation Movements.

    c) Establishment of a Black-Anti-Defamation League which will protect our African image.

"9. We call for the establishment of a Black University to be funded with $130,000,000 to be located in the South. Negotiations are presently under way with Southern University.

"10. We demand that IFCO allocate all unused funds in planning budget to implement the demands of this conference."

Many of the remaining members of the congregation, who did not hastily exist in hot pursuit of their fleeing minister to avoid hearing what they were to correct in their preachings, listened to Mr. Forman; many nodded their head in agreement or dis- agreement with the demands, and also indicated other gestures of pleasure or displeasure, but they never-the-less listened to the pleading of a group of African-Americans who had an indictment

against the callousness of organized institutional "Western Religions" and its alignment with government, money, and racism. But
in this citadel of European-American Anglo-Saxon Protestantism,
where White middle-class "liberalism" is preached each and every
Sunday of the year on the subject of "...AID TO MINORITY GROUPS,"
and echoed over its F.M. Radio Station news broadcast, the representatives of Jesus Christ on earth - the clergy - display none
of the compassionate feelings they always claim for their God
and Saviour - Jesus Christ. Why the alarm? A "...handful of irresponsible Negroes"[66] had entered "...the house of God...", Riverside Church, and tried "...to take their troubles and leave it
on the doorstep of the Lord;"[62] just as the Christian hymnal suggested all these hundreds of years to the Blacks of the United
States of America.

The indictment against this Protestant sect had followed an
earlier confrontation between Mr. Forman and his followers against
the hierarchy of the inner-circle of the Presbyterian sect that
listened to their demands, but had very little to say with respect
to commitments of their financially plush institution towards the
illimination of the ills mentioned in the "Manifesto." Yet, the
demands dealt with fellow-Christian brothers and sisters of the
Black community from whence the Reverend Dr. Martin Luther King,
Jr., their alleged hero, was born, raised, and was martyred for the
cause of White America and organized religions - two of the so-called
"WESTERN RELIGIONS" (Judaism, Christianity).

Christianity was not the only religion Mr. Forman intended
to call upon, as he had indicated in so many press conferences
before and after the Riverside Church's non-violent demonstration,

294

which so many million European-Americans claim is "..the right way;" yet, they rejected such action when it happened in their own backyard. As such, the news got to Rabbi Maurice N. Eisendrat of the equally wealthy Temple Emmanuel, most noted of the Reformed sects of Judaism (located at the northeast corner of 61st Street and Fifth Avenue, a plush residential area where very few - if any - African-American Christian, Moslem,or Jew could secure residence).

The mere suggestion that this very small non-violent group of African-American protestors were supposed to place its demands during the Omeg Shabbath (Friday Evening Service) of the Temple brought out some of the not so non-violent Jewish Defense League, whose members were reported to have had "...tire irons, car chains, baseball bats," and other such "non-violent weapons" awaiting the unarmed "non-violent protestants." Newspaper and radio reports indicated that Rabbi Perlman of Temple Emmanuel protested the presence of the Jewish Defense League, which he claimed not to have invited or knew in advance would be there.

Strange as it may appear, no one (including the same "Negro" religious leaders and "Negro Jews" - called Hatzaad Harishon, who had been extremely vocal in protesting about "Negro anti-Semitism") cried out in shock against this wantonly "violent" display of White Jewish anti-Blackism. The irony of it all is that neither Mr. Forman,nor any of his followers indicated any definite intent of visiting Temple Emmanuel, and did not. Stranger yet, not one of the Civil Rights Organizations' "Negro leaders" who alligned themselves against "Black Studies" courses and "community control in Black communities" who are always available to condemn "Negro anti-

Semitism," raised a single voice of protest against the weapons-
bearing non-violent Jewish Defense League members that awaited
a physical confrontation with Mr. Forman and his unarmed group
of African-Americans (Blacks).

The Prophet Elijah Mohammed, Rev. Bishop "Sweet Daddy Grace," Rabbi
Wentworth Matthews, Honourable Marcus Moziah Garvey, and other
major religious personalities and political figures who have not
received the 'GOOD NEGRO SEAL OF APPROVAL' from the allegedly
White "LIBERAL MIDDLE-CLASS COMMUNITY OF THE UNITED STATES OF
AMERICA' (Jews, Christian, Moslem, Christian Science, etc.) are
none-the-less heroes and saints - or even saviours and redeemers -
among Black peoples who are aware of the fact that 'HE WHO PAYS
THE FIDDLER CALLS THE TUNES.'

CONCLUSION

Many African-Americans have recently moved from their "I know a good Negro family in my church..,etc.," window dressing role to positions of minor non-policy making participation in White America's religious institutions. The "GOOD NEGROES," never-the-less, have decided to act upon , rather than remain quietly within the White Christian religion. They are presently asking:

How is it that all of the White "liberal" religious leaders of every creed allow their respective institutions to become tied to the operations of the national government; at the same time preaching"the separation of church and state?" Why is religion protecting slum lords in "Negro" communities? Why is religion (Jewish, Christian, Moslem) a part of big business, including being slum lords? Why is there no place in religion for the White poor, much-less the Black ones? Why is there no chair set at the table of the White Jewish home for the stranger in the Temple (be he Black, White, or technicolor) as commanded in Hebrew Scriptures, including Black Jews? Why is it that European-style Christianity (Protestants and Roman Catholic sects alike) ignoring the command of their leader - Jesus Christ - Who said: "Who-so-ever receives one such as these in my name, receives me?"[62a] Is it enough to send a pitiful check to the National Association for the Advancement of Colored People, and other so-called "responsible Negro organization" on occasion, or take part in a Martin Luther King, Jr., type demonstration to prove brotherhood of man? Or, was the African-American struggle for rights already guaranteed in the United States of America's Federal Constitution - the "BILL OF RIGHTS - completed with the sacrifice of the Reverend Dr. Martin Luther King, Jr's bier when it rolled down the streets of Alabama to its final resting place as White America and her members of the clergy followed in hot pursuit? And; Did the closing of stores for a few hours hours, shedding of tears, ringing of church bells, releasing of statements against "violence" when applied by Blacks (only) in condemnation of "anti-Semitism," but ignoring 'anti-Blackism,' talking about "love thy neighbor" while the poor watch billions of pounds of food rot in warehouses while more is plowed under as the clergy of all religions stand idly by? How can these display of utter dis-

297

regard for justice in the African-American (Black) communities by the clergy stop? Is it to be expected, continuously that is, that the Black Americans are to remain non-violently watching their kinfolk exterminated for another four-hundred (400) years plus (1619 - 1970 C.E.), which they have spent in the United States of America and the former British colonies, before they are accepted as mere human beings? Or, are they not to take up weapons and defend themselves against tyranny as the "Fathers" of the United States of America did against the British? What should it be? What is God doing about it?

Black people in the United States of America, be they Jews, Christians, Moslems, or of traditionally noted indigenous African religious denominations,are also asking"White America" (Jews, Christians and Moslems alike):

Is religion's role and sole purpose for the existence and perpetuation of the powers that allow it to become wealthy?

They further asked of religious leaders, Black ones included:

Is "...thou shalt not kill" only applicable to individuals and not nations? Are the provisions on slavery found in the Jewish, Christian,and Moslem Holy Scriptures ordained by God (Jehovah, Jesus Christ, Al'lah) against Black people of the world alone, as proclaimed by the Calvinists and Later Day Saints (Mormons)?[63] Did the Africans not Pass Over (Pesach) from one part of their homeland - Egypt, Africa (Alkebu-lan) to another part of their land - Mt Sinai - with their fellow African - Moses and thousands more of their fellow African (Black) brothers and sisters - the African HARIBU (Hebrews or Jews)? Was it not from Africa most of what mankind call "Judaism, Christianity" and "Islam" originated? is it not in Africa, around the sources of the Blue and White - Nile Valley, the Olduvai Gorge in Tanzania,and Ethiopia the oldest fossils of man have been found? Is it not in the Black man's continent - Africa (Alkebu-lan) Judaism, Christianity,and Islam got their"TEN COMMANDMENTS" from the "NEGATIVE CONFESSIONS" and other such documents? Was the concept of God not originated among the indigenous Blacks who worshipped the Sun God - RA of Africa?

How long is "Black America"expected to worship a God on its knees and stare into the clouds awaiting the coming or return of

298

the promised "MESSIAH" to free them from their earthly bonds?
Did any group, ethnic or otherwise, ever before free themselves
on their knees by praying? Did any group before allow its women to be dragged off to prison, beaten, spat upon, disrobed in
public, set upon by ferocious dogs - their children included,
while their men stand by passively and watch it all in the name
of God, except the African-Americans? Where in history is it recorded that any other group of human beings stood in down-pouring
showers of torrential rain on their kness praying for a stricken
sheriff, called "Bull Connors,"[64] while his deputies await his commands for another chance to set their vicious dogs (blood hounds)
upon them, and to shock them with electrical charges that were
otherwise used for cattle?* Did the European (White) Christians
pray for America, and did God take it from the so-called "Indians," the
only true indigenous peoples of the United States of America, and
gave it to them non-violently? Did Bishop Bartolome de LasCasas
of the Roman Catholic Church[65] receive permission from God (Jesus
Christ) to force Africans into slavery for the benifit of European and European-American Christians, and later on Jews, throughout the Americas, when he initiated the infamous "slave trade" in
the year 1506 C.E. from his base on the Island of Hispaniola (today's Haiti and Santo Domingo) with the approval of the Pope in
Rome and the King and Queen of Spain? Were the reported bestial
acts of the Pharoah (King), Rameses II, of Sais (Egypt) against
the African Hebrew peoples (all of the tribes); King Saul of

---

* Dr Martin Luther King, Jr.'s non-violent movement was involved
in a prayer session in a down-pour of rain asking Jesus Christ
to save the life of the same sheriff - Bull Connors - who had
not too long before shocked Black women with electric cattle prods.

Palestine against the Hittites, Amalaskites, Moabites, Zebusites, and others; Emperor Caracalla against the Christians;[66] the Chris - tian Crusaders against the Moslems; the Moslems in their "jihads" (Holy Wars) against the Africans of North, East,and West Africa; Dictator Adolph Hitler of Nazis Germany against the Jews of Europe, especially the Warsaw Ghetto[67] and other Ghettos? Are these depraved acts more contemptuous to the Gods of Judaism, Christianit and Islam than the enslavement of the African-Americans in the Americas? Are the Gods of Ju Ju, Voodoo, Damballah Ouedo, Witch- craft, Obyah (who also witnessed their sons and daughters captured, shackled and shipped off from Africa as slaves to the Americas) less concerned than Jehovah, Jesus Christ or Allah? Or, are the Gods of the indigenous African peoples, whose religions are described by so many non-Africans as "paganistic heathenism," and a host of other invectives (which are never used in relationship to any other peoples' religions of Europe) not entitled to respect? Why no reparations for those who have slaved for over three-hundred (300) years, suffered all forms of genocide, and still suffer every type of human degradation and mental slavery in the "LAND OF THE FREE AND THE HOME OF THE BRAVE "[68] while they watch others col- lect reparations from the German and Japanese governments for the loss of their kinfolk,and personal properties? The African-American losses were more than fifteen milions (15,000,000) exterminated, while countless thousands more were destroyed mentally, only to be offered "forty acres of land and a mule, each..."; none of which they have collected to date in these United States of America But, those who are generally called "the GOOD PEOPLE,""the RESPONSI BLE PEOPLE," pass off such atrocities with the following: "GOD WILL TAKE CARE OF IT ALL." Which God? When? Where? How?

300

Maybe the God of Mount Sinai (Jehovah or Yahweh), Jerusalem
(Jesus Christ), Mecca (Al'lah), or all of them, have no place
in their PARADISE for people with BLACK SKIN, THICK LIPS, WOOLLY
HAIR (kinky), and of INDIGENOUS AFRICAN ORIGIN, even though these
same people established the basis for said GODS and said RELI-
GIONS. Maybe these Gods are removing all references to the African
peoples of Sais (Egypt) and Kush (Cush or Ethiopia) from their
"HOLY SCRIPTURES?" Maybe they are returning the "TEN COMMANDMENTS"
and restoring them to the "NEGATIVE CONFESSIONS" of the "MEMPHITE
OSIRIAN DRAMA as recorded in the Pyramids and on the papyri of the
MYSTERY SYSTEMS OF THE NILE VALLEYS back to their original indigenous African ancestors who created them? Maybe these Gods are
not as COLOR BLIND as they were supposed to be, or maybe they are
not "SPIRITS" after all? Maybe these Gods are all a combination
of Anglo-Saxon-Semitic-Hamitic Caucasians who have no housing for
Blacks to rest, restaurants for Blacks to eat, fountains for Blacks
to wet their thirst, jobs for Blacks to work and to feed their offsprings, schools for Blacks to study and learn, churches - synagogues - mosques and other places of worship for Blacks to
pray in? And maybe these Gods will just pay off the Blacks for the
hundreds and thousands of lives they have given to genocide in the
Americas for hundreds of years, along with their enslavement; beginning in 1506 in the Caribbeans, and 1619 in Jamestown, Virginia, United States of America (from colonial days) to the present
day - 1970 C.E., and it will be perfect? Then everyone shall say:

    AMEN. AMEN. **AMEN**: THE SINS OF THE FATHER WILL NO
    LONGER FALL UPON THE CHILDREN UNTO THE FOURTH (4th)
    GENERATION, SAYETH THE LORD - GOD - JEHOVAH (Yahweh) [69]

and everything and everyone can feel relieved of it all, say, as
if it had never happened. This way...AFRICAN, AFRICAN-AMERICAN

301

STUDIES, and all other studies dealing with the Black peoples' contributions to world civilization, can be ignored once more, because it would not have existed; therefore, no more need for "BLACK COMMUNITY CONTROL"; of course, no more I.S. 201, nor OCEAN HILL BROWNSVILLE schools for African-American and Puerto Rican "INFERIOR CHILDREN" to spoil the "SUPERIOR" European-American "PURE WHITE CHILDREN."

Voodoo, Obyha, Damballah Ouedo, and Magic (Black or any other color), like Judaism, having originated in Africa, will be respected one day as the forerunner of what is today still being called "WESTERN RELIGIONS" (all denominations and creeds); only then shall further studies not have to reveal the true ties between these religions, and others not mentioned herein. The "Spirituals, Blues," and of course, "Jazz," may then also receive their deserving place and attention along with European music. The religious message Blues and Jazz carried for years to the peoples of the world may then receive its just recognition. But, as one examines either Blues or Jazz, one sees the basic religious musical significance that is a part of Voodoo and Judaism – also in Christianity and Islam – come into focus. They reveal one common indigenous African origin and denominator; an origin that includes the religious music of indigenous Africans from as far south as MONOMOTAPA,* far north as SAIS,* far west as GHANA,* and to the far-off extremes of East Alkebu-lan (Africa) – which was known as PUNT.*

Disclaimers on this subject make students of Voodoo and other traditionally noted African indigenous religions wonder why so many "Western" historians (Jews and Christians alike) refer to "Judaism in West Africa," but fail very conveniently to mention

---

* Monomotapa was the original name of what is today called the Republic of South Africa. Sais is the original name of Egypt. Ancient Ghana included much of the nations of today's West Africa. Punt was located where the Somalias and parts of Kenya now stand.

302

about "Ju Ju-ism and Voodooism in Israel and the United States of America," other parts of the Americas, and Europe. In so wondering, one must stop and examine why African influences on European life are continually restricted to music and other forms of entertainment, and of course free labor. The same applies to the United States of America. In so doing, one must realize the proper recognition of African origins of Voodooism and other contributions not directly connected with North Africa would integrate Jewish and Christian scriptures beyond presently accepted quotas for Black people in so-called "WESTERN RELIGIONS." Equally, it would mean that there would no longer be any "lily white heaven." Tremendous economic burdens would ensue upon all sects to recreate new religious tracts for distribution dealing with blackened images for biblical personalities - from Abraham, to Moses, to Jesus Christ, to Mohamet. It would also mean that Sais (Egypt) and all other lands of North and East Africa will have to return to the African continent and be redeclared African lands.[70] Furthermore, it would require the full recognition that the Egyptians* were no different than any other indigenous Africans. When these things have been initiated, it would follow that the entire educational system of the "Western World" would have to be completely revamped to speak of man's contributions - all of mankind, not just starting with the ancient Greeks and relating everything around them. These efforts, at this point, appear to be unrealistic to those who are responsible for such appropriate and meaningful changes. Why? Be-

---

* The Greek historian - Herodotus, who learned history and other disciplines from the indigenous Africans of Egypt from 450 B.C.E., described them in his HISTORIES, Book II, in the following way: "The Egyptians, Colchians and Ethiopians have thick lips, broad noses, woolly hair, and they are burnt of skin." Herodotus' description fits any "Negro" in the Harlems of the United States of America.

cause mankind loves power, even the power to enslave his fellow
men. Because of this power-love, power is not very often surrendere
voluntarily by any group throughout the history of mankind.

Strange as it may seem to the African-American, this is how
the "conclusion" adds up. But, this is providing youthful"Black
America"is willing to remain on its knees like their middle-aged
and older forerunners have been doing lately, while awaiting
their "Messiah" to come and "deliver" them."Yeah... there is ah
great day a'comin';[71] but not in the sense of the "Negro Spiritual" of resignation in which these words were written by downtrodde
Africans in the United States of America, when at that time, the
only hope seemed to be "...I'm ah comin', I'm ah comin', for my
head is bending low."[72] No! It is not even "...Joshua fit de battle
of Jericho." It is African-Americans (Black) and their "Human
Rights."[73] guaranteed them by the mere virtue of their birth, and
by the world community of nations in its "Declaration of Human
Rights." "Rights" which found much of their fundamental origins in
the religious philosophies of the so-called "AFRICANS SOUTH OF THE
SAHARA" - "BLACK AFRICA."

There can be no doubt that "WESTERN RELIGIONS" is a misnomer
of the "nth" degree. It is as racist as it sounds. "WESTERN
RELIGIONS," like "GREEK PHILOSOPHY," cannot escape its indigenous
African origin, and the inheritors of their African origin -
presently indigenous Africans and their descendants in the Caribbeans, the Americas, Europe, and elsewhere.

WHAT MAKES ONE GOD BETTER THAN THE OTHER? RELIGIOUS BIGOTRY
DOES, AND RACISM SUPPORTS IT. ANY RELIGION IS AS GOOD AS THE OTHER.
EITHER "RACE" IS A FRAUD OR THE RELIGIOUS TEACHINGS OF AN "ADAM

AND EVE IN THE GARDEN OF EDEN" IS.

PREFACE NOTES

1. Sir E. A. Wallis-Budge, BOOK OF THE DEAD; also his OSIRIS.

2. A German Roman Catholic Priest who broke away from the Church in a fight against the hierarchy in Rome to reform its teachings, practices, and dogmas. Luther's revolt led to his own excommunication in 1520 C.E.

3. Ghandi (1869-1947 C.E.) was the leader of India's non-violent struggles against Imperial Britain for independence. He was the world's most outstanding figure in the field of protest through positive pacifism. He was assasinated in 1947 C.E. by a fellow Hindu after leading India to final victory over Britain. See BHANDI, by Geoffrey Ashe, Stein and Day, New York, 1968.

4. Jesus Christ and God are said to be "Spririts." African spirits are called "ancestors," or "ancestral spirits."

5. European and European-American words generally applied to religions that are not common to those of Judaeo-Christian-Islamic origin. These terms are derogatory in use and intent.

5a. See Dr. Albert Churchward, ORIGIN AND EVOLUTION OF FREEMASONRY; ARCANA OF FREE MASONRY, 1915; and, ORIGIN AND EVOLUTION OF THE HUMAN RACE, 1921.

6. Note that the Nile River receives its sources of water from the highlands of Ethiopia (the Blue Nile from Lake Tana, and the Atbara River - north of Lake Tana), also the highlands of Uganda (the White Nile from Lakes "Albert" and "Victoria" - Nyanza Mwanza). The White and Blue meet at Khartoum, Sudan; the Atbara meets at Atbara in Sudan. See landscape maps of this area showing the elevations of the landmass; also BLACKMAN OF THE NILE, by Y. ben-Jochannan, Alkebu-lan Books, New York, N.Y., pps.140,220,257-268.

7. The Hebrew, Christian, and Islamic "Holy Books" (Bible, etc.) were even in this name by most "Westerners" and Asians of the Moslem faith. The religious "truths" of other peoples are called "myths" and other names that indicate "inferiority to the Holy Scriptures." This is common practice among most "Western" writers on that which is called "Western Religions."

8. See, STOLEN LEGACY, by G.G.M. James, New York Philosophical Library, New York, 1954.

9. See Note No. 7. Also give special attention to the last sentence.

10. The ethnic title - "Greek"- added to the "Philosophy" eliminates the possibility of any other peoples involvement.

11. These are terms which have been used to describe the continent the Greeks and Romans labeled "AFRICA," among other names in the ancient past.

INTRODUCTION NOTES

1. See, RELIGION OF THE SEMITES, by Smith Robertson.

2. See, EXODUS, Chapter 20, Verses 13 & 15; also, HYMN OF ADO-RATION OF THE GOD OSIRIS, Chapter I, Note 55.

3. Professor James' STOLEN LEGACY is a critical analysis that shows the Egyptian (African) origin of that which is being called "GREEK PHILOSOPHY" and "WESTERN RELIGIONS." He has taken great care to trace every detail of Africanism in Greek culture, and expose them as such.

4. Count C.C. Volney, in his book - RUINS OF EMPIRES, like Baron Denon's, TRAVELS IN UPPER AND LOWER EGYPT, saw the Sphinx of Ghizeh (Giza) in 1789 C.E., before Emperor Napoleon Boneparte's French troops blasted away its thick lips and broad nose with cannon fire as target practice. Baron Denon even drew the Sphinx in its original image - as seen on page 140 of BLACK MAN OF THE NILE, by Y. ben-Jochannan, New York, 1970. His picture of the Sphinx is considered an art treasure and should be seen if at all possible.

5. See, BOOK OF THE DEAD, by Sir E. A. Wallis-Budge, pp 66-98; also, OSIRIS, pp 62-166.

6. Ibid.

7. EXODUS, Chapter 20, Verse 3.

8. Like so many others, Reverend Placide Temples made the mistake of believing he knew "...how the Africans think...;" solely on the basis that he lived amongst them for a number of years. He failed to note the master and slave relationship that existed between himself and other European representatives of the colonial system against the indigenous Africans he believed he realy knew.

308

9.   These words are only used to describe non-European religious beliefs. Their purpose is to established in peoples' mind the inferiority of **Black things** as against White, thus translated as between European-Americans - vs - African-Americans.

10. This was brought on by the 1964 C.E. killing of a 14 year old Black boy named Powell at Yorkville, New York City, New York, by an off-duty White police lieutenant named Gilligan. The controversy over this killing caused whole-scale rioting in many Black communities that followed the lead of Harlem, New York City, New York, in protest.

11. Such as Father Divine, Marcus Moziah Garvey, Prophet Sweet Daddy Grace, Prophetess Mother Horne, and many others.

12. See, Note No. 35, Chapter I.

1. Mogen David - Hebrew (Jewish) Star. Crucifix - Christian Cross
    with an idol purporting to be Jesus Christ, or a plain cross.
    Ka'aba (Al-Ka'aba, representing a piece of fallen meteor from
    Ethiopia; once worshipped by the peoples of Mecca and other
    parts of Arabia until the time of Mohamet - the Prophet and
    founder of Islam).

2. Common custom during the communion ceremonies in most Chris-
    tian orders (sects), from Roman Catholicism to Holy Rollers.
    Instead of palm wine, the Christians use grape wine.

3. The Hebrews, like most of the ancient peoples, had sacrifices
    of fellow Hebrews. This custom changed to animals in the action
    of "Sacrificial Lambs." The Christians even considered their
    Jesus Christ a "sacrifice," and continue to do so at "Lent;'
    just as the Moslems with Mohamet at Rammadan.

3a. The words in parenthesis indicate the equivalent indigenous
    African religious customs and practices which Jews, Christians
    and Moslems call "paganism."

4. The words "pagan," "uncivilized" and "cannibals" are always in
    quotes in this work, as they relate to stereotype castigations
    by people who are prejudice against others whose religion
    not meet their own specifications.

5. The Druids were an ancient people and society. See, ANACALYPSIS,
    by Sir Geoffrey Higgins, Vol. I & II; and Dr Albert Churchward,
    ORIGIN OF FREEMASONRY.

6. Among certain orders (sects) of Jews, Christians, and Moslems
    musical instruments in religious services are objectionable;
    whereas, among others the services must have them. The choice
    of instruments are as varied as there are orders (sects).

7. God is male and female. It all depends upon which religion is
    being referred to at any given time. God takes on a masculine
    form in the three religions most commonly used in Europe and
    the Americas.

7a. The Fourteenth Ammendment (July 9, 1968 C.E.) came more than
    two-hundred and forty-nine (249) years after the first African
    slaves landed in the United States of America - when it was
    still a British colony (1619 or 1620 C.E.).

8. For centuries European and Europeam-American Christian mission-
    aries preached this type of "Christ's message."

8a. The Pharoah in this reference was Rameses II, who supposedly
    drove Moses and other African-Hebrews (Jews) from western Egypt
    to eastern Egypt (Mt. Sinai) around 1298-1232 B.C.E.

310

9. Most African-Americans have refrained from this "Anthem" because of certain "civil rights movements" that opposed "Negroes having their own National Anthem." James Weldon Johnson was once Executive Director of the National Association
for the Advancement of Coloured People (N.A.A.C.P.), Imperial
Potentate of the "Negro Elks," poet, and master musician. Ole
Man River is avoided by the sophisticates who wish that their
history of slavery can be ignored out of existence.

10. Another name for "BLACK MAGIC." In its truest form, a name of
an African religion equal to Judaism, Christianity, and Islam.
Billy Daniels, an African-American ("Negro") entertainer,
made a song with this title. He made this religion appear to
be a sexpot symbol with his antics as he sang a song by the
name - "THE OLD BLACK MAGIC." Miguelito Valdez, another entertainer (from the Island of Cuba in the Caribbean) did likewise to the God Baba Loa in his song of the same name. Valdez
should have known that this God is sacred among his indigenous
"AFRO-CUBAN" peoples as much as Jesus Christ is among others.

11. Reverend Placide Temples,' BANTU PHILOSOPHY, translated to
English from the French original entitled..."LA PHILOSPHIE
BANTOUE," by Dr. A Rubbens (from Father Temples original work.
The Rev., Colin King, translator, Imprimatur, Victor Petrus
Keuppens, Vic. Ap. de Lulua, Luabo - Kamina, May 30, 1952.
Imprini Potest, Kanzenze, December 2, 1952, p. Simeon, O.F.M.
Sup. Reg.).

11a.Typical position of the Christian missionaries, as stated in
their writings up to the mid-twentieth century.

12. See, GOD, JUJU, AND ALLAH, by Jack Mendelsohn, Beacon Press,
Boston, 1962.

13. See, THINGS FALL APART, by Chinua Achebe, Obolensky, New York,
1959, pp 185-186.

14. Ibid, pp. 186-187.

15. Ibid, p. 187.

16. Ibid, pp. 187-188.

17. Many books dealing with the African slave trade to the Americas
deal with the role of the slave runner - the Reverend John Hawkins - and his slaveship "JESUS (CHRIST) deLOBIC."

17a Deuteronomy, Chapter 7, Verses 6-8. See, Fishberg's, THE JEW;
also, Rogers,' SEX AND RACE, Vol. I.

17b See, THE JEW, by M. Fishberg; also, SEX AND RACE, by J. A.
Rogers; HEBREW MYTHS, by R. Patai; and, HISTORY OF MANKIND, by
Ratzel.

18. See, BANTU PHILOSOPHY, by Placide Temples; also Note No. 2

of this Chapter.

19. Ibid, pp. 45-46: THE GENERAL LAWS OF VITAL CAUSALITY.

19a. The Oracle of Anon caused Alexander "the Great", in 332 BCE, to invade Egypt and conquer its low land cities (Lower Egypt).

20. From the HOLY BIBLE, Revised Standard Version (Old and New Testaments), Meridan Books, the World Publishing Company, Cleveland and New York, pp. 86-87; Leviticus, Chapter I, Verses 1-17.

21. Ibid, Chapter IV, Verses 32-35.

22. See, AFRICAN MYTHOLOGY, by Geoffrey Parrinder, pp. 23-24, Paul Hamlyn, London, 1967.

23. The HOLY BIBLE - The First Book of Moses (Genesis), Chapter I, Verses 1-25.

24. Ibid, Verses 26-31.

25. Ibid, Chapter II, Verses 15-25.

26. Ibid, Chapter III; Chapter IV, Verses 1-17.

27. See, FACING MT. KENYA, by Jomo Kenyatta, pp. 224-225, Vintage Books, New York. The word "KIKUYU" is used by Europeans instead of "MU-GIKIYU" singular, or "AGIKUYU" plural - used by the indigenous Africans themselves). Jomo Kenyatta explained this on the first page of the preface of his book under footnote No. One. He decided to use the more popular "Gikuyu" for both singular and plural purposes.

28. Ibid, p. 227.

29. Ibid, pp. 5-7.

29a See Professor M.D.W. Jeffreys' "The Negro Enigma," (in: THE WEST AFRICAN REVIEW, September, 1951).

30. See, AFRICAN MYTHOLOGY. Ibid, Note 22 this Chapter, first paragraph.

31. Ibid; second paragraph.

32. The HOLY BIBLE, Genesis, Chapter I, Verse 26.

33. See pp. 1-24, first line of Note No. 22 of this work; also, AFRICAN MYTHOLOGY, by Geoffrey Parrinder, p. 23.

34. See pp. 1-25, first line of Note No. 23 of this work, the HOLY BIBLE, Genesis, Chapter I, Verse 1.

35. See pages 1-27, first line of Note No. 27 of this work; also

FACING MT. KENYA, by Jomo Kenyatta, p. 224.

36. See chronology of Moses in the TORAH (Five Books of Moses - or Holy Bible).

37. According to Matthew, Chapter IV, Verses 17-20 (Holy Bible - New Testament).

37a See, WORLD'S GREAT MEN OF COLOR, by J. A. Rogers, Vol. II; also HISTORY OF THE ARABS, by P. K. Hitti.

38. See Chapter Four of this work, Chronology of Mohamet.

39. See quotation of the Scriptures in Chapter Three, pp 3-28 and 29 of this work; also the HOLY BIBLE - Numbers, Chapter XII, Verses 1-2.

40. See Al-Jahiz' account of the life of the Prophet Mohamet and other noted founders of Islam in Chapter Four of this work.

40a. It is the feeling of some African-American musicians that "JAZZ IS A DEROGATORY NAME GIVEN TO SERIOUS MUSIC OF BLACK PEOPLE BY WHITES WHO DO NOT UNDERSTAND ITS MEANING. THEY MADE IT AN EXTENSION OF SEXUAL SENSATIONS AND WITH CONNECTION TO THE BROTHELS OF ST LOUIS DURING THE DAYS OF RECONSTRUCTION."

40b. Mary Baker Eddy was the founder of the CHRISTIAN SCIENCE "sect" (First or Mother Church) in 1879 C.E. at Boston, Massachusettes, United States of America. It is based upon the view that Christianity is a science, and has physical healing powers. See, SCIENCE AND HEALTH WITH A KEY TO THE SCRIPTURES, by Mary Baker Eddy (first published 1876); also her, MANUAL OF THE MOTHER CHURCH.

41. See, AFRICAN MYTHOLOGY, by Geoffrey Parrinder, pp. 15-16.

42. Hebrew peoples that existed in Kush (Cush or Ethiopia) before Moses "left Egypt for the Promise Land." One of their numbers married Moses -"the daughter of the High-Priest of Kush." They are presently located around the Lake Tana region - around the countryside of the City of Gondar. These Hebrews (Jews) twice ruled Ethiopia; the last time in the 9ᵗʰ Century C.E., when their queen, Judith, recaptured the government of Ethiopia in the year 840 C.E. Another group of these people entered Kush during the reign of the glorius Queen of Sheba (Makeda), upon her return from Israel after visiting with King Solomon - for whom she became pregnant and bore him her only child - a son named Menelik, who became the first Emperor of Ethiopia upon the abdication of the throne by his mother in his favor; at this period in history Axum was the capital of Ethiopia. See Hebrew, Christian and Islamic religious scriptures for further accounts of this report on the Solomon-Sheba episode. Also see the KEBRA NEGAST, Ethiopia's CHRONICLES.

43. Hebrews (Jews) that lived in the Arabian country of Yemen un-

313

til their removal by the government of Israel after the creation of the Jewish State by European and European-American Jews. They are generally dark-brown in colour; however, not as dark as the average Black Jews of Ethiopia - generally. They look somewhat in complexion as the Yemenite Moslems (Arabs) with whom they lived for over two-thousand years. These people are now being forced to stop their polygamous way of life, which they,like the Falashas of Ethiopia,have practised from biblical times.

44. Most European and European-American religious writers seem to claim that their religious declarations are the only "true scripture;" this of course is in keeping with the general superiority syndrome of Europeanism.

45. First Commandment of the Jewish, Christian, and Islamic religions as "received by Moses on Mount Sinai," according to their Holy Bible or Koran.

46. Practised as a religious rite amongst many Christian sects; but not universally a part of Christian teachings. It has been adopted as a health requirement by most hospitals and physicians.

47. Piercing of the female hymen for physical and religious reasons.

48. See Note No. 22 of this Chapter; last paragraph of quotation.

49. See, FIRST BOOK OF MOSES - Genesis (The Holy Bible).

49a Taken from the APOSTLE'S CREED: "I believe in God the Father Almighty, maker of heaven and earth...," etc.

50. See, MAN AND HIS GODS, by Homer W. Smith, p. 64, Little, Brown and Company, Bostom, 1953.

51. See, RUINS OF EMPIRES, by Count C. C. Volney, pp. III-IV (publisher's Preface, by Peter Eckler, New York, January 3, 1890). See description of "...the flat nose, thick lips, and Negro features of the Egyptian Sphinx."

52. See "Epilogue"(in: MAN AND HIS GODS, by Homer W. Smith, p. 441, paragraph 2).

53. Ibid, paragraph 2.

54. Ibid, pp. 441-442, paragraph 3.

55. The PYRAMID TEXTS, as per Nebseni Papyrus (ca. 1600 B.C.E.) without the "SALUTATIONS." Pages 43-44 of MAN AND HIS GODS.

56. ALKEBU-LAN is the ancient name the Ethiopians and Moors called the continent which the ancient Greeks and Romans renamed "Afric These are only two of the numerous names Africa has been called over the past few thousand years. Among others are the following

314

"ORTEGIA, AMONIS, LYBIA, ETHIOPIA, OCEANIA", and "HESPERIA."
See, BLACK MAN OF THE NILE, by Y. ben-Jochannan, Alkebu-lan
Books, New York, 1970, p. 252.

ST. AUGUSTINE: CHAPTER II - NOTES

1. St Augustine gave very extensive accounts of his own background
   in his CONFESSIONS. There are many English translations of the
   original Latin text, most of which are entitled "CONFESSIONS OF
   ST AUGUSTINE."

1a. Constantine "the Great" was responsible for changing the course
   of world history when he converted to Christianity and led
   Rome and all of Europe into Christendom. He made Rome the
   second Christian nation in the world at that time, second only
   to the Christian Empire of Ethiopia (Kush), East Africa - which
   became a Christian nation more than one-hundred years before
   Rome did.

2. The Ethiopian Emperor, Abraha, converted to Christianity while
   he was still a prince. His father, Emperor Johannes, had him
   study the "new religion" from Phoenician and Koptic merchants
   passing through Ethiopia. Upon mounting the throne Abraha declared Ethiopia a "CHRISTIAN EMPIRE." This took place about
   120 C.E.

3. Martyrdom was (during this period) a kind of _fad_ among the
   Christians who were "...expecting the second coming of the
   Messiah" (Jesus Christ) " any day ." within their own lifetime.

4. C. P. Groves was Professor of Missions in the Selly Oak Colleges
   in Birmingham, and"an outstanding author on Christian Church
   history." PUNIC is an ancient word for PHOENICIA.

5. See, THE VANISHED CITIES OF NORTHERN AFRICA, by Mrs.Stewart
   Erskine, p. 80; also the CATHOLIC ENCYCLOPEDIA.

6. See, HEBREWISM IN WEST AFRICA, by J. J. Williams.

7. This princess is immortalized in Virgil's work under the name
   of "DIDO." He speaks of her in relationship to the City of Troy.

8. GIBRALTAR is a Spanish corruption of the words "GIBRAL TARIKH"
   which means "Rock of Tarikh," or "Mount Tarikh." General Tarikh
   was an indigenous African (Black man) who led the African-Moors
   into Spain in 711 C.E. as conquerors, defeated the Spaniards and
   occupied the town of Algciras. Later on, on his second invasion
   of Spain, he took Heraclea and other towns, which drew forth the
   war that meted Tarikh against King Roderic of Spain in the Battle
   of Andalusia near Xeres, in which the Africans were supreme, and
   the entire Iberian Peninsula became African territory.

9. Septimus Severus was born at Leptis Magna (today's Tripolitan-
    ia), and died at York, Britain, in February, 211 C.E. See,
    COAST OF BARBARY, by Jane Soames; also, ROMAN BRITAIN, by R.
    G. Collingwood; and, THE VANISHED CITIES OF NORTHERN AFRICA,
    by Mrs. Stewart Erskine.

9a. Note that STOICISM was the prevailing philosophy followed by
    the Romans. This emperor was it's protector.

10. Augustus Caesar was originally called "OCTAVIANUS." He was
    the Isperator Caesar Octavianus (Emperor Octavius Caesar),
    who ruled Palestine (Israel) when "...the birth of Jesus
    Christ was proclaimed." He ruled Egypt (Aegypt) as his private
    estate through one of his Prefects (Praefectus Aegypt).

10a Adopted from, AN ENCYCLOPEDIA OF WORLD HISTORY, (4th ed.) as
    compiled and edited by William Langer, Houghton Mifflin Co.
    Boston, 1986, p. 113.

11. Professor C. Eric Lincoln wrote a book by the name of BLACK
    MUSLIMS, which brought to the general public certain facts
    about these African-Americans of which so many were otherwise
    ignorant.

12. Senator Joseph McCarthy was a post War II U.S.A. Senator, who
    made his national fame through investigations and public ex-
    posures of the U. S.A. Communists during his tenure on the
    Un-American Committee of the Senate. This Committee and the
    Senator met with public ridicule and the censure of his colleag
    in the Senate. It also led to the destruction of the public
    life of hundreds of government employees; such as Alger Hiss (a
    high positioned State Department official) and Professor J.
    Robert Oppenheimer (one of the fathers of the Atomic Bomb).

13. This title is the equivalent of the ancient "MINISTER OF WAR"
    still in use in many lands today.

14. This was reported in the works of Eusebius of Caesarea (c260-
    339 C.E.).

15. Tertullian's, De ANIMA, XXX (as quoted by Harnack in MISSION
    AND EXPANSION, Vol. III, p. 275.).

16. See, THE VANISHED CITIES OF NORTHERN AFRICA, by Mrs Stewart
    Erskine, p. 80.

17. Ibid, Note No. 4, this Chapter.

18. Ibid, Note No. 16, p. 81.

19. Ibid.

20. See, COAST OF THE BARBARY, by Jane Soames, p. 60.

21. Lbid, Note 16, p. 81.

22. See, A HISTORY OF POLITICAL THEORY, by George H. Sabine.

23. Madauros was also the birthplace and site where another of the world famous indigenous African writer, APULEIUS, wrote his major work called "THE GOLDEN ASS."

24. Popes during Tertullian's lifetime (?155-222 C.E.): St. Anicetus 155-c166 (he became Pope the year of Tertullian's birth); St. Soter, c166-c175; St. Eleuterus c175-189; St. Victor I, 189-199; St. Zephysinus 197-217; and St. Calictus I, 217-222 (he died the same year Tertullian did (222 C.E.)
Popes during St. Cyprian's lifetime (date of his birth unknown. It is known, however, that he was born during the late days of Tertullian's lifetime, and died some time before the birth of St. Augustine. And that he was at least forty-six (46) years old when he received his "HEAVENLY CALL AND BIRTH."
Popes during St. Augustine's lifetime (354-430 C.E.): St. Liberius ruled at the time of St. Augustine's birth - 352-366; Felix II (anti-Pope) 353-365; Damasus I, 366-383; Ursinus (anti-Pope) 366-367; St. Siricius 384-399; St. Anastasius I, 399-401; St Inocent I, 401-417; St. Zosimus, 417-418; St. Boniface I, 418-422; Eulalius (anti-Pope) 418-419; and St. Celestine I, 422-432 C.E. (during whose Papacy St. Augustine died at the age of seventy-six years of age).

25. See, CONFESSIONS: CITY OF GOD; and ON CHRISTIAN DOCTRINES (in: Great Books of the Western World, Vol. 18 - Augustine. Edited under Editor-in-CHIEF Robert Maynard Hutchins, formerly President of the University of Chicago, Ill.). This work is translated from Augustine's original Latin works. Published by Encyclopedia Britanica, Inc., Chicago, Ill., U.S.A. The CITY OF GOD is translated by Marcus Dodds; and ON CHRISTIAN DOCTRINE, translated by J. F. Shaw; CONFESSIONS, by Edward B Pussey.

26. Crusades (1096-1291 C.E.): The first was ordered by Pope Urban II (1096-1147); the second by Conrad III and Louis VII (1147-1189); the third by Richard I and Frederick Barbosa (1189-1202); the fourth through eight ("the weening years") Abigensian - Waldensian Children's; Bohemian of Nicopolis - led by Sigismund of Hungary; Varna (1202-1291).

27. Augustine wrote this poem after he decided to follow letters in preference to law, which his father insisted be learned and make his career. He also served as a teacher of grammar at Tagaste, and subsequently established himself as a rhetorician at Carthage.

28. Augustine's first book was written some time between 377 and 383 C.E.

29. These two works were edited by Augustine from conversations he recorded while in the company of his mother, his son, some friends and pupils (when they were awaiting his conversion as Cassiciacum). He published them as philosophical diologues.

30. This is the only book of a series Augustine wrote that survived
He wrote them immediately after his conversion to Christianity,
while leading a type of monastic life before his departure
from Africa to Europe (Milan and Rome).

31. This work caused Augustine his first controversy with the older
thinkers of his ear, both laymen and the clergy. It dealt with
his own values "On Christian Doctrines." It also included certa.
philosophical concepts he developed after his stay in Rome for
over one year. Augustine sold all the properties he had amassed
after writing this work; the proceeds went to the poor. It was
his last writing before he established his "MONASTERY," which
he occupied with his son and two friends - along with followers
that joined them in a life of study and prayer.

32. The first of three books on the subject, which he took thirty-
one years to complete. This one was completed about 397 C.E., tl
exact year is questionable.

33. He started this work after the completion of his three volume
work of thirty-one years (397-428 C.E.). He published it between 398 and 400.

34. One of his greatest doctrinal treatises. He began this treatise
the same year he completed a previous volume.

35. This work seems to be the result of his disagreement with the
Roman officials over the fall of the Eternal City (Rome). It
cited the relationship of the Roman Catholic Church and the
Roman Empire. It was started in 413 C.E. as a serial, which
appeared for thirteen consecutive years - 413-426 C.E. These
writings were mainly reflections on his previous works, which
he brought up-to-date in preparation for his successor as
Bishop of Hippo Rigius in 426 C.E. Augustine wrote that its
purpose was..."to compile and point out all those things
which displease me in my works."

36. CONFESSIONS, VIII.

37. Ibid, VIII (VI). 13, Psalm, 19. 14.

38. Ibid, VIII (VII). 17.

39. Ibid, IX (IV) 7. The three disputations against Academics.
Augustine's De VITA BEATA, and his two other books - De
ORDINE, are in question 4. The SOLILOQUIES (2 books). Au-
gustine's conversation with himself. According to Luke, 3: 5.
See Psalm 19: 6.

40. Ibid, (V) Psalm, Ver. 8, Vulgate Bible 21, I Corinthian, 15:
54. Psalm, 9: 9, Vulgate Bible.

41. Ibid, IX (V) 13. Cf. CITY OF GOD, Book XVIII, 29.

42. Ibid, X. 46. Titus, I. 15. Romans, 14. 20. I Timothy, 4: 4

318

I Corinthians, 8.8. Col., 2. 16. Romans, 13. 23. Opposition
to the denial of eating as suggested by the Manichees. Genesis, 9. 13. I Kings, 17. 6. The Manichees views on in-
sects as the most deplorable food. Matthew, 13. 4. Genesis, 25.
34. II Samuel, 23.15-17. Matthew, 4.3. and Numbers, I.

43. Augustine supported the Platonists against other philosophers
with respect to the fellowship of man and his God. See, THE
CITY OF GOD, VIII, Chapter 5.

44. THE CITY OF GOD, Chapter 28. Augustine challenged the ignor-
ance of non-believers, not being able to see his newly found
Jesus Christ in the same manner.

45. THE CITY OF GOD, XV, Chapter II, Methuselah's age. THE CITY
OF GOD, Book XVII, Chapters 42-44. The HEBREW TORAH set Methuselah's age at one-hundred and eighty-seven (187) years.

46. ON CHRISTIAN DOCTRINE, I, Chapter 2. See also Matthew, 13.12,
and Matthew, 14.17, etc., 20.34, etc.

47. Ibid, Chapter 6.

48. Ibid, Book II, Chapter 42.63.

49. Ibid, Book III, Chapter 14.22. Matthew 7.12. Cf. Tobit, 4.15.

50. See, STOLEN LEGACY, by G.G.M. James, with respect to Aristotle's alleged authorship of most of the Africans' work
attributed to him.

52. Manetho, the Egyptian High Priest, was forced to train Greek
students brought into Egypt, Africa, by Aristotle and the
self-declared Pharoah, General Soter – who took on the title
PTOLEMY I. He was not allowed to train his fellow African students.

53. Many of these students are accredited "Western
Philosophers", etc. No credit for their education is given to
the indigenous (Black, Negroes, etc.) Africans that trained
them, nor for the source of the materials and documents they
used.

54. Manetho served under the self-declared Pharoah (King), Ptolemy
I (the former Macedonian general – Soter – of Alexander "the
Great's" army that captured and colonized Egypt).

55. See, BOOK OF THE DEAD, by Sir E. A. Wallis-Budge; RUINS OF
EMPIRES, by Count C.E. Volney; MAN AND HIS GODS, by Homer W.
Smith; THE GOLDEN BOUGH, by Sir James Fraizer; and, OSIRIS,
by Sir E.A. Walis-Budge. These are only a few of the hundreds
of books on this subject.

56. See the CONFESSIONS, Book III, Chapter XI-XII.

57. Ibid, Book I & II.

58. From, THE PATRIARCHS.

59. See, CITY OF GOD, Chapter 16.

59a Charles Ist of Spain to Charles Vth (last Roman Emperor, crowned by the Pope at Balonga) 1519-1558 C.E.

59b Raymond Lull was a lay missionary of the Roman Catholic Church who twice tried to turn the North Africans against their Arab conquerors religion - ISLAM. See AFRICAN GLORY, by Professor J.C. deGraft-Johnson, for the best account of this era of the history of the North African Church.

60. The first English version of the Christian Bible was made from the Vulgate. However, in 1560(when Roman Catholicism was outlawed in England) the British brought out their own English version of the Vulgate Bible. This forced the remaining British Roman Catholics to develop another bible of their own, which was designed to maintain their own interpretations as they understood the "Christ story." The result was the Rheims and Douay "version." Why the name "Rheims?" Because the New Testament (Christian text) was printed and published in Rheims in 1582 C.E. "Douay" came from the 1609-10 C.E. printing of the Old Testament section in that city. The entire undertaking was directed by Dr. Gregory Martin on commission by Rome and the Holy See. This Bible remained "the official English translation" from the original Latin Vulgate Bible until about 1773 C.E.; at which time Bishop Challoner, Vicar Apostolic of the London District, England, decided to have it changed to meet the new meanings of the ancient traditional teachings. He felt that the Douay "Version" had also become archaic for that period. In 1775 C.E. the Bishop Challoner's English language "version" of the Douay Bible was printed and published. In 1810 C.E. the Roman Catholic Archbishop of Baltimore, Maryland, U.S.A., made the Challomer's "version" the official United States of America Roman Catholic community bible. The Archbishop was joined in his approval by all of the other American Catholic (R.C.) Bishops. In 1858 C.E. The Ninth Provincial Council of Baltimore proposed further revisions of the Challomer's "version", which the Sacred Congregation de Proproganda Fide (The Sacred Society for the Propogation of the Faith) accepted and entrusted it to a team of outstanding Roman Catholic theologians and other scholars and specialists. This was the development of the current New Testament Bible used by Roman Catholics in the United States of America that differs so greatly with St. Augustine's comments. It is therefore very important that

320

commentators who follow St. Augustine's era and
decide to give critiques on his works be able to
react and understand the Vulgate "version." This
suggestion also applies to the works of the other
two African "Church Fathers," St. Cyprian and
Tertullian, as seen in the last pages of this
Chapter.

61. St.Cyprian, THE LAPSED, pp. 15-16 (as translated by Maurice
    Bevenot, S.J, The Newman Press, Westminister, Maryland, 1957).

62. St.Cyprian, THE UNITY OF THE CATHOLIC CHURCH, pp. 43-43, (Ibid).

63. Basic religious doctrine of the Roman Catholic Church.

64. Tertullian, THE TREATISE AGAINST HERMOGENES, pp. 26-27 (as
    translated by J.H. Waszink, The Newman Press, Westminister,
    Maryland, 1957).

65. Ibid, pp. 27-29.

66. Ibid, pp. 31-32.

67. Ibid, p. 85.

MOSES: CHAPTER IV NOTES

1. A SHORT STORY OF THE WORLD, by H.G. Wells, p. 59.

2. C.P. Snow's comments (In: JOHN O'LONDON'S WEEKLY, 1952), and
   THE NEXT MILLION YEARS, by Sir Charles Darwin, Jr., 1952.

3. NEW YORK TIMES, April 1, 1969.

4. There are Jews of every hue, physical characteristic, and nationality.

4a. Pharoah Rameses I ruled Egypt, North Africa, from 1320 to
    1318 B.C.E. Moses left Egypt about c1232 B.C.E. See the BOOK
    OF EXODUS, Chapter 7, Verse 7.

4b. See Note No. 14b following.

5. THE HISTORY OF EGYPT, by J.H. Breasted; A HISTORY OF EGYPT,
   by Sir E.A. Walis-Budge; STOLEN LEGACY, by G.G.M. James; and
   EGYPT, by Josephus.

5a. See, ANCIENT EGYPT, by L. Liebevitch; HISTORY OF EGYPT, by J. H. Breasted; also, THE ORIGINS OF CHRISTIANITY, by S. Robertson.

5b. Ibid.

6. EXODUS, Chapter 1, Verse 22.

7. Ibid, Chapter 2, Verses 1-9.

8. Ibid, Chapter 2, Verse 10.

9. Ibid, Chapter 2, Verses 11-12. Note that Egypt had laws against violence; and that Moses was charged with "committing murder" before the Hebrews had their FIVE BOOKS OF MOSES (Torah); also before Moses reached Mt Sinai.

10. Up until the time when Moses killed his fellow African of Egypt, of the religion of the God RA, - according to Exodus, Chapter 2, Verses 11-12 - there is no record of him being interested in the plight of the Hebrew people cited in the Torah.

11. EXODUS, Chapter 2, Verses 13-35; and Chapter 3, Verses 1-16.

11a See pages 1-46 and 1-47, Chapter I of the HYMN OF ADORATION TO OSIRIS.

11b Ibid, Chapter 3, Verses 7-9.

12. EXODUS, Chapter 3, Verse 5. African-Americans are now carrying their plight into religious institutions.

12a William F. Allen, Charles P. Ware and Lucey M. Garrison (eds.), SLAVE SONGS OF THE UNITED STATES. A. Simpson, New York, 1867, p. 76.

13. EXODUS, Chapter 12, Verses 37-38.

14. Ibid, Chapter 12, Verses 43-44.

14a Ibid, Chapter 12, Verse 45.

14b See, TEL-el-AMARA (14th Century B.C.E. Egyptian dispatches) account of the Haribu (Hebrews or Jews) and Hittites entrance into Upper Egypt, Africa. Also, see the HISPARICAL BACKGROUND OF THE BIBLE, by J. N. Schofield.

15. GENESIS, Chapter 12, Verses 10-16.

15a These dates vary, but not sufficiently to cause concern of inaccuracy of the events themselves.

16. 4100 B.C.E. See most books dealing with ancient Egypt historically - including, STOLEN LEGACY; HISTORY OF EGYPT; and LEGACY OF EGYPT (these books have already appeared in this work).

17. See, EBERS PAPYRUS, London Museum, London, England.

18. See, EDWARD C. SMITH PAPYRUS, Brooklyn Museum, Brooklyn, N.Y.

19. Bibliography on this entire chapter is included in this work following these notes.

19a These Verses are taken from A HISTORY OF ISRAEL, by Osterley & Robinson, 1934.

20. See, NEGRO SLAVE SONGS IN THE UNITED STATES, by Fisher; also, BOOK OF AMERICAN NEGRO SPIRITUALS, by James and Rosamond Johnson.

21. See, SECOND BOOK OF MOSES - Exodus, Chapter 2, Verses 1-10.

22. See Chapter V for information on Garvey, founder and first president of the U.N.I.A.

23. Herzl was one of the Jews' earliest writer demanding a separate Jewish homeland somewherre in the world. He was born in Austria during 1860 C.E. He was the founder of the first ZIONIST CONGRESS, in 1897, at Basel, Switzerland. MY PEOPLE: THE STORY OF THE JEWS, by Abba Eban, p. 324-26. See his writings signed "from the Jewish State" (In: Abba Iban's book, p. 283).

24. See Chapter V for outline on the "Civil Rights Movement" martyr and Noble Peace Prize winner.

25. A few European Jews also served as slave masters in the south and the Caribbeans in the same manner as the European Christians. See, ANTI-SLAVERY, by D. W. Dumond; FROM SLAVERY TO FREEDOM, by John Hope Franklin; also, AMERICAN NEGRO SLAVE REVOLTS, by Herbert Aptheker.

26. See, GENESIS (First Book of Moses), and EXODUS (Second Book of Moses), for Jewish origins in Africa. Also, BOOK OF THE DEAD; THE HISTORY OF EGYPT (by countless writers); HEBREW ORIGINS; ARE THE JEWS A RACE?; THE JEW; WORLD'S GREAT MEN OF COLOR.

27. Jews move from neighborhoods whenever Black Americans begin moving in just as any other White American does. Review cases of discrimination in housing against landlords of whom a proportionate number are Jews in neighborhoods designated "ghettos" or "slums."

28. EXODUS, Chapter 20, Verse 16 - "You shall not bear false witness against your neighbor."

29. See U.S.A. Census reports over the past fifty years relating to Jews. Most European-American Jews are registered as "Caucasians" or " Whites." In some places White Jews exclude Blacks, including Black Jews, from their places of cultural and

social involvement. Jews are a part of "White" or Caucasian
America and cherish their European origin as much as Christ
ians and Moslems from Europe.

30. Joel E. and Arthur B. Joel founded the SPINGARM AWARDS in
    1914 C.E. First Chairman of the Board.

31. Joel E., as Chairman until his death. Arthur B., as President
    until his retirement on January 2, 1966; at which time Kirie
    Kaplan, a wealthy Bostonian Jew, succeeded in the post. See,
    THE NEGRO ALMANAC, pp. 166-168.

32. There is never any poling in Black communities as to what the
    people want done for themselves. No Blacks of the "...target
    population..." designated "poor" or "irresponsible" for whom
    the N.A.A.C.P. was allegedly founded.

33. The "poor" and "irresponsible" are never consulted or allowed
    to vote on who will be the Executive Director of the N.A.A.C.P.,
    the Urban League, or any other such social agency for "coloured
    folks."

34. See, Note No. 28, this Chapter.

35. This word is used in its classic sense, not in the sense as to
    who is left or right of capitalism or socialism. "Militancy"
    is dependent upon who is in or out of the power that is being
    attacked at any given time.

36. The national headquarters of most "Negro Civil Rights Move-
    ments" are located in White commercial neighborhoods. The
    Congress of Racial Equality (C.O.R.E.) is an unusual excep-
    tion but it also had its headquarters in the White neighbor-
    hood when it had White members that controlled it (1942-67).

37. "UNCLE TOM" and "AUNT THOMASINA" are male and female names for
    "Negro" lackies or stoogies.

38. Sammy Davis is a radio, television,and Hollywood personality
    of very noted fame. He was married to former White actress
    Mae Britt, who bore him a child. He was cited in the public
    media a few years ago for having converted from Christianity
    to Judaism. He is a Black man. Mr Davis is also very much in-
    volved in the "Civil Rights Movement" (non-violent aspect of
    it).

39. THE JEW, by M. Fishberg, pp. 117, 147-148, London, 1911; also
    BOOK OF THE BEGINNINGS, by G. A. Massey, Vol. II, Part 2; and,
    BRIEF VIEW OF THE CAST SYSTEM, by Nesfield. All of these works
    speak of the "NEGRO ORIGINS OF THE JEW."

40. SEX AND RACE, Vol. I, by J. A. Rogers, p. 91. Also his , NATURE
    KNOWS NO COLOR LINE, p. 40 (both books published by Helga Rog-
    ers, New York, N.Y.).

40a See, ANACALYPSIS, by Sir Geoffrey Higgins, Vols. I & II, London, 1840.

41. Among the Beta Israel (Falashas or Black Jews) only members who completed their Confirmation (Bamitzvah) can become involved in the processing of foods under the laws of the THIRD BOOK OF MOSES, Leviticus. See, FALASHA ANTHOLOGY, by Wolf Leslau; also writings in Yiddish by Dr Jacques Faitalovitch at the Herzl Center's Library, located at 59th Street and Park Avenue, New York City, N.Y.

42. The name "FALASHA" (Falasa in the Amheric language of Ethiopia, East Africa) means "immigrant" or "stranger." In reality, the word has the same connotation as "Negro" or "Coloured", with respect to Blacks. Ethiopians of non-Falasha origin often translate the term into the following phrase....."The do'nt touch me." This latter expression comes from the fact that the "Falashas" (Beta Israel) have voluntarily isolated themselves from the rest of the other peoples of Ethiopia, beginning about 840 C.E., at which time they had lost their final control over the Ethiopian nation under Queen Judith. The only proper for these Jews is "BETA ISRAEL" - Children of the House of Israel or House of Israel. See, JEWISH ENCYCLOPEDIA; FALASHA ANTHOLOGY, by Wolf Leslau; and, KEBRA NEGAST (Ethiopian Chronicles - The History of Ethiopia).

43. There is no person alive who has kept, or can produce, any proof of direct descendency from King Solomon, much less from Abraham, Jacob, Isaac, Moses and all of the others who came into, or were born, in Egypt - Africa; also those that left Africa during the Passover (Pesach).

44. Kibutzim are communal communities in Israel of the type indigenous Africans all over the continent of Africa have had for thousands of years before the coming of the Europeans to Africa in the 15th century C.E. They are somewhat similar to the method of living the Jews of Ethiopia, East Africa, are accoustomed. They are also agriculturally based, with local headmen and headwomen, whose responsibility it is to administer them. Kibutz is singular. See, JEWISH ENCYCLOPEDIA.

45. They are Black Jewish communities in the Bronx, Brooklyn, Queens and Manhattan - New York City, New York. There are others in Chicago, Ill; Philadelphia, Pensylvania; Boston, Mass; Washington, D.C.; New Haven, Conn; and in most major cities of northeastern United States of America.

46. "BIAFRA" was the self-proclaimed "independent" Eastern Province of the Federal Government of the Republic of Nigeria, West Africa. There was a civil war between the government in Lagos (the capital of the Federal Government) and the "rebel" break-away Eastern Province. The Central Government is headed by General Yakubu Gowon, and the rebel government was under the leadership of General Odumegwu Ojuku. There were thousands, possibly millions, of European-Americans engaged

in maligning the Central Government on alleged charges of "genocide against the Ibos" (the dominant "ethnic" group of the Eastern Province). These same people have ignored "genocide" in South Africa, Rhodesia, Angola, Portuguese Guinea, Mozambique, and Sudan for over twenty years, at least, without a word of protest on their part, even to this very day.

47. This was one of the many propaganda slogans of the "SAVE BIAFRA" liberals who seemed to have unlimited funds and connections with the mass media.

48. Mozambique and Angola are Portuguese colonies where thousands upon thousands of indigenous Africans die daily in a death struggle against Portuguese slavery and genocide in their efforts to free themselves. See UNITED NATIONS SECURITY COUNCIL REPORTS.
Rhodesia, named for "the butcher" - Cecil Rhodes (rated by most African historians on colonialism to be one of the most despotic and cruel masters of genocide in history), remains one of the very few colonies in Africa that is forcibly European controlled. The rule of this self-proclaimed "White racist" government is patterned after South Africa's apartheid.
Ian Smith declared this country "an independent nation" in 1968, to be "ruled by Whites only." Britain, the ruler-in-fact over this colony from the time it was taken from Cecil Rhodes and his gang of colonialist of the worst order in 1878, ruled it until the above date, when a handful of more than 300,000 Europeans (most of them Britishers) seized control of it. The correct name of this land is "ZIMBABWE,"[31] the name of its indigenous African people before the arrival of the Europeans in East Africa.

49. In the State of Mississippi, Sotuh Carolina, Alabama, and others of the so-called "deep South," African-Americans die daily of malnutrition and starvation without a twinkle of an eye being raised in horror against it by those who were most voiceferous about the civil war in Nigeria, West Africa.

50. From the Passover drama in Exodus, Chapter 12, Verses 14-20.

51. LEVITICUS, Chapter 3, Verses 1-17.

52. Ibid, Chapter 4, Verses 1-12.

53. The Jews of Ethiopia (the Falashas) know about the TALMUD'S existence, but they have not endorsed its usage. They follow the literary commands of the TORAH as handed down to them from generations after generations for the last three-thousand years, and more.

54. This quotation comes from the SECOND BOOK OF MOSES, Exodus, Chapter 10, Verses

55. This is typical in Christian teachings; that "...the Jews killed Christ." There was an attempt made by Pope John 22nd

326

to change this tradition when he released an encyclical denying any responsibility of the Jews for said act. See Pope John 22nd Encyclical.

56. The word "SEMITIC" comes from the word "SHEM" - the oldest of the sons of Noah in the Hebrew Torah. See the FIRST BOOK OF MOSES, Genesis, Chapter 10, Verse 1: Thus; "These are the generations of the sons of Noah, Shem, Ham and Japheth; sons were born to them after the flood...," etc. See also Genesis, Chapter 5, Verse 32; thus...."After Noah was five-hundred years old, Noah became the father of Shem, Ham,and Japheth... etc."

57. FIRST BOOK OF MOSES - Genesis, Chapter 9, Verses 1-20.

58. Ibid, Verse 32.

59. NUMBERS, Chapter 12, Verses 1-16. It would seem that Mirriam was not "WHITE", as she turned "...white as snow." She was Moses sister, and had the same two parents.

59a Tacticus wrote..."Many again say that they"(the Jews) "were a race of Ethiopian origin," in his Book V, Chapter 2. See also, HUMAN HISTORY, by Professor Elliot Smith, p. 134; the Moslem Koran's "...And he" (Moses) "drew forth his hand out of his bosom and behold it appeared white unto the spectators."(Chapter VII, p. 128)..."And put thy right hand under thy left arm; it shall come forth white" (translation by Sabe, AL KORAN, p. 257, 1784). According to Mohammedan traditions... "Moses was a Black man" (Sir T. W. Arnold, THE PREACHING OF ISLAM, p. 106).

60. The Jews were in Hellenic Greece when they wrote most of the modern Jewish texts in existence today. See, WORLD HISTORY, p. 87; also, HEBREW ORIGINS, by T.J. Meek; and, THE RELIGION OF ISRAEL, by B.D. Erdmans; THE CULTIC PROPHET IN ANCIENT ISRAEL, by A.R. Johnson; or, STOLEN LEGACY, by G.G.M.James.

61. Rabban Johanan ben-Zakhai died in the year 80 C.E. There is no definite date known of his birth. Among the most outstanding Rabbis throughout the history of Rabbinic Judaism. He is considered to have been "...one of the greatest Rabbi..." by most Hebrew (Jewish) scholars.

62. The Romans placed Judaea under an Imperial Procurator about 4 B.C.E. By the end of Herod Agrippa II reign (50-100 C.E.) all of Palestine was a Roman Province. The Romans destroyed Jerusalem about 132-135 C.E. and dispersed the Hebrew peoples. See, AN ENCYCLOPEDIA OF WORLD HISTORY, p. 115 (edited by W. L. Langer). Also, JEWISH ENCYCLOPEDIA.

63. See, THE JEW, by M. Fishberg, pp. 117, 147-148; 120-134, London, 1911.

64. HISTORY OF MANKIND, by Ratzel, Vol. II, P. 246.

65. HISTORY OF THE CALIPHS, by Suyuti (as translated by H.S. Jarrett), p. 342, Calcutta, 1881.

66. THE SPANISH INQUISITION took place in 1487-1490 C.E. It was the period in Spanish history when the Christians of Spain tried to suppress the Jewish (Hebrew) Religion and committed wholescale genocide against the Jews of the Iberian Peninsula.

67. The Nazis of Germany, under the dictatorship of Adolph Hitler, committed mass genocide on the Jews throughout Europe to the tune of more than "8,000,000 million men, women, and children." They were exterminated between 1936-1945 C.E. The Reformed Jews of Germany were as much a part of Germany as were the Christians up to the period when Hitler first usurped the German Chancellory and declared himself "DICTATOR OF GERMANY." Their influence on the German government was, more or less, as it is now in the United States of America.

68. THE PREACHING OF ISLAM, by Sir T. W. Arnold, p. 358, London, 1913.

69. See, LA MONETE del' HALIA ANTICA, Parte Secunda, LXXV, 11, 12, 13, 14, 15, Roma, 1885.

70. Plutarch; Alexander "the Great;" Diodorus Siculus, Book XVII, Chapter 2; Clavier, BIOG. UNIVERSELLE, Vol. VIII, p. 461 (1844).

71. See, POWER OF SYMPATHY, by Keneln Digby, p. 76, London, 1660; also, ETHIOPIAN HISTORY, by Helibdorus, 1857, (London, 1895).

72. EXODUS, Chapter 20, Verse 16.

73. Terminologies used for "NEGROES" acting contrary to the interest of the African-American (Black) communities. Generally used against Blacks in the establishment of White owned and financed Black organizations - such as the N.A.A.C.P.

74. "THE BLACK EXPERIENCE" is a term which basically refers to the Africans experience in the Americas from 1503 C.E., when they were first brought to Hispaniola (Hayte or Haiti) as slaves through the efforts of the Right Reverend Bishop Bartolome de LasCasas of the Roman Catholic Church. It also has major emphasis on the role of the Black people in the United States of America from c1619 or 1620 C.E. in Jamestown, Virginia, to the prsent "LIBERATION STRUGGLES." From slavery to semi-slavery.

75. The Black (African-American) Jewish communities have isolated themselves in fear of taking any stand which would find them in the Black-White confrontation.

76. This is the present smoke screen being used in some White Jewish quarters as a means of combating Black community control.

328

77. This period marked the time when Jesus Christ was allegedly
"...Crucified by the Jews and nailed to the Cross..." during
the reign of Romanemperors over Israel. Pontius Pilot, the
Roman Governor (Perfectus) of the colony – Israel, being completely absolved from the crime they were alleged to have
committed, since it is supposed to have been "...the Jews
that condemned Jesus...." See, NEW TESTAMENT of the Christian
Bible (any Version).

78. Ibid.

79. The African–American "anti-Semitism" has resulted from their
experiences with Christian anti-Semitism. They are victims of
their own religious teachings within the Christian clergy, and
lately because of their current involvement with Islamic
studies and local nationalism.

80. See, "Story of Abraham" in the FIRST and SECOND BOOK (Genesis
and Exodus) OF MOSES, or OLD TESTAMENT.

81. See pp. 3-29 of this Chapter dealing with the Rabbinate and
the Great Synagouge.

82. It has failed to hold on to the young Black Jews, because it
does not relate to their secular needs. It has become a place
for prayer and no community action, except on conformity of
the recipients; thereby ignoring the social institutions and
forces within the overall Black communities it must operate
within. The net result is that the young Black Jew finds his
affiliations with his Black Christian and Muslim brothers and
sisters much more meaningful.

83. See, JUDAISM, (edited by Authur Hertzberg), Chapter One,
PEOPLE, p. 21.

BILAL: CHAPTER IV – NOTES

1. Dictionaries differ on the meaning of this word to the extent
thatrone of them can be considered authoritative. The colloqui-
al expression is derogatory towards Black people, mostly directed at African-Americans in particular.

2. "ASIATIC" is a term which is strictly European and European-
American. The peoples of Asia call themselves "ASIANS."

2a. This is a phrase commonly used by the late Malcom X (el Hajj
Malik Shabazz).

3. See, AFRICAN GLORY, by J.C. deGraft-Johnson; WEST AFRICAN
   KINGDOMS, by Basil Davidson; AFRICA SPEAKS, by Leo Froebeni-
   us; AFRICAN BEFORE THE WHITE MAN, by H. Labourete.

4. THE ARABS: A SHORT HISTORY, by P.K. Hitti; also, COAST OF THI
   BARBARY, by Jane Soames; WORLD's GREAT MEN OF COLOR, by J.A.
   Rogers; and, THE ARABS, by E.C. Hodgkin.

5. Ibid.

6. Ibid.

7. A MODERN SLAVERY, by H. Nivinson; THE BELGIAN CONGO, by R.
   Slade; THE AFRICAN SLAVE TRADE, Basil Davidson; POLITICS IN
   THE CONGO, by C. Young; and, STANLEY IN AFRICA, by Donkere
   Wildernissen.

8. Africans such as Bilal, Al-Hajjis, Al-Jahiz, Al-Masoudi, and
   others were but a few who helped in creating the religion and
   civilization of Islam. See, WORLD'S GREAT MEN OF COLOR, by J.
   A. Rogers; LIFE OF MOHAMET, by Baldwin; THE ARABS, by P.H.
   Hitti; also MAKERS OF ARAB HISTORY.

9. AFRICAN KINGDOMS, by Basil Davidson, also , THE AFRICAN PAST
   AFRICAN GLORY, by J.C. deGraft-Johnson; AFRICA BEFORE THE
   WHITE MAN, by H. Labourete; and, AFRICA SPEAKS, by L. Froe-
   benius.

10. See, HOLY KORAN: WORLD'S GREAT MEN OF COLOR, by Rogers; and,
    THE LIFE OF MOHAMET, by Baldwin.

11. See, HISTORY OF THE ARAB WORLD, by Hitti; THE RAPE OF AFRICA
    by Sonnersen; also,WORLD'S GREAT MEN OF COLOR, by Rogers.

12. The "LAND OF BILAL." Consult early Arab maps and literature
    on Africa for further proof. See Note No. 8 of this Chapter;
    also Note No. 10.

13. The Europeans renamed many areas of Africa that were already
    renamed from their original African names. See, THE MAP OF
    AFRICA BY TREATY, by Sir Edward Hertslet (3 Vols.); IMPERIAL-
    ISM AND WORLD POLITICS, by Parker T. Moon; THE AFRICAN PAST,
    by Basil Davidson; and, PORTUGAL IN AFRICA, by James Duffy.

14. See Note No. 4, 8, 10-11 and 12 of this Chapter.

15. Ibid.

16. Ibid, Special attention to WORLD'S GREAT MEN OF COLOR, by J.
    Rogers, Vol. I, with regards to Bilal.

17. St Augustine's, CONFESSIONS; HOLY CITY OF GOD; and his, ON
    CHRISTIAN DOCTRINES. See also, Chapter II of this work.

18. Promised in the Koran. Physical virginity that reproduces i

330

self spontaneously. See also, WORLD'S GREAT MEN OF COLOR, by J. A. Rogers, Vol. I; also the , KORAN.

19. Ibid.

20. The emphasis in this area is quite inaccurately compiled, because African-Americans generally keep their offsprings born out of wedlock; whereas European-Americans generally surrender theirs for adoption. Secondly, legal abortions are much more readily available to European-Americans.

21. See, WORLD's GREAT MEN OF COLOR, by J.A. Rogers, Chapters on Bilal and Mohamet.

22. The HOLY KORAN, the HOLY BIBLE (Christian NEW and OLD Testaments) and the TORAH are as inter-related; yet neither Jews, Christians or Moslems accept all three as "...the words of God."

23. A soldier in the cause of Islam is the highest role of the faithful. At death a soldier automatically enters "Paradise," as shown in subsequent paragraphs in this Chapter.

23a Ethiopia's Hebrew and Christian population employed these customs for centuries before Islam was born.

24. Bilal was born in Ethiopia and carried off to Arabia as a slave. See, BILAL, in J.A. Rogers', WORLD'S GREAT MEN OF COLOR Vol. I.

25. Ibid.

26. Ibid.

27. Ibid.

28. Ibid.

29. See, LIFE AND LETTERS OF LAFCADIO HEARN, by Bisland, Vol. I, p. 281, Boston, 1923; MOHAMMED, by W. Koelle, London, 1889; also, LIFE AND TEACHING OF MOHAMMED, by Ameer Ali Syed, London, 1891.

30. See, GENESIS and EXODUS, the First and Second Books of the Hebrew Torah (Bible).

31. See, Note No. 24 of this Chapter.

31a Malcom X was the outspoken minister who propagandized Elijah Mohammed's Black Muslims (Nation of Islam) into prominence. He broke with Mohammed and formed his own movement. He was assassinated on February 20, 1967.

32. Elijah Mohammed was a former African-American Baptist preacher He converted to Islam and began his own brand of the Muslim

religion. His headquarters is located in Chicago, Ill.

33. See, WORLD'S GREAT MEN OF COLOR, by J.A. Rogers; THE ARABS, by H. K. Hitti; MAKERS OF ARAB HISTORY, by H.K. Hitti.

34. Ibid. (With emphasis on the Chapter of the Life of Mohammed).

35. See accounts of the birth, life, and death of Moses and Jesus Christ, according to the Hebrew (Jewish) FIVE BOOKS OF MOSES and CHRISTIANS Holy Bible (New Testament).

36. See Note No's. 4, 8, 10-12 of this Chapter.

37. See, LIFE OF MOHAMMET, by Baldwin; WORLD'S GREAT MEN OF COLOR by J.A. Rogers; HISTORY OF ISLAM, by Hitti; and HISTORY OF THE ARABS, by Hitti.

38. See, A SHORT HISTORY OF THE WORLD, by H.G. Wells, p. 188.

39. In every Moslem country there are translations of these works. He is the most quoted of the Moslem religious poets.

40. See, ESSAYS ON THE EASTERN QUESTION, by C. Palgrave, pp. 292-296, London, 1872.

41. THE ENCYCLOPEDIA OF ISLAM, Vol. II, p.1, p423.

42. See, ARABIC LITERATURE, by H.A.R. Gibb, pp. 377-349, London, 1926.

43. Also, WORLD'S GREAT MEN OF COLOR, by J.A. Rogers.

44. Ibid. (Chapter on Al-Jahiz).

45. Ibid. See following note also.

46. Excerpts from Al-Jahiz', KITAB al-SUDAN wa al - BIDAN (as translated into English by G. VanVoltan in his TRIA OPPOSCULA AUCTORE ABU OTHMAN AMIR IBN BAHR ALSJAHIZ, Basrensi, Leyden, 1903). See also, SEX AND RACE, by J.A. Rogers, Vol. I, pp 95-96, 284, J. A. Rogers, New York, 1951; and, WORLD'S GREAT MEN OF COLOR, pp. 90-95.

47. See Professor M.D.W. Jeffreys,' "The Negro Enigma" (in: THE WEST AFRICAN REVIEW, September, 1951); and , Donald Weidner, A HISTORY OF AFRICA SOUTH OF THE SAHARA.

48. see, THE SUPERIORITY IN THE GLORY OF THE BLACK RACE OVER THE WHITE, by Al-Jahiz (as translated from the Arab text).

49. See, BLACK MUSLIMS, by C. Eric Lincoln.

50. See Note No. 46 this Chapter.

DIVINE, MOHAMET AND KING: CHAPTER V - NOTES

1. Ray pleaded guilty to Dr. King's murder in a Tennesse Court on March 10, 1969 C. E. He received a "ninety-nine year" jail sentence for his crime.

2. A story that met with Roman Catholic Church endorsement. A pamphlet to this effect was distributed to young people for them to learn about this African-American of South America.

3. Martin Luther was a Roman Catholic priest that fought the corruption of religious practices in the Church. He was ex-communicated in 1520 C.E. following his destroying a Papal Bull submitted to him by Johann Eck during their discussion with Andreas Bodenstein (called Karlstadt). He was born in 1483, died in 1546. Son of a miner in his native town of Eisleben, Germany. He became a priest in 1507; a professor at Willenberg in 1508; visited Rome in 1511 because of his dispute with the Pope on Christian teachings and Church ethics.

4. The teachings of present Christian leaders of religion, which dates back before the original "Fathers of the Church" of North Africa. Much of this premise stems from the writings of these three Africans, however. Their emphasis is upon this aspect of CHRISTIAN DOCTRINES which assured its acceptance as "...the desire of God."

5. A "call" is an expression used among members of the African-American Christian clergy. It denotes that they were "...called by Jesus Christ to serve His ministry." They refused the idea that their job was a choice of their own, as any other person making a selection of employment or vocation. See, APOSTLE OF FREEDOM, by Rev. Richard Allen, Washington, D.C., 1935; also, THE LIFE, EXPERIENCE AND GOSPEL LABORS OF RT. REV. RICHARD ALLEN, Philadelphia (n.d.).

6. The Yoruba people of West Africa are mostly found in Eastern and Western Nigeria. Of the religions of Africa still being practised in the Americas the Yorubas is the largest and oldest. There is another group in Harlem that is led by an African-American called Nana Adefumi.

7. Richard Allen founded the "African Methodist Episcopal (AME) Church" of the United States of America.

7a. The Black Muslims, by C. Eric Lincoln; also, BLACK NATIONAL-ISM, by Esium-Odom.

7b. Ahases, Gulam Bougans, Mohammed Rassouli, Elijah Muck Muhd, born October 7, 1897 C.E. Wife - Clara Evans.

8. The last of the New York City "HEAVENS" is located at West 128th Street, between Lenox and Fifth avenues. Today very few people are aware of their existence in the Harlem community.

9. Father Divine's followers have refused to accept his death. They have maintained his "...ascendency into the greater heaven beyond; bodily."

10. GENESIS, Chapter 3, Verses 16-17.

11. This is a common belief and teaching among the vast majority of Christians, that "...Jesus Christ arose from the dead and ascended into Heaven on Easter Sunday morn, where He sit at the Right Hand of God the Father Almighty."

12. Father Divine was subjected to many civil law suits in New York State. This barred him from the City, except for Sundays and Holidays, etc., in order to avoid service of supeona.

13. The "RECONSTRUCTION MOVEMENT" in Judaism was started by a European-American Rabbi, Dr. Mordecai Kaplan, more than forty years ago. This movement did not grow to any large number, but it lingers on just as Father Divine's movement.

14. The current TALMUD was re-written during the 12th Century C.E. by Hebrew (Jewish) scholars in Europe under the leadership of Moses ben-Maimon, also known as "MAIMONIDES," (1135-1206 C.E.) He is rated by most "Western" Jewish scholars on Judaism as "...one of the all time great scholars on the Torah."

15. The Story of Queen Esther (Hadas'sah) according to the Hebrew Scriptures in the BOOK OF ESTHER.

16. Integrated Black and White synagogues are rare in American Jewish communities of the United States of America. American racism has affected Judaism as well as it has any other religion or religious institution within the jurisdiction of the U.S.A., or under U.S.A's influence.

17. The vast majority of the Black Jews in the United States of America are from background which dates back to the Universal Negro Improvement Association (UNIA) founded by the late Marcus Moziah Garvey (the "Black Moses") in 1918 C.E. This has helped to keep them a separate group as much as White Jewish Zionist movements have been separated from other White Americans.

18. The condemnation was issued as a means of support for Albert Shanka's UNITED FEDERATION OF TEACHERS UNION struggle against the experimental complexes at Ocean Hill Brownsville in Brooklyn, and the Arthur Olonzo Schomburg Intermediary School (I.S. 201) group in Harlem - the major and over-riding issue being "Black community control in Black and Puerto Rican communities of the City of New York," New York, against "continued White control" in these areas.

19. It has been customary for years to refer to "Egypt and Africa" as if Egypt was located at a remote place from Africa. This is to give the impression that Egypt was an exclusive "Caucasian

334

nation" - as suggested by most White historians. They project
this one-sided fact that "the Egyptians brought in Negro slaves
from Nubia (Sudan)," but conveniently forget that Egyptians
and Nubians made slaves of each other.

20. PROPHET and PROPHETESS are names of commonality within Afri-
    American religions, especially in Christianity and other
    sects related thereto.

21. Archbishop Alexander McGuire was appointed by Mr. Garvey.
    See, PHILOSOPHY AND OPINIONS OF MARCUS GARVEY, (as edited
    by Amy Jacques Garvey).

22. These pictures of the "ETHIOPIAN JESUS CHRIST" are still
    available at the AFRICAN NATIONAL MEMORIAL BOOK STORE, West
    125th Street, between Lenox and Seventh Avenues, Harlem, New
    York City, New York.

23. Sung in most Christian churches of Protestant sects.

24. See, PHILOSOPHY AND OPINIONS OF MARCUS GARVEY, Part I, Chapt-
    er III, page 25.

25. Ibid, pp 32-33, "THE UNIVERSAL NEGRO IMPROVEMENT ASSOCIATION
    and FRIENDS IN THE CAUSE OF AFRICAN REDEMPTION."

26. Ibid, pp 33-34.

27. Ibid, p 33, Chapter II.

28. Ibid, p 22, Chapter II.

29. See, WHERE THE TWAIN SHALL MEET, by Mary Gaunt, John Murray,
    London, 1922, pp. 170-215; THE HISTORY OF JAMAICA OR A GENER-
    AL SURVEY OF THE ANTIENT, by Edward Long, T. Lowndes, London,
    1744, Vol. II, pp 338-350; and, BLACK MOSES, by Edmund D.
    Cronon, The University of Wisconsin Press, Madison, Milwaukee,
    and London, 1968, p 5.

30. Jamaica was taken from Spain by Britain in the year 1565 C.E.
    and became politically independent in 1965 C.E. under indi-
    genous African-Caribbeans (Blacks).

31. The figures on the total membership of the UNIA differ
    with as many people who are writing on Mr. Garvey and his
    organization. Such figures run from a low 5,000,00 to a high
    15,000,000. One thing about them is certain it ran into the
    millions. See, BLACK MOSES, by E. D. Cronon; and, PHILOSOPHY
    AND OPINIONS OF MARCUS GARVEY, (edited and compiled by Amy
    Jacques Garvey - Garvey's second wife, and mother of his two
    children, both sons).

32. Christopher Columbus (Cristobal Colombo) misnamed the indi-
    genous Americans - "INDIANS," because he thought America was
    "INDIA."

33. Both the UNIA and the African Orthodox Church were mentioned
and described before. The Church was a unit of the UNIA, yet
it operated in religious matters with a great degree of independence.

36. This song has maintained its "NEGRO SPI ITUAL" identity, but
it too has lost its original resignation of being weary of
the slavery Blacks were subjected too, and like most of the
others it became a wailing song of forgiveness instead.

37. For Christians this song is like the BATTLE CRY OF THE REPUB-
LIC. Its militaristic character reminds one of the many colonial invasions by the European Christians against the so-
called "pagan Moslems" during their six "CRUSADES."

38. Benjamin J. Tanner was a Bishop in the AME. He once claimed
that this Curch was "...the Ecclesiastical Court House as well
as the Church." See, UNWRITTEN HISTORY, by L.J. Coppin, Philadelphia, 1920, p. 127; also, AN APOLOGY FOR AFRICAN METHODISM,
by Benjamin T. Tanner, Baltimore, 1867.

39. Marcus M. Garvey – BLACK MOSES – was deported from the United
States of America in the year 1927 C.E., having served two of
years and three months of a jail sentence of four years; all
of which was due to the trial and conviction on a trumped-up
charge of "MAIL FRAUD." See, BLACK MOSES, by J.Cronon.

40. See, HARLEM'S RELIGIOUS ZEALOTS, by Frank Rasky (in: TOMORROW,
Vol. 9, November, 1949). This movement is still alive.

41. A Georgia girl turned prophetess. See, BLACK GODS OF THE ME-
TROPOLIS, by Arthur H. Fauset, Chapter II.

42. See, THE INCREDIBLE MESSIAH, by Robert A. Parker; also, HAR-
LEM'S RELIGIOUS ZEALOTS, by Frank Rasky (In: TOMORROW, Vol.
9, November, 1949).

43. Ibid. See also copies of, THE NEW DAY, published during the
1930's. It is still being published by the successors of
Father Divine.

44. See, THE INCREDIBLE MESSIAH, by Robert A. Parker, pp 58-59.

45. See, HARLEM'S RELIGIOUS ZEALOTS, by Frank Rasky (In: TOMORROW,
Vol. 9, November, 1949).

46. See, BLACK GODS OF THE METROPOLIS, by Arthur H. Faucet; also,
HARLEM'S RELIGIOUS ZEALOTS, by Frank Rasky.

47. Like Father Divine, Daddy Grace's followers believed he was
"GOD," and his death was just a method he used to prove his
"ONENESS WITH GOD." That "he is returning in the same body in
the not to distant future." One can visit his Temple at the
S.E. corner of West 125th St., and 8th Avenue, Harlem, New York
City, New York.

336

48. The story of the African-American as a non-existent reality acting in a culture which fails to recognize him.

49. The protest literature of the "NEGRO" in the major metropolis and the life of Wright himself.

50. Hughes' SATIRE OF THE SOCIAL PROBLEMS OF THE NEGRO IN AMERICA. The humor African-Americans developed for survival.

51. African poetess brought to the British colonies from Togoland at the age of 14. Sent to France by her slave owner who bore the name Whitley. She became America's (the U.S.A.) greatest poetess at the same time Edgar Allen Poe was America's greatest poet.

52. Harriet Tubman was the "UNDERGROUND RAILROAD" conductor that led hundreds of her fellow Africans (Blacks) to freedom (relatively that is) from Southern slavery. There are many books written about her life and times. She was one of the greatest heroine the African peoples in the United States of America had during their struggles for independence. Her shrine and memorial is the home in which she lived and died, in up-State New York.

53. Dr. W.E.B. DuBois - former editor of the CRISIS MAGAZINE of the NAACP, a Social Anthropologist, author and lecturer. He led many of the Pan-African Congress'conventions. He lived through 1868 - 1963 (the year he died) C.E. He died in Ghana, West Africa, at the time he was engaged in the completion of a multi-volume "ENCYCLOPEDIA AFRICANA" for the Government of Ghana, which was at the same period under the leadership of President Dr. Kwame Nkrumah - the "Father of African Pan-Africanism." DuBois and Garvey were both bitter enemies during the 1920's, yet they were both dedicated towards the complete freedom of Africa and the African peoples. However, each had different goals as to how this was to be achieved.

54. Marcus M. Garvey was the founder of the African Nationalist movement theory in the Americas. He was the forerunner of all so-called "BLACK NATIONALISTS" of today. He was the first person to introduce what is today being called "THE LIBERATION FLAG OF BLACK PEOPLES" - the RED, BLACK AND GREEN - or as he called it -"THE TRI-COLORS OF AFRICA".See, BLACK MOSES, by Cronon; and, PHILOSOPHY AND OPINIONS OF MARCUS GARVEY,(as edited by Amy Jacques Garvey).

55. These two towns are still predominantly African- Puerto Rican. However, as time passes the ratio of Blacks to Whites becomes incrasingly evened. These Blacks are the descendants of Africans imported into the island when it was still called "BORINQUEIN" by the indigenous peoples, later on "PUERTO RICO" (Rich Port) by the Spaniards. It is to be noted that Africans also arrived as free men under the title of "CONQUISTADORES" with other Spaniards, however they were in the minority of the majority of the Blacks that came to the island. These Africans

became the ancestors of the vast majority of the present
Carolinians and Louisians of Puerto Rico. Their culture was
amalgamated with that of the Moorish (African and Arab) -
Spanish culture and that of the indigenous peoples of the
islands - Los Caribes (The Caribs). Their rich cultural heritage from Africa is seen in the "Plena" and other locally
developed music and dances; also in all other religious and
cultural involvement of this land.

56. See, HARLEM'S RELIGIOUS ZEALOTS, by Rasky; THE INCREDIBLE
    MESSIAH, by R.A. Parker; and, BLACK GODS OF THE METROPOLIS,
    by A.H. Fauset, p.26.

57. See, THE NEGRO CHURCH IN AMERICA, by E. Franklin Frazier,
    p. 64. See, also, BLACK GODS OF THE METROPOLIS, by Fauset,
    Chapter II.

58. This is seen in the THIRD BOOK OF MOSES - Leviticus, in which
    the burial of the dead and other things are restricted for
    certain handlers who must take ritual baths before returning
    to their community.

59. The Yemenite Jews have been removed from Yemen, Asia, and re-
    settled in the State of Israel. They offer the most ancient
    customs and traditions of Hebrew culture and religion along
    with the Falashas of Ethiopia, East Africa. Next to the Afri-
    can Hebrews (Jews) - the Falashas - and those of Cochin, India
    - the "COCHIN JEWS" - they are the blackest, or darkest, Jews
    in the world. They and the other Jews from Africa and Asia
    find segregation and discrimination there because of the color
    of their skin, and their lack of familiarity with things
    European or European-American. This is partly due to the
    fact that the government of Israel is predominatly controlled
    by European and European-American (White-skinned) Jews.

60. EXTRACTS from the "BLACK MANIFESTO" of the National Black Eco-
    nomic Conference as adopted at Detroit, Michigan, USA, on 26
    April, 1969; and as presented on Sunday, 11 May, 1969.

61. This is a common expression usually reserved for any group of
    Blacks that protest against their being inhumanly treated by
    the United States of America and groups of Whites "purporting
    to be Liberals," and of course those from the far right. Any
    Black person not using the prescribed method of voicing their
    dissent or opposition to society's values that oppress them,
    as approved by the "Liberals," find themselves bearing the
    label - "IRRESPONSIBLE." The measure of "RESPONSIBILITY" is
    that which is set forth for "NEGROES" as seen through the eyes
    of the NATIONAL URBAN LEAGUE and NATIONAL ASSOCIATION FOR THE
    ADVANCEMENT OF COLORED PEOPLE (NAACP), and other such inte-
    grationist organizations that have the blessings of the "White
    Liberals" of the governing monies that operate them through
    "responsible Negro leadership."

338

62. From a Christian hymn which is very often sung in most African-
American churches.

62a As stated in the Christians HOLY BIBLE, according to Mark,
Chapter 8, Verses 36-37. Jesus Christ speaking to his disciples
while holding a little child on his knees. It is common practice for Christian missionaries to hold non-Christians to re-
dicule as "...little childresn," in light of the quotation
from the statement of Jesus Christ in their "Sacred Scriptures."

63. Founded by Bingham Young in 1840 C.E. It is fundamentally
racist in its belief and outlook with respect to Black
people being slaves. It holds to the view that "GOD," as
they interpret religion, "MADE THE NEGORES TO SERVE THE WHITE
MAN." Young, himself, ran from religious persecution in New
England, but he founded his own sect of Christianity based
upon racial segregation and religious bigotry. For years they
had refused to have Blacks among their midst as members of
their religion. They now have "Negroes", but they are not allowed to become officials or ministers (leaders or elders). It is
one of America's most segregated religious sects. Many of the
United States of America's so-called "liberals" are members
of this Christian sect, including one of President Nixon's
Cabinet Members - George Romney, Secretary of Housing, etc.

64. The Sheriff of Selma, Alabama, who had his diputies set their
blood-hounds (police dogs) on the non-violently protesting
African-Americans against the inhuman treatment they were receiving from the United States of America and specifically the
State of Alabama; all of which dealt with the denial of their
"HUMAN RIGHTS" and "CIVIL RIGHTS" under the "UNITED STATES OF
AMERICA'S Federal CONSTITUTION. He also had his deputies use
electric proding rods which cowhands generally use for shocking
cattle - against Black women and children. Bull Connors inhuman and racist tactics were condemned in the halls of the
UNITED NATIONS ORGANIZATION and other international bodies
and governments throughout the entire world.

65. Bishop Bartolome de LasCasas was mentioned earlier in this
work as the man most responsible for starting the infamous
slave trade that saw millions upon millions of Africans up-
rooted from Africa and forced into chattel slavery throughout
the Americas - the so-called "New World." He was a Roman
Catholic Bishop on the Island of Hispaniola (today's Santo
Domingo and Haiti). See, LasCasas, HISTORIA de las INDIAS,
1519; also , LIFE OF BARTOLOME de LASCASAS, by Liciado, Madrid
1565.

66. Caracalla was the indigenous African (Black) Emperor of Rome
(the son of Emperor Septimus Severus - the African who captured England, where he also died)"that fed the Christians to the
the lions." This was also charged to his father - Emperor
Septimus Serverus (also indigenous to Africa).

67. Thousands of Jews were mercilessly murdered (exterminated) by
the Nazis in a segregated area "for Jews only" called the
WARSAW GHETTO," Warsaw, Poland, Eastern Europe. These helpless victims of Nazi genocide were forced to fight the Nazis'
army without any aid whatsoever from outside of their walled
city. The last of them were exterminated on Passover, 19 April,
1943, on direct orders of Adolph Hitler. See, MY PEOPLE:
THE STORY OF THE JEWS, by Abba Iban, p. 411.

68. This statement is commonly used by Americans in boasting of
their "patriotism." It is written in the "National Anthem"
(THE STAR-SPANGLED BANNER), which was formerly a poem written
by Francis Scott Key, on 13 September, 1814, during the WAR
OF 1812.

69. This warning was made by Moses to the Jews in the name of Yvah
(God) because of their behavior in reverting back to their
"pagan ways." See, FOURTH BOOK OF MOSES - Numbers, Chapter 14,
Verses 18-19.

70. It has been the practice for most European historians, and
European-Americans, to write of "EGYPT AND AFRICA," "ETHIOPIA
AND AFRICA," as if other parts of North and East Africa were
not connected to these two parts. They seem to forget that the
entire continent of Africa takes in the North, South, East, West
and Central areas - all 11,000,000 plus, square miles.

71. These words are from a famous "NEGRO SPIRITUAL," which was in
reality a protest song by the Africans that were enslaved in
the United States of America by Europeans and European-Americans
of whom a few were Jews, the overwhelming majority being
Christians. Today it is seen by many only for its religious
overtone and message. See, NEGRO SLAVE SONGS OF AMERICA, by
M. Fisher; BOOK OF NEGRO SPIRITUALS; also, SECOND BOOK OF
NEGRO SPIRITUALS, (both), by James Weldon and Rosmond Johnson.

72. From the slave song "OLE BLACK JOE," which carried the carica-
ture of the "NEGRO" as a sloth. See books of Note No. 71 of
this Chapter, above.

73. The "UNIVERSAL DECLARATION OF HUMAN RIGHTS, as published by
the United Nations Organization, United Nations Plaza, New
York City, New York. The Commission on Human Rights released
its report in the year 1948 C.E. This document has been endorsed by most of the nations of the world as the basic mini-
mum rights each human being is entitled to solely on the basis
of birth. There are no stipulations as to <u>race</u>, <u>creed</u>, <u>color</u>,
sex, <u>national origin</u> or <u>physical handicap</u> mentioned upon which
any of these rights may be abridged by an person or nation.
This work was started in January, 1947 C.E., under the Chair-
manship of Mrs. Eleanor Roosevelt - wife of President Roosevelt (both of whom are deceased), and was completed on 10
December, 1948; at which time it was adopted by the GENERAL
ASSEMBLY by a vote of 18 in favor, 8 abstentions, and no negative votes. On 3 December, 1950, the GENERAL ASSEMBLY passed
a RESOLUTION requesting all nations of the Wordl to observe

DECEMBER 10th of each year as "HUMAN RIGHTS DAY." This
practice is common today in many nations around the
entire world.

This volume is the only comprehensive presentation of the BLACK MAN as originators of the fundamental concepts, principles, and philosophy of the MAJOR "WESTERN RELIGIONS" - Judaism, Christianity, and Islam.

Professor ben-Jochannan has exceeded his own scholarly work, BLACK MAN OF THE NILE, in this volume, as he entered this area of religious myths and taboos, and cites their historical origins and background which have been for so long concealed from the general public.

These revelations uncover many of the basic misconceptions of the mythology within Judaism, Christianity, and Islam - such as the TRUE origin of the TEN COMMANDMENTS coopted from the Africans of the Nile Valleys NEGATIVE CONFESSIONS in the COFFIN TEXTS, rather than from MOSES, through JEHOVAH, on MOUNT SINAI.

Although prepared for college level courses in the history of that which is misnomered "WESTERN RELIGIONS" (Judaism, Christianity, and Islam), Professor ben-Jochannan's documented historical revelations are recorded in a manner whereby the average reader can comprehend thereby providing the masses with insight into TRUTHS which were heretofore obscure.

CARRY-OVERS of AFRICANISMS into the Judaeo-Christian-Islamic in the "New World, especially the United States of America, have been boldly cited and detailed, resulting in disclosures of many basic facts about African-American religious personalities and their effects upon religious thought which have been ignored and/or suppressed for over three-hundred and fifty (350) years.

Olahdio Kinta-Odalgo
Hougan (Priest)
Rep. of Hayte, W.I.
July 1, 1970 C.E.

342

Select Bibliography

Secular Books Quoted and Otherwise Cited

Achebe, Chinua. *Things Fall Apart*. New York: McDowell, Obolensky, 1959.

Al–Jahiz, Amr ibn Bahr. "The Book of Animals." vols. 1–7. In *The Life and Works of Jahiz*. Berkeley: University of California Press, 1969.

————. "Eloquence and Conciseness." In *The Life And Works of Jahiz*. Berkeley: University of California Press, 1969.

————. "The Merits of the Turks." In *The Life and Works of Jahiz*. Berkeley: University of California Press, 1969.

————. "In Praise of Tradesmen and Disparagement of Officialdom." In *The Life and Works of Jahiz*. Berkeley: University of California Press, 1969.

————. "The Superiority of Speech to Silence." In *The Life and Works of Jahiz*. Berkeley: University of California Press, 1969.

————. "The Superiority of the Blacks to the Whites." In *The Life and Works of Jahiz*. Berkeley: University of California Press, 1969.

Ali, Ameer. *The Life and Teachings of Mohammed*. London: Allen and Company, 1891.

Allen, Richard. *The Life, Experience, and Gospel Labors of the Right Reverend Richard Allen*. Philadelphia: A.M.E. Publishing House, 1887.

Allen, William F., Charles P. Ware and Lucy M. Garrison. *Slave Songs of the United States*. New York: A. Simpson and Company, 1867.

al–Suyuti. *History of the Caliphs*. Translated by Henry S. Jarrett. Calcutta: Asiatic Society, 1881.

Apuleius Madaurensis. *The Golden Ass*. Translated by William Adlington. London: W. Heinemann, 1915.

Aptheker, Herbert. *American Negro Slave Revolts*. New York: Columbia University Press, 1943.

Arnold, Thomas W. *The Preaching of Islam*. London: Constable, 1913.

Ashe, Geoffrey. *Gandhi*. New York: Stein and Day, 1968.

Augustine, Aurelius. *Against the Academics*. Translated by John J. O'-Meara. Westminster, MD: Newman Press, 1950.

————. *The Catholic and Manichaean Ways of Life*. Translated by Donald A. Gallagher and Idella J. Gallagher. Washington, D.C.: The Catholic University of America Press, 1966.

————. *The City of God*. Translated by Marcus Dods. vols. 1–2. Edinburgh: T. and T. Clark, 1871.

————. *Confessions*. Translated by Edward B. Pusey. New York: Dutton, 1950.

————. *De Beata Vita*. Cologne: Ulrich Zell, 1470.

————. *Divine Providence and the Problem of Evil, . . . St. Augustine's De Ordine*. Translated by Robert P. Russell. New York: Cosmopolitan Science and Art Service Company, 1942.

————. *Dramatic Poems*. n.p., n.d.

————. *On Christian Doctrine*. Edinburgh: T. and T. Clark, 1892.

Select Bibliography

_____. "On Order." In *The Retractions*. Translated by Mary I. Bogan. Washington, D.C.: The Catholic University of America Press, 1968.

_____. *On the Beautiful and the Fit.* n.p., n.d.

_____. *On the History of Life.* n.p., n.d.

_____. *The Retractions.* Translated by Mary I. Bogan. Washington, D.C.: The Catholic University of America Press, 1968.

_____. *St. Augustine on Music.* Translated by Robert C. Taliaferro. Books 1–6. Annapolis, MD: The St. John's Bookstore, 1939.

Balfwil, M. *The Life of Mohamet.* n.p., n.d.

ben–Jochannan, Yosef. *Black Man of the Nile.* New York: Alkebu–lan Books, 1970.

Blyden, Edward W. *Christianity, Islam and the Negro Race.* London: W. B. Whittingham and Company, 1888.

Breasted, James H. *A History of Egypt from the Earliest Times to the Persian Conquest.* New York: C. Scribner's Sons, 1905.

Budge, Ernest A. *The Book of the Dead.* New York: Bell Publishing Company, 1960.

_____. *Osiris.* vols. 1–2. New Hyde Park: University Books, 1961.

Burton, Richard F. *The Kasidah of Haji Abdu el–Yezdi.* London: Privately printed, 1880.

Casas, Bartolome de las. *Historia de las Indias.* vols. 1–5. Madrid: Impr. de M. Ginesta, 1875–76.

Churchward, Albert. *The Arcana of Freemasonry.* New York: Macoy Publishing and Masonic Supply Company, 1915.

_____. *The Origin and Evolution of Freemasonry Connected With the Origin and Evolution of the Human Race.* London: G. Allen and Unwin, 1920.

_____. *Origin and Evolution of the Human Race.* London: G. Allen and Unwin, 1921.

Cicero, Marcus T. *...De Officiis.* Translated by Andrew P. Peabody. Boston: Little, Brown and Company, 1883.

Clavier, A. *Biographie Universelle.* vol. 8. Paris: n.p., 1844.

Collingwood, Robin G. *Roman Britain.* Oxford: The Clarendon Press, 1932.

Coppin, Levi J. *Unwritten History.* Philadelphia: A.M.E. Book Concern, 1919.

Cronon, Edmund D. *Black Moses.* Madison: University of Wisconsin Press, 1969.

Cyprian, Saint. *The Lapsed.* Translated by Maurice Bevenot. Westminster, MD: Newman Press, 1957.

_____. *On the Unity of the Catholic Church.* London: The Manresa Press, 1924.

Darwin, Charles G. *The Next Million Years.* London: R. Hart–Davis, 1952.

Davidson, Basil. *African Kingdoms.* New York: Time, Inc., 1966.

_____. *The African Past.* Boston: Little, Brown, 1964.

_____. *The African Slave Trade; Precolonial History, 1450–1850.* Boston: Little, Brown, 1961.

DeGraft–Johnson, John C. *African Glory.* London: Watts, 1954. Reprint. Baltimore: Black Classic Press, 1986.

Denon, Dominique V. *Travels in Upper and Lower Egypt, During the Campaigns of General Bonaparte.* vols. 1–2. London: B. Crosby and Company, 1802.

Digby, Kenelm. *Of Bodies, and of Man's Soul. To Discover the Immortality of Reasonable Souls. With Two Discourses of the Powder of Sympathy, and of the Vegetation of Plants.* London: Printed for J. Williams, 1669.

Diodorus Siculus. *Diodorus Siculus*. Cambridge, England: n.p., n.d.

Dumond, Dwight L. *Antislavery; The Crusade for Freedom in America.* Ann Arbor: University of Michigan Press, 1961.

Eban, Abba S. *My People: The Story of the Jews.* New York: Behrman House, 1968.

Eddy, Mary Baker. *Manual of the Mother Church.* Boston: The Christian Science Publishing Society, 1899.

_____. *Science and Health; With a Key to the Scriptures.* vols. 1–2. Boston: The Author, 1883.

Erdman, B. D. *The Religion of Israel.* New York: n.p., n.d.

Erskine, Beatrice Steuart. *Vanished Cities of Northern Africa.* London: Hutchinson and Company, 1927.

Essien–Udom, Essien U. *Black Nationalism.* Chicago: University of Chicago Press, 1962.

Fauset, Arthur H. *Black Gods of the Metropolis.* Philadelphia: University of Pennsylvania Press, 1944.

Fishberg, Maurice. *The Jews: A Study of Race and Environment.* London: The Walter Scott Publishing Company, Ltd., 1911.

Fisher, Miles M. *Negro Slave Songs in the United States.* Ithaca: Cornell University Press, 1953.

Franklin, John H. *From Slavery To Freedom.* New York: Knopf, 1967.

Frazier, Edward F. *The Negro Church in America.* New York: Schocken Books, 1964.

Frobenius, Leo. *The Voice of Africa.* vols. 1–2. London: Hutchinson and Company, 1913.

Garrucci, Raffaele. *La Monete Dell' Italia Antica Raccolta Generale.* Part 2. Roma: Coi Tipi Del Cav. V. Salviucci, 1885.

Garvey, Marcus. *Philosophy and Opinions of Marcus Garvey.* Edited by Amy Jacques–Garvey. vols. 1–2. New York: The Universal Publishing House, 1923–25.

Gaunt, Mary E. *Where The Twain Meet.* London: J. Murray, 1922.

Gibb, Hamilton A. R. *Arabic Literature, An Introduction.* London: Oxford University Press, 1926.

Gibb, Hamilton A. R., B. Lewis and J. Schacht, et al. *The Encyclopaedia of Islam.* Leiden: E. J. Brill, 1960.

Graves, Robert and Raphael Patai. *Hebrew Myths; The Book of Genesis.* Garden City: Doubleday, 1964.

Groves, Charles P. *The Planting of Christianity in Africa.* vols. 1–4. London: Lutterworth Press, 1964.

Harnack, Adolf von. *The Mission and Expansion of Christianity in the First Three Centuries.* Translated by James Moffatt. vols. 1–2. London: Williams and Norgate, 1908.

Hearn, Lafcadio. *The Life and Letters of Lafcadio Hearn.* Edited by Elizabeth Bisland Wetmore. vol. 1. Boston: Houghton, Mifflin and Company, 1906.

Heliodorus, of Emesa. *An Aethiopian History.* Translated by Thomas Underdowne. London: D. Nutt, 1895.

345

Select Bibliography

Herodotus. *Herodotus: The Histories.* Book 2. Translated by Aubrey de Selincourt. Baltimore: Penguin Books, 1954.

Hertslet, Edward. *The Map of Africa By Treaty.* vols. 1–3. London: Harrison and Sons, 1909.

Hertzberg, Arthur, ed. *Judaism.* New York: G. Braziller, 1961.

Higgins, Godfrey. *Anacalypsis.* vols. 1–2. London: Longman, 1836.

Hitti, Philip K. *History of the Arabs.* London: Macmillan and Company, Ltd., 1937.

_____ . *Makers of Arab History.* New York: St. Martin's Press, 1968.

Hodgkin, E. C. *The Arabs.* London: Oxford University Press, 1966.

Jahn, Janheinz. *Muntu.* Translated by Marjorie Grene. New York: Grove Press, 1961.

James, George G. M. *Stolen Legacy.* New York: Philosophical Library, 1954.

Johnson, Aubrey R. *The Cultic Prophet in Ancient Israel.* Cardiff: University of Wales Press Board, 1944.

Johnson, James Weldon and John R. Johnson. *The Books of American Negro Spirituals.* New York: Viking Press, 1940.

Kenyatta, Jomo. *Facing Mount Kenya.* New York: Vintage Books, 1962.

The Koran: Commonly called the Alkoran of Mohammed. Translated by George Sale. New York: American Book Exchange, 1881.

Labouret, Henri. *Africa Before The White Man.* Translated by Francis Huxley. New York: Walker, 1963.

Langer, William L., ed. *An Encyclopedia of World History, Ancient, Medieval and Modern.* Boston: Houghton Mifflin, 1952.

Leibovitch, J. *Ancient Egypt.* Cairo: L. Baroukh, 1938.

Leslau, Wolf. *Falasha Anthology.* New Haven: Yale University Press, 1951.

Lincoln, Charles E. *The Black Muslims in America.* Boston: Beacon Press, 1961.

Lull, Raymond. *Lull Reports.* London: n.p., n.d.

Massey, Gerald. *A Book of the Beginnings.* vol 2. London: Williams and Norgate, 1881.

Meek, Theophile J. *Hebrew Origins.* New York: Harper and Brothers, 1936.

Mendelsohn, Jack. *God, Allah, and JuJu.* New York: Nelson, 1962.

Moon, Parker T. *Imperialism and World Politics.* New York: The Macmillan Company, 1936.

Muir, William. *The Life of Mahomet from Original Sources.* London: Smith, Elder and Company, 1894.

Nesfield, John C. *Brief View of the Caste System of the North–Western Provinces and Oudh.* Allahabad: North–Western Provinces and Oudh Government Press, 1885.

Nevinson, Henry W. *A Modern Slavery.* New York: Harper and Brothers, 1906.

Ortiz Fernandez, Fernando. *La Africania de la Musica Folklorica de Cuba.* Habana: Ministerio de Educacion, Direccion de Cultura, 1950.

Palgrave, William G. *Essays On Eastern Questions.* London: Macmillan and Company, 1872.

Parker, Robert A. *The Incredible Messiah; The Deification of Father Divine*. Boston: Little, Brown and Company, 1937.

Parrinder, Edward G. *African Mythology*. London: Hamlyn, 1967.

Ploski, Harry A. and Roscoe C. Brown, Jr. *The Negro Almanac*. New York: Bellwether Publishing Company, 1967.

Plutarch. *Plutarch's Life of Alexander, the Great*. Translated by Thomas North. Boston: Houghton, Mifflin and Company, 1900.

Ratzel, Friedrich. *The History of Mankind*. vols. 1–2. London: Macmillan and Company, Ltd., 1896–97.

Robertson, Archibald. *The Origin of Christianity*. New York: International Publishers, 1962.

Robinson, Theodore H. and William O. Oesterley. *A History of Israel*. vols. 1–2. Oxford: Clarendon Press, 1932.

Rogers, Joel A. *Nature Knows No Color–Line*. New York: J. A. Rogers Publications, 1952.

_____. *Sex and Race*. vol. 1. New York: J. A. Rogers Publications, 1940.

_____. *World's Great Men of Color*. vol. 1. New York: J. A. Rogers Publications, 1946.

Sabine, George H. *A History of Political Theory*. New York: Holt, Rinehart and Winston, 1961.

Schofield, John Noel. *The Historical Background of the Bible*. London: T. Nelson and Sons, Ltd., 1938.

Slade, Ruth M. *The Belgian Congo*. London: Oxford University Press, 1961.

Smith, Grafton E. *Human History*. New York: W. W. Norton and Company, Inc., 1929.

Smith, Homer W. *Man and His Gods*. London: Cape, 1953.

Smith, William R. *The Religion of the Semites*. New York: Meridian Books, 1956.

Soames, Jane. *The Coast of Barbary*. London: J. Cape, 1938.

Sonnerson, S. *Rape of Africa*. n.p., n.d.

Stanley, Henry M. *In Darkest Africa*. vols. 1–2. New York: C. Scribner's Sons, 1890.

Tanner, Benjamin T. *An Apology for African Methodism*. Baltimore: n.p., 1867.

Tempels, Placide. *Bantu Philosophy*. Paris: Presence Africaine, 1959.

Tertullian, Quintus S. *De Anima*. Amsterdam: Holland Publishing Company, 1947.

_____. "Against Hermogenes." In *The Writings of Quintus Septimius Florens Tertullian*. Translated by P. Holmes. vol. 2. Edinburgh: T. and T. Clarke, 1869.

Volney, Constantin F. *The Ruins; or, A Survey of the Revolutions of Empires*. London: Freethought Publishing Company, 1881. Reprint. Baltimore: Black Classic Press, 1991.

Wells, Herbert G. *A Short History of the World*. New York: Penguin Books, 1946.

Wiedner, Donald L. *A History of Africa South of the Sahara*. New York: Random House, 1962.

Wildernissen, D. *Stanley in Africa*. vols. 1–2. Germany: n.p., 1887.

Young, Crawford. *Politics in the Congo*. Princeton: Princeton University Press, 1965.

Select Bibliography

Religious Books and Documents Quoted and Otherwise Cited

Talmud. *The Babylonian Talmud*. Translated by Isidore Epstein. vols. 1–34. London: Soncino Press, 1935–48.

Coffin Texts. *The Egyptian Coffin Texts*. Edited by Adriaan DeBuck and Alan H. Gardiner. vols. 1–7. Chicago: The University of Chicago Press, 1935–61.

"The Exordium." In *The Holy Koran*. London: R. Carlile, 1822.

The Holy Bible. Authorized King James Version. New York: Oxford University Press, 1963.

The Holy Koran. London: R. Carlile, 1822.

"Hymn of Adoration." In *The Egyptian Coffin Texts*. Edited by Adriaan De-Buck. vol. 2. Chicago: The University of Chicago Press, 1938.

MacDonald, Alexander. *The Apostle's Creed*. London: K. Paul, Trench, Trubner and Company, Ltd., 1925.

McGlinchey, James M. *The Teaching of Amen–em–ope and the Book of Proverbs*. Washington, D.C.: The Catholic University of America, 1939.

"Negative Confession." In *The Book of the Dead*. Translated by Ernest A. Budge. New Hyde Park: University Books, 1960.

"The Proverbs." In *The Holy Bible*. Authorized King James Version. New York: Oxford University Press, 1963.

The Torah, The Five Books of Moses. Philadelphia: Jewish Publication Society of America, 1963.

Periodicals, Documents, Paintings, etc., Quoted and Otherwise Cited

Edwin Smith Surgical Papyrus. *The Edwin Smith Surgical Papyrus*. Translated by James H. Breasted. vols. 1–2. Chicago: The University of Chicago Press, 1930.

"Encyclical of Pope Clement XIII (1758–1769)." In *Catholic Church*. Pope. *The Papal Encyclicals in Their Historical Context*. Edited by Anne Fremantle. New York: The New American Library, 1963.

"Encyclical of Pope John XXIII (1958–1963)." In *Catholic Church*. Pope. *The Papal Encyclicals in Their Historical Context*. Edited by Anne Fremantle. New York: The New American Library, 1963.

Ford, Arnold J. *The Universal Ethiopian Anthem*. New York: n.p., 1919.

Galerius. *Imperial Edict of May*. n.p., n.d.

Jeffreys, M. D. W. "The Negro Enigma." *West African Review*, vol. 22, no. 288 (September 1951): 1049–1050.

Manifesto of the National Black Economic Conference. Detroit: n.p., April 26, 1969.

"Map of Africa." In *Black Man of the Nile*. Yosef ben–Jochannan. New York: Alkebu–lan Books Associates, 1970.

Muhammad Speaks. Chicago: The Nation of Islam, vol. 4, no. 8 (January 1, 1965).

The New Day. Newark, NJ: New Day Publishing Company, vol. 1, no. 1 (May 21, 1936).

Papyrus Ebers. *The Papyrus Ebers.* Translated by Bendix Ebbell. London: Oxford University Press, 1937.

"Protestant Churches Divided On Their Urban Crisis Programs." *The New York Times,* (Sunday, May 18, 1969): 80.

Rasky, Frank. "Harlem's Religious Zealots." *Tomorrow,* vol. 9, no. 3 (November 1949): 11–17.

Tell–el–Amarna tablets. *The Tell–el–Amarna tablets.* Edited by Samuel A. B. Mercer. vols. 1–2. Toronto: Macmillan Company of Canada, 1939.

United Nations. General Assembly. *Universal Declaration of Human Rights.* Lake Success: United Nations Dept. of Public Information, 1949.

United States. Bureau of the Census. *Census of Population: 1920–1960; The Fourteenth–Eighteenth Decennial Census of the United States.* Washington, D.C.: U.S. Government Printing Office, 1922–61.

Verlat. *Christ and Barabbas.* Antwerp: Royal Museum of Antwerp, Belgium, n.d.

Supplementary Bibliography
Used, but not quoted or cited in text

Adamson, Robert. *The Development of Greek Philosophy.* Edited by William R. Sorley and Robert P. Hardie. London: W. Blackwood and Sons, 1908.

al–Maqqari, Ahmad ibn Muhammad. *The History of the Mohammedan Dynasties in Spain.* vol. 1. London: Printed for the Oriental translation fund of Great Britain and Ireland, 1840.

al–Mas udi. *Les Prairies D'or.* Translated by Barbier de Meynard, Charles A. and Abel J. Pavet de Courteille. vol. 7. Paris: l'Imprimerie Imperiale, 1878.

Andrea, Tor. *Mohammed: The Man and His Faith.* n.p., 1936.

Armattoe, Raphael E. *The Golden Age of West African Civilization.* Londonberry: The Londonberry Sentinel, 1946.

Arnold, Edward V. *Roman Stoicism.* Cambridge, England: The University Press, 1911.

Arnold, Thomas W. and Alfred Guillaume, eds. *The Legacy of Islam.* Oxford: The Clarendon Press, 1931.

Augustine, Aurelius. *Basic Writings of Saint Augustine.* Edited by Whitney J. Oates. New York: Random House, 1948.

_____. *The First Catechetical Instruction.* Translated by Joseph P. Christopher. Westminster, MD.: The Newman Bookshop, 1946.

_____. *The Greatness of the Soul.* Translated by Joseph M. Colleran. Westminster, MD.: Newman Press, 1950.

_____. *The Lord's Sermon on the Mount.* Translated by John J. Jepson. Westminster, MD.: Newman Press, 1948.

Ayandele, E. A. "External Influence on African Society." In *Africa in the Nineteenth and Twentieth Centuries.* Edited by Joseph C. Anene and Godfrey N. Brown. Ibadan: Ibadan University Press, 1966.

Select Bibliography

Bacon, Reginald H. *Benin, the City of Blood*. London: Arnold, 1897.

Bailey, Cyril. *The Greek Atomists and Epicurus, A Study*. Oxford: The Clarendon Press, 1928.

Barns, Thomas A. *An African Eldorado, the Belgian Congo*. London: Methuen and Company Ltd., 1926.

Beier, Ulli, ed. *The Origin of Life and Death: African Creation Myths*. London: Heinemann, 1966.

Biobaku, Saburi O. *Religion in Contemporary African Literature*. New York: n.p., 1966.

Blackman, Aylward M., et al. *The Psalmists*. Edited by David C. Simpson. London: Oxford University Press, 1926.

Blyden, Edward W. *West Africa Before Europe*. London: C. M. Phillips, 1905.

Bourke, Vernon J. *Augustine's Quest of Wisdom*. Milwaukee: The Bruce Publishing Company, 1945.

Bourne, Henry R. Fox. *Civilization in Congoland: A Story of International Wrongdoing*. London: P. S. King and Son, 1903.

Breasted, James H. *Ancient Records of Egypt*. vols. 1–5. Chicago: The University of Chicago Press, 1906–1907.

Brode, Heinrich. *Tippoo Tib, the Story of His Career in Central Africa, Narrated from His Own Accounts*. London: E. Arnold, 1907.

Brooks, Charles H. *A History and Manual of the Grand United Order of Odd Fellows in America*. Philadelphia: n.p., 1893.

Bruce, Philip A. *The Plantation Negro As A Freeman*. New York: G. P. Putnam's Sons, 1889.

Buber, Martin. *At the Turning; Three Addresses On Judaism*. New York: Farrar, Straus and Young, 1952.

Buchler, Adolf. *Die Tobiaden Und Die Oniaden Im II*. Wien: Israel– Theol. Lehranstalt, 1899.

Budge, Ernest A. *Egypt*. New York: H. Holt and Company, 1925.

_____. *From Fetish to God in Ancient Egypt*. London: Oxford University Press, 1934.

Burnet, John. *Early Greek Philosophy*. New York: Meridian Books, 1957.

_____. *Greek Philosophy, Thales to Plato*. New York: Macmillan, 1960.

Burnet, John, ed. *The Works of Plato*. In *Oxford Classical Texts*. vols. 1–5. New York: n.p., 1888.

Burridge, William. *Destiny Africa: Cardinal Lavigerie and the Making of the White Fathers*. London: G. Chapman, 1966.

Capes, William W. *Stoicism*. London: Society for Promoting Christian Knowledge, 1880.

Caton–Thompson, Gertrude. *The Zimbabwe Culture*. Oxford: The Clarendon Press, 1931.

Chilcote, Ronald H. *Portuguese Africa*. Englewood Cliffs: Prentice–Hall, 1967.

Cook, Stanley A. *The Religion of Ancient Palestine in the Light of Archaeology*. London: Oxford University Press, 1930.

Cooley, William D. *The Negroland of the Arabs Examined and Explained*. London: J. Arrowsmith, 1841.

Coulange, R. *The Revolution of the Mass*. n.p., n.d.

Cowley, Arthur E., ed. *Jewish Documents of the Time of Ezra*. New York: The Macmillan Company, 1919.

Dallas, Robert C. *The History of the Maroons.* vols. 1–2. London: T. N. Longman and O. Rees, 1803.

Danquah, Joseph B. *The Akan Doctrine of God.* London: Lutterworth Press, 1944.

_____. *Gold Coast: Akan Laws and Customs and the Akim Abuakwa Constitution.* London: G. Routledge and Sons, Ltd., 1928.

Dawson, Christopher H. *The Making of Europe.* New York: Meridian Books, 1956.

Dellagioacona, V. *An African Martyrology.* Italy: n.p., 1965.

Demos, Raphael. *The Philosophy of Plato.* New York: C. Scribner's Sons, 1939.

Desai, Ram, ed. *Christianity in Africa as Seen By Africans.* Denver: A. Swallow, 1962.

Dittenberger, Wilhelm. *Corpus Inscriptionum Graecarum.* n.p., n.d.

_____. *Corpus Inscriptionum Latinarum.* n.p., n.d.

_____. *Corpus Inscriptionum Semiticarum.* n.p., n.d.

_____. *Orientis Graeci Inscriptiones Selectae.* vols. 1–2. Lipsiae: S. Hirzel, 1903–05.

_____. *Sylloge Inscriptionum Graecarum.* vols. 1–5. Lipsiae: S. Hirzelium, 1915–24.

Dixon, Roland B. *The Racial History of Man.* New York: C. Scribner's Sons, 1923.

Dodge, Ralph E. *The Unpopular Missionary.* Westwood: F. H. Revell Company, 1964.

Dodgson, C. *Tertullian.* Part 1. Oxford: n.p., 1842.

Doob, Leonard W. "Psychology." In *The African World: A Survey of Social Research.* Edited by Robert A. Lystad. New York: Frederick A. Praeger, 1965.

Du Bois, William E. B., ed. *The Negro Church.* Atlanta: The Atlanta University Press, 1903.

_____. *The World and Africa.* New York: International Publishers, 1965.

Dupont–Sommer, Andre. *The Dead Sea Scrolls, A Preliminary Survey.* Oxford: Blackwell, 1952.

Erdmann, Johann E. *A History of Philosophy.* Translated by Williston S. Hough. vol. 1. London: Swan Sonnenschein, 1910.

Erman, Adolf. *Die Literatur der Aegypter.* Leipzig: J. C. Hinrichs, 1923.

Eusebius Pamphili. *Ecclesiastical History.* Translated by Roy J. Deferrari. vols. 1–2. New York: Fathers of the Church, 1953–55.

Evans–Pritchard, Edward E. *Theories of Primitive Religion.* Oxford: Clarendon Press, 1965.

Farrington, Benjamin. *Science and Politics in the Ancient World.* London: Allen and Unwin, 1965.

Fickling, Susan M. *Slave Conversion in South Carolina, 1830–1860.* M. A. Thesis. Columbia, South Carolina: University of South Carolina, 1924.

Finbert, Elian J. *Dictionnaire des Proverbes Du Monde.* Paris: R. Laffont, 1965.

Finkelstein, Louis. *The Jews; Their History, Culture, and Religion.* vols. 1–2. New York: Harper, 1949.

Foakes–Jackson, Frederick J. and Kirsopp Lake, eds. *The Beginnings of Christianity.* London: Macmillan, 1920–33.

351

Select Bibliography

Fortes, Meyer. *Oedipus and Job in West African Religion*. Cambridge, England: University Press, 1959.

Frazer, James G. *The Golden Bough; A Study in Magic and Religion*. vols. 1–13. London: Macmillan, 1911–36.

_____ . *Passages of the Bible Chosen for Their Literary Beauty and Interest*. London: n.p., 1895.

Freyre, Gilberto. *The Masters and the Slaves: A Study in the Development of Brazilian Civilization*. New York: A. A. Knopf, 1946.

Gard, Richard A., ed. *Great Religions of Modern Man: Buddhism*. New York: George Braziller, Inc., 1962.

Garrucci, Raffaele. *Le Monete Dell'Italia Antica Raccolta Generale*. Part. 2. Roma: Coi Tipi Del Cav. V. Salviucci, 1885.

Geddes, Michael. *The Church–History of Ethiopia*. London: Printed for Ri. Chiswell, 1696.

Gibbon, Edward. *The History of the Decline and Fall of the Roman Empire*. vols. 1 and 4. Dublin: W. Hallhead, 1781.

Gluckman, Max. "The Logic of Witchcraft." In *The Study of Africa*. Edited by Peter J. M. McEwan and Robert B. Sutcliffe. London: The Camelot, 1965.

Greene, Lorenzo J. *The Negro in Colonial New England*. New York: Atheneum, 1968.

Gressman, Sange. *Dar Weisbeitsbuch Des Amen–Em–Ope*. Translated by R. Griffith. n.p., 1925.

Griffith, R. *The World's Best Literature*. n.p, 1897.

Hall, Harry R. *The Ancient History of the Near East*. London: Methuen, 1947.

_____ . *Great Zimbabwe*. n.p., 1905.

Harper, Robert F., ed. *The Code of Hammurabi, King of Babylon, about 2250 B.C.* Chicago: The University of Chicago Press, 1904.

Herskovits, Melville J. *The Myth of the Negro Past*. New York: Harper and Brothers, 1941.

Hibbert, Eleanor. *The Spanish Inquisition*. New York: Citadel Press, 1967.

Higgins, Godfrey. *The Celtic Druids*. London: R. Hunter, 1827.

Hinde, Sidney L. *The Fall of the Congo Arabs*. London: Methuen and Company, 1897.

Hitti, Philip K. *Arabic Literature*. London: n.p., 1926.

Homer. *The Odyssey of Homer*. Translated by Alexander Pope. vol. 2, Book 18. Philadelphia: J. Crissy, 1828.

Hooke, Samuel H. *Myth and Ritual*. London: Oxford University Press, 1933.

Hooper, John. *Ad Uxorem*. London: n.p., 1550.

Horne, Melvill. *Letters On Missions*. Bristol: Bulgin and Rosser, 1794.

Huart, Clement I. *Litterature Arabe*. Paris: A. Colin, 1902.

Huxley, Thomas H. *Man's Place in Nature and Other Anthropological Essays*. Essay 4. London: Macmillan and Company, 1906.

Ibn Khallikan. *Biographical Dictionary*. Translated by MacGuckin De-Slane. vol. 1. Paris: n.p., 1843.

Inge, William R. *The Philosophy of Plotinus*. vols. 1–2. New York: Longmans, Green and Company, 1929.

Ions, Veronica. *Indian Mythology*. London: Hamlyn, 1967.

Irby, Charles L. and James Mangles. *Travels in Egypt and Nubia, Syria and the Holy Land*. London: J. Murray, 1844.

Irenaeus. *Against the Heresies*. London: n.p., 1916.

Jack, James W. *The Date of the Exodus in the Light of External Evidence*. Edinburgh: T. and T. Clark, 1925.

Jaeger, Werner W. *Aristotle; Fundamentals of the History of His Development*. Oxford: The Clarendon Press, 1934.

Johnson, Samuel. *The History of the Yorubas*. London: G. Routledge and Sons, Ltd., 1921.

Kaplan, Mordecai M. *The Future of the American Jew*. New York: Macmillan Company, 1948.

Kautsky, Karl. *Are the Jews a Race?* New York: International Publishers, 1926.

Keane, Augustus H. *Man; Past and Present*. Cambridge, England: The University Press, 1920.

Kellner, Karl A. *Tertullians Ausgewahlte Schriften*. vol. 7, Book 1. Kempten: J. Kosel, 1912.

Kidd, Beresford J. *A History of the Church to A. D. 461*. vols. 1–3. Oxford: The Clarendon Press, 1922.

Kramers, Johannes H. *The Legacy of Islam*. New York: n.p., 1931.

Latourette, Kenneth S. *A History of the Expansion of Christianity*. vol. 2. London: Eyre and Spottiswoode, 1939.

Loisy, Alfred F. *The Birth of the Christian Religion*. Translated by Lawrence P. Jacks. London: G. Allen and Unwin, 1948.

Long, Edward. *The History of Jamaica: or, General Survey of the Ancient and Modern State of That Island*. vols. 1–3. London: T. Lowndes, 1774.

Lopes, Duarte. *A Report of the Kingdom of the Congo*. Translated from Italian by Philippo Pigafetta; Translated by Abraham Hartwell. London: Iohn Wolfe, 1597.

MacMichael, Harold A. *A History of the Arabs in the Sudan*. vols. 1–2. Cambridge, England: The University Press, 1922.

Malinowski, Bronislaw. *Magic, Science and Religion*. Boston: Beacon Press, 1948.

Margoliouth, David S. *Yaquet's Dictionary of Learned Men*. Lyden: n.p., 1907.

Maurier, Henri. *Religion et Developpement; Traditions Africaines et Catecheses*. Mame: Esprit et Mission, 1965.

Mays, Benjamin E. and Joseph W. Nicholson. *The Negro's Church*. New York: Institute of Social and Religious Research, 1933.

Meek, Charles K. *A Sudanese Kingdom*. London: K. Paul, Trench, Trubner and Company, Ltd., 1931.

Mendelssohn, Sidney. *The Jews of Africa, Especially in the Sixteenth and Seventeenth Centuries*. New York: E. P. Dutton and Company, 1920.

Meyerowitz, Eva L. R. *Akan Traditions of Origin*. London: Faber and Faber, 1952.

_____. *The Sacred State of the Akan*. London: Faber and Faber, 1951.

Michelet, Raymond. *African Empires and Civilization*. Translated by Edward Cunard. Manchester: Panaf Service, 1945.

353

Select Bibliography

Mitchell, Robert C. and Harold W. Turner. *A Comprehensive Bibliography of Modern African Religious Movements*. Evanston: Northwestern University Press, 1966.

Morel, Edmund D. *The Black Man's Burden*. New York: B.W. Huebsch, Inc., 1920.

_____. *King Leopold's Rule in Africa*. New York: Funk and Wagnalls Company, 1905.

Moses ben Maimon. *The Guide for the Perplexed*. Translated by Michael Friedlander. London: G. Routledge and Sons, Ltd., 1904.

Muhammad, Elijah. *The Supreme Wisdom*. vol. 1. Chicago: The University of Islam, 1957.

The Negro Pew: Being an Inquiry Concerning the Propriety of Distinctions in the House of God on Account of Color. Boston: Isaac Knapp, 1837.

Nketia, J. H. Kwabena. *Art, Ritual and Myths in American Negro Studies*. Accra: n.p., 1966.

Northcott, William C. *Christianity in Africa*. Philadelphia: Westminster Press, 1963.

Nottingham, Elizabeth K. *Methodism and the Frontier*. New York: Columbia University Press, 1941.

Oehler, Franz. *Quinta Septimu Florentis Tertullian Quae Supersunt Omnia. I.* Leipzig: n.p., 1853.

Ovington, Mary W. *The Walls Came Tumbling Down*. New York: Harcourt, Brace, 1947.

Palmer, H. H. *Haroun–Al–Rachid*. London: n.p., 1881.

Parkes, James W. *The Jew and His Neighbour*. New York: R. R. Smith, Inc., 1931.

Parrish, Lydia. *Slave Songs of the Georgia Sea Islands*. New York: Creative Age Press, Inc., 1942.

Pascoe, Charles F. *Two Hundred Years of the S.P.G.: An Historical Account of the Society for the Propagation of the Gospel in Foreign Parts*. vols. 1–2. London: Published at the Society's Of–fice, 1901.

Peet, Thomas E. *Egypt and the Old Testament*. Liverpool: University Press of Liverpool, 1922.

Phillips, Ulrich B. *American Negro Slavery*. New York: D. Appleton and Company, 1929.

_____. ed. *Plantation and Frontier Documents: 1649–1863*. vols. 1–2. Cleveland: The H. H. Clark Company, 1909.

Plato. *The Myths of Plato*. Translated by John A. Stewart. London: Macmillan and Company, Ltd., 1905.

Plotinus. *The Enneads*. Translated by Stephen Mackenna and Bertram S. Page. vols. 1–6. London: The Medici Society, 1917–30.

_____. *Select Works of Plotinus*. Translated by Thomas Taylor. London: G. Bell and Sons, 1909.

Purchas, Samuel. *Purchas, His Pilgrimage; or, Relations of the World*. London: Printed by William Stansby, 1614.

Ramos, Arthur. *The Negro in Brazil*. Translated by Richard Pattee. Washington, D.C.: The Associated Publishers, Inc., 1930.

Rattray, Robert S. *Ashanti Law and Constitution*. Oxford: The Clarendon Press, 1929.

Rolland, A. *Remain Intermediare des Chercheurs et des Cusieux*. vol. 34. n.p., n.d.

Russell, John H. *The Free Negro in Virginia, 1619–1865*. Baltimore: The Johns Hopkins Press, 1913.

Russell, Michael. *Nubia and Abyssinia*. New York: Harper, 1869.

Rylands, Louis G. *The Beginnings of Gnostic Christianity*. London: Watts and Company, 1940.

Sabine, George H. *A History of Political Theory*. New York: H. Holt and Company, 1937.

Schure, Edouard. *Les Grands Inities*. Paris: Perrin, 1929.

Shinnie, Margaret. *Ancient African Kingdoms*. London: Edward Arnold, 1965.

Smith, Edwin W. *The Golden Stool*. Garden City: Doubleday, 1926.

Southon, Arthur E. *Gold Coast Methodism*. London: The Cargate Press, 1934.

St. John, Spenser B. *Hayti; or, The Black Republic*. London: Smith, Elder, and Company, 1889.

Stace, Walter T. *A Critical History of Greek Philosophy*. London: Macmillan and Company, Ltd., 1920.

Steindorff, George and Keith C. Seele. *When Egypt Ruled the East*. Chicago: The University of Chicago Press, 1942.

Steward, Theophilus G. *Fifty Years in the Gospel Ministry, from 1864 to 1914*. Philadelphia: Printed by A.M.E. Book Concern, 1914.

Stewart, John A. *Plato's Doctrine of Ideas*. Oxford: The Clarendon Press, 1909.

Stoddard, Theodore Lothrop. *The Rising Tide of Color Against White World–Supremacy*. New York: Scribner, 1920.

Tacitus, Cornelius. *The Histories*. Book 5. London: Macmillan and Company, 1913.

Talbot, Percy A. *Some Nigerian Fertility Cults*. London: Oxford University Press, 1927.

Telles, Balthazar. *The Travels of the Jesuits in Ethiopia*. London: Printed for J. Knapton, A. Bell and J. Baker, 1710.

Tertullian, Quintus S. *Treatises On Marriage and Remarriage: To His Wife, An Exhortation To Chastity, Monogamy*. Translated by William P. LeSaint. Westminster, MD: Newman Press, 1951.

_____. *Treatises On Penance: On Penitence and On Purity*. Translated by William P. LeSaint. Westminster, MD: Newman Press, 1959.

Thelwall, S. *Tertullian*. New York: n.p., 1925.

Thornton, C. "The Treatise of St. Caecilius Cyprian." In *Library of the Fathers of the Holy Catholic Church*. vol. 3. Oxford: n.p., 1839.

Tritton, Arthur S. *The Caliphs and Their Non–Muslim Subjects*. Bombay: Oxford University Press, 1930.

Turner, Lorenzo D. *Africanisms in the Gullah Dialect*. Chicago: University of Chicago Press, 1949.

Van Volten, G. *Tria Opposcula Auctore Abu Othman Amr Ibn Bahr Al–Jahiz*. Leyden: n.p., 1903.

Vittorino, D. *An African Martyrology*. Verona, Italy: n.p., 1965.

Volney, Constantin F. *Travels Through Syria and Egypt, in the Years 1783, 1784 and 1785*. vols. 1–2. London: G. G. J. and J. Robinson, 1787.

355

Select Bibliography

Voorhis, Harold V. B. *Negro Masonry in the United States.* New York: H. Emmerson, 1940.

Wakigorski, A. *The Jews in Africa.* Cairo: n.p., 1966.

Wallis, R. E. "The Writings of St. Cyprian." In *Ante–Nicene Christian Library.* vol. 8. Edinburgh: n.p., 1868.

Wand, J. and M. John. *Our Sudan: Its Pyramids and Progress.* London: n.p., 1905.

Warren, Ruth. *Muhammed, Prophet of Islam.* New York: F. Watts, 1965.

Washington, Booker T. *The Story of the Negro.* vols. 1–2. New York: Doubleday, Page and Company, 1909.

Watkins, Sylvestre C., ed. *Anthology of American Negro Literature.* New York: The Modern Library, 1944.

Welch, Galbraith. *Africa Before They Came.* New York: Morrow, 1965.

_____. *The Unveiling of Timbuctoo.* New York: W. Morrow and Company, 1939.

Werner, Alice. *Myths and Legends of the Bantu.* London: G. G. Harrap and Company, Ltd., 1933.

Westermann, Diedrich. *Africa and Christianity.* New York: Oxford University Press, 1937.

Wheless, Joseph. *Forgery In Christianity.* New York: A. A. Knopf, 1930.

_____. *Is It God's Word?* New York: A. A. Knopf, 1926.

Whittaker, Thomas. *The Neo–Platonists; A Study in the History of Hellenism.* Cambridge, England: The University Press, 1901.

Widney, Joseph P. *Race Life of the Aryan Peoples.* vols. 1–2. New York: Funk and Wagnalls Company, 1907.

Williams, Eric E. *Capitalism and Slavery.* Chapel Hill: University of North Carolina Press, 1944.

_____. ed. *Documents on West Indian History, 1492–1655.* vol. 1. Port–of–Spain, Trinidad: PNM Publishing Company, 1963.

_____. *The Negro in the Caribbean.* Washington, D.C.: The Associates In Negro Folk Education, 1942.

Williams, John A., ed. *Islam.* New York: G. Braziller, 1961.

Williams, Joseph J. *Hebrewisms of West Africa.* London: G. Allen and Unwin Ltd., 1930.

Williamson, Sydney G. *Akan Religion and the Christian Faith; A Comparative Study of the Impact of Two Religions.* Accra: Universities Press, 1965.

Windsor, Rudolph R. *From Babylon to Timbuktu.* New York: Exposition Press, 1969.

Woodson, Carter G. *The Education of the Negro Prior to 1861.* New York: G. P. Putnam's Sons, 1915.

_____. *The History of the Negro Church.* Washington, D.C.: The Associated Publishers, 1921.

Yinger, John M. *Religion, Society and the Individual.* New York: Macmillan, 1957.

Young, Crawford. *Politics in the Congo; Decolonization and Independence.* Princeton: Princeton University Press, 1965.

Zeller, Eduard. *A History of Eclecticism in Greek Philosophy.* Translated by Sarah F. Alleyne. London: Longmans, Green and Company, 1883.

_____. *A History of Greek Philosophy From the Earliest Period to the Time of Socrates*. Translated by Sarah F. Alleyne. vols. 1–2. London: Longmans, Green and Company, 1881.

Periodicals and Journals

Beynon, Erdmann D. "The Voodoo Cult Among Negro Migrants in Detroit," *The American Journal of Sociology*, vol. 43 (July 1937–May 1938): 894–907.

Daniel, Vattel E. "Ritual and Stratification in Chicago Negro Churches," *American Sociological Review*, vol. 7, no. 3 (June 1942): 352–361.

De Meynard, Barbier. "Ibrahim, Fils de Mehdi," *Journal Asiatique*, (March–April 1869): 201–342.

Fernandez, James W. "Politics and Prophecy: African Religious Movements," *Practical Anthropology*, vol. 12, no. 2 (March–April 1965): 71–75.

Fitchett, E. Horace. "The Traditions of the Free Negro in Charleston, South Carolina," *The Journal of Negro History*, vol. 25, no. 2 (April 1940): 139–152.

Garrett, Romeo B. "African Survivals in American Culture," *The Journal of Negro History*, vol. 51, no. 4 (October 1966): 239–245.

Jernegan, Marcus W. "Slavery and Conversion in the American Colonies," *The American Historical Review*, vol. 21, no. 3 (April 1916): 504–527.

Lovell, Jr., John. "The Social Implications of the Negro Spiritual," *The Journal of Negro Education*, vol. 8, no. 4 (October 1939): 634–643.

Makdisi, Nadim. "The Moslems of America," *The Christian Century,* vol. 76, no. 34 (August 26, 1959): 969–971.

Woodson, Carter G. "The Negroes of Cincinnati Prior to the Civil War," *The Journal of Negro History*, vol. 1, no. 1 (January 1916): pp. 1–22.

Index

Index

Index

Index

Index